The Value of Systems and Complexity Sciences for Healthcare

Joachim P. Sturmberg
Editor

The Value of Systems and Complexity Sciences for Healthcare

Springer

Editor
Joachim P. Sturmberg
Department of General Practice
The University of Newcastle
Newcastle, NSW, Australia

ISBN 978-3-319-79909-4 ISBN 978-3-319-26221-5 (eBook)
DOI 10.1007/978-3-319-26221-5

Springer Cham Heidelberg New York Dordrecht London

Softcover reprint of the hardcover 1st edition 2016

Printed on acid-free paper

Springer International Publishing AG Switzerland is part of Springer Science+Business Media (www.springer.com)

In memory of my late father
Paul E. Sturmberg (1924–2000)
who first introduced me to the notion of
unintended consequences.

Preface

This has been the *1st International Conference on Systems and Complexity Sciences for Healthcare*, an event more than two decades in the making. Having reached this landmark, not possible without the enthusiasm, passion and persistence of those attending and those unable to do so, it is time to reflect on the journey, an inevitably part of celebrating *firsts*.

Each of us has had their own long and often lonely journey to understand and make sense of the many obvious complexities we encounter in daily practice that could not, cannot and never will be accounted for by the prevailing scientific frame based on reductionism. We represent an alternative frame, *holism*, one that describes and studies phenomena based on the dynamics of the interactions between connected entities—the larger the number of entities, the greater is the dimension of its complexity. Collectively we represent all the knowledge entities relating to *health*, the sciences basic to medicine, healthcare delivery, ethics, education, healthcare organisations and health policy. As individual agents in a holistic frame, we are interconnected in a web of relationships whose interactions allow us to learn, to create new knowledge and to find answers to questions that have not yet emerged.

Before reading on reflect for just a moment on your own journeys.

My journey entails two childhood experiences and a crisis in the early years as a medical practitioner. I learnt from my father, a mechanical engineer, the notion of *unintended consequences*; his designs of new machinery to make it possible to build very high precision products, like the spindles for the canal lift at Henrichenburg or the magnets for the first hadron collider at CERN, meant that highly qualified tradesmen would lose their jobs, and with it manufacturing would lose a unique set of valuable but underappreciated skills solely residing in these men, something that weighed heavily on his social conscience. The exposure to Donella Maedows' *Limits to Growth* provided a different way of seeing and thinking that of *interconnected and interdependent systems* and their *nonlinear system dynamics behaviour*. Unfortunately medical school pushed all of this to the side, only to hound me in my early career in general practice.

At the time of crisis in my early years, two eminent persons came to my rescue. Ian McWhinney helped me to understand my role in healthcare. He emphasised the importance of understanding the contextual dimensions—*sensitivity to initial condition*—and the underlying *feedback* relationships that characterise the patient's illness experience.[1]

> Complex natural systems are "particulars". To make general inferences from studies in these sciences we must have good descriptions of the contexts in which they were conducted. ... A complex, self-organizing system does not respond to change in a simple unidirectional manner. Reciprocal effects and feedback loops are circular, not linear processes.

Ed Pellegrino opened my eyes to the epistemology of medicine as a discipline whose *essential focus* is on both health and disease.[2]

> ... the principal conception of medicine, health, and disease are necessarily related to, and acquire their meaning from, the epistemological features of clinical interaction. Both health and disease are essential conceptions of medicine as a discipline. To the objection that health and disease are definientia only of organ systems, one must counter with the large body of evidence that both concepts are evaluative; that is, they include in their meaning the values of patients, societies, and cultures (p. 63).

Whilst Paul Cilliers introduced me to the philosophical foundations of complexity sciences,[3] Dave Snowden provided a pragmatic framework, the Cynefin[4] model, to appreciate the different dimensions of understanding with different levels of connectedness between its agents, their underlying dynamics and the different approaches required to meaningfully engage within and between these differing domains.[5]

Systems and complexity science methodologies have been applied to answer questions encountered in every domain affecting the health professions. The chapters in these *Proceedings* describe the approaches and results of high-profile researchers from across the discipline and should serve as encouragement for especially our younger colleagues to engage with *systems and complexity sciences* in their clinical and research work.

Newcastle, NSW, Australia — Joachim P. Sturmberg
April 2015

[1] McWhinney I. 'An acquaintance with particulars ...'. Family Medicine 1989;21(4):296–298.

[2] Pellegrino E and Thomasma D. A Philosophical Basis of Medical Practice. Towards a Philosophy and Ethic of the Healing Professions. New York Oxford: Oxford University Press; 1981.

[3] Cilliers P. Complexity and Postmodernism. Understanding Complex Systems. London: Routledge; 1998.

[4] A Welsh word most closely meaning 'place of belonging'.

[5] Kurtz CF and Snowden DJ. The new dynamics of strategy: Sense-making in a complex and complicated world. IBM Systems Journal. 2003;42(3):462–483.

Acknowledgements

It is my great pleasure to acknowledge the wonderful team that made this conference possible—Howard Federoff, Sona Vasudevan, Carmel Martin, Renee Crichlow, Beverley Ellis, Lauren Wolkoff, Brian Castellani, Elliott Crooke, Stewart Mennin, Mark Smith, Sean Hawkins, Mohammed El-Khatib and the large team of volunteers who supported the conference on the day. My special thanks to *Georgetown University* and *MedStar Institute of Innovation* for hosting the *1st International Conference on Systems and Complexity Sciences for Healthcare* and Khristine Queja for her editorial support of these Proceedings.

Front: Renee Crichlow, Stewart Mennin, Sona Vasudevan, Carmel Martin and Beverley Ellis
Back: Howard Federoff, Martin Konitzer, Elliot Crooke, Sean Hawkins, Joachim Sturmberg and Lauren Wolkoff

Contents

Part I Complexity in Clinical Care

1 **"Returning to Holism": An Imperative for the Twenty-First Century** 3
Joachim P. Sturmberg

2 **Systems Biology: Unravelling Molecular Complexity in Health and Disease** 21
Amrita K. Cheema, Massimo S. Fiandaca, Mark Mapstone, and Howard J. Federoff

3 **Complicated vs. Complex, Disease vs. Illness: Rethinking Diagnosis, Therapy, and Restoring Health** 29
S. Lee Hong and Simeon J. Hain

4 **A System for Systems Epidemiology: The Example of Inference from Agent-Based Models** 39
Abdulrahman M. El-Sayed

5 **Coping with Complexity and Uncertainty: Insights from Studying Epidemiology in Family Medicine** 51
Martin Konitzer, Waltraud Fink, Vilen Lipatov, Gustav Kamenski, and Thorsten Knigge

6 **Anticipation in Complex Systems: Potential Implications for Improving Safety and Quality in Healthcare** 69
Thomas O. Staiger

7 **Extreme Variability is Typical Not Normal** 79
Bruce J. West

8 **Monitoring Variability and Complexity at the Bedside** 91
Andrew J.E. Seely, Kimberley D. Newman, and Christophe Herry

9 **Heterogeneity Mediated System Complexity: The Ultimate Challenge for Studying Common and Complex Diseases** ... 107
Henry H. Heng, Steven D. Horne, Joshua B. Stevens, Batoul Y. Abdallah, Guo Liu, Saroj K. Chowdhury, Steven W. Bremer, Kezhong Zhang, and Christine J. Ye

10 **Multimorbidity: Through a Glass Darkly** 121
Carmel M. Martin

11 **Viewing Mental Health Through the Lens of Complexity Science** 133
David A. Katerndahl

12 **Quantitatively Demonstrating the Complex Nature of Intimate Partner Violence** 147
David A. Katerndahl, Sandra Burge, Robert Ferrer, Johanna Becho, and Robert Wood

13 **Depression: Not Just a Top–Down Phenomenon** 163
Jeanette M. Bennett and Joachim P. Sturmberg

Part II Complexity and the Healthcare System Ethics, Organisation Policy, and Politics

14 **Ethical Complexities in Systems Healthcare: What Care and for Whom?** 177
Kevin T. FitzGerald

15 **Systematic Reviews: Beyond Cochrane to Complexity** 187
Frances Griffiths and Jane Goudge

16 **Agent-Based Modelling of Organizational Performance** 197
Russell S. Gonnering and David Logan

17 **Leading the Emergency Department as a Complex Adaptive System** 205
Paola Camorlinga and Sergio Camorlinga

18 **The Value of Systems and Complexity Thinking to Enable Change in Adaptive Healthcare Organisations, Supported by Informatics** 217
Beverley S. Ellis

19 **Using a Team Approach to Address Avoidable Emergency Department Utilization and Re-hospitalizations as Symptoms of Complexity Through Quality Improvement Methodology** 231
Jacqueline Morse, Andrew S. Valeras, Dominic Geffken, Daniel Eubank, A. John Orzano, Douglas Dreffer, Amanda DeCook, and Aimee Burke Valeras

20 Access to Primary Care: A Complex Adaptive Systems Lens on Acuity 239
Carmel M. Martin and David Emanuel Surate Solaligue

21 "If the Facts Don't Fit the Theory, Change the Theory": Implications for Health System Reform 247
Joachim P. Sturmberg

Appendices 261

Index 281

List of Contributors

Batoul Y. Abdallah Department of Pathology, Center for Molecular Medicine and Genetics, Karmanos Cancer Institute, Wayne State University School of Medicine, Detroit, MI, USA

Johanna Becho Family & Community Medicine, University of Texas Health Science Center at San Antonio, San Antonio, TX, USA

Jeanette M. Bennett Ph.D. Program in Health Psychology, The University of North Carolina at Charlotte, Charlotte, NC, USA

Department of Psychology, The University of North Carolina at Charlotte, Charlotte, NC, USA

Steven W. Bremer Department of Pathology, Center for Molecular Medicine and Genetics, Karmanos Cancer Institute, Wayne State University School of Medicine, Detroit, MI, USA

Sandra Burge Family & Community Medicine, University of Texas Health Science Center at San Antonio, San Antonio, TX, USA

Paola Camorlinga Department of Emergency Medicine, University of British Columbia, Vancouver, BC, Canada

Sergio Camorlinga Department of Applied Computer Science, University of Winnipeg, Winnipeg, MB, Canada

Amrita K. Cheema Department of Oncology, Georgetown University Medical Center, Washington, DC, USA

Department of Biochemistry, Georgetown University Medical Center, Washington, DC, USA

Department of Molecular & Cellular Biology, Lombardi Comprehensive Cancer Center, Georgetown University Medical Center, Washington, DC, USA

Soraj K. Chowdhury Research Department, VA John Dingell Medical Center, Detroit, MI, USA

Amanda DeCook Concord Hospital Family Health Center, New Hampshire Dartmouth Family Medicine Residency, Concord, NH, USA

Douglas Dreffer Concord Hospital Family Health Center, New Hampshire Dartmouth Family Medicine Residency, Concord, NH, USA

Abdulrahman M. El-Sayed Department of Epidemiology, Mailman School of Public Health, Columbia University, New York, NY, USA

Detroit Health Department, City of Detroit, Detroit, MI, USA

Beverley S. Ellis Health Informatics Team, School of Health Sciences, College of Health and Well-being, University of Central Lancashire, (UCLan) Preston, UK

Daniel Eubank Concord Hospital Family Health Center, New Hampshire Dartmouth Family Medicine Residency, Concord, NH, USA

Howard J. Federoff Departments of Neurology, Georgetown University Medical Center, Washington, DC, USA

Robert Ferrer Family & Community Medicine, University of Texas Health Science Center at San Antonio, San Antonio, TX, USA

Massimo S. Fiandaca Departments of Neurology, Georgetown University Medical Center, Washington, DC, USA

Waltraud Fink Vienna University, Department of Public Health, Academic Teaching Practice, Straning, Austria

Kevin T. FitzGerald Center for Clinical Bioethics, Georgetown University, Washington, DC, USA

Department of Oncology, Georgetown University Medical Center, Georgetown University, Washington, DC, USA

Dominic Geffken Concord Hospital Family Health Center, New Hampshire Dartmouth Family Medicine Residency, Concord, NH, USA

Russell S. Gonnering Medical College of Wisconsin, Elm Grove, WI, USA

Jane Goudge School of Public Health, Centre for Health Policy, University of the Witwatersrand, Johannesburg, South Africa

Frances Griffiths Social Science and Systems in Health Research Unit, Division of Health Sciences, University of Warwick, Warwick Medical School, Coventry, UK

Simeon J. Hain Heritage College of Osteopathic Medicine, Ohio University, Athens, OH, USA

Henry H. Heng Department of Pathology, Center for Molecular Medicine and Genetics, Karmanos Cancer Institute, Wayne State University School of Medicine, Detroit, MI, USA

Christophe Herry Ottawa Hospital Research Institute, Ottawa, ON, Canada

S Lee Hong Heritage College of Osteopathic Medicine, Ohio University, Athens, OH, USA

Steven D. Horne Department of Pathology, Center for Molecular Medicine and Genetics, Karmanos Cancer Institute, Wayne State University School of Medicine, Detroit, MI, USA

David A. Katerndahl Family & Community Medicine, University of Texas Health Science Center at San Antonio, San Antonio, TX, USA

Gustav Kamenski Vienna University, Department of Public Health, Academic Teaching Practice, Angern, Austria

Thorsten Knigge Family Physician, Hambühren, Germany

Martin Konitzer Hannover Medical School (MHH), Department of Family Medicine, Academic Teaching Practice, Schwarmstedt, Germany

Karl Landsteiner Institute for Systematics in General Medicine, Angern, Austria

Vilen Lipatov Compass Lexecon, Brussels, Belgium

Guo Liu Department of Pathology, Center for Molecular Medicine and Genetics, Karmanos Cancer Institute, Wayne State University School of Medicine, Detroit, MI, USA

David Logan Marshall School of Business, The University of Southern California, Los Angeles, CA, USA

Mark Mapstone Department of Neurology, University of Rochester School of Medicine, Rochester, NY, USA

School of Medicine and Dentistry, University of Rochester Medical Center, Rochester, NY, USA

Carmel M. Martin Department of Public Health and Primary Care, Trinity College, College Green, Kelvin Grove, Brisbane Qld, Dublin, Ireland

Jacqueline Morse Concord Hospital Family Health Center, New Hampshire Dartmouth Family Medicine Residency, Concord, NH, USA

Kimberley D. Newman Ottawa Hospital Research Institute, Ottawa, ON, Canada

A. John Orzano Concord Hospital Family Health Center, New Hampshire Dartmouth Family Medicine Residency, Concord, NH, USA

Andrew J.E. Seely Thoracic Surgery & Critical Care Medicine, University of Ottawa and Scientist, Ottawa Hospital Research Institute, Ottawa Hospital - General Campus, Ottawa, ON, Canada

David Emanuel Surate Solaligue Max Plank Institute Bad Nauheim, MBML (Molecular Biology and Medicine of the Lung), Hessen, Germany

Thomas O. Staiger Department of Medicine, University of Washington, Seattle, WA, USA

Joshua B. Stevens Department of Pathology, Center for Molecular Medicine and Genetics, Karmanos Cancer Institute, Wayne State University School of Medicine, Detroit, MI, USA

Joachim P. Sturmberg Department of General Practice, School of Medicine and Public Health, Faculty of Health and Medicine, The University of Newcastle, Newcastle, Wamberal, NSW, Australia

Andrew S. Valeras Concord Hospital Family Health Center, New Hampshire Dartmouth Family Medicine Residency, Concord, NH, USA

Aimee Burke Valeras Concord Hospital Family Health Center, New Hampshire Dartmouth Family Medicine Residency, Concord, NH, USA

Bruce J. West Mathematics and Information Sciences Directorate, U.S. Army Research Office, Research Triangle Park, Durham, NC, USA

Robert Wood Family & Community Medicine, University of Texas Health Science Center at San Antonio, San Antonio, TX, USA

Christine J. Ye The Division of Hematology/Oncology, University of Michigan Comprehensive Cancer Center, Ann Arbor, MI, USA

Kezhong Zhang Department of Pathology, Center for Molecular Medicine and Genetics, Karmanos Cancer Institute, Wayne State University School of Medicine, Detroit, MI, USA

Part I
Complexity in Clinical Care

The prevailing mode of dealing with complexity in clinical care is simplification—reducing the problems into their constituent components. While this approach may gain valuable insights into the structure and function of small parts, it unfortunately fails to guide the management of the problem in the *particular patient* in front of us, or patient groups in a particular context. The contributions in the first part of the *Proceedings* untangle the notion of complexity inherent in the clinical context, and highlight how the application of complexity sciences helps us to better understand, approach and solve some clinical problems.

It is hoped that some readers will be encouraged to explore complexity science approaches in their area of interest and present their insights at the next meeting in 2016.

Chapter 1
"Returning to Holism": An Imperative for the Twenty-First Century

Joachim P. Sturmberg

Each of us has had their own long and often lonely journey to understand and make sense of the many obvious complexities we encounter in daily practice that could not, cannot and never will be accounted for by the prevailing scientific frame based on reductionism. These *Proceedings* present an alternative frame—*holism*—that describes and studies the dynamics of the interactions between connected entities. The larger the number of entities, the greater the dimension of complexity. Collectively, the authors of the *Proceedings* represent all the knowledge domains relating to *health*, the sciences basic to medicine and health care practices, ethics, education for work in the health professions, health care organisations, and health policy development. As individual agents in a holistic frame, we are interconnected in a local web of relationships whose interactions lead to adaptive actions which lead to system-wide change and learning, creating new knowledge and practices and looking for new questions that have not yet been asked and the adaptive actions which have yet to emerge.

It was the *constraints* of the prevailing reductionist way of thinking in medicine and healthcare [1] that precipitated my crisis. I had to widen my gaze to embrace the contextual interdependencies of the multiple facets that constitute a *health* delivering health care system (Fig. 1.1).

I postulate a framework for understanding health and health systems grounded in the *principles* of systems and complexity science. The paper makes ample use of *narrative* and *metaphorical images* to illustrate system structures and dynamics.

It addresses firstly some of the epistemic and historical developments that limit the prevailing "restricted" scientific framework before outlining issues and

J.P. Sturmberg (✉)
Department of General Practice, School of Medicine and Public Health, The University of Newcastle, Newcastle, PO Box 3010, Wamberal, NSW 2250, Australia
e-mail: jp.sturmberg@gmail.com

J.P. Sturmberg (ed.), *The Value of Systems and Complexity Sciences for Healthcare*, DOI 10.1007/978-3-319-26221-5_1

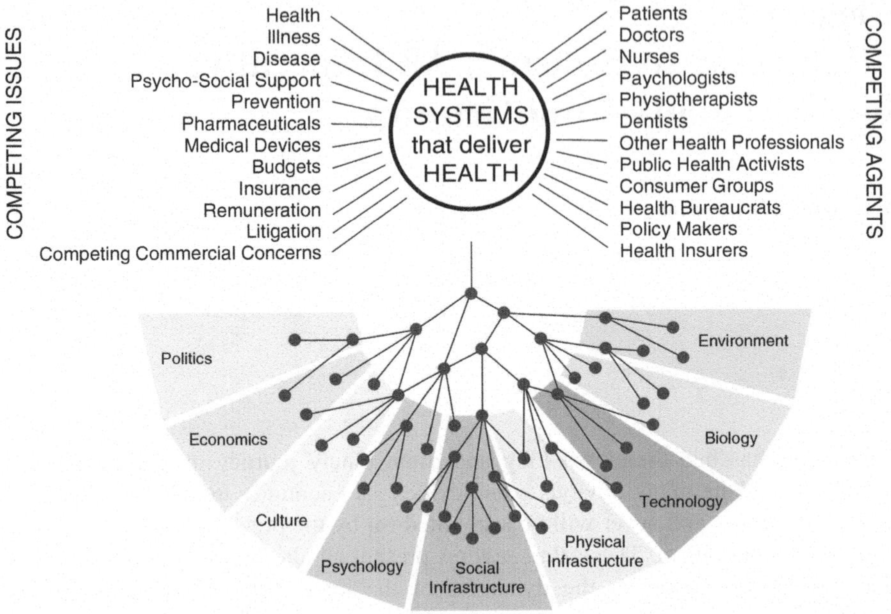

Fig. 1.1 The complexities of a *Health System that delivers Health*. A health system has many competing agents and issues, all of which are interconnected in a complex network of subsystems and their various sub-, subsub- etc. systems

challenges for the renewal of *health care*[1] that meet a person's interdependent needs to achieve *health*. The remaining chapters of these *Proceedings* deal with some of the particular nodes of a *health-delivering* healthcare network.

1.1 Models: Mental Representations of Reality

Reductionism and complexity sciences are two ways of exploring issues, each approach based on a different mental model. Models are defined as "*an external and explicit representation of part of reality as seen by the people who wish to use that model to understand, to change, to manage and to control that part of reality*" [2]. Einstein already pointed out that even physical models are the product of our mind, and Wittgenstein alluded to the fact that our ideas determine the scope of our observations and their representation.

Our mental models reflect a particular way of seeing and thinking about reality. Reductionism breaks reality into parts and then studies the parts to seek understanding of the whole. Complexity sciences explore the relationships and

[1]Note the distinction between "health care", the activity, and "healthcare" the organisational unit.

Table 1.1 Reductionist and complexity frameworks for problem solving

Confirmatory models	Exploratory models
• General rules and control	• Context and insight
• Cause and effect	• Meaning and purpose
• Explain and predict	• Describe and understand

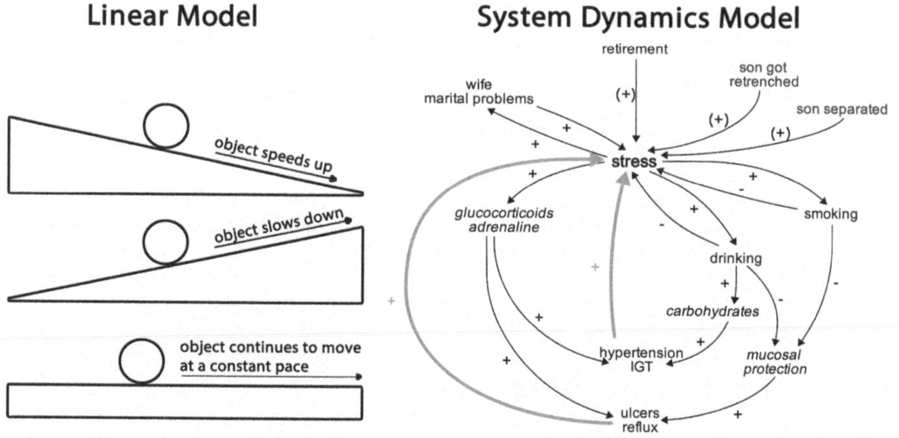

Fig. 1.2 Linear (Newtonian) model of acceleration (*left*) and non-linear system dynamics model (*right*)

interdependencies among members of the system under particular conditions. They are different ways of asking questions and approaching problems that can be summarised as confirmatory and exploratory (Table 1.1), and arise from different sets of underlying assumptions (see Fig. 1.2). Neither mode can provide a complete picture of reality [3], however, as Gorge Box pointed out, while "*... all models are wrong, ... some are useful*" [4].

Life consists of interconnected networks, an inescapable reality. We recognize complex adaptive phenomena in nature and in society; however, we generally lack knowledge and understanding about the dynamics of complex adaptive systems (CAS). Accordingly we attempt to reduce complex problems into simple ones and thus end up, in Russell Ackoff's words, *with simple—if not simple-minded solutions* [5]. How can this be?

Dörner [6] explored this question and found that the human brain has a limited capacity to deal with more than a few things (on average 7 ± 2) at any one time. We have difficulties to easily detect connections between seemingly unconnected objects or facts, and we cannot easily anticipate—especially non-linear—behaviours more than a step or two ahead. Successfully dealing with complex problems requires the skill to observe dynamic changes over time, to understand the observed dynamics, and to *respond anticipatorily* in small increments (Table 1.2).

Table 1.2 Characteristics of successful problem solvers (adapted from Dörner [6])

- Make more decisions
- Consider not just the primary goal of any given measure but also its potential effect on other sectors of the system
- Act "more complexly". When making decisions they take different aspects of the entire system into account, not just one aspect
- Test hypotheses frequently
- Ask more *why* questions (as opposed to *what* questions), i.e. ask more *exploratory* than *descriptive* questions
- Are more interested in the causal relationships behind events, in the causal network that made up …, dig deeper in their analyses
- Use similar decision strategies over time
- Focus on the same topics within the problem area
- Reflect more on own behaviour, comment critically on it, and make efforts to modify it
- More structured behaviour, thinking out loud, more frequently displaying sequencing patterns like "First I have to deal with A, then with B, but I shouldn't forget to think about C as well"

1.2 Distributions in Living Systems

These cognitive difficulties are compounded by a prevailing perception that objects in the living world behave in mechanistic ways that are predictable based on the average observed behaviour. It is assumed that any change in input will result in a proportional change in output. Mathematically these behaviours are expressed as means and standard deviations (Gauss distributions). However objects in the living world typically follow non-linear patterns (Fig. 1.3). Firstly, objects in the living world are distributed in a long tail or inverse power-law distribution (Pareto distributions). Secondly, their behaviour to an input typically results in disproportional outputs. Mathematically these behaviours are described by the median [7, 8].

1.3 Characteristics of CAS

CAS consist of a number of agents that are linked in a networked fashion. Implicitly all systems are nested—every system simultaneously is part of a larger system (i.e. it is a sub-system) and a larger system containing smaller systems (i.e. it is a supra-system) (Fig. 1.4). CAS are bounded which provides constraints that limit the possibilities of interactions between agents. All interactions occur without external supervisory influence. The interactions are recursive and fed back on each other to create feedback loops which can be either "*self-reinforcing* (vicious cycles)" threatening the stability of the system or "*self-stabilising*" therefore maintaining it. Behaviour in CAS is emergent and hence non-deterministic, i.e. the resulting

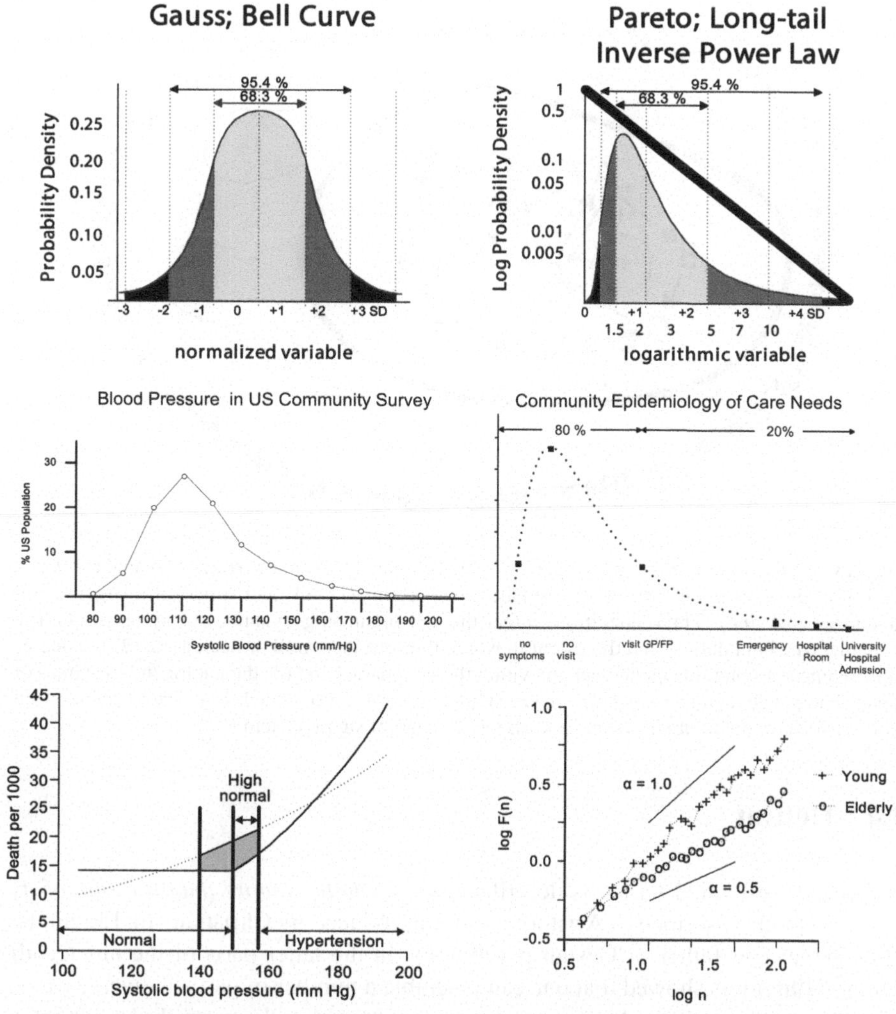

Fig. 1.3 Comparison between Gauss and Pareto distributions (*top*). Blood pressure distribution in the US community survey 1999 (*middle left panel*) [9], care needs from White's community health study 1961 (*middle right panel*) [10], absolute mortality and blood pressure for a 50-year-old from the Framingham study (*bottom left panel*) [11] and F(n) by log(n) of gait variability over time of a young and elderly showing the decreasing scaling exponent α with ageing (*right panel*) [12]

outcomes cannot be precisely predicted. Table 1.3 provides an overview of definitions of the key terms of systems sciences and their effects on CAS behaviours.

Complexity increases exponentially with the number of agents interacting—a system with ten agents can have a maximum of 45 different connections; increasing the number of agents to 1000 (a 100-fold increase) results in 499,500 different connections (a 10,000-fold increase)—a power law distribution.

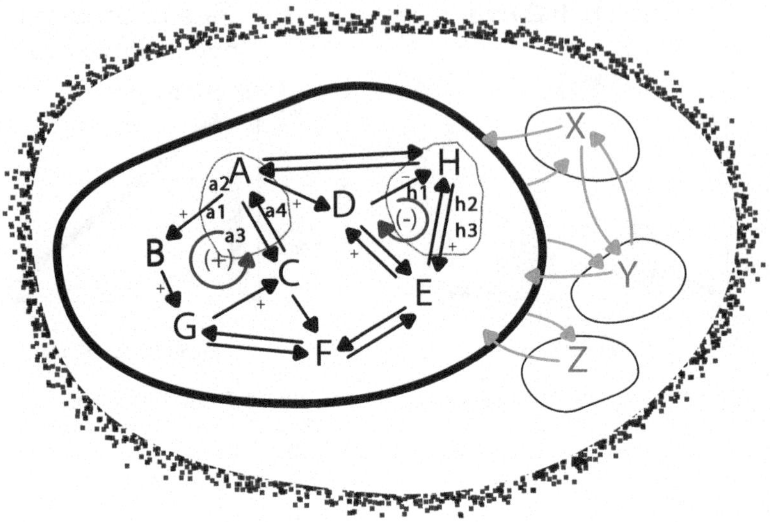

Fig. 1.4 Systems are collection of agents (A–H) contained within a permeable boundary (*black circle*), where each agent represents a smaller sub-systems (a1–a4) and is part of a larger supra-system (*dotted line*). Three conditions affect the self-organising dynamics of systems: (1) The container (the boundaries) and the extent to which they are increased or decreased; (2) the degree of differences among the agents that are within the boundaries and (3) the nature and dynamics of the exchange between the agents involved. Whilst systems are bounded they receive inputs from and provide outputs to other systems (X–Z) within a larger supra-system

1.4 Holism

Holism, in colloquial terms, is described as *the whole is more than the sum of its parts*—a phrase ascribed to Aristotle[2] and reintroduced by Christian von Ehrenfels, philosopher and father of Gestalt psychology, in the latter parts of the nineteenth century. Ehrenfels showed that one can assemble a number of parts in diverse ways, giving them forms that exhibit properties not contained in the parts. Today we refer to this observation as *non-separability*: the state of the whole is not constituted by the states of its parts—or more precisely, *the whole is more* ***and different*** *than the sum of the parts*.

Philosophy of science juxtaposes two approaches to studying holism described in "The Stanford Encyclopedia of Philosophy" as methodological holism and methodological reductionism.

[2] *In the case of all things that have several parts and in which the whole is not like a heap, but is a particular something besides the parts, there must be some such uniting factor.* [Aristotle. (1952). Metaphysics (R. Hope, Trans.). Ann Arbor, MI: University of Michigan Press. (Book Eta, 1045a8–10)].

Methodological Holism: An understanding of a certain kind of complex system is best sought at the level of principles governing the behavior of the whole system, and not at the level of the structure and behavior of its component parts.
Methodological Reductionism: An understanding of a complex system is best sought at the level of the structure and behavior of its component parts.
(http://plato.stanford.edu/entries/physics-holism/)

Whilst in physics the methodological argument has long been settled in terms of the former approach, this is not yet the case in the medical and social sciences. While it certainly is helpful to understand the structure and function of an individual cell, it is not possible to infer the ordered interactions of cells within an organ or

Table 1.3 Properties of complex adaptive systems (CAS)

Non-linearity	• results not proportional to stimulus • can lead to sudden massive changes of the system • sensitive to initial conditions
Open to environment	• a system continuously interacts with its environment, e.g. • exchanging material, energy, people, capital and information • non-linear responses to the external environment can lead to sudden massive and stochastic changes
Self-organization	• relies on three basic principles o recursive feedback (positive & negative) o balance of exploitation and exploration (exploitation of familiarity and exploration of novelty) o multiple interactions
Emergence	• occurs when a number of simple entities (agents) operate in an environment whose conditions promote self-organisation resulting in the emergence of more complex behaviours as a collective • arises from intricate causal relations across different scales and feedback—interconnectivity • the emergent behaviour or properties are not a property of any single such entity, nor can they easily be predicted or deduced from behaviour in the lower-level entities: they are irreducible
Pattern of interaction	• different combinations of agents lead to the same outcome, or • the same combination of agents leads to different outcomes
Adaptation and evolution	• changes involve the whole system and are not restricted to a few measurable factors • adaptation leads to a new homoeostasis with new dynamic interactions
Co-evolution	• each agent in the exchange is changed • parallel development of a sub-system with new characteristics and dynamics

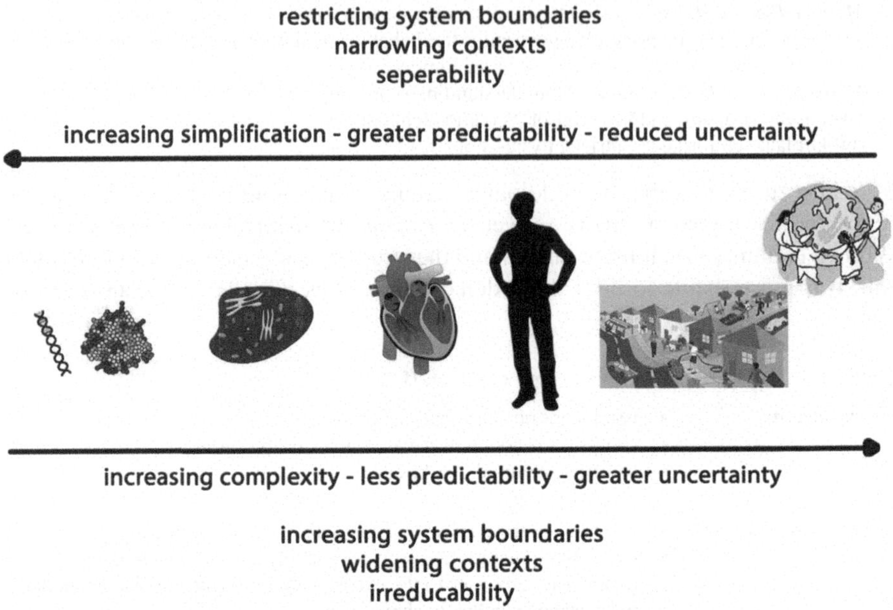

Fig. 1.5 The interrelationship between reductionist and holistic perspectives

the disordered behaviour of cells in a tumour from the understanding of a single malignant cell. Similarly understanding the attitudes and behaviours of an individual person does not infer the function of a group or society. Obviously the reverse inference is not possible either (Fig. 1.5).

Understanding the whole arises from studying the dynamics of the interconnections between its component parts, an insight that has led to the emergence of new academic fields like systems biology, psycho-neuro-immunology, systems medicine and network medicine.

1.5 Re-framing Health

How can we understand health and health care from a holism/complexity perspective?

1.5.1 Health as a Dynamic Entity

The most widely recognised definition of heath is that of the WHO: *Health is a state of complete, physical, mental and social well-being and not merely the absence of disease and infirmity* [13]. This definition presents a largely static and idealised picture and stands in contrast to the dynamic notions suggested by many other thinkers over the last 100 years [14].

Contrast this with just three dynamically focused definitions:

- Illich pointed to health as a positive state that dynamically spans across the stages of life—*The ability to adapt to changing environments, to growing up and to ageing, to healing when damaged, to suffering and to the peaceful expectation of death* [15];
- Ingstad emphasised indigenous people's experience of health as an interdependent sense of integrity, dignity and communal and environmental belonging—*Health depends on many interconnected aspects of life: belonging to one's local environment/land, the sense of freedom, cultural and spiritual belonging, and the sense of dignity and security* [16]; and
- Husserl stressed the holistic ability to function well in one's life—*Health is a holistic ability to relate properly to and function well in the whole life-world in all its aspects, and disease a disturbance of this ability, on any of a variety of levels or in any of a variety of dimensions* [17].

1.5.2 Health and Dis-ease as Experiential States

These considerations also entail that health, like disease, are subjective rather than objective states, or as Per Fugelli [18] put it, the "objective of disease" only exists when you experience it.[3] We have seen a marked shift from the etymological origins of these terms over time. Health comes from the old-English *hal* meaning whole; disease, *des*—without and *aise*—ease, meaning to be "without ease", hence better spelled as "dis-ease" reflecting the experience of discomfort, inconvenience and distress. The modern meaning of disease as an objective pathological/pathophysiological state has major implications for research, the praxis of health care and the planning of health services and policy.

How do we recognise the experience at the physiological level?

Johannes Peter Müller, the father of modern physiology, noted that external experiences like pressure on our skin are transmitted via sensory nerves to our brain where they get translated to provide us with the awareness of the stimulus. In his 1840 *Handbook of Human Physiology* he put it this way:

> Sensory perception is not the result of the transmission of a quality or state of the external objects to consciousness, but the transmission of a quality or a state of a sensory nerve elicited by an external stimulus to consciousness. These qualities, which are different in the various sensory nerves, are the qualities of the senses [19].

---

[3]The exact quote is: ... *disease does not exist, only the experience of disease* [does].

His observation was taken one step further by Jacob von Uexküll who noted that living things respond to the stimuli of their environment (Umwelt), where the stimulus acts as a "sign or symbol" that is decoded to have a particular "meaning" that results in a response—the first *bio-cybernetic* model (Fig. 1.6). He posited that living things experience their environment on a subjective level; they create what Husserl termed "their inner life-world". The ability to interpret the many objective physical, chemical and other triggers in one's environment is the basis of the concept of bio-semiotics[4] [20].

Primates and humans retain memory of their life experiences and within their inner life-world humans can imagine an external reality and experience the consequences of imagination resulting in the clinical picture of somatisation. Psycho-Neuro-Immunologists have described the physiological feedback pathways that link the physical with the emotional/cognitive, and the emotional/cognitive with the physical experiences [21]. It is only for our convenience that we separate them into different categories, when in fact they are one thing.

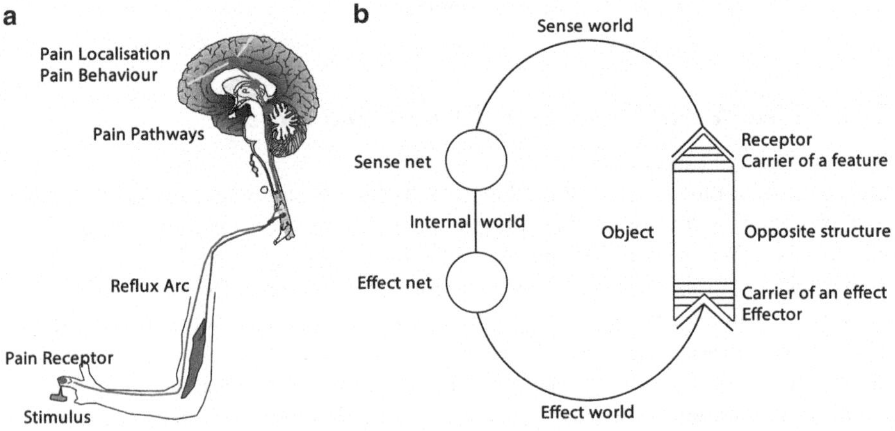

Fig. 1.6 The translation of a sensory stimulus by a pain receptor via a sensory nerve to (**a**) trigger the reflex movement away from the stimulus and (**b**) stimulation of the brain's pain centres and resultant translation of that information to pain location site and pain behaviour patterns (*left*). Jacob von Uexküll's early bio-cybernetic diagram, linking the sense world with the *internal world* and the effect world (1920)

[4]From the Greek *bios* meaning "life" and *semeion* meaning "sign", first used by Friedrich S. Rothschild in 1962.

1.5.3 *Operationalising Health as a Complex Adaptive State: The Somato-Psycho-Socio-Semiotic Model*

Whilst the bio-psycho-social model of health has long been accepted, the semiotic aspects remain neglected. In 2000 Pauli, White and McWhinney summarised the state of thinking in the following way, and there is no indication that anything has changed by late 2014:

> ...it might be argued that molecular and genetic biology have identified, or are on the way to identifying, many of the agents of life processes and their disturbances. Without minimizing the tremendous insights into biological structures and functions that have been achieved in these fields it has to be stressed that molecular or genetic entities are not the messages (signs and information) but the chemical carriers of messages (i.e. messengers) that maintain life processes. Likewise, functional phenomena, such as the interaction of transmitter substances with the receptors on cellular surfaces or the flow along neural and transmembrane potential gradients, allow no conclusion concerning the content (the meaning) of the information (sign or message) that flows. They are merely phenomena of transmission without evidence of their significance for life processes in general. To use a mechanistic analogy, there is a profound difference between radio transmitters or receivers and the music transmitted. ... Medicine ... tends to confine its conceptual thinking to a much narrower range of ideas focused largely on reductionistic processes. ... In our view [medicine] more realistically [ought to end its association with the] predominance of a mathematical/materialistic paradigm, as fascinating and productive as it has been, and [accept] a systemic/biosemiotic paradigm [22].

Health and disease have been described from different perspectives as biological or somatic, psychological or emotional, social, and semiotic or cognitive in nature. However, health and disease result from the dynamic interplay between these dimensions and are experiential in nature—health reflecting an optimal state between these dimensions (Fig. 1.7—top). These experiences can occur as much in the—rare—case of evident disease, i.e. the objective state of identifiable pathology (disease), as in its absence. Figure 1.7 (bottom) illustrates two different patients that have suffered an acute ischaemic myocardial event leading to two very different functional outcomes. The person with very significant loss of cardiac function (EF 18 %) experiences health, however, for the other person the experience has resulted in significant disease despite recovering with full cardiac function (EF >50 % [23, 24].

This somato-psycho-socio-semiotic model of health outlines the interdependencies between the various domains and, being backed by physiology, can be used as much as a diagnostic as therapeutic tool. The direction of the deviation towards one of the domains provides the "label" for the condition; besides addressing the condition's immediate concerns, returning to an optimal state requires great attention to the opposite three dimensions. In other words, the four domains of the model are dynamically interdependent.

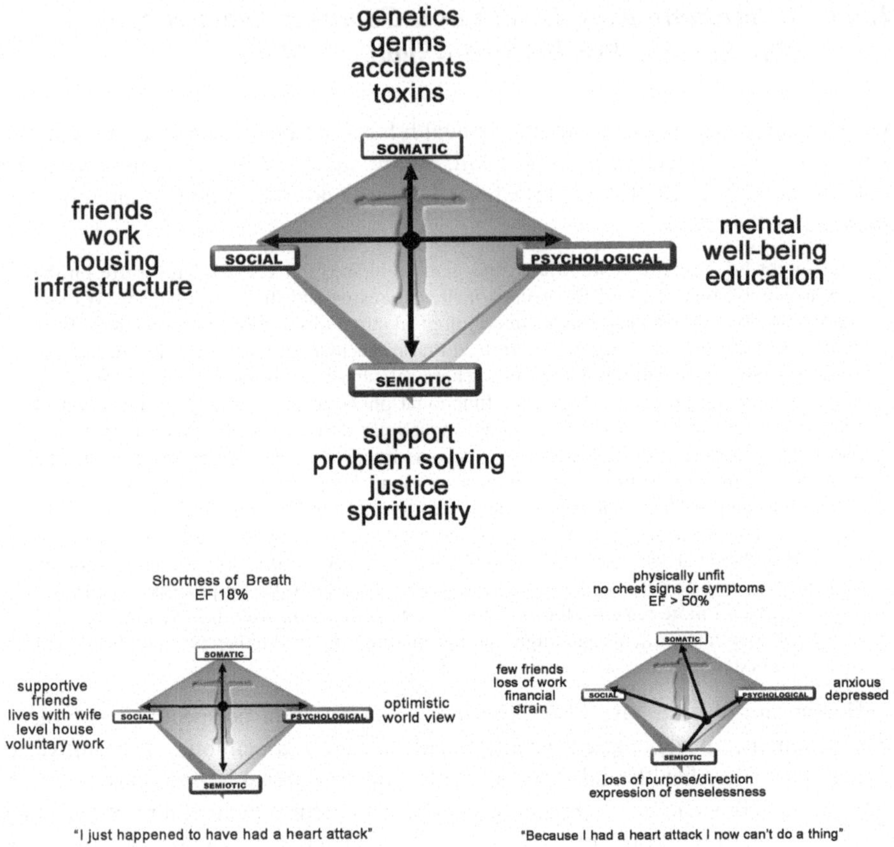

Fig. 1.7 Health resulting from the interplay of the four main dimensions of health (*top*), and their net effect in light of a specific disease

1.5.4 Dynamics of Health

The state of the components of each of the health domains changes constantly, resulting in continuous change in the experience of health. Usually, day to day changes are barely noticeable but occasionally they can be rather dramatic. When plotted in phase space, these changes result in the familiar patterns we refer to as acute illness, chronic illness, mental illness or somatisation [23] (Fig. 1.8).

This somato-psycho-socio-semiotic model of health shows the dynamic changes of health as a consequence of the four main dimensions impacting on every person's health, and explains the remarkable robustness of health at an experiential level. Adaptation to changing circumstances, be it in physiological function, emotional experience, social connectedness, cognitive appreciation, and combinations thereof, is a hallmark of health and a prerequisite for survival.

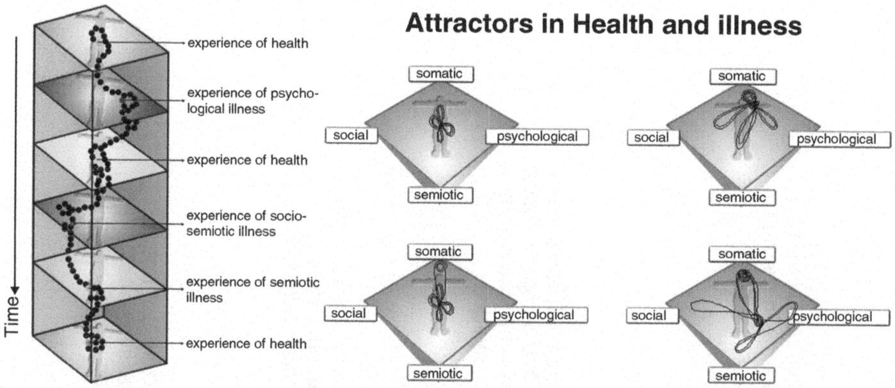

Fig. 1.8 Phase space representation of health and illness. Plotting the day-to-day changes of health (*left*) in a phase space the characteristic patterns of *health* (*top centre*), *chronic illness* (*top right*), *acute self-limiting illness* (*bottom centre*) and *somatisation* (*bottom right*) emerge

1.6 Health as the Organising Principle for a Twenty-First Century Health System

The epidemiology of health experiences in a community follows a Pareto (power law) distribution (see Fig. 1.3), meaning the majority of people feel either healthy or healthy enough not to require medical attention. Of those perceiving the need for medical care the majority have health problems requiring no disease-specific interventions. Only very few experience health problems requiring tertiary medical care.

Our health systems ought to cater for this scale-free distribution of care need. Who is the busiest hub in the system? The person—he meets most of his care needs by self-care, most of his acute and chronic illness needs through continuing, co-ordinated and person-centred care from primary/community health professionals, most of his disease-specific needs through episodic interventions by "parts-focused" health professionals, and his occasional need for catastrophic conditions through the high-technology supported interventions in a tertiary hospital setting.

Whilst the health system as a whole has to maintain a central focus, a *core value*, to allow the emergence of the most adapted or "fit-for-purpose" configuration and interactions between its agents, this will result in many different but mutually agreeable system configurations. Such *variability* is a *sign of the health of a complex system*, contrary to the belief expressed by top-down models of health system organisation.

A truly "fit-for-purpose" health system requires the whole of the system to focus on the person and his needs, with all in the various parts of the health system providing inputs to meet these needs.

The health vortex illustrates the structure and dynamics of a "fit-for-purpose" health system for the twenty-first century (Fig. 1.9).

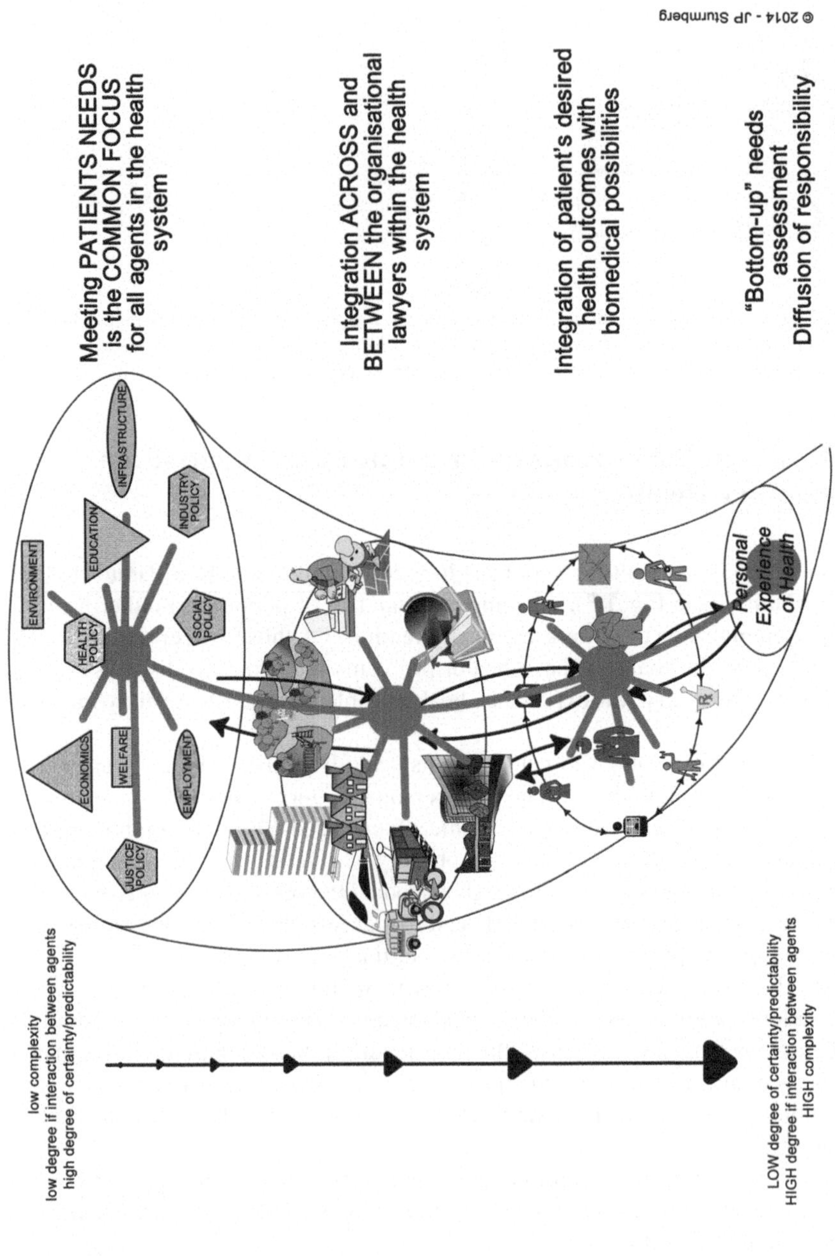

Fig. 1.9 The health vortex—connecting the elements

The changing scale from the general to the specific is associated with loss of complexity. Greater complexity is a sign of health and provides resilience, loss of complexity increases with the severity of disease. Hence it is not surprising that primary care encounters show greater complexity compared to disease-focused encounters [25].

1.7 Implications for the Twenty-First Century

"Systems and complexity" as a terminology may be new, however, our ancient colleagues already were well aware that connected things have properties that are not present in their parts. They also understood that context matters, i.e. things behave differently under varying constraints.

Any issue confronting the health system is highly interconnected with a wide range of other issues and, therefore "predictably", offers multiple perspectives to understanding. Invariably such issues are not amenable to finding the "one right" solution, and solutions will change with changing the focus (or re-framing)—we are continually dealing with *wicked problems*.

This paper has outlined the science behind the notion of *health being a personal complex adaptive state*. Consequently *health* care as a system needs to focus on the *person's needs for care*; the health vortex metaphor offers a pragmatic framework for understanding the different *scales* of a seamlessly integrated health system focused on *need*.

Finally here are some of the issues we need to address on the journey towards a truly holistic health system:

- Holism is a scientific endeavour whose foundations are based on the study of the structure and dynamics of networks at all scales—molecular, cellular, organ, person, family, community and societies
- Non-linear distributions are the rule in CAS and linear relationships define special and more limited situations
- Health and disease are states that result from the dynamic non-linear interactions between the somatic, psychological, social and cognitive/semiotic dimensions of life
- External conditions (environmental contexts) as well as specific causative agents contribute to the development of disease
- The dynamic interactions of the somatic, psychological, social and cognitive/semiotic dimensions of life modulate the physiological pathways that define the clinical pictures of somatisation and discrete diseases
- Healthcare equals care for the specific condition and its specific environmental context
- Health care providers need to distinguish "markers *associated with* health and disease" from "their *interactional function* in disease"

As a movement, we need to build a scale-free network amongst all researchers and practitioners to allow us to shape the developments towards a health system that delivers care that *meets the needs of each patient*, i.e. is "fit-for-purpose". These needs are distributed in a power law distribution with preventive care > general care > specific care. The art of practising the science of medicine is to move seamlessly along this path in light of the changing needs of the person's illness trajectory.

It's high time to translate our insights into actions. Rudolf Virchow[5] already called for system wide actions on improving health in the 1850s: "Medicine is a social science and politics is nothing else but medicine on a large scale. Medicine as a social science, as the science of human beings, has the obligation to point out problems and to attempt their theoretical solution; the politician, the practical anthropologist, [and the person-centered health professional[6]] must find the means for their actual solution."

References

1. West BJ. Where medicine went wrong. rediscovering the path to complexity. Singapore: World Scientific Publishing Company; 2006.
2. Pidd M. Tools for thinking: modelling in management science. 3rd ed. Chichester, UK: Wiley; 2010.
3. Cilliers P. Complexity and postmodernism. Understanding complex systems. London: Routledge; 1998.
4. Box GEP, Draper NR. Empirical model building and response surfaces. New York, NY: Wiley; 1987.
5. Allio RJ. Russell L. Ackoff, iconoclastic management authority, advocates a "systemic" approach to innovation. Strateg Leadersh. 2003;31(3):19–26.
6. Dörner D. The logic of failure: recognizing and avoiding error in complex situations. New York: Metropolitan Books; 1996.
7. West BJ. Homeostasis and Gauss statistics: barriers to understanding natural variability. J Eval Clin Pract. 2010;16(3):403–8.
8. West BJ. Mathematical principles: tales of tails. In: Sturmberg JP, Martin CM, editors. Handbook of systems and complexity in health. New York: Springer; 2013. p. 63–80.
9. Schwartz L, Woloshin S. Changing disease definitions: implications for disease prevalence. Eff Clin Pract. 1999;2(2):76–85.
10. White K, Williams F, Greenberg B. The ecology of medical care. N Engl J Med. 1961;265(18):885–92.
11. Port S, Demer L, Jennrich R, Walter D, Garfinkel A. Systolic blood pressure and mortality. Lancet 2000;355(3):175–80.

[5]Rudolf Carl Virchow (1821–1902) was a German doctor, anthropologist, pathologist, prehistorian, biologist, writer, editor, and politician, known for his advancement of public health. He is known as "the father of modern pathology" because his work helped to discredit humorism, bringing more science to medicine. He is also considered one of the founders of social medicine.

[6]My addition.

12. Hausdorff JM, Mitchell SL, Firtion R, Peng CK, Cudkowicz ME, Wei JY, et al. Altered fractal dynamics of gait: reduced stride-interval correlations with aging and Huntington's disease. J Appl Physiol. 1997;82(1):262–9.
13. WHO. Declaration of Alma-Ata. International Conference on Primary Health Care, Alma-Ata, USSR; 1978 Sep 6–12. Geneva: World Health Organisation.
14. Sturmberg JP, Martin CM. Handbook of systems and complexity in health. New York: Springer; 2013.
15. Illich I. Limits to medicine. medical nemesis: the expropriation of health. London: Marion Boyars Book; 1976.
16. Ingstad B, Fugelli P. "Our health was better in the time of Queen Elizabeth": the importance of land to the health perception of the Botswana San. In: Hitchcock RK, Ikeya K, Lee RB, Biesele M, editors. Updating the san: image and reality of an African people in the 21st century (Senri Ethnological Studies No 70). Osaka, Senri: National Museum of Ethnology; 2006.
17. Husserl E. The basic problems of phenomenology: from the lectures, winter semester, 1910–1911. Dordrecht: Springer; 2006.
18. Fugelli P. Clinical practice: between Aristotle and Cochrane. Schweiz Med Wochenschr. 1998;128:184–8.
19. Müller JP. Handbuch der Physiologie des Menschen, Band 2. Coblenz: Hölscher; 1840.
20. Uexküll TV, Pauli HG. The mind-body problem in medicine. Adv J Inst Adv Health. 1986;3(4):158–74.
21. Slavich GM, Cole SW. The emerging field of human social genomics. Clin Psychol Sci. 2013;1(3):331–48.
22. Pauli HG, White KL, McWhinney IR. Medical education, research, and scientific thinking in the 21st century (Part two of three). Educ Health (Abingdon). 2000;13(2):165–72.
23. Sturmberg JP. Health: a personal complex-adaptive state. In: Sturmberg JP, Martin CM, editors. Handbook of systems and complexity in health. New York: Springer; 2013. p. 231–42.
24. Sturmberg JP. The personal nature of health. J Eval Clin Pract. 2009;15(4):766–9.
25. Katerndahl DA, Wood R, Jaen CR. A method for estimating relative complexity of ambulatory care. Ann Fam Med. 2010;8(4):341–7.

Chapter 2
Systems Biology: Unravelling Molecular Complexity in Health and Disease

Amrita K. Cheema, Massimo S. Fiandaca, Mark Mapstone, and Howard J. Federoff

2.1 Introduction

Complexity in a biological system arises from a constant and dynamic interaction between different components of a living system which leads to non-linear perturbations [1]. As such, efforts to improve quality and efficacy of medical care are inextricably linked to complexity science and monitoring variability at both the level of the population and the individual [2]. Systems thinking, therefore, encompasses a holistic understanding of how things influence one another systemically [3]. In nature, examples of systems thinking include ecosystems in which various elements such as air, water, plants, and animals work together to survive or perish.

A.K. Cheema
Department of Oncology, Georgetown University Medical Center, Washington, DC, USA

Department of Biochemistry, Georgetown University Medical Center, Washington, DC, USA

Department of Molecular & Cellular Biology, Lombardi Comprehensive Cancer Center, Georgetown University Medical Center, 37th and O Streets, N.W., Washington, DC 20057, USA
e-mail: akc27@georgetown.edu

M.S. Fiandaca • H.J. Federoff (✉)
Department of Neurology, Georgetown University Medical Center, 37th and O Streets, N.W., Washington, DC 20057, USA

Department of Neuroscience, Georgetown University Medical Center, 37th and O Streets, N.W., Washington, DC 20057, USA
e-mail: mfiandac@uci.edu; federoff@uci.edu

M. Mapstone
Department of Neurology, University of Rochester School of Medicine, Rochester, NY, USA

School of Medicine and Dentistry, University of Rochester Medical Center, 601 Elmwood Ave, Box 673, Rochester, NY 14642, USA
e-mail: mark.mapstone@uci.edu

J.P. Sturmberg (ed.), *The Value of Systems and Complexity Sciences for Healthcare*, DOI 10.1007/978-3-319-26221-5_2

In organizations, systems consist not only of people, but also the structures, and processes that combine to make the enterprise healthy, or unhealthy. To date, traditional healthcare relies on treatment methods that are typically focused on speciality care, or one organ system at a time (e.g. cardiology or urology). This classic approach, however, does not always yield optimal results since it does not account for the complex and often subtle interactions between organ systems, arising from the micro-environment within and surrounding a diseased organ, and the influence of more general environmental modulators. These interactions are especially evident in the complex physiologies associated with cancer and Alzheimer's disease, that take decades to develop [4, 5]. Thus, focusing research efforts, drug development strategies, and treatment modalities on one component of the system rather than the sum of the interacting parts is likely to blind us to the operating disease mechanisms. Complexity science is based on the premise that health and disease result from non-linear interactions between the somatic, psychological, social and cognitive dimensions of life. In the example of Alzheimer's disease, while preferentially displaying anatomical localization, its inherent systemic characteristics are evident in the pre-clinical stages and recognized using comprehensive molecular phenotyping approaches [6]. Such a complex system has multiple parts, with a variety of combinations between the entities: One part may interact with multiple adjacent or remote parts; one part may provide multiple functional capabilities; and/or, many parts providing singular overlapping functions. In such a complex biological system, each component part may respond differently to a variety of environmental stimuli. Such a differential response is based on either a set of intrinsic phenotypic operating rules that help shape how extrinsic influences affect the specific component part, or the direct alteration of phenotype by the extrinsic effects. In a biochemical system, for example, such an extrinsic effect could lead to modulation of metabolic pathways that would ultimately result in an altered phenotype for a component of or the entire organism. Several studies have shown that the ageing process not only leads to structural and functional modifications of individual components of the central nervous system, as well as the musculoskeletal system, but also in a system-wide re-wiring of interactions within and between the different levels and functional domains [7, 8]. Examining and treating different biological components in isolation, therefore, leads to loss of important context and information about the relationships that exist between the specific component and the entire system. Complexity science encourages researchers, medical educators and clinicians to incorporate a more holistic view of the human biological system for more accurate diagnostic and efficacious therapeutic purposes [9].

2.2 Holism: An Imperative for the Twenty-First Century

The concept of holism is based on the premise that the whole is more than the sum of its parts. To understand the entire system, therefore, you must also appreciate the intricate inter-relationships between components, in addition to understanding each individual component. Understanding a complex system, therefore, is best directed to the level of governing principles influencing the behavior of the whole system, and not at the level of the structure and function of its component parts [10]. Thus, a holistic concept involves the study of the structure and dynamics of interacting components, forming networks at multiple levels, including molecular, cellular, organ, person, family, community and society. For the complex biological system existing in humans, the systemic interactions observed provide evidence for nearly constant change and increased uncertainty. Health and disease states, therefore, result from variations within physiological pathways resulting from a complex series of gene/environment interactions [11].

2.2.1 Disease Complexity: Malfunction of Molecular Networks

The P4 (Predictive, Preventive, Participatory, Personalized) medicine paradigm involves comprehensive understanding of regulation and dysregulation of complex molecular networks that dictate the phenotype of an individual [12]. Disease can be perceived as a consequence of aberrant reprogramming of cellular and molecular networks that lead to organ dysfunction. The interaction of the diseased organ with the entire being often leads to a cascade of multiple dysregulated networks, resulting in associated disease co-morbidities. Systems medicine aims to characterize specific perturbations resulting from alterations in genomic expression and metabolic networks that identify the inter-individual differences that augment or detract from monitoring responses to therapy. The information obtained from analyzing big data is likely to significantly decrease health care costs by personalizing care and treating the specific causes rather than the symptoms of disease [13]. Recent technological advances in genomic, proteomic and metabolomic technologies have provided researchers with unprecedented leverage in interrogating different levels of cellular expression. With the requisite bioinformatic integration of these data together with the individual clinical and social demographic strata of information, perturbations within the complex system can truly be developed on an individual basis, approaching the *cura personalis* goal.

2.2.2 Ethical Complexities in Systems Medicine

The systems biological approaches afforded by the technological advances seen in the twenty-first century have the potential to revolutionize healthcare and specifically the approach to patient care, in positive and negative ways. Both ramifications, together with an open and broad dialogue of specific issues raised by various technological advances, will minimize the risk to the "*primum non nocere*; first, do no harm" medical credo. The exploding knowledge base, mechanistic understanding, and technological advances provided through investigations in network biology are impacting society's ability to interdict in various disease states and promote well-being. Unfortunately, such rapid advances in molecular methods are transforming the caring art of medicine, more and more, into an exact, often impersonal science. Caregivers must continue to pay attention to keeping the patient and their family foremost in consideration when novel diagnostic and therapeutic options are being proposed for development and implementation. As per the systems approach in general, it is important to remember that there are complex interactions within the entire person and to their surrounding environment (e.g. family and friends, co-workers, employer) related directly to options and actions we may offer as healthcare providers. In certain cases, having the capability of offering a diagnostic or treatment doesn't necessarily translate into a single right answer. An example could include an elderly individual with severe spinal pathology making it more difficult or impossible for them to walk, due to weakness or pain. Although surgical treatment options for their spinal pathology are present, should they be offered to that specific patient? Certain diagnostics and treatments need to be weighed as to their overall effects on the system (patient + environment), risks, best/worse case scenarios, and not just related to a specific disease or condition. The moral dilemmas and complex approaches required for achieving a determination of proper conduct in these situations are growing in parallel with the sophisticated innovations in science. Recent minimally invasive biomarkers for Alzheimer's disease are being developed and provide highly accurate measures of risk of developing the disease in asymptomatic subjects. What are the important issues to consider prior to offering such a test to a person, especially in the current environment where there are no viable therapeutic options to offer? Furthermore, how will the diagnosis affect the individual with regard to future planning, end of life decisions, and their concept of personhood? Approaches to ethics and ethical patterns of behavior will require expanded consideration and implementation in dealing with the growing complexities in healthcare arising from our scientific and technological advances. The holistic approach to systems biology demands it.

2.2.3 Improving Healthcare Through Complexity Science

Improving prevention and treatment of a given pathophysiology depends on increasing knowledge of the pathogenic basis with the promise of personalizing interventions based on an intimate knowledge of individual and their environment. It is broadly stated that the "omics" technologies will enable personalized medicine, and reverse the scourge of poor health care outcomes arising from inter-individual heterogeneity. Fundamental questions remain, however, as to how personalized medicine can be enabled, and how implementation of personalized medicine might augment the evolution to customized therapeutics. Significant questions remain unanswered pertaining to the correlation of complex disease onset, progression, and prognosis, and the underlying genetic and environmental influences, as well as the role of the microbiome. Conversely, the identification and characterization of therapeutic- or nutritional-responsive gene expression and metabolism that could lead to restoration of homoeostasis requires a concerted research effort. Specifically, how does gene expression and metabolism differ qualitatively and quantitatively in health and disease? What can a systems approach reveal about the gene–environment interaction? What are the earliest anticipatory changes that can be detected to help predict the risk of disease development? What are the key intracellular and extracellular nutritionally dependent signals that trigger disease onset? The integration of data obtained from different "omics" technologies is likely to provide a roadmap for pathway-based responses that may be more effectively employed in the clinical management of a given disease phenotype. From a clinician's point of view, by encountering the full spectrum of variability in response to specific treatment in patient population with similar disease presentation, a patient-centric systems medicine approach is likely to address why some individuals respond to therapy while others do not [14]. The goal of achieving an integrated data portal containing clinical, environmental, family history, pathology, and molecular data would provide greater depth of information, leading to more thoughtful and comprehensive treatment and care decisions under the "personalized medicine" paradigm [15, 16]. By integrating a variety of clinical and molecular data elements, and facilitating rapid analysis thereof, the practice of systems medicine will be enabled in future clinical settings, including personalized strategies for disease prevention and modification. The ultimate goal of such approaches would be advanced within a population health paradigm that incorporates such data acquisition and consideration for each individual, from cradle to grave, for the benefits provided to the individual and society as a whole.

2.3 Experimental Design for Systems Biology

In recent decades, several clinical cohort and studies using animal models have utilized various "omics" approaches for dissecting dysregulated molecular networks in health and disease. The results of these studies, however, are challenging to interpret and compare due to biological, analytical and pre-analytical variability [17]. Contributing factors to the intra- and inter-individual biological variability include environmental factors (e.g. diet, lifestyle), circadian rhythm, biological age, genetics, epigenetic factors and differences in the microbiome [18–22]. In recently reported blood and urine studies using human cohorts [23, 24], substantial intra-individual variability was found for several biomarkers, thereby diminishing the power to detect disease associations. While this variability may be less problematic when using inbred strains of animals for models, especially with controlled diet and environment, it is not absent [18, 25]. Results from mouse or other animal models [26], however, are not always predictable for human based applications and hence human clinical investigations are critical for developing biomarkers that can be validated in independent cohorts and ultimately be developed for clinical use.

Other confounds exist and need to be controlled even with clinically defined biological data, for proper interpretation. Pre-analytical variability is caused by inconsistency in sample collection and storage procedures. Analytical variability arises primarily within the diagnostic laboratory and from institutional differences in standard operating procedures. Both of these components of overall variability typically lead to a decrease in signal to noise ratio [17]. Thus the importance of study design that accounts and controls for these variables cannot be over-emphasized. Standard protocols have been proposed for different types of investigations and there have been calls for a central reporting database for investigators, that would detail various contamination parameters (e.g. the presence of blood in tissues), sample stability in storage, and possible changes in the properties of the analytical system accounting for batch to batch inconsistencies [27]. Furthermore, the challenge of comparing data from different batches affects many, if not all, high-throughput methods [28]. In addition data acquisition should include randomization of cases and controls [27, 28], and the use of pooled quality controls interspersed throughout the batch acquisition course of the run [27] so as to generate high quality data. In summary, experimental study design that minimizes pre- and post-analytic variables would ultimately lead to meaningful data with potential clinical relevance and utility [29].

2.4 Conclusions

It is evident that human physiology is remarkably flexible owing to evolutionarily selected, inherent compensatory mechanisms. It remains to be seen whether human behavioral biology can also respond positively to the changes required for a truly holistic approach to medicine. Such a transition from the conventional to the holistic, as described in this chapter is likely to result in marked improvements in healthcare delivery. Even when an individual is asymptomatic, the dysregulation of molecular networks or dysfunctional interactions between system components that eventually leads to organ malfunction or a diseased phenotype, may be accessible to our diagnostic queries. A full understanding of complex disorders such as cancer or neuro-degenerative diseases requires a comprehensive analysis of all of the factors that ultimately dictate the specific phenotype. It is increasingly evident that such an approach includes many factors beyond the genome. A systems medicine strategy to understanding human disease will requisitely analyze the combined impact of biological, environmental, ethical and socio-economic factors on disease progression. Identification of individual biomarkers, or more likely collections of orthogonal biomarkers, associated in certain cases with specific environmental factors, will allow diagnosis of disease stage, and prediction of therapeutic success or failure for certain interventions. If successful, such approaches will facilitate adoption of evidence-based clinical strategies that can be broadly applied to the healthcare of individuals as well as populations.

References

1. Hawe P. Lessons from complex interventions to improve health. Annu Rev Public Health. 2015;18(36):307–323.
2. Ahmad S, Tejuja A, Newman KD, Zarychanski R, Seely AJ. Clinical review: a review and analysis of heart rate variability and the diagnosis and prognosis of infection. Crit Care. 2009;13(6):232.
3. Leykum LK, Lanham HJ, Pugh JA, Parchman M, Anderson RA, Crabtree BF, et al. Manifestations and implications of uncertainty for improving healthcare systems: an analysis of observational and interventional studies grounded in complexity science. Implement Sci. 2014;9(1):165.
4. Gomes AP, Blenis J. A nexus for cellular homeostasis: the interplay between metabolic and signal transduction pathways. Curr Opin Biotechnol. 2015;34C:110–7.
5. Schluesener JK, Zhu X, Schluesener HJ, Wang GW, Ao P. Key network approach reveals new insight into Alzheimer's disease. IET Syst Biol. 2014;8(4):169–75.
6. Fiandaca MS, Mapstone ME, Cheema AK, Federoff HJ. The critical need for defining preclinical biomarkers in Alzheimer's disease. Alzheimers Dement. 2014;10(3 Suppl):S196–212.
7. Sleimen-Malkoun R, Temprado JJ, Hong SL. Aging induced loss of complexity and dedifferentiation: consequences for coordination dynamics within and between brain, muscular and behavioral levels. Front Aging Neurosci. 2014;6:140.
8. Hong SL. The dynamics of structural and functional complexity across the lifespan. Nonlinear Dyn Psychol Life Sci. 2007;11(2):219–34.
9. Guarinoni MG, Motta PC, Petrucci C, Lancia L. Complexity of care: a concept analysis. Ann Ig. 2014;26(3):226–36.
10. Sturmberg JP. Emergent properties define the subjective nature of health and disease. J Public Health Policy. 2014;35(3):414–9.
11. Topolski S, Sturmberg J. Validation of a non-linear model of health. J Eval Clin Pract. 2014;20(6):1026–35.
12. Hood L, Auffray C. Participatory medicine: a driving force for revolutionizing healthcare. Genome Med. 2013;5(12):110.
13. Flores M, Glusman G, Brogaard K, Price ND, Hood L. P4 medicine: how systems medicine will transform the healthcare sector and society. Pers Med. 2013;10(6):565–76.
14. Vogt H, Ulvestad E, Eriksen TE, Getz L. Getting personal: can systems medicine integrate scientific and humanistic conceptions of the patient? J Eval Clin Pract. 2014;20(6):942–52.
15. Tian Q, Price ND, Hood L. Systems cancer medicine: towards realization of predictive, preventive, personalized, and participatory (P4) medicine. J Intern Med. 2012;271(2):111–21.
16. Spiegel AM, Hawkins M. 'Personalized medicine' to identify genetic risks for type 2 diabetes and focus prevention: can it fulfill its promise? Health Aff (Millwood). 2012;31(1):43–9.
17. Bielohuby M, Popp S, Bidlingmaier M. A guide for measurement of circulating metabolic hormones in rodents: Pitfalls during the pre-analytical phase. Mol Metab. 2012;1(1):47–60.
18. Johnson CH, Gonzalez FJ. Challenges and opportunities of metabolomics. J Cell Physiol. 2012;227(8):2975–81.
19. Norman AW. Sunlight, season, skin pigmentation, vitamin D, and 25-hydroxyvitamin D: integral components of the vitamin D endocrine system. Am J Clin Nutr. 1998;67(6):1108–10.
20. Lee S, Lenton E, Sexton L, Cooke I. The effect of age on the cyclical patterns of plasma LH, FSH, oestradiol and progesterone in women with regular menstrual cycles. Hum Reprod. 1988;3(7):851–5.
21. Wallace M, Hashim Y-Y, Wingfield M, Culliton M, McAuliffe F, Gibney M, et al. Effects of menstrual cycle phase on metabolomic profiles in premenopausal women. Hum Reprod. 2010;25(4):949–56.
22. Katz FH, Romfh P, Smith JA. Diurnal variation of plasma aldosterone, cortisol and renin activity in supine man. J Clin Endocrinol Metab. 1975;40(1):125–34.

23. Sampson JN, Boca SM, Shu XO, Stolzenberg-Solomon RZ, Matthews CE, Hsing AW, et al. Metabolomics in epidemiology: sources of variability in metabolite measurements and implications. Cancer Epidemiol Biomarkers Prev. 2013;22(4):631–40.
24. Xiao Q, Moore SC, Boca SM, Matthews CE, Rothman N, Stolzenberg-Solomon RZ, et al. Sources of variability in metabolite measurements from urinary samples. PloS One. 2014;9(5):e95749.
25. Cheema AK, Pathak R, Zandkarimi F, Kaur P, Alkhalil L, Singh R, et al. Liver metabolomics reveals increased oxidative stress and fibrogenic potential in Gfrp transgenic mice in response to ionizing radiation. J Proteome Res. 2014;13(6):3065–74.
26. Fiandaca MS, Federoff HJ. Using viral-mediated gene delivery to model Parkinson's disease: do nonhuman primate investigations expand our understanding? Exp Neurol. 2014;256:117–25.
27. Want EJ, Masson P, Michopoulos F, Wilson ID, Theodoridis G, Plumb RS, et al. Global metabolic profiling of animal and human tissues via UPLC-MS. Nat Protocols. 2013;8(1):17–32.
28. Leek JT, Scharpf RB, Bravo HC, Simcha D, Langmead B, Johnson WE, et al. Tackling the widespread and critical impact of batch effects in high-throughput data. Nat Rev Genet. 2010;11(10):733–9.
29. Kreutz C, Timmer J. Systems biology: experimental design. FEBS J. 2009;276(4):923–42.

Chapter 3
Complicated vs. Complex, Disease vs. Illness: Rethinking Diagnosis, Therapy, and Restoring Health

S. Lee Hong and Simeon J. Hain

The end of the twentieth century and beginning of the twenty-first century have brought about advancements in medicine that are among the greatest in man's existence. As technologies emerge and political and economic forces find their way into medicine, the physician of the twenty-first century has the challenge of simultaneously embracing the new wave of culture and adoption to industry, while holding steadfast to the roots of medicine's foundation. The centre of this foundation is and always has been the patient. Our modern system has embraced a disease care model. Disease in a pathologic sense is the scientific construct of our tools of investigation and observations in a lab. These tools allow us to define a set and distinct entity that is a theoretical construct, but the reality of disease for the patient is experienced quite differently. Science and objective data aid the clinician in understanding a patient's disease, but the protean manifestations of illness are only understood relative to the individual. In this way of thinking, "Disease, then, is an abstraction; illness, a process ... It happens to a single individual over a restricted period of time and will never happen again in precisely the same way," (Delp [1], p. 1). We must orient the available evidence and management to the unique individual rather than tailoring the individual to a system of disease. This forces the modern physician to go back to the bedside, listen and examine the patient, and construct a thoughtful approach to care with the individual at the centre of management, rather than guidelines or diseases. From this perspective (which follows throughout this chapter), disease is a disruption or significant alteration to physiological function. Disease is "objective" and can be measured directly from a single biomarker that is outside "normal limits". Illness, on the other hand, is "qualia", a subjective experience of a state of health or lack thereof.

S.L. Hong (✉) • S.J. Hain
Heritage College of Osteopathic Medicine, Ohio University,
Grosvenor Hall, Athens, 45701 OH, USA
e-mail: Slhong.iub@gmail.com; hain@ohio.edu

J.P. Sturmberg (ed.), *The Value of Systems and Complexity Sciences for Healthcare*, DOI 10.1007/978-3-319-26221-5_3

To address the dichotomy between a "disease focus" and a focus on illness, we turn to the growing field of complex systems to provide a framework for the workings of human physiology in health and disease. There is now the opportunity for this process to be guided by a conceptual orientation that understands the *limitations* of science in the context of a complex system such as the human body. If we start with the view that the patient's complaints are manifestations of a myriad of complex interactions unique to the individual, then disease can be interpreted as a process within an individual context.

3.1 Complex vs. Complicated Systems

What exactly is a complex system? Is a personal computer a complex system, with all of its many chips and transistors working together to process information while handling input and output? A personal computer is a complicated system, with many interacting components. But, each and every component serves a single function, reflecting a one-to-one mapping between the component and its function. If the hard drive is damaged and no longer functional, there is simply no way for the stored data to be accessed. If one component is not functioning appropriately, the entire system becomes completely dysfunctional. Yet, because of the one-to-one mapping of component to function, diagnosing a "disorder" in a computer is a simple process. "Treatment" is also easy, as once the damaged component(s) are replaced, the computer is fully functional.

Contemporary medicine relies heavily on a view of human anatomy and physiology from the "complicated system" perspective. Physiologic feedback loops are drawn out on a piece of paper as if a simultaneous sequence of events. A goes up, B goes down, which in turn activates C, and so on. From the disease biomarker perspective, illness is measured based on detecting values of a particular physiological marker that is outside the norm, i.e., too much of X, or too little of Y.

Unlike the computer, the human body is a complex system, where there are many-to-one and one-to-many mappings of different anatomical structures to their functions. A single anatomical structure or even its physiological output can play many different roles in affecting overall physiological function. The liver is a good example of this many-to-one mapping. Among its many functions, the liver serves as a storage space for glucose as glycogen, it also plays a role in protein synthesis, and the breakdown of red blood cells. Another example of many-to-one mapping is blood pressure modulation, a process that can be initiated via baroreceptor, chemoreceptor, and neurotransmitter action. An important benefit of the many-to-one mapping is that unlike the computer, disease or dysfunction affecting a single anatomical component does not necessarily lead to a complete breakdown of the entire system because the human body is capable of compensatory adaptation to address the dysfunction by altering the functions of other physiological systems. What imbues the body with the capacity for "self-healing" is known as "self-organization" within a complex system where multiple interacting components adapt to the outputs of one another.

3.2 The Primacy of Dynamic Patterns in Health and Illness

We often hear the phrase "the whole is greater than the sum of its parts" used to describe complex systems such as the human body. Human physiological systems are in constant flux, pulsing and oscillating and at a variety of different rates and rhythms. Nothing remains at a perfectly steady-state. On the surface, it would seem that a system that is constantly fluctuating would be difficult to control, let alone possess integrated functions. Instead, it is the dynamic nature of the body that affords the functionality of the human body. With the many different physiological processes occurring at different rates and on different time-scales, each physiological process possesses its own natural dynamics. Through a complex interaction, collective behaviours emerge driving the individual physiological dynamics away from their natural patterns, through competition and cooperation. The best way to conceptualize this collective behaviour would be the constructive or destructive collision of waveforms, the waves in the ocean being a great physical example. Sometimes, waves collide and extinguish their collective behaviour. At other times, the interactive dynamics of the waves generate a constructive, synchronized action, leading to high magnitude waves.

Within the human body, we know there are many pulsatile processes and wave actions, such as blood flow, peristalsis, and even insulin secretion. Greater emphasis could be placed on their dynamic patterns. One example would be a situation where a patient presents with high fasting blood glucose, yet has a normal response on the glucose tolerance test. Such an example reflects a situation where the problem is not just more glucose, but rather, an individual capacity to effect change on the blood glucose level over time. While much of medical science is based on standardization and normalization for the purposes of reliability and validity, what is often forgotten is that every patient is a unique, complex combination of physiological processes that are constantly in flux. An awareness of the dynamic patterns gives another perspective from which to appreciate the significance of this flux.

Another consequence of the generally wave-like and pulsatile nature of human physiology is a need to reconsider the concept of "blockage" and impingement of an anatomical or physiological process. Most often, physicians rely on imaging to detect such obstructions to normal function. However, imaging approaches such as magnetic resonance imaging (MRI) require the accumulation of data over a period of time, e.g., 2–3 s for a clear "static" image, obscuring any dynamics of the given anatomical or physiological process. A good example of a dynamic problem hidden by a static image would be shoulder pain with no clear lesion or impingement on an MRI. Yet, the patient continues to complain of pain in that joint, perhaps, especially during movement. It is quite possible that the dynamics of the muscles that span the shoulder are pulling against one another in a manner that results in pain. Adjacent structures may require shoulder compensation.

Such dynamic phenomena should also be considered in other forms of obstruction, e.g., vascular, lymphatic, and digestive. If a nearby anatomical structure pulses with a phase relationship with the structure in question that creates a destructive collision of waveforms, then a dynamic blockage is created. This type of blockage can arise as whenever the primary structure is about to achieve its zenith along its wave form, it is met with a counter motion of equal and opposite magnitude from the nearby structure. If these waveforms are synchronized (albeit out-of-phase), there is a destructive, cancelling process, where the process has been obstructed in a manner that cannot be detected through static images.

3.3 Disrupted Dynamic Patterns on the Pathway to Illness and Disease

In order to illustrate the phenomenon how aberrant physiological dynamics can lead to disease, an overview of a medical case is presented. Here, a patient presents with atrial fibrillation (AF), yet, does not possess any common risk factors for the disease, which would include history of coronary disease or hypertension, alcohol abuse, thyroid disease, diabetes, kidney disease or family history of atrial fibrillation. When asked about recent trauma history, the patient replied that approximately 1 month prior, she had tripped at a junction falling forward face first striking the concrete ground with her chin and breaking her jaw, which was still very tender. As a result, the fall and ensuing jaw injury was the only remarkable factor in her medical history.

Thus, a question arises as to a possibility of how such a traumatic event so far from the chest could result in a disruption of cardiac function. Landing on the tip of the chin would effectively stretch the longus coli, sternothyroid and sternohyoid musculature. The mandible itself would be compressed and act as a lever lifting the tracheal and oesophageal fascia's in the pre-tracheal fascial compartment. This would likely create leverage into the mediastinum and put longitudinal tension into the pulmonary trunk. There would also be circumferential compression along the tensed tissues (including the carotid sheath) supplying afferent and efferent nervous supply to the heart. The pulmonary trunk region is where the electrical isolation between the pulmonary veins and atrial pacemaker cells resides. A similar cascade of events involving the muscles of mastication and their anatomic relationship with the mandible and cranial base would occur in this strain and is likely the reason for her jaw movement abnormalities.

These alterations to the musculature have the effect of leading to hypertonicity in the neck flexors and hypotonicity in the neck extensors. In order to allow movement, joints must be spanned and acted upon by two or more muscles. Each muscle generates a torque to create angular motion about the joint and movement is achieved by shifting the equilibrium points of both the flexor and extensor [2]. The compliance or "stiffness" of the joint, i.e., its resistance to force can then be achieved by shifting the force-length relationship for each muscle, allowing a greater resistance to external forces. Effectively, the illness is a disruption in the dynamic balance between the muscles of the neck.

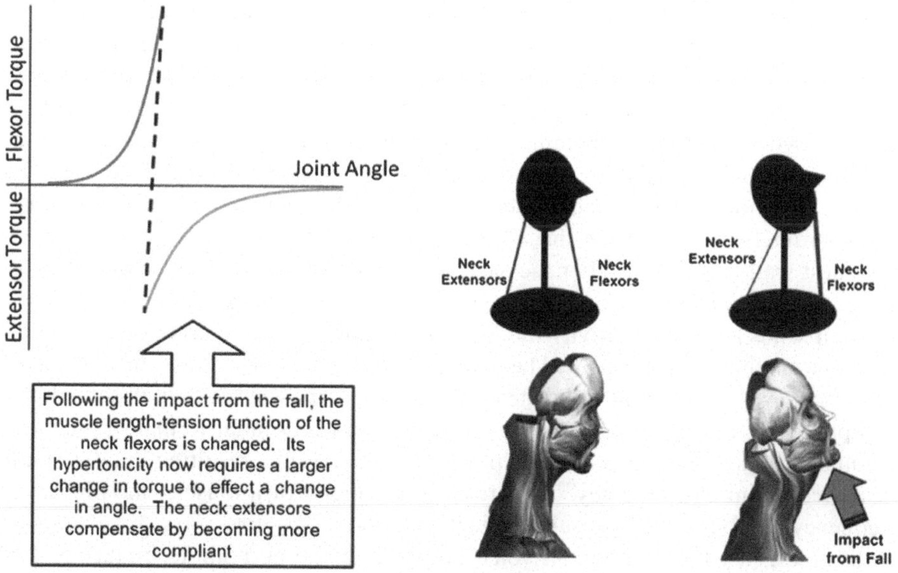

Fig. 3.1 Effect of jaw impact on altering the equilibria of the neck muscles. The result of the impact is a tonic imbalance, leading to aberrant coordinated muscle activity dynamics

Via the blow to the jaw, the neck flexor muscles will be rapidly stretched, resulting in a deviation in their equilibrium points. However, because normal day-to-day function (e.g., looking around, eating, etc.) requires the general resting position of the neck to be maintained to look ahead, the extensor muscles have to shift their equilibrium points in order to adapt to the trauma chronically (Fig. 3.1). As a result, the length-tension relationships have been changed, leading to two problems: (1) lengthening of the flexors with a greater force needed to accompany a change in length, i.e., stiff flexors; and (2) shortened extensors that are actually more compliant in that they require a smaller force to change the angle at the neck. This is consistent with the principle of a complex dynamic self-organizing system as there was a compensatory change in the agonist-antagonist relationship at the neck in response to the trauma of the fall.

One clear possibility is that a change in mechanical tension of the musculature surrounding the chest wall (and increased tension of pretracheal-pericardial structures) alters the mechanics of each heartbeat. It is more important to keep in mind that mechanical actions of the muscles and the electrical activity that would be evident in an electromyogram are synonymous [3]. Simply, muscle activity from the point of its mechanics and electrophysiology are one in the same. This is where the idea of the body as a dynamic unit becomes essential.

At this juncture, it is important to remember that atrial fibrillation is characterized by the lack of organized atrial activity (quivering or "chaotic" conduction of electrophysiological activity in the heart) with an irregularly irregular ventricular response [4]. A normal sinus rhythm allows the completion of clear beat cycles from the atria to the ventricles. When the rate is quivering, there is a greater proportion of higher frequency activity that is reflected in chaos or chaotic fluctuations (see Williams [5]) in the electrical activity of the heart. Chaos in the electrical activity will overwhelm the sinus rhythm, leading to the quivering activity seen as atrial fibrillation. Consequently, the overall heartbeat will be negatively affected.

The next question to be addressed is where such complex patterns could arise from an interaction between the normal activity in the atria and the muscles of the chest wall and ribcage. For the sake of simplicity, we can consider a situation where the heart and muscle wall interact as a summative process. Each time the atria beats, it sends a pulse of activity into the musculature. As these processes "collide" with one another, waveforms will become superimposed onto one another. When all of these waves at different frequencies are summed up, what is then observed is a complex pattern of fluctuations. One analogy would be similar to that of plucking a guitar string, where the heartbeat "plucks" on the muscle, resulting in a vibration of a given primary frequency. The greater the tonicity of a muscle, the higher its frequency will be, just like a guitar string.

Muscles, just like the human voice do not oscillate at a single frequency, but rather over a broad range of harmonic frequencies, which arise from a variety of mechanical and neural sources [6]. The patterns of muscle oscillations are extremely complex as the muscle interacts with connective tissues. Especially if one considers potential distant effects from other joints and connective tissues in more remote regions of the body, as in pre-tracheal fascial connections in this case, the dynamics of the behaviour of any single muscle will contain a broad range of oscillation frequencies and amplitudes. In a situation without somatic dysfunction around the ribcage, the musculature is sufficiently compliant, allowing for a low frequency, slower vibrations at the level of the muscles that do not interfere with the normal dynamics of the heart. But, when the tonicity of the musculature is excessive, the tension on the "guitar string" leads to a high pitched vibration, leading to high frequency oscillations that overwhelm the atrial p-waves.

To capture this, we create a simple example of this phenomenon using a computational model. On the left panel of Fig. 3.2, we observe a condition where there is a normal level of tonicity in the neck flexors. Using powernoise.m (created by Little et al. [7]) in MATLAB, we create a muscle response in the chest wall that is dominated by low frequency activity. The net effect of both cardiac and muscle processes is the sum of the two signals. When tonicity results in low frequency dynamics, a slow drift in net output is observed, but the p-waves are maintained overall. This drift is similar to that which is observed in everyday electrocardiographical measurements. When there is hypertonicity in the neck flexors, the muscle response contains a greater presence of high frequency activity from the muscles of the chest wall. The net result is a "destruction" of the original p-waves and a chaotic pattern of atrial activity.

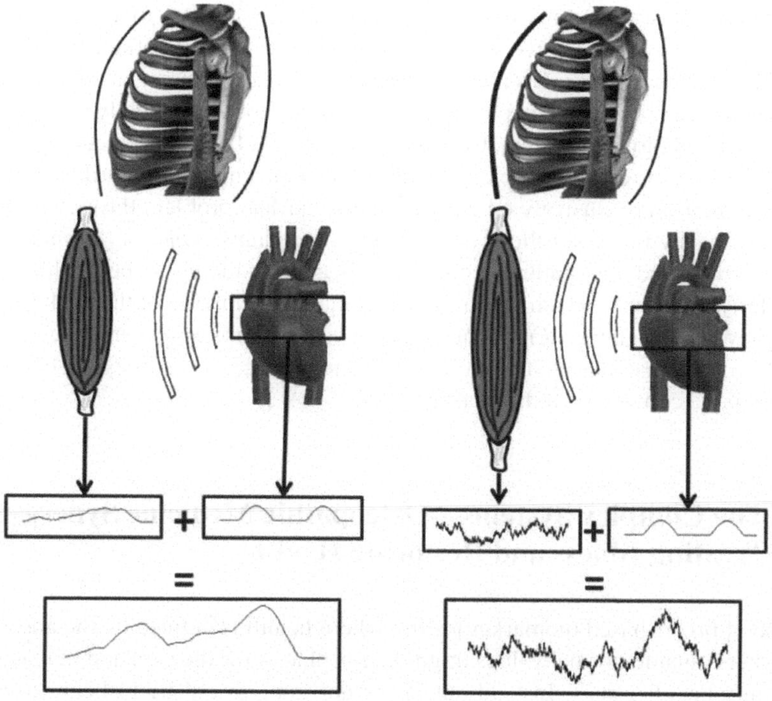

Fig. 3.2 A simple model of how atrial fibrillation can arise from hypertonicity in the musculature. *Left panel* shows how normal p-waves would be affected by low frequency oscillations in muscle. The shape of the p-waves is maintained, with the introduction of a slow drift normally seen in ECGs. *Right panel* demonstrates the effects of hypertonicity, which contaminate the p-waves with high frequency oscillations. The net result is a chaotic oscillation in the ECG signal, which overwhelms the p-waves

3.4 Disease and Illness: Chicken or Egg?

The problem that a complex system dynamics perspective raises is whether disease necessarily has to precede illness. Because of the inherent compensatory capacity of human physiology, the body is remarkably flexible. However, the process of diagnosing illness seems more difficult, only becoming apparent once a few different physiological systems become dysfunctional simultaneously. Perhaps this is why some illnesses are insidious. As mentioned in a preceding section, even if a single or multiple physiological systems suffer from disease, an illness is not necessitated, but depends on the body's capacity to adapt and compensate for the diseased systems. Yet, by convention, there is an expectation that a single physiological system becomes affected by disease initially that eventually begins to affect other physiological systems, giving rise to illness. From this perspective disease is a well-defined entity that leads to the understanding of the vagaries, often communicated as symptoms that are the patient's experience of illness. Because of the compensatory, adaptive nature, and its complex organization, this does not always have to be the case. Even in the absence of disease, illness, i.e., dysfunctional interactions between the many physiological systems could eventually lead to failure of a single physiological system. Effectively, this would be illness preceding disease.

Returning to the case of the patient with AF, by convention, standard medical care would be focused exclusively on alleviating the cardiac problem through treatment with rate or rhythm controllers or with anti-coagulants. Once a "normal" sinus rhythm is restored, the patient would have been considered to be healthy, while the underlying illness, which was a dysfunctional coordination of the neck muscles, would have been ignored. From the perspective of complex systems, medical care should require that the dysfunction in the musculature be addressed before the patient can be considered to be healthy.

3.5 The Complex Systems—Osteopathic Medicine Synergy: Treating Illness and Restoring Health

The use of broad-based biomarker testing where health is defined by the absence of biomarkers outside normal values might be misplaced for the care and management of chronic health issues. Instead, an important goal would be to begin to detect illness, by seeking out holistic patterns of dysfunction. If this could be achieved before the onset of disease, considerable morbidity and mortality may be prevented, allowing our healthcare system to evolve into a true *health*care system. Osteopathic Medicine, since its inception, looks beyond the focus on treatment of diseases and tries to better understand the integrated components that make up health in the individual. This approach does not in any way mitigate or ignore disease, but rather broadens the scope of search for a more complete understanding of a patient's problems. Attempts to delve further into the minutiae have driven medicine for the past century and yielded incredible levels of understanding. The time has come to begin the monumental task of putting these pieces back together from a complex systems perspective and attempt to, "take a crude look at the whole," as Murray Gel-Mann, Nobel laureate put it.

The *complexity* of the human body is not reducible to complicated pieces, but rather stands alone as a whole. By observing the principles of a non-linear dynamic system, for the body in action, possibilities emerge that allow inherent bodily forces to drive health. This complexity, when viewed as a whole, is an opportunity for modern medicine to evolve into a search for health dynamic and complex—rather than maintaining a primary (largely unitary) focus on fighting disease. Health and the accompanying patterns of integrated function are ongoing processes that, when dysfunctional, precede the onset of disease in essentially every case. True patient centred care attempts to *restore health* to the unique individual not just fight or prevent disease. The dynamic complex systems perspective offers the opportunity to more fully realize this patient-focused approach to health and medicine.

In conclusion, diseases are not lurking in the shadows waiting to pounce on unsuspecting victims, but rather represent a perturbation of the coordinated dynamics of many different physiological systems. In this light, targeting a single biomarker and "restoring" it to normal levels may not be a viable solution. From a complex systems perspective, the causes of illness are almost always multi-factorial and involve a broad range of influences that may be inherited over generations within families, acquired by poor dietary habits, accumulated in a lifetime of traumas, be it physical, environmental and mental. At no time are any individual factors independent from the interactions with the whole. In many ways, disease is not much more than a label, while illness is the eventual manifestation of alterations to the overall functions of the many components that make up the individual. Health then is far more than the absence of disease, and is best understood only in the context of the complex system that is the individual. Complex systems and complexity theory offer a scientific orientation to such a broad and all-encompassing global view of health and disease. More importantly, it provides an intellectual framework from which novel therapeutic methods and modalities of addressing health problems at the level of the individual can be developed.

References

1. Delp MH, Manning RT, Major RH. Major's physical diagnosis. Philadelphia: WB Saunders Company; 1975.
2. Feldman AG. Once more on the equilibrium-point hypothesis (lambda model) for motor control. J Mot Behav. 1986;18(1):17.
3. Hof AL. EMG and muscle force: an introduction. Hum Mov Sci. 1984;3(1):119–53.
4. Longo D, Fauci A, Kasper D, Hauser S, Jameson J, Loscalzo J. Harrison's principles of internal medicine. 18th ed. New York: McGraw-Hill; 2011.
5. Williams GP. Chaos theory tamed. Washington, DC: Joseph Henry Press; 1997.
6. Elble RJ, Koller WC. Tremor. Baltimore: Johns Hopkins University Press; 1990.
7. Little MA, McSharry PE, Roberts SJ, Costello DA, Moroz IM. Exploiting nonlinear recurrence and fractal scaling properties for voice disorder detection. BioMed Eng OnLine. 2007;6(1):23.

Chapter 4
A System for Systems Epidemiology: The Example of Inference from Agent-Based Models

Abdulrahman M. El-Sayed

4.1 Systems and Epidemiology: The Conceptual Argument

The dynamics of populations, in terms of health and disease, emerge from the behaviors and interactions of the heterogeneous individuals that comprise them. In this way, interaction undergirds many of the mechanisms that mediate the production of health and disease. These interactions may operate both on the macro-scale between exposures acting at multiple levels and on the micro-scale between individuals within populations. Interactions challenge the current epidemiologic toolkit in several ways. As factors may interact in complex ways to determine health and disease risk, the current "risk factor" approach to epidemiology, which emphasizes decontextualized, independent effect measures for exposures may not be appropriate [3, 4]. Furthermore, variability in health may be mediated by the degree and nature of social interaction within and between social groups. In this regard, several studies have shown that social interaction may transmit non-infectious disease outcomes [5–8]. Furthermore, research about the health influences of social

---

This chapter draws directly from two previously published papers [1, 2].

A.M. El-Sayed (✉)
Department of Epidemiology, Mailman School of Public Health,
Columbia University, New York, NY, USA

Detroit Health Department, City of Detroit, 3245 E. Jefferson Ave,
Ste 100, Detroit, MI 48207, USA
e-mail: ame2145@columbia.edu; abdul.m.elsayed@gmail.com

J.P. Sturmberg (ed.), *The Value of Systems and Complexity Sciences for Healthcare*, DOI 10.1007/978-3-319-26221-5_4

interactions suggests that population-level modes of social interaction, such as social cohesion, social capital, and social support, may shape population health and disease distribution [9–11]. Ultimately, however, social interaction does not lend itself to the reductionist analytic paradigm that we employ, as potentially important social interactions between individuals in a population violate the central assumption of independence of observations in regression approaches. Second, population dynamics feature nonlinearity, whereby change in disease risk is not always proportional to the change in exposure, and feedback, where disease can modulate exposure just as exposure can modulate disease. These dynamics are not often explored in social epidemiology, although they may have profound implications for population health. For instance, a central observation in social epidemiology is that low social status predicts poor health [12]. However, poor health can also predict low social status [13]. Therefore, mutually reinforcing in a positive feedback loop, low social status and poor health may ultimately converge, with reinforcing implications for a third social ill-inequality (which itself plausibly feeds back on low social status and poor health) [14, 15]. As is characteristic of positive feedback loops, the relationships between social status, health, and inequality are likely to feature nonlinear, accelerating behavior because of amplification at each turn of the loop. As an illustration of the inability of the current epidemiologic paradigm and toolset to negotiate these dynamics, consider the use of directed acyclic graphs (DAGs) in traditional epidemiologic analyses. DAGs are mental models used to specify and formalize the causal relationships between exposures and outcomes. However, like the regression models they educate, these mental models, by definition, forbid cyclical relationships between exposure and outcome, and therefore the feedback and reciprocity that likely characterize the true relationships between them. Third, the counterfactual conceptual framework that underpins epidemiologic inquiry falls short when considering both fundamental social causes and macrosocial causes of disease. Our etiologic understanding of the social determinants of disease rests on the counterfactual exercise of contrasting outcome occurrence probabilities corresponding to two or more mutually exclusive exposures [3, 4]. However, social factors, of fundamental importance in social epidemiology, such as race, ethnicity, and gender, are attributes of individuals, rather than exposures. Because these attributes are fundamental to identity, authors have argued that the counterfactual approach is theoretically implausible [15–18]. Similarly, understanding macrosocial causes requires the assumption that a counterfactual universe could be unchanged barring a large-scale social cause. However, causes across levels are inevitably interlinked, suggesting that an alternate universe comparable to the present universe, save changes in a macrosocial influence, may also be implausible. These three challenges may be limiting the progress of epidemiology, and have resulted in calls to adopt newer methods that can overcome them [18–21]. Several authors have suggested the adoption of systems approaches in epidemiology as a way past these challenges [22–24]. "Systems thinking" suggests that complex dynamic systems, such as populations, which feature multiple interdependent components whose interactions may include feedback, non-linearity, and lack of centralized control [25], are best understood holistically [26]. This epistemological approach is best contrasted to "reductionism," which suggests that systems are best understood by aggregating information gathered via the independent study of their components. By contrast, a systems approach implies that the dynamics and behavior of a system are different, qualitatively, from those of the sum of its parts. A systems approach, therefore, emphasizes the dynamics of relationships between components of a system, rather than the characteristics of those components themselves [26, 27].

4.2 Systems and Epidemiology: An Empirical Example

Computerized simulation approaches, such as agent-based models, are of growing interest in population health research [22, 23]. Agent-based models are computerized simulation models that can be used to simulate individuals nested in simulated environments over simulated time. The simulated individuals behave according to programmed rules that define baseline characteristics, locations in space, and interactions with their environments and with one another. These simulated individuals are dynamic and adaptive over time, autonomous from one another, and heterogeneous with regard to baseline characteristics. Moreover, they can be nested within networks that can simulate diverse motifs of human interaction, such as households, families, social networks, neighborhoods, and communities. We propose the use of agent-based counterfactual (ABC) simulations, simulations of counterfactual universes that use artificial computerized models, to allow for discrete in silico "policy experiments" from which researchers can infer the influences of perturbations within particular exposure parameters on outcomes of interest within the simulation.

Although this approach is only in its early stages, there are already fruitful examples of the use of ABC simulations in epidemiologic inquiry. For example, two recent studies used similar computerized simulations to characterize the mechanisms underlying social disparities in walking behavior and food choices, respectively. Yang et al. [28] used an agent-based model in which walking choices were influenced by demographic and spatial characteristics as well as distances to different activities, walking ability, and attitudes toward walking to simulate walking behaviors within a city. By comparing walking behavior across four counterfactual simulations, each with different levels of safety and walkable land use, the authors demonstrated that differences in these factors in more deprived compared with less deprived neighborhoods might explain socioeconomic disparities in walking behavior. Another study [29] used an agent-based model to understand socioeconomic disparities in healthy food consumption. In this model, aggregate household food preferences in a neighborhood, which are products of household socioeconomic status, predicted the availability of stores offering healthy food in that neighborhood. The authors demonstrated that with socioeconomic segregation, stores offering healthy food became less prevalent in low-income neighborhoods. Furthermore, through a series of simulations, they demonstrated that both increasing healthy food preferences in low-income households and decreasing the price of healthy foods were necessary to improve availability of healthy food in low-income settings.

In the present analysis, we had two aims. First, we used an ABC simulation model to explore the implications of interventions targeting social networks to reduce obesity. To do this, we simulated the relative efficacy of interventions that target the most highly connected individuals in a social network relative to those targeting individuals at random. Second, we illustrated the potential of ABC simulations as a powerful tool in etiological inference building on observational analyses in settings where randomized social interventions are impractical.

4.2.1 Model

We used data from the Health Surveys for England in 1999 and 2004 as well as data about the relative risk of obesity among those with obese contacts compared with those without obese contacts from Christakis and Fowler [6] to design an agent-based social network model of obesity in England among a simulated birth cohort born in 1981.

Initial conditions for the baseline model were as follows: Each agent was stochastically assigned gender, ethnicity, social class, and educational level, adherent to distributions of each characteristic in England, such that the proportion of Asian, black, and white agents, for example, mimicked that of the English population overall. Each agent was nested within 1 of 6 spatial contexts, representing different ethnic and social class compositions, and was placed in a context preferentially by demographic characteristics (ethnicity and social class). A proportion of the population was assigned obese status at the model outset by demographic and neighborhood allocation similar to the population 18 years of age who are obese in England. Each agent represented an individual 18 years of age at the model outset, aging by 1 year for each time step, each agent's risk for developing obesity in that time step was calculated as a function of gender, ethnicity, social class, education, and social contacts and was implemented (Web Appendix available at http://aje.oxfordjournals.org/).

To model the effects of social networks on the spread of obesity, agents were also nested within a segregated social network that was generated by using a biased preferential attachment growth model to create a scale-free (Barabsi-Albert model) [30] social network with assortative mixing. The network was initialized from a seed network composed of a small number of agents. Each new agent added to the network was connected to up to four existing agents with a probability of connecting to an existing agent that was proportional to the number of connections that existing agent already had. Moreover, an additional bias was included to preferentially connect agents with like characteristics. Whereas 25 % of new agents to the network were connected without regard to their characteristics (i.e., ethnicity, social class, education), 50 % of new agents to the network were restricted to connecting with existing agents of similar ethnicity, again with a probability of connecting to existing agents with the same ethnicity that was proportional to the number of connections that agent already had. Twenty-five percent of new agents added to the network were restricted to connecting with existing agents of similar ethnicity and social class, again with a probability of connecting to an existing agent with the same ethnicity and social class that was proportional to the number of connections that agent already had.

For contacts of obese nodes, we assigned a higher probability of becoming obese in each time step on the basis of findings from Christakis and Fowler [6], such that if an agent's contact became obese in a previous time step, that agent had a 1.16 times higher risk of developing obesity in the current time step. For more detailed information about the construction of the model and its limitations, please see the original article [2].

4.2.2 Simulations

We tested two interventions. The first was a prevention intervention that rendered a proportion of the population incapable of becoming obese throughout the simulation. It was administered first among 10 % of the population at random and then among the most well-connected 10 % of the population. The second intervention featured a treatment for obesity, which returned a proportion of the entire obese population back to normal body mass index each year. It was implemented among 10 % of the obese population each year, first at random, and then among the most well-connected 10 % of the population. To understand the influence of the strength of the network effect of obesity on our findings, we tested each of these interventions both on the baseline model and by using an altered model in which the parameter indicating the relative risk of developing obesity if a network contact became obese in the previous time step was increased from 1.16 (the Christakis and Fowler parameter) to 10.

We ran further simulations to ensure the robustness of our findings to the population scale of each intervention as well as to differences in network topology as discussed above. To account for the potential for different outcomes by intervention scale, we simulated each of the interventions applied to 30 % of the population as well. To account for potential sensitivity to network topology, we replicated each of our simulations by using a segregated Erdős–Rényi model and a clustered network (construction described in detail in the Web Appendix).

To further characterize the mechanism underlying our findings regarding the effects of targeting our treatment intervention, we ran two further simulations. By using the scale-free network model with an artificially high network communicability parameter of 10 (the relative risk of developing obesity if a network contact became obese in the previous time step), we implemented a permanent treatment intervention whereby in each time step, 10 % of the obese population reverted back to normal weight and was made incapable of developing obesity in future time steps.

This intervention was implemented both at random and by targeting the most well-connected individuals in the population.

All intervention simulations were compared with a control simulation (with the same network effect parameter and network topology) without any intervention. All results were subject to Monte Carlo simulation with 100 iterations.

4.2.3 Findings

Among the most well-connected 10 % of individuals in the scale-free social network, the mean number of contacts was 25.4 per agent, and the median number of contacts was 17 (not shown). Among the remaining agents in the model, the mean number of contacts was 6.1 per agent, and the median number of contacts was 5 (not shown).

Figure 4.1 shows obesity prevalence by age among 10,000 agents representing a cohort born in 1981 in England in a simulation without intervention (baseline), simulating an intervention that prevented 10 % of the population from becoming obese at random, and simulating an intervention that prevented the most well-connected 10 % of the population from becoming obese. There was almost no difference in the prevalence of obesity throughout the life course between simulations that included interventions and the baseline simulation. Similarly, there

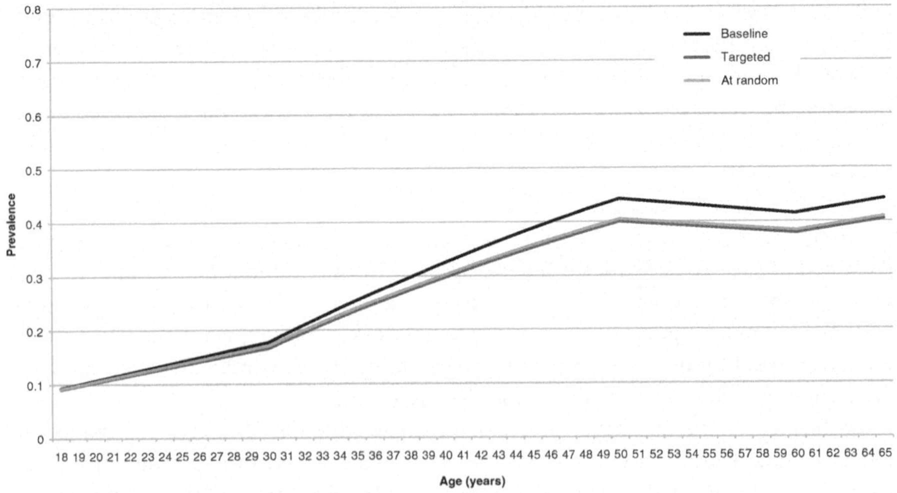

Fig. 4.1 Obesity* prevalence and 95 % confidence intervals by age among 10,000 agents representing a cohort born in 1981 in England (a) without intervention (b) simulating an intervention which prevented 10 % of the population from becoming obese at random, and (c) simulating an intervention which prevented the most well-connected 10 % of the population from becoming obese. *Obesity calculated as BMI $> 30\,\mathrm{kg/m^2}$

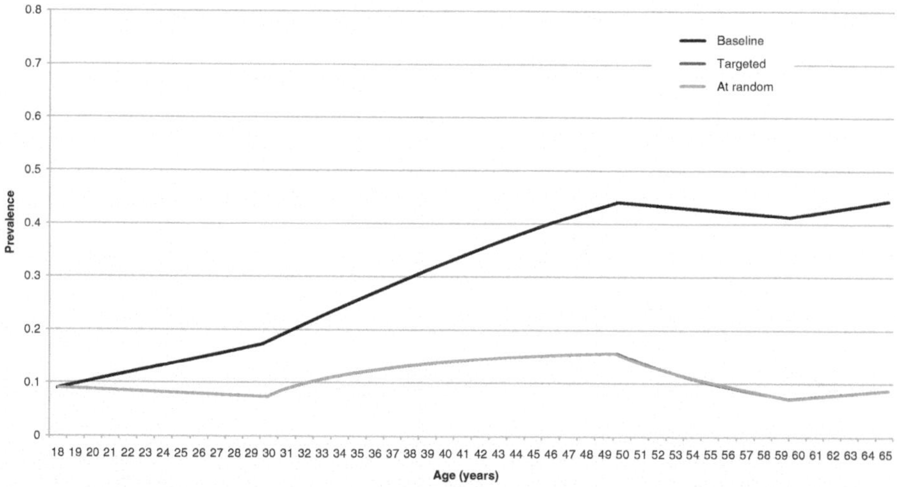

Fig. 4.2 Obesity* prevalence and 95 % confidence intervals by age among 10,000 agents representing a cohort born in 1981 in England (a) without intervention, (b) simulating an intervention that treated obesity among 10 % of the obese population each year, and (c) simulating an intervention that treated obesity among the most well-connected 10 % of the obese population each year. *Obesity calculated as BMI > 30 kg/m^2

was no difference in the prevalence of obesity between the simulation featuring the intervention implemented among the most well-connected individuals and that featuring the intervention implemented at random. Similarly, Fig. 4.2 shows differences in obesity prevalence in a simulation without intervention (baseline), in a simulation of an intervention that treated obesity among 10 % of the obese population each year at random, and in a simulation of an intervention that treated obesity among the most well-connected 10 % of the obese population each year, with similar findings. Although both intervention simulations showed lower prevalence of obesity throughout the life course than the baseline simulation, the targeted intervention did not outperform the intervention implemented at random in reducing obesity prevalence.

Figures 4.3 and 4.4 are analogous to the previous two figures, although demonstrating the results of simulations run in the model with the artificially high network effect on obesity risk. Figure 4.3 shows the results of preventive interventions implemented both among the most well-connected individuals and at random relative to baseline. The lowest prevalence of obesity occurred in the simulation with the intervention targeting the most well-connected obese individuals, followed by the simulation featuring the at-random intervention, and then the baseline simulation with no intervention. By contrast, Fig. 4.4, which shows the results of the treatment intervention implemented both among the most well-connected individuals and at random relative to baseline, demonstrates the lowest prevalence of obesity in the simulation featuring the intervention implemented at random, followed by the simulation featuring the targeted intervention, and then the baseline simulation.

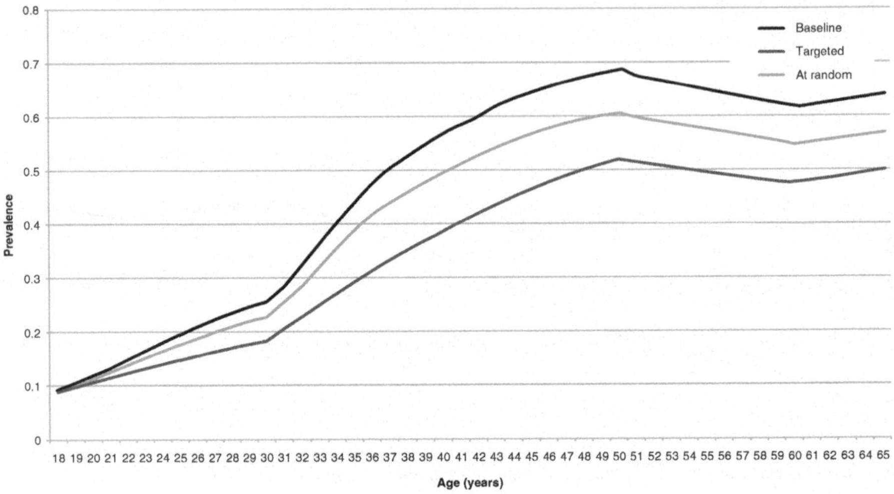

Fig. 4.3 Obesity* prevalence and 95 % confidence intervals by age among 10,000 agents representing a cohort born in 1981 in England in simulations with artificially high network effects on obesity risk[1] (a) with no intervention, (b) simulating an intervention which prevented 10 % of the population from becoming obese at random, and (c) simulating an intervention which prevented the most well-connected 10 % of the population from becoming obese. *Obesity calculated as BMI $> 30\,\text{kg/m}^2$. [1]In these simulations, if a network contact became obese, an agent's odds of becoming obese increased to 10 as compared to 1.16 in the baseline model

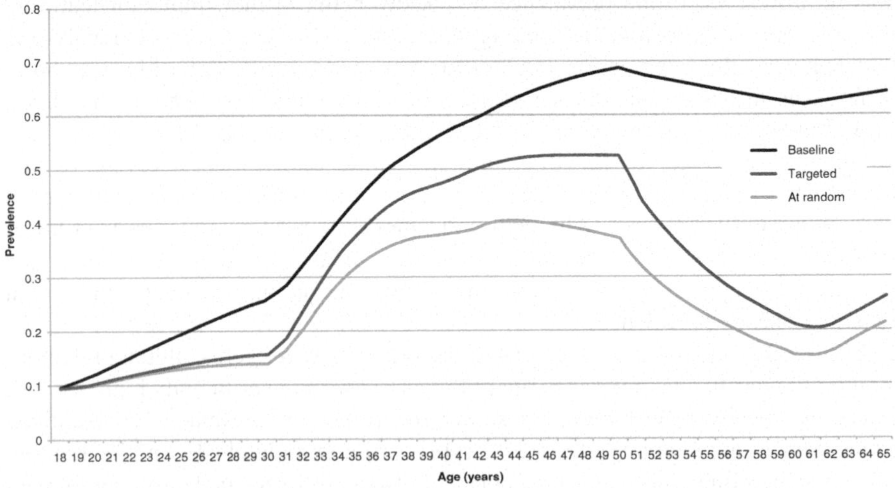

Fig. 4.4 Obesity* prevalence and 95 % confidence intervals by age among 10,000 agents representing a cohort born in 1981 in England in simulations with artificially high network effects on obesity risk[1] (a) at baseline, (b) simulating an intervention that treated obesity among 10 % of the obese population each year, and (c) simulating an intervention that treated obesity among the most well-connected 10 % of the obese population each year. *Obesity calculated as BMI $> 30\,\text{kg/m}^2$. [1]In these simulations, if a network contact became obese, an agent's odds of becoming obese increased to 10 as compared to 1.16 in the baseline model

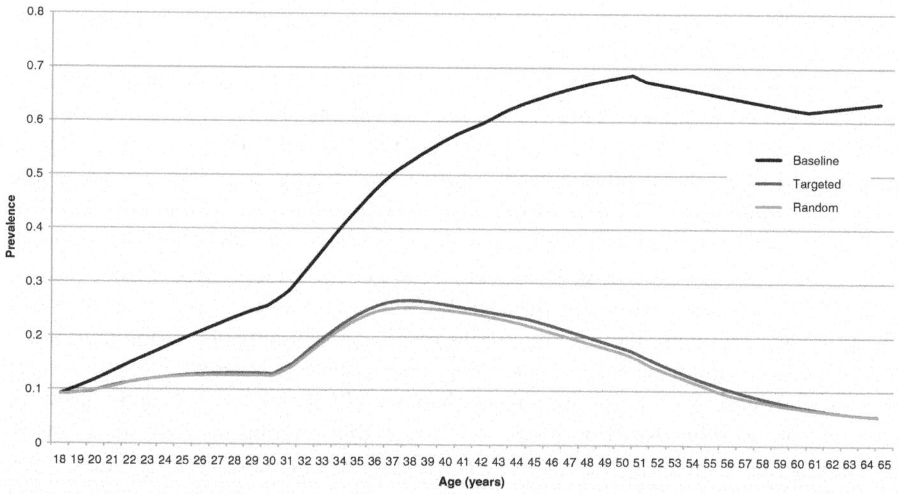

Fig. 4.5 Obesity* prevalence and 95 % confidence intervals by age among 10,000 agents representing a cohort born in 1981 in England in simulations with artificially high network effects on obesity risk[1] (a) at baseline, (b) simulating an intervention that permanently[2] treated obesity among 10 % of the obese population each year, and (c) simulating an intervention that permanently[2] treated obesity among the most well-connected 10 % of the obese population each year. *Obesity calculated as BMI $> 30\,\text{kg/m}^2$. [1]In these simulations, if a network contact became obese, an agent's odds of becoming obese increased to 10 as compared to 1.16 in the baseline model. [2]Following treatment, agents were no longer capable of developing obesity at any further point in time

Results in Figs. 4.1, 4.2, 4.3, and 4.4 were replicated across network topologies and intervention scales with no qualitative differences in findings.

Figure 4.5, analogous to Fig. 4.4, shows the results of a permanent treatment intervention wherein treated individuals were made incapable of becoming obese again in future time steps. Relative to Fig. 4.4, which shows the results of treatment interventions that imposed no restrictions on individuals' future risks of developing obesity, Fig. 4.5 demonstrates that eliminating future risk of obesity eliminated nearly the entire gap in efficacy between the intervention implemented at random and that targeting the most well-connected individuals in the population.

4.2.4 *Implications*

In this ABC simulation of the progression of obesity through a densely interconnected social network among a simulated population of 10,000 individuals representing an English cohort born in 1981 between ages 18 and 65 years, we found no difference in the progression of obesity when either preventive or treatment interventions were applied differentially to well-connected individuals in a network or randomly across the population.

Our study adds to a small but growing literature that has simulated obesity interventions predicated on epidemiologic observations about the spread of obesity through social networks. Bahr et al. [31] used social networks to test hypotheses with regard to effective interventions against the obesity epidemic. By using the body mass index (calculated as weight (kg)/height(m)^2) distribution from US data in 2000 to initialize their network, as well as the basic rule that the likelihood of progression between classes of body mass index (underweight, appropriate weight, overweight, or obese) was a function of the body mass index class of the majority of an agent's contacts, they found stable results across network topologies (e.g., lattice, random, small-world, or scale free). They concluded that weight loss among friends of friends was more important than weight loss among friends alone in affecting the weight loss of an index individual, that pinning the body mass index of random individuals in the network could promote a more healthy body mass index distribution, and that interventions among well-connected individuals would be more effective than interventions among individuals at random.

Arising from this literature are a number of important considerations regarding where and how to intervene. While the literature remains nascent in this area, our findings, alongside other literature, yield several important insights. Primarily, information about social networks for targeting social networks to improve the efficiency of public health interventions may not merit the investment this might require, and public health institutions may better invest resources elsewhere to maximize efficiency. By contrast, individuals interested in mitigating weight gain or improving weight loss may seek to identify friends of their friends.

However, our findings demonstrate the value of systems simulation to educate public health. Further research regarding systems simulation methods, including parameterization, calibration, and validation are needed. Furthermore, there are many more public health issues for which these methods may yield important insights: addressing the spread of smoking, drug use, risky sexual behavior, and other potentially socially transmitted activities.

References

1. El-Sayed AM, Scarborough P, Seemann L, Galea S. Social network analysis and agent-based modeling in social epidemiology. Epidemiol Perspect Innov. 2012;9(1):1.
2. El-Sayed AM, Seemann L, Scarborough P, Galea S. Are network-based interventions a useful antiobesity strategy? An application of simulation models for causal inference in epidemiology. Am J Epidemiol. 2013;kws455.
3. Greenland S, Robins JM, Pearl J. Confounding and collapsibility in causal inference. Stat Sci. 1999;14:29–46.
4. Kaufman JS, Kaufman S, Poole C. Causal inference from randomized trials in social epidemiology. Soc Sci Med. 2003;57(12):2397–409.

5. Andrews JA, Tildesley E, Hops H, Li F. The influence of peers on young adult substance use. Health Psychol. 2002;21(4):349.
6. Christakis NA, Fowler JH. The spread of obesity in a large social network over 32 years. N Engl J Med. 2007;357(4):370–9.
7. Fowler JH, Christakis NA. Dynamic spread of happiness in a large social network: longitudinal analysis over 20 years in the Framingham heart study. Br Med J. 2008;337:a2338.
8. Pearson M, West P. Drifting smoke rings. Connections. 2003;25(2):59–76.
9. Cohen SE, Syme S. Social support and health. New York: Academic; 1985.
10. Hawe P, Shiell A. Social capital and health promotion: a review. Soc Sci Med. 2000;51(6):871–85.
11. Kawachi I, Kennedy BP, Glass R. Social capital and self-rated health: a contextual analysis. Am J Public Health. 1999;89(8):1187–93.
12. Link BG, Phelan J. Social conditions as fundamental causes of disease. J Health Soc Behav. 1995;80–94.
13. Goldman N. Social inequalities in health. Ann N Y Acad Sci. 2001;954(1):118–39.
14. Marmot M, Wilkinson RG. Psychosocial and material pathways in the relation between income and health: a response to Lynch et al. Br Med J. 2001;322(7296):1233.
15. Wilkinson R, Pickett K. The spirit level: why greater equality makes societies stronger. New York: Bloomsbury Publishing; 2009.
16. Holland PW. Statistics and causal inference. J Am Stat Assoc. 1986;81(396):945–60.
17. Kaufman JS. Epidemiologic analysis of racial/ethnic disparities: some fundamental issues and a cautionary example. Soc Sci Med. 2008;66(8):1659–69.
18. Kaufman JS, Cooper RS. Seeking causal explanations in social epidemiology. Am J Epidemiol. 1999;150(2):113–20.
19. Diez Roux AV. Integrating social and biologic factors in health research: a systems view. Ann Epidemiol. 2007;17(7):569–74.
20. Kaplan GA. Whats wrong with social epidemiology, and how can we make it better? Epidemiol Rev. 2004;26(1):124–35.
21. Roux AVD. Towards a realistic and relevant public health: the challenges of useful simplification. J Public Health. 2008;30(3):230–1.
22. Auchincloss AH, Roux AVD. A new tool for epidemiology: the usefulness of dynamic-agent models in understanding place effects on health. Am J Epidemiol. 2008;168(1):1–8.
23. Galea S, Hall C, Kaplan GA. Social epidemiology and complex system dynamic modelling as applied to health behaviour and drug use research. Int J Drug Policy. 2009;20(3):209–16.
24. Galea S, Riddle M, Kaplan GA. Causal thinking and complex system approaches in epidemiology. Int J Epidemiol. 2010;39(1):97–106.
25. Ladyman J, Lambert J, Wiesner K. What is a complex system? Eur J Phil Sci. 2013;3(1):33–67.
26. Meadows DH. Thinking in systems: a primer. White River Junction: Chelsea Green Publishing; 2008.
27. Skyttner L. General systems theory: problems, perspectives, practice. Singapore: World Scientific; 2005.
28. Yang Y, Diez Roux AV, Auchincloss AH, Rodriguez DA, Brown DG. A spatial agent-based model for the simulation of adults' daily walking within a city. Am J Prev Med. 2011;40(3):353–61.
29. Auchincloss AH, Riolo RL, Brown DG, Cook J, Diez Roux AV. An agent-based model of income inequalities in diet in the context of residential segregation. Am J Prev Med. 2011;40(3):303–11.
30. Barabsi A-L, Albert R. Emergence of scaling in random networks. Science. 1999;286(5439):509–12.
31. Bahr DB, Browning RC, Wyatt HR, Hill JO. Exploiting social networks to mitigate the obesity epidemic. Obesity. 2009;17(4):723–8.

Chapter 5
Coping with Complexity and Uncertainty: Insights from Studying Epidemiology in Family Medicine

Martin Konitzer, Waltraud Fink, Vilen Lipatov, Gustav Kamenski, and Thorsten Knigge

Between 1950 and 1980 pioneers of Family Medicine observed a number of paradoxes. Austrian GP Braun [1, p. 168] and [2, pp. 278 ff] showed that paradoxically 80 % of general practice consultations end with an outcome label belonging to the 20 % least certain "diagnoses". British epidemiologist Cochrane [3, pp. 197ff] found a skewed Gaussian distribution of intraocular pressure, however glaucoma occurred widely across the distribution even below mean pressure readings. British GP Marinker [4] experienced encounters he could not handle with the skills of his Balintian training but only cope with by hermeneutics of chaos borrowed from Foucault and Borges.

M. Konitzer (✉)
Hannover Medical School (MHH), Department of Family Medicine, Academic Teaching Practice, Bahnhofstr. 5, D-29690 Schwarmstedt, Germany
e-mail: m-konitzer@t-online.de

W. Fink
Vienna University, Department of Public Health, Academic Teaching Practice, Haus Nr. 142, A-3722 Straning, Austria
e-mail: waltraud.fink@gmx.at

V. Lipatov
Compass Lexecon, 23 Square de Meeus (7th Floor), Brussels 1000, Belgium
e-mail: vlipatov@compasslexecon.com

G. Kamenski
Vienna University, Department of Public Health, Academic Teaching Practice, Ollersbachgasse 144, A-2261 Angern, Austria
e-mail: kamenski@aon.at

T. Knigge
Family Physician, Hasenheide 5, D-29313 Hambühren, Germany
e-mail: ctknigge@gmx.de

J.P. Sturmberg (ed.), *The Value of Systems and Complexity Sciences for Healthcare*, DOI 10.1007/978-3-319-26221-5_5

For the first time these pioneers described implicitly the complexity of Family Medicine. Some readers might have recognised that Braun's and Cochrane's skewed distributions follow Pareto's 1909 graphs of wealth distribution [5, pp. 192ff], i.e. 80 % of "events" occur in 20 % of the "population". However only recently have these complexities been made explicit by complexity researchers in medicine [6].

We trace Braun's epidemiological studies of family medicine encounters which emphasised its high level of diagnostic complexity and associated uncertainties, which is in stark contrast to speciality practice whose encounters end with well-defined diagnoses and low uncertainty.

5.1 Braun's Law, Distribution, Grid and Protocols: An Implicit Handling of Epidemiological Complexity

Over the years national [7–9] and international [10–12] epidemiological studies have shown similar patterns of distributions of illness in primary care. Braun was one of the first to publish these patterns, formulate a law and draw out the implications for daily general practice.

5.1.1 Braun's Law

Sixty years ago, based on his own as well as British GPs' Horder [13], McGregor [14] and Logan [15] studies, Austrian GP Robert N. Braun stated his epidemiological law:

> Populations of at least 1,000 unselected persons living under similar conditions present to Family Medicine in similar annual frequency rates of old and new episodes of illness (= cases) [16].

Braun's international comparison from 1957 [1] shows that the epidemiology of clinical encounters follows a power law or Pareto distribution [5, 17]. He *implicitly* unveiled the complexity and uncertainty properties inherent in this distribution as suggested by systems philosopher Luhmann [18], however, rather than exploring the properties of these distributions theoretically, he successfully reduced their *complexity* for practical application in the clinical setting (Fig. 5.1).

5.1.2 Distribution

To make sense of the distribution's pattern Braun initially referred to German economist Wilhelm Lexis' theory of illnesses' distributions as "biological mass phenomena" [19, pp. 6–13], a reference provided by an attendant of his Vienna lecture in 1955 [20, p. 84].

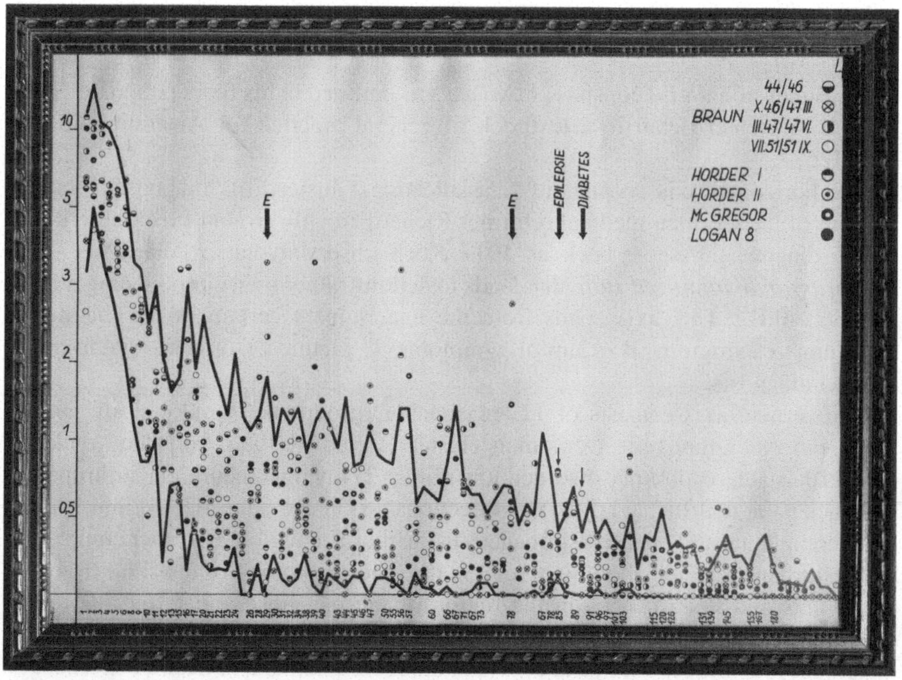

Fig. 5.1 Braun's original graph from 1957 showing ranking (abscissa) and frequency (ordinata, scale logarithmically compressed) of diagnoses from his own and colleagues' practices

Co-working with statistician Karl Freudenberg of the Lexis School Braun focused primarily on Lexis' theory itself and not on the theory's fruitful consequences for risk classification as described by Keynes in his "Treatise on Probability" [21, pp. 391ff]. Otherwise perhaps he would have noted Keynes' theory of irreducible uncertain risks [22, p. 84ff] which are inherent in the distribution of economic data as in his own observations on diagnoses. Mandelbrot [23] analysed such economic data distributions during the early 1960s, the same time Braun published his data.

Braun's attempts, stimulated by Wittgenstein's *Tractatus* [24, 25, p. 56], to reach a firm diagnoses by the logical deduction of *true/untrue* statements was unsuccessful. He realised that diagnoses cannot be reduced to binary sets of *diagnosis/no diagnosis* as they "logically progress" along a continuum of ***symptom—group of symptoms—picture of disease—diagnosis***—the foundation of his diagnostic grid.

5.1.3 Grid

His bi-dimensional grid consists of two axes as outlined in his first textbook of 1970 [2] and in greater detail in a textbook of general practice for Australian GPs in 1982 [26].

The horizontal axis consists of “classifications” instead of “diagnoses”, taking account of the German medical reformer Richard Koch’s ground-breaking critique of the diagnosis. As far back as 1917 Koch observed that a “diagnosis” is a *temporary individualized state* that leads to actions rather than simply being a label [27, pp. 70ff].[1] This axis spans from the uncertain to certain of the diagnostic spectrum: **A** symptom, **B** group of symptoms, **C** picture of disease (syndromes), **D** exact diagnosis.

The vertical axis consists of 12 “reasonable” groups or “windows” of *consultation outcomes* that reflect common clusters sorted by their frequency ranking: (1) febrile state, respiratory disorder, tonsillitis; (2) myalgia, neuralgia, arthropathy, low back pain, neuritis; (3) pyogenic infections—skin and adnexae; (4) injuries; (5) other complaints and health disturbances in the thoracic region; (6) other complaints and disturbances in the abdominal region; (7) other pathology of the skin; (8) other complaints and disturbances in the region of the ear, nose and throat; (9) other complaints and disturbances in the urogenital region; (10) other complaints and disturbances in the region of the eye; (11) other complaints and health disturbances concerning the “nerves” and psyche; (12) other complaints and health disturbances.

Figure 5.2 illustrates the *certainty distributions* in the 12 “windows” from Braun’s original work.

Globally general practice outcomes show a certainty distribution [() = examples of respiratory problems for illustration purposes] of:

- **A** symptom 25 % (cough)
- **B** group of symptoms 25 % (cough, rhinitis, sore throat and fever)
- **C** disease picture (syndromes) 40 % (picture of scarlatina)
- **D** diagnosis 10 % (evidence of beta haemolytic streptococcus)

The bottom line shows the distribution across all presentations.

[1] Die Diagnose ist also ein Ausdruck für die Summe der Erkenntnis, die den Arzt zu seinem Handeln und Verhalten veranlasst. … Diagnostiziert wird nicht ein Krankheitsbegriff, sondern der Zustand eines einzelnen. [The diagnosis is an expression of the sum of insights that cause the physician to act and respond. … We do not diagnose the label for the person’s illness experience, i.e. the diagnosis, but rather the state of experience of that person.]

	A classification of symptoms	B classification of unnamed syndromes	C classification of named syndromes	D diagnoses	A-D total of lines, absolute percentage of total of episodes of care
1 uncharacteristic febrile syndrome	330 (number of cases) 28,25 (percentage in this line)	791 67,72	46 3,94	1 0,09	1168 14,7
2 muscular pain, pain in joint and joints, sacral and sacroiliac pain, neuritis	351 36,15	496 51,08	104 10,71	20 2,06	971 12,2
3 abscess, furncle, boil	1 0,35	10 3,52	270 95,07	3 1,06	284 3,6
4 Injuries	18 2,92	43 6,98	248 63,92	14 3,61	388 4,9
5 other disorders in thoracical region, cough	57 14,69	69 17,78	248 63,92	14 3,61	388 4,9
6 other disorders in the abdominal region	218 30,19	218 30,19	179 24,79	107 14,82	722 9,1
7 other disorders of skin	81 9,16	47 5,32	641 7,51	115 13,01	884 11,1
8 other disorders in the otonasopharyngeal region	58 21,01	7 2,54	158 42,63	53 19,20	276 3,5
9 other disorders in the urogenital region	125 28,80	30 6,91	185 42,63	94 21,66	434 5,5
10 other disorders in the region of the eyes	22 9,82	13 5,80	126 56,25	63 28,13	224 2,8
11 other disorders of psyche and the nerves	75 16,30	94 20,43	244 53,04	47 10,22	460 5,8
12 other disorders and complaints	481 31,60	119 7,82	804 52,83	118 7,75	1522 19,1
total of column absolute %	1817 22,90	1937 24,4	3298 41,50	897 11,30	7949 100,0

Fig. 5.2 Braun's bi-dimensional grid. Note the marked variability of diagnostic accuracy between each of the 12 "reasonable clusters". The *bottom row* shows the overall distribution of "diagnostic certainty"

5.1.4 Protocols

As Braun states in his Australian textbook this *reduction of complexity* aims to *reduce diagnostic uncertainty.*

> The classification of "Results of Consultation" just described is fundamental to appreciation of what really goes on in general practice. It frees practitioners from the feeling of compulsion to make a "diagnosis" when it is really quite unjustifiable to do so. It also provides a realistic base on which to construct a suitable programme for the patient involving both prognosis and a plan of action [26, Chap. 1].

Diagnostic programmes according to Braun are founded in standardizing the clinical approach:

...individual processes of history taking and examination intuitively produced by conscientious doctors. Repetitive collection of a series of such processes derived from similar cases can lead to the preparation of a process list protocol which may then be tested by applying it to like "Reasons for Consultation" in the future [26, Chap. 5].

Diagnostic programmes are primarily founded in common sense logical operations grounded in the experience as a lay person as well as the professional intuition based on knowledge and prior experience:

When the beginner in general practice undergoes the unfamiliar experience of being called to his first patient with an "uncharacteristic fever", he usually proceeds according to his hospital experience modified only by his previous experience as a layman. This lay experience is derived from what he has observed when he himself, a member of his family or a close acquaintance has been similarly afflicted and possibly attended by the family doctor. From this lay experience he knows at least something of the excellent prognosis and likely rapid recovery of patients under similar circumstances. Conversely he may also have heard of some others who have fallen sick in this way with serious or eventual fatal consequences and carry this prior conditioning with him into the new situation.
As the doctor becomes more experienced in practice, repetitive involvement with frequently met "uncharacteristic" reasons for consultation unconsciously builds up useful working programmes in his mind specific for the problems appropriate for use in general practice [26, Chap. 5].

As these quotes highlight Braun's central concern as a general practitioner remained that of diagnostic accuracy, embodied by his fundamental question: *It looks like, but what is it really?* [27, 28, p. 94]. Hence he aimed to develop diagnostic programmes to discriminate different causes amongst similar symptoms, or—semiotically speaking—processing similarity.

During the 1950s New Zealand's SR West and Braun independently developed diagnostic protocols, first published in 1960. Braun remarked that *Communication with West had made it clear, where identical "Reasons for Consultation" had been worked on, nearly identical protocols had been produced independently* [26, Chap. 5, third page].

Braun's protocols have been refined over time and are now in its fifth German edition [29]. They consist of 82 protocols and follow the 12 windows or "reasonable clusters" approach from the Braunian grid as shown in Fig. 5.3.

5.2 Braun's Work in Its Historical Context

Whilst Braun's classification system was highly regarded in Great Britain, Australia and France [26, 30–32], and his important concepts like "reason for consultation/encounter", "result of consultation/encounter", "avoidable dangerous courses of disease" (French: "scenes du danger") have been widely adopted, Braun did not succeed in defining family medicine as a discipline.

Three reasons have been postulated all of which relate to differences between "academic" and "pragmatic practitioner" viewpoints throughout the 60s–90s:

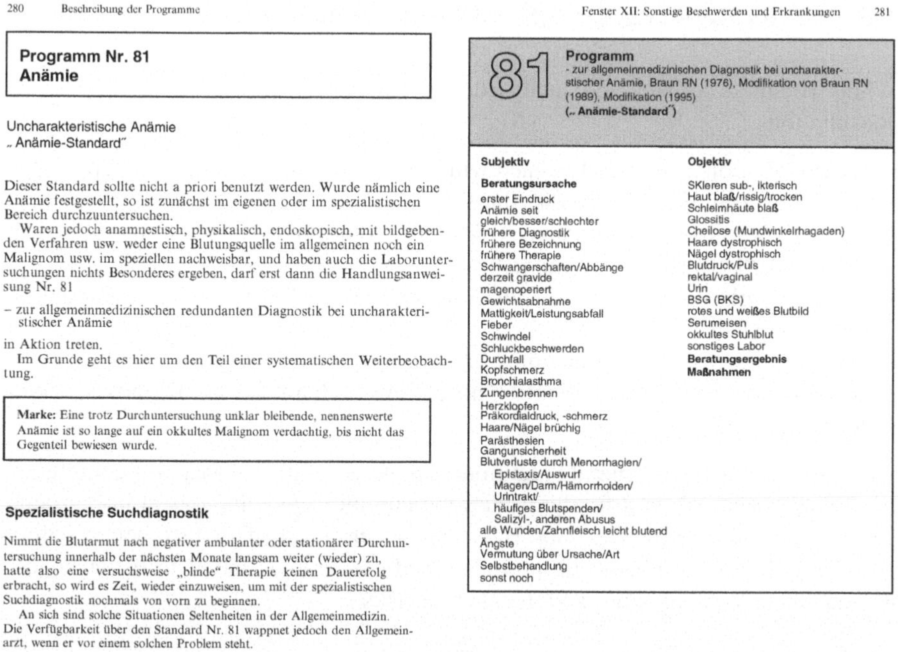

280 Beschreibung der Programme

Programm Nr. 81
Anämie

Uncharakteristische Anämie
„ Anämie-Standard"

Dieser Standard sollte nicht a priori benutzt werden. Wurde nämlich eine Anämie festgestellt, so ist zunächst im eigenen oder im spezialistischen Bereich durchzuuntersuchen.

Waren jedoch anamnestisch, physikalisch, endoskopisch, mit bildgebenden Verfahren usw. weder eine Blutungsquelle im allgemeinen noch ein Malignom usw. im speziellen nachweisbar, und haben auch die Laboruntersuchungen nichts Besonderes ergeben, darf erst dann die Handlungsanweisung Nr. 81

– zur allgemeinmedizinischen redundanten Diagnostik bei uncharakteristischer Anämie

in Aktion treten.

Im Grunde geht es hier um den Teil einer systematischen Weiterbeobachtung.

Marke: Eine trotz Durchuntersuchung unklar bleibende, nennenswerte Anämie ist so lange auf ein okkultes Malignom verdachtig, bis nicht das Gegenteil bewiesen wurde.

Spezialistische Suchdiagnostik

Nimmt die Blutarmut nach negativer ambulanter oder stationärer Durchuntersuchung innerhalb der nächsten Monate langsam weiter (wieder) zu, hatte also eine versuchsweise „blinde" Therapie keinen Dauerefolg erbracht, so wird es Zeit, wieder einzuweisen, um mit der spezialistischen Suchdiagnostik nochmals von vorn zu beginnen.

An sich sind solche Situationen Seltenheiten in der Allgemeinmedizin. Die Verfügbarkeit über den Standard Nr. 81 wappnet jedoch den Allgemeinarzt, wenn er vor einem solchen Problem steht.

Fenster XII: Sonstige Beschwerden und Erkrankungen 281

81 **Programm**
- zur allgemeinmedizinischen Diagnostik bei uncharakterstischer Anämie, Braun RN (1976), Modifikation von Braun RN (1989), Modifikation (1995)
(„ Anämie-Standard")

Subjektiv

Beratungsursache
erster Eindruck
Anämie seit
gleich/besser/schlechter
frühere Diagnostik
frühere Bezeichnung
frühere Therapie
Schwangerschaften/Abbänge
derzeit gravide
magenoperiert
Gewichtsabnahme
Mattigkeit/Leistungsabfall
Fieber
Schwindel
Schluckbeschwerden
Durchfall
Kopfschmerz
Bronchialasthma
Zungenbrennen
Herzklopfen
Präkordialdruck, -schmerz
Haare/Nägel brüchig
Parästhesien
Gangunsicherheit
Blutverluste durch Menorrhagien/
Epistaxis/Auswurf
Magen/Darm/Hämorrhoiden/
Urintrakt/
häufiges Blutspenden/
Salizyl-, anderen Abusus
alle Wunden/Zahnfleisch leicht blutend
Ängste
Vermutung über Ursache/Art
Selbstbehandlung
sonst noch

Objektiv

SKleren sub-, ikterisch
Haut blaß/rissig/trocken
Schleimhäute blaß
Glossitis
Cheilose (Mundwinkelrhagaden)
Haare dystrophisch
Nägel dystrophisch
Blutdruck/Puls
rektal/vaginal
Urin
BSG (BKS)
rotes und weißes Blutbild
Serumeisen
okkultes Stuhlblut
sonstiges Labor
Beratungsergebnis
Maßnahmen

Fig. 5.3 Example of a Protocol—Anaemia—from Braun RN, Mader FH. Programmierte Diagnostik in der Allgemeinmedizin. 5th. ed. Heidelberg, New York: Springer; 2005

1. The implementation of ICPC rather than ICD had major advantages for the academic perspectives on family medicine, however it did not advance Braun's "pragmatic practitioner" concern of enhancing diagnostic certainty in an epidemiologic environment of high uncertainty.
2. In Braun's opinion evidence based medicine's Bayesian inference model—also favoured by academic family medicine—is inappropriate for decision making in low prevalence environments and high levels of diagnostic uncertainty.
3. Braun's personality [25, 31], being passionately committed to defend his rigorous scientific approach to "pragmatic" general practice, prevented collaboration with those offering differing perspectives.

However, Braun's conceptualisation of the complexities of family medicine with its high level of diagnostic uncertainty again attracts scientific interest, especially under interdisciplinary aspects of risk management in low risk environments [33] and diagnoses' distributions as an issue of quantitative linguistics, e.g. Zipf's law [34–36].

5.3 Understanding Complexity in Clinical Practice

While Braun described and analysed the complex nature of general practice consultations,

- the distributions are fractal as each window of consultation outcomes repeats the overall pattern of the whole distribution
- 80 % of all consultations receive 20 % of all "consultation outcome labels" which define the "least certain diagnoses"
- the long tail contains 20 % of all consultations and 80 % of all "consultation outcome labels"
- 90 % of all consultation outcomes fall within more or less well-defined "classification categories", but only 10 % have a "well characterised diagnoses" (refer to Fig. 5.2)

it is our task to help all general practitioners to successfully manage this complexity in daily practice. We will firstly discuss the complex epidemiological background (fractality, Pareto properties, non-Bayesian uncertainty) of daily practice before proposing the use of diagnostic protocols and casugraphic tables to better handle the discipline's complexities and its inherent risks.

5.3.1 Fractality

The term "fractality" was coined by Mandelbrot [23] meaning that a broken part or "fractus" repeats the pattern of the part it is broken from and that this repetition can be done from fractus to fractus again and again, i.e. it is "scalefree". Fractal properties are evident in many diverse domains—snowflakes (nature), Russian dolls (artefacts) or epidemiology distributions (bio-sociological hybrids).

5.3.2 The Linguistic Properties of the Braun's Distribution and Their Practical Consequences

Braun's data can also be assessed from a linguistic perspective, i.e. what are the natural language terms used to describe the conditions observed, and what does this mean for clinical practice. The distribution of word frequencies on the ordinata and their ranking on the abscissa results in a distribution very similar to that of the diagnoses distribution, i.e. the natural language use in clinical practice also follows a Pareto pattern and is described by linguists as a Zipf distribution (for explanation see Fig. 5.4) [36].

Zipf named the ordinata "force of unification" or "speaker's economy" and the abscissa "force of diversification" or "auditor's economy" highlighting that speakers

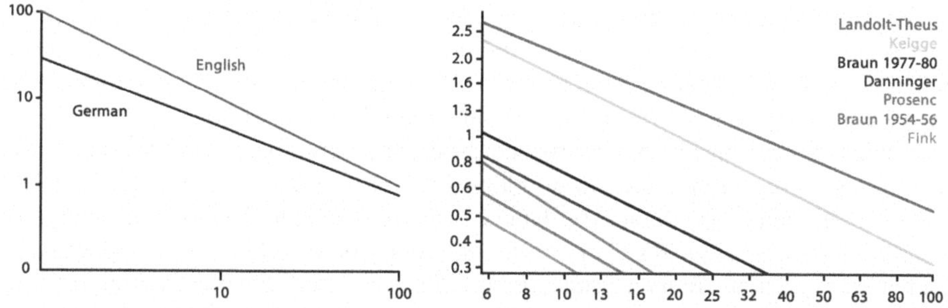

Fig. 5.4 Zipf distribution of word usage in the English and German languages (*left*) and "natural language diagnoses" distribution in various German-speaking general practices (*right*). The equal distribution of "speaker's economy" and "auditor's economy", plotted on a log–log curve shows a slope of $p = 1$—present in the English but not in the German language with a slope $p < 1$. For example German uses three different articles—*der, die, das*—where English uses only one—*the* (for more details refer to Umstätter [37]). Note the differences in the use of diagnostic language by individual German speaking practitioners and over time (Braun's language has become more precise between 1954 and 1980). The different slopes indicate the different frequencies of the high volume uncertain diagnostic labels of *symptoms* (Braun class **A**) and *group of symptoms* (Braun class **B**)

and auditors have contrary interests concerning the effort of expressing *meaning* through words. The ideal speaker's economy is "a vocabulary that consisted exclusively of one single word—a single word that would mean whatever the speaker wanted it to mean" [36, p. 20] whereas the ideal auditor's economy is "a vocabulary of such size that it possessed a distinctly different word for each different meaning to be verbalized" [36, p. 21]. Consider the following—the doctor's economy of speech economy reduces the number of unspecific abdominal symptoms to the diagnosis of *irritable bowel syndrome*, whereas the patient requires a number of words to describe *his experience* in a diverse way as *boring, burning, crampy, tender, bloated, etc.*

Zipf concluded that the ideal communication would have a balanced distribution of word use, the "principle of the least effort", an ideal realised in the English language that has a symmetrical distribution of word frequency and ranking. The German word distribution also follows a Zipf-pattern, but its fit is less perfect.

We demonstrated that comparing Braun-distribution with other commonly used classifications like ICD and ICPC [9, 38], do not show Pareto/Zipf properties as proved by us [33]. However, other natural language systems around the world, including Japanese natural language coded diagnoses [34] and diagnoses codes based on "medical knowledge network"—like the one constructed from Harrison's "Principles" [35]—also show Pareto/Zipf distribution properties. Coding systems based on natural language vocabulary from daily medical practice more accurately reflect the real work in clinical care, or as our Japanese colleagues' put it: "This mutual influence of medical knowledge and clinical practice may control the similar structures and distributions" [35].

The importance of the linguistic perspective on diagnoses reflects the way health professionals and patients understand the presenting problem and the uncertainties inherent in it. Uncertainty directly relates to the appreciation of risk and risk management, an ever increasing concern in a more litigious world.

The right panel in Fig. 5.4 shows the different practitioners' use of uncertainty to certainty description of patient problems [39]. Different slopes indicate different shares of the uncertain diagnostic labels *symptoms* (Braun class **A**) and *group of symptoms* (Braun class **B**). Two different groups of labellers can be identified, higher users of high-frequency uncertain diagnoses (Landolt-Theus, Knigge) from those using certain and uncertain diagnoses more evenly (Braun, Danninger, Fink, Prosenc).

The problem of high proportions of uncertain diagnoses as identified here on the basis of linguistics is typical of Pareto/Zipf-distributions and has been termed by Taleb as the "black swan" phenomenon [40]. Its importance to medical and especially primary care practice will be discussed in the next section.

5.3.3 Uncertainty = Risk

More recently the understanding of risk in terms of Keynes' probability theorem has been further developed by Skidelsky [22, p. 42, p. 84], Taleb [40] and Cooper [41, pp. 141ff] in the context of understanding economical hazard.

Skidelsky explores three types of probabilities bearing a specific kind of risk in accordance with Keynes: "cardinal", "ordinal" and "uncertain" probabilities.

> The first is **cardinal** or measurable probability, according to which all probabilities can be compared by distances between numbers and their absolute values. For example, the statement "There is a one in six chance of your house catching fire in the next year" means that the chance of fire is 16.7 %. This is the domain of *risk* proper. ... The second type of probability is **ordinal** probability, where the only information to be had is that of the relative position of the event in a ranking. One can say that X is more likely to pass the exam than Y, without being able to say that he is twice as likely to pass. Keynes thought this was by far the largest class of probability. We reason that some events, based on our evidence, are more likely to occur than others, but not how much more likely, because we don't have enough observations to make a proper statistical inference. We have entered the domain of uncertainty. Ordinal probabilities fall between statistical frequency and irreducible uncertainty and represent what one might call "vague knowledge". The difference between this and cardinal probability is between qualitative and quantitative judgements of probability. ... The third type of probability in Keynes' universe of probabilities is unknown probability. This is the domain of irreducible **uncertainty**. It arises from non-comparable premises. ... Keynes would have said that most of them are unforeseeable [22, p. 85].

Cooper termed the *ordinal risk* the "known unknowns". In terms of family medicine these are the firm but rarely seen diagnoses that reside beyond the 300 most frequent ones the average family physician will encounter during a year.

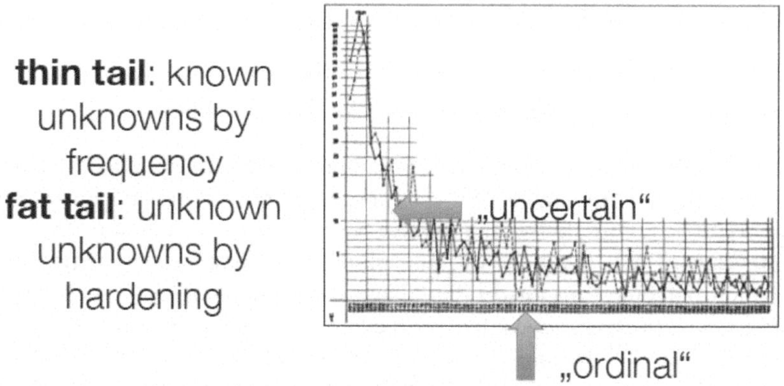

Fig. 5.5 Long tail "ordinal" and fat bulk "uncertain" risks

Cooper named the *uncertain risk* the "unknown unknowns". In terms of family medicine these are the highly uncertain consultation outcomes of unspecific "diagnoses" *(symptom, group of symptoms and disease picture/syndromes)* the average family physician encounters on a daily basis.

Taleb coined the metaphor of the "black swan" for events that come as a surprise, have major—often negative—effects, and which are regularly, but inappropriately, rationalized after the fact with the benefit of hindsight. In medicine this typically occurs following the realisation of an "avoidable dangerous course of action", like having misdiagnosed an acute coronary syndrome thinking the complaint and signs are those of left sided shoulder pain.

By applying these criteria to the Braun-distribution the two risks clearly can be demonstrated (Fig. 5.5):

- the long tail's risk is "ordinal" (known unknowns) because of the low frequency, whereas
- the fat bulk's risk is "uncertain" (unknown unknowns) because of the poor differentiation.

5.3.4 Bayesian Heuristics Are Not the Answer to Managing Uncertainty/Risk in Primary Care

Bayes theorem[2] relates current probability to prior probability. In medical terms we talk about positive predictive value (PPV) being determined by *prevalence* and

[2] $P(A|B) = \frac{P(B|A)P(A)}{P(B)}$; where A and B are events.
$P(A)$ and $P(B)$ are the probabilities of A and B independent of each other.

sensitivity and thus can be written as suggested by Praetorius [42]:

$$\text{PPV} = \frac{\text{SEN} * \text{PRE}}{\text{SEN} * \text{PRE} + (1 - \text{SPE}) * (1 - \text{PRE})}.^{3}$$

Family medicine is rightly called a low-prevalence discipline based on two observations: firstly in any given year a family physician has a low ordinal probability to be confronted with a disease beyond the most common 300 diseases (low prevalence) and secondly the discipline's low diagnostic sensitivity (most consultation outcomes are unspecific "diagnoses": *symptoms, group of symptoms and disease picture/syndromes*). Family medicine operates—in terms of Keynesian probabilistic—in the domain of uncertainty. However, Bayesian heuristics are problematic for generalist disciplines as Bayes statistics require "specified initial conditions" which are usually unknown in their environment, an issue already alluded to by the clinical psychologist Meehl [43].[4]

Accepting these limitations a modification to the Bayesian approach has been promulgated, the "step by step" examination of patients' symptoms [44, 45] where every new step is seen "as an opinion modifier, updating a prior probability of disease to generate a posterior probability". This approach however can be criticised as "mimicry" of Bayes theorem [42], and does not add anything to understanding or solving the many undifferentiated thus uncertain presentations of family medicine's complex problems.[5]

For family medicine to achieve greater diagnostic certainty we need diagnostic protocols as mentioned earlier, accompanied by complementary casuistic tables—or in Braunian terms, "casugraphies". Figure 5.6 provides an example for the symptom "dyspnoea". The casugraphic table describes four strategies:

- *refer to protocols, standardized* ***examinations/tests***,
- *consider the degree of diagnostic* ***certainty***,
- *evaluate avoidable dangerous courses vs natural limited* ***courses***, and
- *employ watchful waiting or other* ***strategy*** [46, p. 101].

$P(A|B)$, a conditional probability, is the probability of A given that B is true.
$P(B|A)$ is the probability of B given that A is true.

[3]SEN Sensibility; PRE Prevalence; SPE Specificity.

[4]Also see NN Taleb, Fooled by Randomness (2004, pp. 269–270). Taleb reiterated Meehl's critique of the "clinical expert" in the 1950s.

[5]Note: The Bayesian approach is not a tool designed for problems involving high degrees of uncertainty, like *undifferentiated presentations in primary care*. Bayes requires well-defined data, usually gained from specific sources (e.g. cardiac catheter examination) whose sensitivities and specificities are well known.

5.1 Dyspnea

Complaints and the way they are presented

Shortness of breath of shorter or longer duration under various circumstances, feeling of getting not enough air

Result of the problem-oriented investigation

No allocation to typical disorders or diseases which are characterized by dyspnea is possible

Checklist (standardized investigation)

Program no. 30 "Dyspnea"

Degree of diagnostic certainty

(according to Braun`s classification (A) standing for symptom, (B) for a group of symptoms, (C) for "picture of disease" and finally (D) for certified diagnosis

Classification: **A (Symptom)**
B (Group of symptoms)
C (Picture of disease)
Diagnosis: D (Diagnosis)

Natural course and usual duration

Variable course, short control intervals are recommended

Examples of **competing/ concurrent conditions** and of **potentially life-threatening conditions** (i.e. avoidable dangerous courses of a disease)	
• **Pulmonary embolism**	*ebd00085*; K5.43***
• **Cardiac insufficiency**	*ebd00069; K4.70* *ebd00071; K4.72*
• Pulmonary hypertension	*ebd00077; K4.90*
• Bronchial asthma	*ebd00108; K6.30*
• COPD (Chronic obstructive pulmonary disease)	*ebd00112; K6.34*
• **Malignant tumor / pleural effusion**	*ebd00118; K6.50* *ebd00127; K6.80*
• **Coronary heart disease**	*ebd00066; K4.63*
• **Pneumonia**	*ebd00101; K6.11*
• **Anemia**	*ebd00300; K15.20*
• **Pneumothorax**	*ebd00123; K6.61*

Links to the Finish EbM-guidelines* (internet version) and corresponding book chapters** in German

Suggestions for coding in ICD or ICPC, respectively

ICD 10: R06.0 A Dyspnea

ICPC 2: R02 Shortness of breath/dyspnea

Fig. 5.6 Casugraphy example for the symptom of *Dyspnoea*, courtesy of Gustav Kamenski

5.4 Coming to Terms with Uncertainty: The Challenge for the Future of Family Medicine

Braun's central concern was that of diagnostic accuracy in an environment of high uncertainty, paraphrased as: *It looks like, but what is it really?* Family medicine's epidemiological complexity—high levels of unspecific symptoms, infrequent specific diagnoses—poses a formidable challenge.

First, we communicate our problems through heuristics and emphasize "similarity" as the basis for learning and decision making [47]. However, language entails high degrees of ambiguity.

And secondly, according to Spengler [48, p. 540], there is the "modern" change from mathematical to statistical inference, reflecting the change from handling traditional "mechanics" to handling "chaos".

This statistical—or in Spengler's words "chaotic"—inference in science studies [49] is actually more commonly used as a tool of excluding or reassuring notions of similarity, working and thinking in analogies of former experiences than with mathematical numerical inference. These operations should be systematized and developed further into diagnostic protocols.

What does this mean for family medicine's research agenda? Three domains shall be highlighted here:

- *Family Medicine Epidemiology*
  Currently we do not have sufficient data to describe the huge variety of diagnoses in family medicine. We require more diagnoses distributions for normal consultation hours as well as special settings (e.g. air plane, kindergartens, prisons, etc.). To accurately capture and compare the work of family medicine these data need to be coded using different coding systems (Braunian, ICD, ICPC).
- *Improving Doctors' Decision-making Skills*
  Currently we have a limited understanding how doctors arrive at diagnoses for undifferentiated diseases. What are the modes of inference used in daily practice? How do physicians handle similarity and uncertainty in light of Braun's classifications of clinical encounters [2, pp. 75–88]? Do they apply means such as Rosch's prototype resemblance categorisation [50] and Sadegh-Zadeh's fuzzy decision-making and similaristic reasoning approaches [51, pp. 603–673]?
- *Developing Advanced Decision-making Tools*
  There is an urgent need to develop diagnostic decision-making tools that take account of the above modes of inference thinking that are concordant with the complex epidemiological properties of family medicine.

The final words should go to a specialist in non-Bayesian heuristics—though less an expert in bedside manner—Dr. House from Princeton's Plainsboro Teaching Hospital while discussing the problem of uncertainty with his assistant Dr. Foreman (http://house.wikia.com/wiki/Zebra):

Dr. Foreman: “You learn it in first year medical school: when you hear hoof beats think horses not zebras.”
Dr. House: “Are you in first year medical school?”

Acknowledgements
Thanks to Frank H. Mader for discussing a faint idea of this manuscript in 2012.
Thanks to Klaus D. Kossow for providing the Praetorius reference [42].
Thanks to Joachim P. Sturmberg for thoroughly editing the manuscript.

References

1. Braun RN. Die gezielte Diagnostik in der Praxis. Stuttgart: Schattauer Verlag; 1957.
2. Braun RN. Lehrbuch der ärztlichen Allgemeinpraxis. München, Berlin, Wien: Urban & Schwarzenberg; 1970.
3. Cochrane AL, Blythe M. One man’s medicine. 2nd ed. Cardiff: Cardiff University Press; 2009.
4. Marinker M. Sirens, stray dogs an the narrative of Hilda Thompson. In: Greenhalgh T, Hurwitz B, editors. Narrative based medicine. London: BMJ Books; 1998. p. 103–9.
5. Pareto W. In: Montesano A, Zanni A, Bruni L, Chipman JS, Mclure M, editors. Manual of political economy. A critical and variorum edition. Oxford: Oxford University Press; 2014.
6. Sturmberg JP, Martin CM. Handbook of systems and complexity in health. New York, NY: Springer; 2013.
7. Göpel H. Beratungsursachen in einer Allgemeinpraxis. Praktischer Arzt. 1975;Heft 12:3508–26.
8. Schach E, Schwartz FW, et al. Die EVaS-Studie. Köln: Deutscher rzte Verlag; 1989.
9. Kühlein Th, Laux G, Gutscher A, Szecsenyi J. Kontinuierliche Morbiditätsregistrierung in der Hausarztpraxis. Vom Beratungsanlass zum Beratungsergebnis - CONTENT. München: Urban & Vogel; 2008.
10. White KL, Williams TF, Greenberg BG. The ecology of medical care. N Engl J Med. 1961;265(18):885–92.
11. Green LA, Fryer GE, Yawn B, Lanier D, Dovey S. The ecology of medical care revisited. N Engl J Med. 2001;344(26):2021–5.
12. Okkes IM, Polderman GO, Fryer GE, Yamada T, Bujak M, Oskam S K, Green LA, Lamberts H. The role of family practice in different health caresystems. A comparison of reasons for encounter, diagnoses, and interventions in primary care populations in the Netherlands, Japan, Poland, and the United States. J Fam Pract. 2002;51:72–91.
13. Horder J, Horder E. Illness in general practice. Practitioner 1954;173(1034):177–87.
14. McGregor RM. The review of a family practice. Health Bull. 1953;11(1):14.
15. Logan WPD. Studies on medical population subjects No.7 and No.9. General Practitioners Records. London: HSMO; 1953.
16. Braun RN. Über fundamental wichtige, bisher unbekannte, die allgemeine Morbidität betreffende Gesetzmäßigkeiten. Vortrag Ges.Ärzte, Wien, 11.3.1955. Klinische Wochenschrift. 1955;12:216
17. West BJ. Mathematical principles: tale of tails. In: Sturmberg JP, Martin CM, editors. Handbook of systems and complexity in health. New York, NY: Springer; 2013. p. 63–80.
18. Luhmann N. Social systems. Stanford: Stanford University Press; 1995.
19. Lexis W. Theorie der Massenerscheinungen. Freiburg i.B.: Fr. Wagnersche Buchhandlung; 1877.
20. Braun RN, Fink W, Kamenski G. Angewandte Medizin und wissenschaftliche Grundlagen. Wien: Facultas; 2004.
21. Keynes JM. A treatise on probability; 1921 (Repr. Rough Draft Breinigsville. PA 2010).

22. Skidelsky R. Keynes: the return of the master. London, New York: Allen Lane an Imprint of Penguin Books; 2009.
23. Mandelbrot B, Hudson RL. The (mis)behaviour of the markets. A fractal view of risk, ruin and reward. London: Profile Books; 2008.
24. Braun RN. Letter to Dr. med.Heinz Brandt, Schildau 30.08.88. Titel L. s. (Fotokopie). 1 f, 2 pp. 8. 4. 1988, s. l.; an Heinz Brandt; H 16/94. Verknüpfung Zettel, 1.Signatur 1282/15-7 Han Autogr. Austrian National Library (ÖNB), Vienna (unpublished)
25. Braun RN. Heilung für die Heilkunde. Autobiography. Sign.: Cod. Ser. n. 38768 Samml.: Han Wien, ÖNB (1991-1992) (unveröffentlicht). Signatur Cod. Ser. n. | Samml.: Han 1.Person Braun, Robert N., 1914–2007 [Verfasser] Titel Heilung für die Heilkunde Zusatz z. Titel Die Geschichte einer Entdeckung Ort lt. Unterlage o.O. Datum normiert 1991-1992 Art, Umfang, Anzahl Manuskript, 2 Mappen, I, 380 Bl. Austrian National Library (ÖNB), Vienna. Unpublished Manuscript; 1992/2012
26. Aitken AM, Braun RN, Fraillon JMG. Understanding general practice. Melbourne - Toorak: the Victorian academy for general practice; 1982 (without page numbers, only chapters numbered).
27. Koch R. Die ärztliche diagnose. 2nd ed. Wiesbaden: Verlag von J.F.Bergmann; 1920.
28. Braun RN, Fink W, Kamenski G. Lehrbuch der Allgemeinmedizin. Horn/NÖ, Wien: Verlag Berger; 2007.
29. Braun RN, Mader FH. Programmierte Diagnostik in der Allgemeinmedizin. 5th ed. Heidelberg, New York: Springer; 2005.
30. Reichenfeld HF. Line and graph case records. J Coll Gen Pract. 1965;10(1):90–2.
31. Rosowsky O, Andral J, Cittee J, Brunel L, De Pouvouville G. Observation de la pathologie on medecin generale. La CASUGRAPHIE. Le concept de cas selon RN Braun dans la gestion du risque en situation diagnostique ouverte. Adaptation a la CIM 10. Saint Maurice: Ed CRI; 1999.
32. Reichenfeld HF. Recent developments in Germany and Austria. J Coll Gen Pract. 1965;10(1):107–8.
33. Fink W, Lipatov V, Konitzer M. Diagnoses by general practitioners: accuracy and reliability. Int J Forecasting 2009;25(4):784–93.
34. Tachimori Y, Tahara T. Clinical diagnoses following Zipfs law. Fractals. 2002;10(3):341–51.
35. Tachimori Y, Iwanagab H, Tahara T. The networks from medical knowledge and clinical practice have small-world, scale-free, and hierarchical features. Physica A. 2013;392(23):6084–9.
36. Zipf GK. Human behaviour and the principle of least effort. An introduction to human ecology. Cambridge: Addison-Wesley Press, Inc.; 1949 (Repr. Martino Publishing Mansfield CT 2012).
37. Umstätter W. Das “Principle of Least Effort” in der Wissenschaft; 2003. www.ib.hu-berlin.de/backsimwumsta/infopub/lectures/leasteffort03a.pdf.
38. Vogt R. Der Beratungsanlass in der allgemeinmedizinischen Konsultationssprechstunde - SESAM. Dissertation Medical Faculty Leipzig University; 2002.
39. Szecsenyi J, Engelhardt N, Wessel M. Eine Methode zur Bestimmung des Denominators in Allgemeinpraxen - Ergebnisse einer Pilotstudie. Gesundheitswesen. 1993;55(Sonderheft):32–6.
40. Taleb NN. The black swan. The impact of the highly improbable. London: Penguin; 2008.
41. Cooper G. The origin of financial crisis. Central banks, credit bubbles and the efficient market fallacy. New York: Vintage Books; 2008.
42. Praetorius F. Bayes-Stadt: Zur Objektivität von Indikationen. DÄB 23 A. 1992;(89)23: 2113–20.
43. Meehl PE. Clinical versus statistical prediction. Minneapolis: University of Minnesota; 1954.
44. Donner-Banzhoff N, Haasenritter J, Bösner S, Viniol A, Becker A. Unsicherheit in der Allgemeinmedizin. A Mathematical Theory of Primary Care. Zeitschrift für Allgemeinmedizin. 2012;88(11):446–51.
45. Schneider A, Dinant GJ, Szecsenyi J. Zur Notwendigkeit einer abgestuften Diagnostik in der Allgemeinmedizin als Konsequenz des Bayes’schen Theorems. Zeitschrift für Ärztliche Fortbildung und Qualitt im Gesundheitswesen. 2006;100(2):121–7.

46. Fink W, Kamenski G, Kleinbichler D. Braun Kasugraphie.(K)ein Fall wie der andere. Benennung und Klassifikation der regelmäßig häufigen Gesundheitsstörungen in der primärärztlichen Versorgung. 3rd ed. Horn/NÖ: Verlag Berger; 2010.
47. Osgood CE. Meaningful similarity and interference in learning. J Exp Psychol. 1946;36(Aug):277–301.
48. Spengler O. Untergang des Abendlandes. Umrisse einer Morphologie der Weltgeschichte. Bd 1. München: C.H. Becksche Verlagsbuchhandlung; 1924.
49. Hofstadter D, Sander E. Surfaces and essences. Analogy as the fuel and fire of thinking. New York: Basic Books; 2013.
50. Rosch E. Principles of categorization. In: Collins A, Smith EE, editors. Readings in cognitive science: A perspective from psychology and artificial intelligence. San Mateo: Morgan Kaufmann; 1988. p. 312–22.
51. Sadegh-Zadeh K. Handbook of analytic philosophy of medicine. New York: Springer; 2012.

Chapter 6
Anticipation in Complex Systems: Potential Implications for Improving Safety and Quality in Healthcare

Thomas O. Staiger

Concepts from complex systems theory are increasingly being applied to healthcare [1, 2]. This paper will provide a brief introduction to anticipatory systems, first described by the theoretical biologist Rosen [3]. In Rosen's anticipatory theory of complex systems, all living systems and virtually all other complex systems require anticipatory models to maintain their organized, far from equilibrium state. The features of anticipatory systems, the potential role of anticipatory systems in promoting safety and quality in healthcare, and whether a broader understanding of anticipatory systems could promote improved safety and quality in healthcare will be discussed here.

As defined by Rosen in *Anticipatory Systems: Philosophic, Mathematic, and Methodological Foundations*, an anticipatory system contains "a predictive model of itself and/or its environment, which allows it to change state at an instant in accord with the model's prediction pertaining to a later instant" [3]. Because the future is always somewhat uncertain, an anticipatory system cannot, of course, produce definitive models of the future. Anticipatory systems are capable of changing in the present based on imperfect models of the future. The case will be made that this is a fundamental and important feature which differentiates anticipatory systems from reactive/recursive systems, in which change never occurs due to the influence of anticipatory models.

A further discussion of the characteristics of anticipatory systems will follow some general remarks about simple and complex system.

T.O. Staiger (✉)
Department of Medicine, University of Washington, Box 356330, Seattle, WA 98195, USA
e-mail: staiger@u.washington.edu; staiger@uw.edu

J.P. Sturmberg (ed.), *The Value of Systems and Complexity Sciences for Healthcare*, DOI 10.1007/978-3-319-26221-5_6

6.1 Simple and Complex Systems

While complex systems are described in a wide variety of ways, commonly accepted features are (1) that the components of a complex system are interrelated and (2) that decomposition of these components leads to a loss of important information about the system [1, 4]. Rosen, in *Life Itself: A Comprehensive Inquiry into the Nature, Origin, and Fabrication of Life*, defines complex systems in similar terms [5]. Rosen defines a *simple systems as one in which all of the information can be captured in a single largest formal model* and *complex systems as those in which all of the information cannot be represented by any single formal model or any finite sets of formal models*.

Modelling relations play a central role in Rosen's descriptions of simple, complex, and anticipatory systems. A detailed discussion of the modelling relationship is presented in Rosen's *Fundamentals of Measurement and Representation of Natural Systems* [6]. As described by the mathematical biologist, A.H. Louie, a student of Rosen's, the common-usual usage of definitions of a model, such as "a simplified description put forward as a basis for theoretical understanding" or "a conceptual or mental representation of a thing" are useful ways of thinking about a model [7]. The best known, and arguably most influential, examples of formal models are the classical and modern models of physics. A description of a formal modelling relationship is as follows (Fig. 6.1):

> Roughly, the essence of a modelling relation consists of specifying an encoding and a corresponding decoding of particular system characteristics into corresponding characteristics of another system, in such a way that implication in the model corresponds to causality in the system. Thus in a precise mathematical sense a theorem about the model becomes a prediction about the system [7].

If Rosen's definitions that all of the information in a simple system can be captured in a largest formal model of the system, and that there is no largest comprehensive formal model of a complex systems are employed, differentiating features between simple and complex systems include the following:

1. A simple system is the exact sum of its components (parts with a function) or its sub-models. A simple system may be complicated due to having many components, however the comprehensive formal model of any given simple

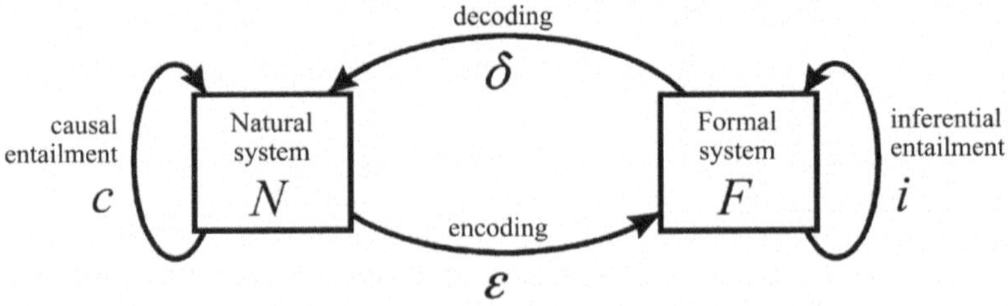

Fig. 6.1 The prototypical modelling relation

system can contain everything knowable about that system. A complex system does not have a largest formal model; the information in a complex system is greater than any finite sum of its components or sub-models.
2. A simple system can be fractionated (broken) into its component or sub-models without loss of information about the system. Fractionating a complex system cannot be accomplished without destroying information about the system, because fractionating a complex system destroys information pertaining to the relationship of the components within a complex system.
3. Simple systems can be simulated, meaning that a computer program could accurately describe its state transitions without losing or distorting information about the system. A simple system can be accurately modelled by the digital information in a simulation. Simulating a complex system inevitably results in loss of information about the system. Simulations can describe some of the behaviours of a complex system, but a simulation cannot provide a comprehensive, explanatory, model of a complex system.

6.2 Recursion

One of the inherent properties of all simple systems is that change is recursive. This was one of Newton's key discoveries about change in physical systems [5]. Recursion in Newtonian mechanics means that what is occurring at a given instant in time (i.e. the positions, velocities, and forces acting on a set of particles) determines what occurs at the next instant in time. As Rosen wrote, "the heart of recursion is the conversion of the present to the future, or the entailment of the future by the present" [5]. In describing the Newtonian paradigm and its impact on scientific thought, Rosen said:

> The essential feature of that paradigm is the employment of a mathematical language with a built-in duality which we may express as the distinction between *internal states and dynamical laws*. In Newtonian mechanics the internal states are represented by points in some appropriate manifold of phases, and the dynamical laws represent the internal or impressed forces. The resulting mathematical image is what is now called a *dynamical system* ... Through the work of people like Poincare, Birkhoff, Lotka, and many others over the years, however, this dynamical systems paradigm or its numerous variants, has come to be regarded as the universal vehicle for representation of systems which could not be technically described mathematically; systems of interacting chemicals, organisms, ecosystems, and many others. Even the most radical changes occurring within physics itself, like relativity and quantum mechanics manifest this framework ...
> This, then, is our inherited *mechanical paradigm*, which in its many technical variants or interpretations has been regarded as a universal paradigm for systems and what they do. These variants take many forms: automata theory, control theory, and the like, but they all conform to the same basic framework first exhibited in the *Principia* p. 78 [5].

Newton's discovery of recursion in nature has substantially influenced how scientific models are formulated and our understanding of causation in the natural world. As Joslyn wrote in a review of *Life Itself*, "... three hundred years of science has been dedicated to the idea that the special class of simulable systems is in fact a *universal* paradigm for explanation of natural phenomena" [8].

The recursive framework for change in systems is present in many, and perhaps most, currently accepted approaches to understanding complexity. For example, a fundamental principle of complexity, according to Paley is that:

> ...a complexity account always takes the same form ...successive states of the system, globally defined, are determined by previous states, locally defined. The function which links the state at t_1 to the state at t_2 is defined as a set of stimulus-response rules ("If ...then ...") applying to individual units (whether cells, ants, termites, birds, or drivers) whose behavior conforms to this function. Normally future global states are unpredictable, given only initial conditions future and the state transition functions; however the systems states are still completely explained by the starting conditions and the rules governing local behavior [9].

6.3 Anticipatory Systems

Roberto Polli, Principle Investigator, UNESCO Chair in Anticipatory Systems said:

> In fact, all human and social sciences have accepted, to varying extents, what is possibly Newton's most important implicit assumption, what Rosen called the Zeroth Commandment: "Thou shalt not allow the future to affect the present" (Rosen, 1991, p. 49 [*Life Itself*]) The Zeroth Commandment implies that all information comes from the past and no information comes from the future. The idea that at least some information can be understood as if it derives from the future is the source of the theory of anticipatory systems [10]. [Brackets are my addition]

Rosen's anticipatory theory of complex systems provides a framework for understanding complex natural systems and explains how complex systems can change in ways that are not recursive. Although anticipatory systems (i.e. organisms) are physical systems in which change does occur recursively, anticipatory systems can also change due to the system's capacity to respond to anticipatory models. As stated by Louie, in "Robert Rosen's anticipatory systems" an excellent concise summary of the key concepts related to anticipatory systems:

> Note, in contrast, that a reactive system can only react, in the present, to changes that have already occurred in the causal chain, while an anticipatory system's present behavior involves aspects of past, present, and future. The presence of a predictive model serves precisely to pull the future into the present; a system with a "good" model thus behaves in many ways as if it can anticipate the future. Model-based behavior requires an entirely new paradigm, an "anticipatory paradigm", to accommodate it. This paradigm extends - but does not replace - the "reactive paradigm" which has hitherto dominated the study of natural systems. The "anticipatory paradigm" allows us a glimpse of new and important aspects of system behavior [7].

Figure 6.2 depicts an anticipatory system. S could be an organism, a social system, or an ecosystem. M is a predictive model of S in which "the corresponding trajectories of M are parametrized by a time variable that goes *faster than real time* ..." so that "...any observable on M, serves as a predictor for the behaviour of some

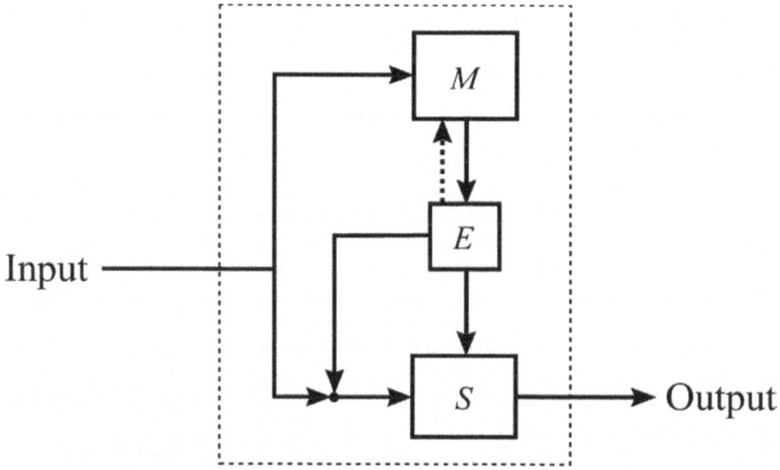

Fig. 6.2 Anticipatory system

corresponding observable of S at that later instant." "... the system M is equipped with a set E of effectors that operate either on S itself or on the environmental inputs to S" [7]. Louie describes how this system functions as follows:

> We shall now allow M and S to be coupled; i.e. allow them to interact in specific ways. For the simplest model, we may simply allow the output of an observable on M to be an input to the system S. This then creates a situation in which a future state of S is controlling the present state transition in S. But this is precisely what we have characterized above as anticipatory behavior. It is clear that the above construction does not violate causality; indeed, we have invoked causality in an essential way in the concept of a predictive model, and hence in the characterization of the system M. Although the composite system (M + S) is completely causal, it nevertheless will behave in an anticipatory fashion [7].

The concept of feed-forward is closely tied to anticipatory systems. Feed-forward is defined in the Miller-Keane Encyclopedia and Dictionary of Medicine, Nursing, and Allied Health as:

> the anticipatory effect that one intermediate in a metabolic or endocrine control system exerts on another intermediate further along in the pathway; such effect may be positive or negative [11].

Descriptions of feed-forward metabolic pathways include:

> Control of a metabolic pathway by a metabolite of the pathway that acts in the same direction as the metabolic flux, i.e. downstream or 'later' in the pathway, e.g. the activation of pyruvate kinase by fructose 1,6-bisphosphate [12].

and:

> Certain pathways, such as those involved in the disposal of toxic compounds, are feed-forward regulated. Feed-forward regulation may occur through an increased supply of substrate to an enzyme with a high Km, allosteric activation of a rate-limiting enzyme through a compound related to substrate supply, substrate-related induction of gene

transcription (e.g., induction of cytochrome P450-2E1 by ethanol), or increased concentration of a hormone that stimulates a storage pathway by controlling enzyme phosphorylation state [13].

Louie elaborates on the role of feed-forward in anticipatory systems with the following description:

> Anticipatory behavior involves the concept of feedforward, rather than feedback. The distinction between feedforward and feedback is important, and is as follows. The essence of feedback control is that it is error-actuated; in other words, the stimulus to corrective action is the discrepancy between the system's actual present state and the state the system should be in. Stated otherwise, a feedback control system must already be departing from its nominal behavior before control begins to be exercised.
>
> In a feedforward system, on the other hand, system behavior is preset, according to some model relating present inputs to their predicted outcomes. The essence of a feedforward system, then, is that the present change of state is determined by an anticipated future state, derived in accordance with some internal model of the world.
>
> We know from introspection that many, if not most, of our own conscious activities are generated in a feedforward fashion. We typically decide what to do now in terms of what we perceive will be the consequences of our action at some later time. The vehicle by which we anticipate is in fact a model, which enables us to pull the future into the present. We change our present course of action in accordance with our model's prediction. The stimulus for our action is not simply the present percepts; it is the prediction under these conditions. I emphasize again that "prediction" is not prescience, but simply "output of an anticipatory model". Stated otherwise, our present behavior is not just reactive; it is also anticipatory [7].

6.4 Most Complex Systems Are Also Anticipatory Systems

In Rosen's anticipatory theory of complex systems a capacity for anticipatory change is a fundamental characteristic of all living systems and of virtually all complex systems [5, 14]. An example of a complex system that is not an anticipatory system is a virus (Louie, personal communication, 2014). A virus is a complex system which accomplishes replication by hijacking the host's metabolic processes, including some of the host's anticipatory processes.

6.4.1 Failure Modes in Simple vs. Complex Systems

Rosen said:

> "In a simple system every global failure of S arises from local failures in the component subsystems Si." "...it is possible for a complex system to exhibit global modes of failure which are not associated with local subsystem failures" [15].

Failures and malfunctions in a simple system can always be traced to the failure or malfunction of a specific component (part with a function) in the system. When a simple system such as a machine breaks, its failure can always be traced to a failure in one or more components. Complex systems can fail when a component in the system fails, but the stability of a complex system is also dependent on the accuracy of its inevitably imperfect models of its present state and on its anticipatory models of future states. Though having a perfectly accurate and comprehensive model of a complex system is, by definition, not possible, the more accurate a complex system's models are of its present state and of future states, the greater the likelihood of the ongoing stability of the system.

6.5 What Does Any of This Have to Do with Safety and Quality in Healthcare?

If Rosen's anticipatory theory of complex systems is correct an enhanced understanding of anticipatory systems and of the characteristics and failure modes of complex systems could supplement existing safety practices and help healthcare organizations reduce the risk of certain serious adverse outcomes. Enhanced individual and organizational understanding of these principles might also help promote greater attention to the importance of promoting common understanding among treating teams, patients, and families and thereby improve the patient experience of care and clinical outcomes which benefit from improved physician–patient communication [16].

If complex systems have no largest formal model, the following are true:

1. Though a clinician could, at least in theory, have a fully comprehensive model of a simple system, no clinician's mental model of a complex system, such as the health status of a patient, can ever be complete.
2. It is impossible for a team of clinicians, or a team of clinicians, patient, and family to ever have a fully congruent "shared mental model" of a patient's complex clinical situation.

If Rosen's anticipatory theory of complex systems is correct, the following propositions are likely to be true:

1. Greater congruence between the models of the current situation and anticipatory models of future states among clinical team members, and among the clinical team, patient, and family increases the likelihood of attaining preferred outcomes. For example, it has been shown that "Agreement between physicians and patients regarding diagnosis, diagnostic plan, and treatment plan is associated with higher patient satisfaction and better health status outcomes in patients with back pain" [17].
2. Inputs from the anticipatory models of clinical team members, patients, and families may be useful for identifying and real time mitigation of some clinical situations in which there is an increased risk of a future serious adverse outcome. Clinicians, patients, or family members who believe, even if based only on a "gut sense" that the diagnosis or plan for a patient is wrong or that a patient is at high risk for an adverse outcome, should be encouraged to speak up.

3. Significantly discrepant present-state or anticipatory mental models between clinical team members or between team and patients/families may indicate an increased risk for an adverse outcome.
4. Clinical teams that recognize that disagreements regarding the appropriate care of a patient may indicate an increased risk of an adverse outcome may be able to create better shared present-state and anticipatory mental modes which could help mitigate future risks.
5. Optimal team functioning should encourage anticipatory inputs from all clinical team members and should include encourage identifying significantly discrepant current state and anticipatory models among clinical team members and between clinical team and patients/families, especially in high-risk situations.
6. Healthcare organizations may be able to reduce certain adverse events by:

   (a) Promoting an awareness of the role of anticipation in complex systems.
   (b) Encouraging clinical team members to recognize that significantly discrepant present-state or anticipatory models may be a source of conflict and may indicate increased safety risks.

Inpatient clinical teams (physicians, RNs, and other treating provider) successfully implementing an anticipatory theory of complex systems in the care of a patient would be expected to:

1. Have high levels of agreement regarding the diagnosis, diagnostic plan, and the treatment plan;
2. Achieve high levels of agreement with patients and families regarding the diagnosis, diagnostic plan, and treatment plans;
3. Actively monitor the clinical team and patient/family agreement on these issues and carefully reassess plans if disagreements are present. A modified version of the instrument mentioned above, developed for patients with back pain, might be useful for assessing and providing feedback on levels of agreement and to help identify instances of significant disagreement; and
4. Carefully reassess plans if anticipatory inputs from team members, patients, or families indicate that the diagnosis or the plan may be wrong.

Ambulatory providers successfully implementing this approach would be expected to achieve high levels of agreement with patients/families regarding the diagnosis, diagnostic plan, and treatment plans, actively monitor for disagreement and reassess plans if disagreement is present, and monitor for personal and patient/family anticipatory inputs suggesting that the diagnosis or plan might be wrong.

These propositions are consistent with and might help extend concepts currently utilized in situational awareness approaches to improving safety in healthcare and in other high-risk domains. Situation awareness:

> involves being aware of what is happening in the vicinity, in order to understand how information, events, and one's own actions will impact goals and objectives, both immediately and in the near future. One with an adept sense of situation awareness generally has a high degree of knowledge with respect to inputs and outputs of a system, i.e. an innate "feel"

> for situations, people, and events that play out due to variables the subject can control. Lacking or inadequate situation awareness has been identified as one of the primary factors in accidents attributed to human error. Thus, situation awareness is especially important in work domains where the information flow can be quite high and poor decisions may lead to serious consequences (e.g., piloting an airplane, functioning as a soldier, or treating critically ill or injured patients) [18].

An enhanced understanding of anticipatory systems and of the characteristics and failure modes of complex systems might help healthcare teams being trained in situational awareness to achieve a better understanding of how to anticipate and plan for future changes in course of a patient's treatment.

6.6 Conclusions and Implications

The anticipatory theory of complex systems provides a novel framework for understanding complex natural systems and provides an explanation for how complex systems can change based on the system's predictions of the future. Applying these concepts in a healthcare environment might help decrease risks for certain adverse outcomes and lead to improvements in some aspects of care quality. Assessing the impact of applying an anticipatory theory of complex systems in a healthcare setting would be a challenging, but potentially highly valuable undertaking.

A broader understanding of these concepts could have great benefit, within and outside healthcare. As Rosen said in closing *Anticipatory Systems*:

> The study of anticipatory systems thus involves in an essential way the subjective notions of good and ill, as they manifest themselves in the models which shape our behavior. For in a profound sense, the study of models is the study of man; and if we can agree about our models, we can agree about everything else p. 370 [3].

References

1. Kannampallil TG, Schauer GF, Cohen T, Patel VL. Considering complexity in healthcare systems. J Biomed Inform. 2011;44:943–7.
2. Sturmberg JP, Martin CM, Katerndahl DA. Systems and complexity thinking in the general practice literature. Ann Fam Med. 2014;12:66–74.
3. Rosen R. Anticipatory systems. 2nd ed. New York: Springer; 2012.
4. Rouse WB. Health care as a complex adaptive system. Bridge. 2008;38:17–25.
5. Rosen R. Life itself. New York: Columbia University Press; 1991.
6. Rosen R. Fundamentals of measurement and representations of natural systems. New York: North-Holland; 1978.
7. Louie AH. Robert Rosen's anticipatory systems. Foresight. 2010;12:18–29.
8. Joslyn C. Book review, life itself. Int J Gen Syst. 1993; 21:394–402.
9. Paley J. The appropriation of complexity theory in healthcare. J Health Serv Res Policy. 2010;15:59–61.
10. Polli R. Project anticipation website. http://www.projectanticipation.org/index.php?option=com_kunena&view=topic&catid=5&id=3&Itemid=504. Accessed Dec. 15th, 2015.

11. Miller-Keane, O'Toole T. Miller-Keane encyclopedia and dictionary of medicine, nursing, and allied health. 7th ed. Amsterdam: Elsevier; 2003.
12. Gen script glossary of biochemistry and molecular biology. http://www.google.com/webhp?nord=1#nord=1&q=gen+script+glossary+of+biochemistry. Accessed Dec. 15th, 2015.
13. Peet A, Lieberman M, Marks AD. Marks basic medical biochemistry. 4th ed. Alphen aan den Rijn: Wolters Kluwer; 2012. https://www.inkling.com/read/marks-medical-biochemistry-lieberman-marks-4th/chapter-9/v--regulation-of-metabolic.
14. Louie AH. More than life itself. Piscataway: Transaction; 2009.
15. Rosen R. Feedforwards and global system failure: a general mechanism for senescence. J Theor Biol. 74:579–90.
16. Doyle C, Lennox L, Bell D. A systematic review of evidence on the links between patient experience and clinical safety and effectiveness. BMJ Open 2013;3:e001570. doi:10.1136/bmjopen-2012-001570.
17. Staiger TO, Jarvik JG, Deyo RA, Martin, B, Braddock CB. Patient-physician agreement as a predictor of outcomes in patients with back pain. J Gen Intern Med. 2005;20:935–7.
18. Situational awareness. Wikipedia. http://en.wikipedia.org/wiki/Situation_awareness. Accessed Dec. 15th, 2015.

Chapter 7
Extreme Variability is Typical Not Normal

Bruce J. West

7.1 Introduction

In my presentation the concept of scientific knowledge is viewed as the top of a three-tiered system of science. The first tier is that of measurement and data, followed by information consisting of the patterns within the data, and ending with theory that interprets the patterns and yields knowledge. Thus, when a scientific theory ceases to be consistent with the database the knowledge entailed by that theory must be re-examined and potentially modified. Consequently, all knowledge, like glory, is transient. With this in mind the focus of my talk is on the variability of data in medicine and how incorrect or unnecessarily restrictive assumptions regarding such statistical properties can lead to unnecessary misunderstanding of the underlying phenomena. This is particularly true when examining the nature of extrema; whether the data is from the statistics of earthquakes or quakes in the brain, from the collapse of bridges to the falling of the elderly, from the failure of economic systems to the collapse of the health care system. Of particular interest are the properties of the extreme values of physiologic time series that are a consequence of the nature of the underlying statistics. What is of concern here is the fact that extreme variability is typical of complex medical phenomena and that variability is not statistically Normal.

Let me address my preliminary remarks to a modified figure from Hayano [1] to indicate what I hope you will take away from this talk. The coloured curves in Fig. 7.1 are the heart rate variability (HRV) statistical distributions taken from a study of a collection of 670 post-AMI (acute myocardial infarction) patients using 24 h Holter monitor data sets yielding heart beat interval variability from the time

B.J. West (✉)
Mathematics and Information Sciences Directorate, U.S. Army Research Office,
Research Triangle Park, Durham, NC, USA
e-mail: bruce.j.west.civ@mail.mil

J.P. Sturmberg (ed.), *The Value of Systems and Complexity Sciences for Healthcare*, DOI 10.1007/978-3-319-26221-5_7

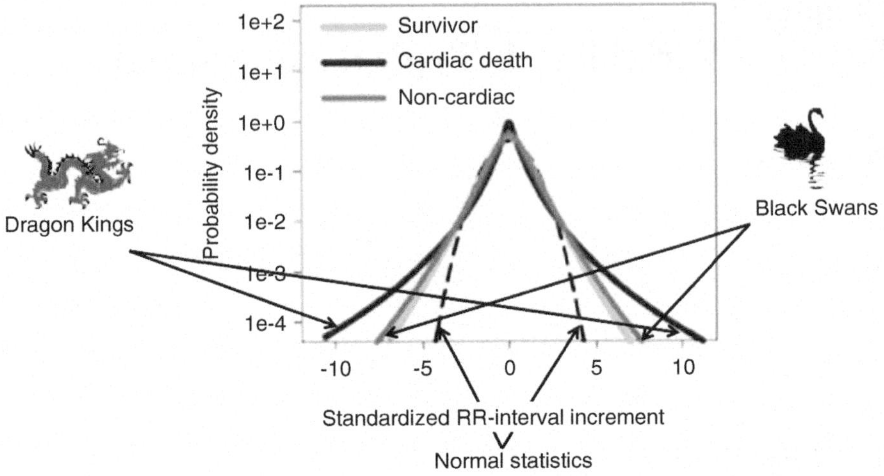

Fig. 7.1 The HRV statistical distributions for 670 post-AMI patients for those that survived, and those that died due to either cardiac or non-cardiac events. The *dashed curve* would be the Normal one in the same normalized variables (adapted from [1])

series. In this study a number of individuals suffered a cardiac death, others died by non-cardiac causes and some survived. The distributions of the three groups are indicated.

The first thing to notice about Fig. 7.1 is that no group had normal statistics, which in terms of the standardized variable would have fallen on the dashed line. Next the survivors and those succumbing to non-cardiac death have essentially the same variability distribution. The extrema for these two processes would constitute the *Black Swans* of Taleb [2] and are unpredictable, but share the statistics of their smaller siblings. The extrema for those that suffer a cardiac death are labelled *Dragon Kings*, a term coined by Sornette [3], and the variability statistics are very different from those that survive and may even contain clues that make them predictable.

My chapter is less about the details of variability statistics, however, and more about complexity and its relation to health. But more importantly it is to convince you that you have been sold a bill of goods when it comes to the Normal distribution. That is because when the phenomena being studied are complex, as is virtually the case for every physiological and biological system in medicine, they are not and cannot have Normal statistics.

The historical strategy adopted to understand complexity was to invent and interpret statistics. At the turn of the nineteenth century the American mathematician Adrian and the German polymath Gauss recognized that experiments never produce the same results twice and in 1808, although separated by an ocean, they simultaneously invented the Normal distribution as a way to interpret the variability of measurements. The next year Laplace established that their bell-shaped curve was more general than either of them had imagined and in 1809 proved the first version of the central limit theorem.

Gauss' initial motivation was to understand why stars twinkle and to provide quantitative measure of their location. The bell-shaped curve that he, Adrian and Laplace developed subsequently morphed into the law of frequency of errors (LFE) and produced such concepts as the average man in a social context and homoeostasis in a medical context. I argued elsewhere that Normal statistics actually presents a barrier to understanding the natural variability of medical phenomena [4]. The LFE captures only a small part of the world but it implicitly assumes that the average coincides with a prediction; all the scatter in the data can be washed away leaving only the deterministic prediction of an equation of motion.

Consequently, even though the individual elements in a population vary, the characteristics of the population as a whole are themselves stable. Statistical stability emerges out of individual variability and has the appearance of order emerging out of chaos, and the orderliness of the LFE eventually led to the assumption that the regularity of the average is more important than the variability of the individual, particularly in medicine. It provided the attractive view of the world in which even the unpredictable is still manageable and the average could be interpreted in terms of physical theory.

A century later the engineer Vilfredo Pareto examined the distribution of wealth in a number of countries and found them to have a common form, that being an inverse power-law (IPL) distribution. Although this latter distribution was subsequently shown to describe all manner of complex phenomena, such as solar flares and sunspots, it did not gain traction in science until the latter part of the twentieth century. This may have been due in part to the fact that not all members of such a statistical population are equivalent; there exists a fundamental imbalance in the distribution of wealth, the data set on which Pareto developed his distribution, and in any other property characterized by the Pareto distribution. In this talk I use the two terms Pareto and IPL distributions interchangeably.

It is the statistical distribution of Pareto and not that of Gauss that leads to the crises described by black swans and dragon kings. The extrema generated by these two kinds of statistics are seen to have much greater probability in the IPL than in Normal distributions as is clear in Fig. 7.2 where the two are compared on log-linear graph paper.

7.2 Two Different World Views

In the world view of Gauss the average value characterizes the phenomenon of interest and that view eventually dominated the physical, social and life sciences. From this perspective phenomena are predictable; a small change in the present state of a process produces a relatively small change in its future behaviour; the output is proportional to the input. Consequently, physical phenomena can be controlled in a straightforward way; the world is stable and the appearance of instability is just that, an appearance, not a reality. But is this the world in which we live?

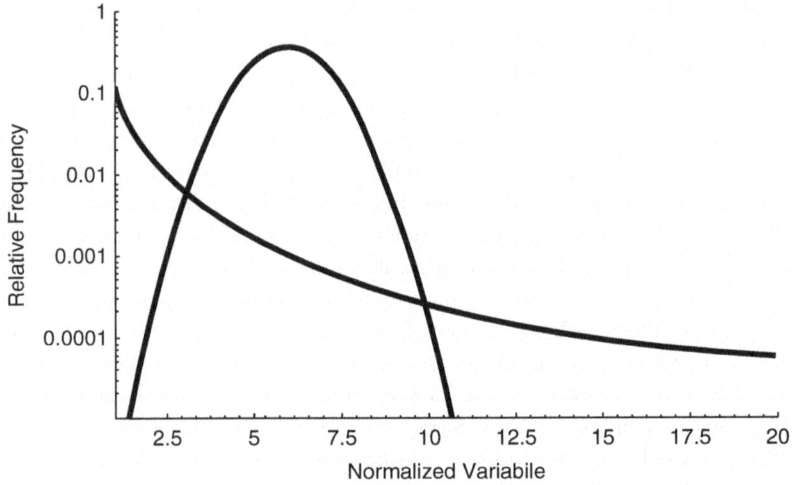

Fig. 7.2 The distribution of Gauss is compared with that of Pareto on log-linear graph paper. The emphasis of the tail of the distribution in the latter case is evident

This comfortable view of the world is implicitly taught to every student that has taken a large survey course during their Freshman year in college. They learn that most students are C's; proportionately fewer are B's and D's and finally there is the rarefied few that are A's and F's. This is euphemistically known as grading on a curve. After taking a sufficient number of these courses the "reality" of the bell-shaped curve becomes second nature and its application is no longer open to doubt.

But where is the evidence to vindicate the use of Normal statistics in learning or at least in the application to the distribution of grades?

I was never comfortable with grading on a curve, but I lacked empirical evidence that it was in fact an improper thing to do. However about a decade ago I ran across a paper that provided the data I was seeking. This paper was based on the university entrance examination data of the Universidade Estadual Paulista (UNESP) given to approximately 60,000 students in the state of Sao Paulo, Brazil [5].

The distribution of grades in the humanities depicted on the top of Fig. 7.3 seems to support the conjecture that they are normally distributed. Whether the grouping was done in terms of income level, type of school or time of day the students attended class, the bell-shaped curve emerged. All these various partitionings of the data were made in [5] and the results all retain the qualitative features of the graph depicted here. Is this a vindication of Normal statistics in an academic setting? It could be, but on the other hand, the distribution of grades in the physical sciences, depicted on the bottom of Fig. 7.3 is completely different from those in the humanities. The mode has vanished and there is the long tail of the IPL. It is certainly not bell-shaped. A similar distribution is obtained for the biological sciences. All this and more are discussed in [5].

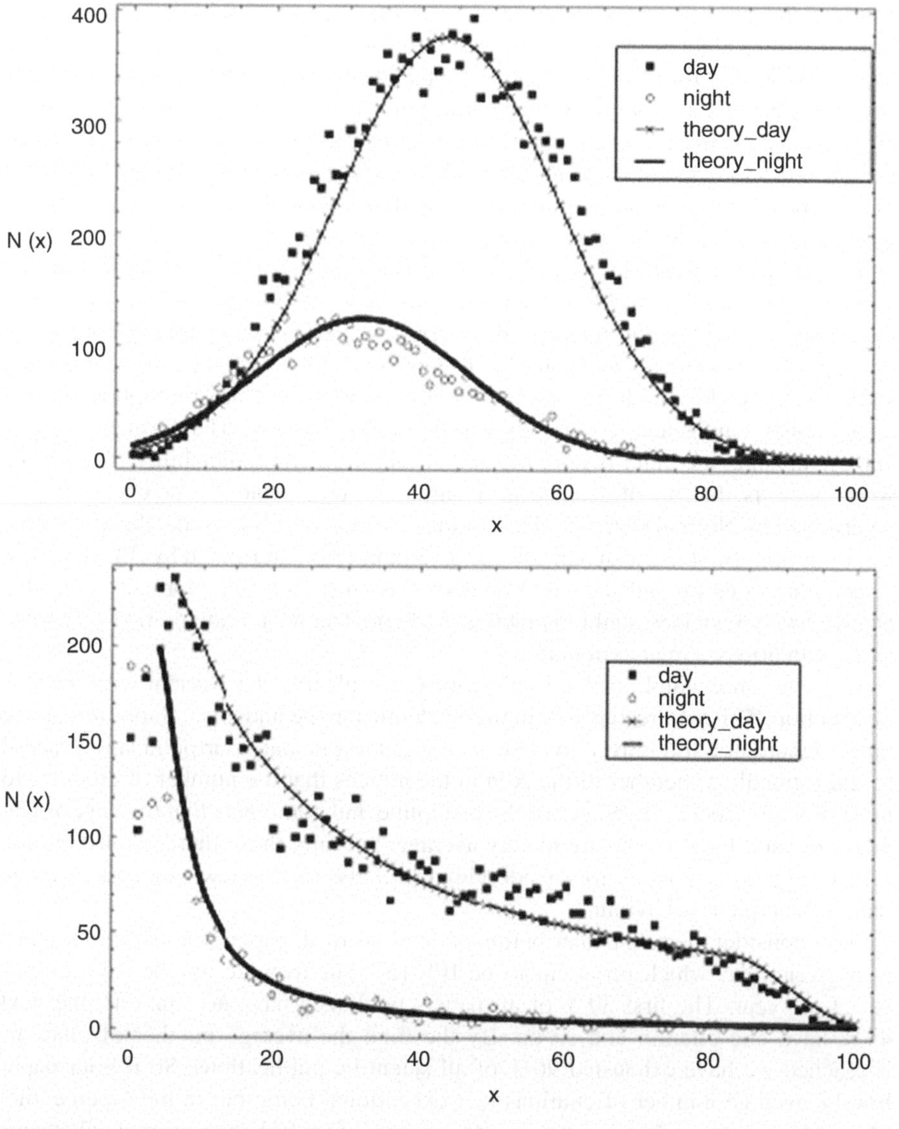

Fig. 7.3 Grade distribution for the university entrance examination of Universidade Estadual Paulista given to approximately 6×10^5 students. *Top*: humanities; *Bottom*: physical sciences; adapted from [5]

One way to account for the different distributions is to notice that the humanities consist of a collection of very different disciplines including history, social studies, philosophy and so on. These disciplines are independent or at most weakly dependent on one another and therefore satisfy the conditions for the central limit theorem. When the grades are added together a Normal distribution is obtained. By way of contrast, the sciences build on a sequence of interdependent subjects, arithmetic is learned before algebra, which is necessary for basic physics and calculus, and the latter is necessary for mechanics and so up the chain. This interdependence violates one of the basic assumptions of the central limit theorem, that the individual errors are independent from one another. Consequently, the bell-shaped curve is replaced by one with a long tail of the kind observed by and subsequently predicted by Pareto. Thus, when data are examined the most familiar applications of Normal statistics turn out to be a fiat of the educator rather than an empirical observation.

Let us now compare the world views of Gauss and Pareto, the simple and the complex. The simple world is linear and proportional as hypothesized by Gauss; the complex world is non-linear as discovered by Pareto where small changes can be amplified to catastrophic failure. In the Gauss world view forces are additive and simple rules yield simple results. In Pareto's view forces are multiplicative and simple rules can generate complex results such as chaos. The former is stable and predictable, the latter is unstable and of only limited predictability. The simple world view is that all of science is quantitative and variability or uncertainty is determined by Normal statistics. The complex world view asserts that the qualitative can be as important as the quantitative and variability is determined by IPL statistics.

So what does this all mean? How does this shift from the Normal to the IPL change how physicians ought to practice medicine and what if anything does it have to do with how we treat extrema?

Consider an example of the implications of replacing the Normal with the IPL distribution. This will resonate with the academics in the audience. Suppose you are up for tenure at a top university. One of the criteria is that your publication record be exceptional. A member of the committee notices that the number of citations to most of your papers is average for the discipline and comments that the department does not want faculty who are merely average, but only those that are outstanding. S/he is, of course, unconsciously adopting the Gauss world view where the average represents typical behaviour.

Now consider the actual distribution of citations to all papers published in science in a given year, which turns out to be IPL [6]. The average number of citations is 3.2 per year. The first 39 % of all papers published have no citations, the next 45 % have one citation and so on. By the time the average number of citations is reached we have exhausted 96 % of all scientific publications. So if your paper has the average number of citations it is exceptional being out in the 4-percentile. This is the Pareto world view, if you are average you are truly exceptional, whether it is in the number of citations your papers receive, the income you earn, the number of papers you publish, how long you live, and on and on. All truly complex phenomena have IPL tails and this significantly changes the traditional interpretation. Thus, when the term average is applied in a situation, whether on a tenure review committee or in a critical care unit, one must be circumspect and think about the underlying distribution before drawing any conclusions.

7.3 Medical Implications

We [7] have argued that scaling in random time series is a novel way of gaining insight into mechanisms of complex systems and that scaling parameters characterize searches for the presence of "essential" uncertainty in outcomes of complex systems. The presence of this type of uncertainty in an emergency system (ES) can point to unusual ways of relieving the financial burden to the health system and improve the public health. An IPL function fit to data can assess "essential" uncertainty. One such measure is the emergency-ward length of stay (EWLS) which was well fit by an IPL, as determined by an aggregated allometric relation [8]. Our analysis indicates that the various hospital dynamic systems embed "essential" uncertainty to various degrees. We concluded that intervention to reduce hospital health care costs must be centered on the interaction and feedback characterizing the ES processing of the patients. The conclusion is no less valid when addressing physiologic systems, since it rests on the properties of complexity as manifest in the statistical distribution and not on specific mechanisms.

Let us now return to the promise I made at the beginning of my remarks and re-examine the cohort of post-AMI patients. The statistics of HRV intervals for this group depicted in Fig. 7.1 deviates markedly from the Normal distribution. The probability of a person surviving with an inter-beat interval that is four standard deviations from the mean is between a factor of ten and one hundred times greater than that given by a Normal distribution. Similarly the probability of such a person dying is about the same as that of surviving, maybe it is a little greater when cardiac events are taken into account. The exact values are not important for the present argument. The point is that the probability density function (PDF) for HRV data is more like the distribution of income that it is the distribution of heights; it is a manifestation of the fact that we live in the world of Pareto and not that of Gauss.

Unfortunately it is difficult to distinguish one IPL from another by direct processing of the data. However the distributions of the extrema in the two cases are quite different. The likelihood of having an extreme value far exceeds what is predicted by the Normal distribution. In Fig. 7.1 it can be seen that the number of non-cardiac deaths given by the black swans exceeds that predicted by a Normal distribution, but even more importantly the number of cardiac deaths, the dragon kings, far exceeds what would be predicted by the black swans. So how do we make use of the difference between the two data sets, given that they both deviate markedly from the Normal.

There is an index that measures the deviation from Normalcy, whose explicit form is not important here [1]. What is important is that this measure of non-Gaussianity has a critical value. Below the critical value the fluctuation distribution describing the variability in HRV intervals of the survivors in the cohort group is determined to be a truncated IPL. Here the unpredictable black swans determine who lives and who dies and the distribution of those that die by means other than cardiac death have the same statistics as those that survive. When the measure of deviation from Gaussianity is above its critical value the dragon kings appear in

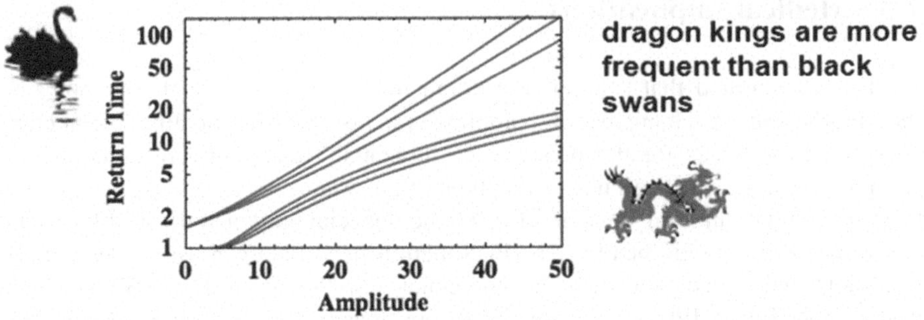

Fig. 7.4 The return time to an event of a given amplitude is given for black swans by the *upper set of curves*. The return time for dragon kings is given by the *lower set of curves*

the IPL tails and these individuals eventually suffer cardiac death. Note that the existence of a physiologic mechanism that produces the observed truncation in the IPL for the black swans has been assumed. The physiological mechanism restricting the variability is suppressed in the IPL for the dragon kings. Thus, the non-Gaussian index might be useful in separating those most at risk for cardiac death from the survivors and potentially suggest a specialized protocol based on the difference in the statistics.

Another possible measure of separation is the return time to an event of a given magnitude as shown in Fig. 7.4. The return time denotes how long you have to wait for the second appearance of a fluctuation of a given size. For the truncated IPL there is nearly a direct proportionality between the amplitude of the event, that being the time interval between beats, and the length of time you need to wait for an interval of that size to again occur. In the HRV data the amplitude is the time interval between successive heart beats. Large events (black swans) are therefore very rare. IPL events without truncation (dragon kings) have a much shorter return time and therefore they occur much more frequently. The frequency and return times of black swans and dragon kings are therefore very different because they are different kinds of extrema.

A second medical example described by IPL variability is a brain-quake; the level of activity within the brain as measured by an EEG during an epileptic seizure. It is remarkable that the PDFs for earthquakes and brain-quakes have been compared and the distributions for the two coincide [9]. What is perhaps most significant in the discussion of brain-quakes for our purposes is the observation first made by Davies et al. [10] regarding inter-quake intervals for fat-tailed PDFs. They asked the question:

> Is it true that, *"The longer it has been since the last event, the longer the expected time till the next?"*.

Figure 7.5 depicts the conditional waiting time as a function of the time since the last event for both seizures and earthquakes [9]. The dashed line is the unconditioned expected waiting time calculated for an underlying exponential PDF. At early

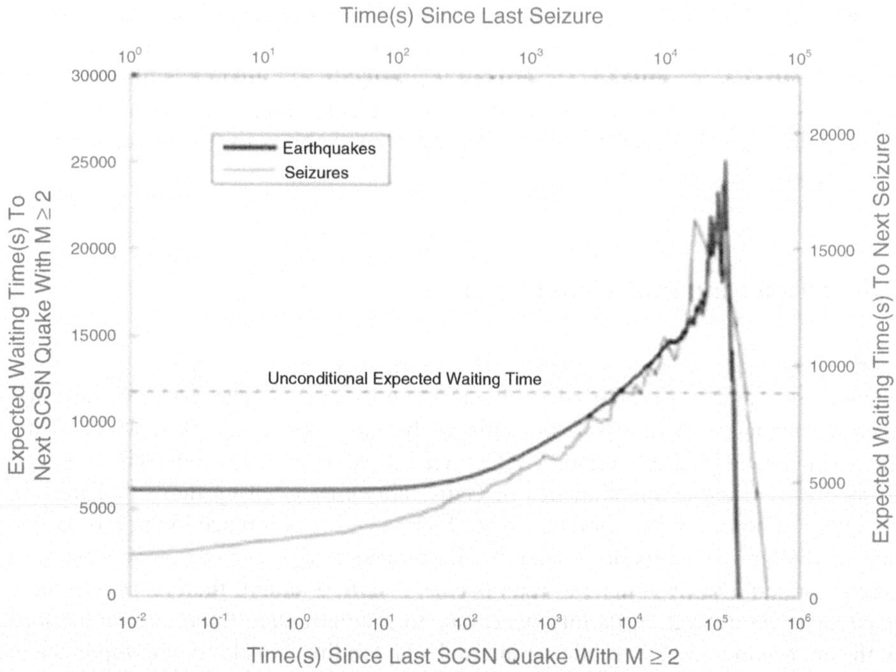

Fig. 7.5 The *blue axes* denote the expected waiting time for earthquakes greater than magnitude 2 and the time in seconds (s) since the last quake of that magnitude. The *red axes* denote the same quantities for seizures or brain-quakes [9] (Colour figure online)

times the conditional expected waiting times are less than the unconditioned value, however at late times, when the asymptotic IPL is expected to be valid, they exceed this value. Thus, at late time the question asked by Davies is answered in the affirmative.

Sornette and Knopoff [11] determine the general conditions under which the question can be answered both positively and negatively. They summarize their finding with the observation that with the exception of the Poisson distribution all statistical descriptions must have a conditional average time from the present time to the next event that depends on the time since the last event. Whether the question is answered positively or negatively depends on whether the waiting time PDF falls off at a rate slower or faster than the exponential, respectively. The exponential is neutral with respect to the question because the time since the last event has no influence on the time of the next event and consequently establishes the statistical crossover between the two states. Huillet and Raynaud [12] re-examine the question and generalize the analysis to renewal events. They find that the question should be replaced with:

> Is it true that: "*The longer it has been since the last earthquake, the longer the median time till the next*".

Note that "expected time" in the original question is replaced with "median time" in the new question since in the analysis the median time is always finite whereas the expected time may in fact diverge as suggested by the figure. Thus, the longer a person survives a dragon king event, the longer is the median survival time until the next dragon king event. In this way the traditional notion of "living on borrowed time" is turned on its head.

7.4 Discussion and Conclusions

In the physical and social sciences the average never characterizes a complex phenomenon and in this regard medicine is no exception. The average and other central tendencies of the PDF are replaced by the slope of the IPL, which is the Pareto index and is simply related to the fractal dimension of the underlying process. Consequently, just as the statistics of Gauss are superseded by those of Pareto in the study of complex phenomena, so too homoeostasis is replaced with a principle that can better accommodate variability. If homoeostasis is seen as the resistance to change in complex systems that are open to the environment, then its replacement must have the natural variability necessary to accommodate fluctuation intrusions of the environment, while retaining internal adaptability. This kind of compliance in long-term evolution and in short-term dynamics has been shown to be a defining characteristic of fractals [13]. In an evolutionary sense a fractal process is pre-adapted to a fluctuating environment and therefore has an evolutionary advantage over processes not sharing this property.

Complex medical phenomena are therefore described by the IPL PDFs of Pareto and not the Normal PDFs of Gauss. This replacement implies that the extrema of the variability of physiologic phenomena is of two kinds, black swans and dragon kings. The former may be described by truncated IPL PDFs, which we postulate to be part of the physiologic process. However when the physiologic mechanism producing the truncation is suppressed due to disease or extreme stress the black swan is transformed into a dragon king [14].

References

1. Hayano J, Kiyono K, Struzik ZR, Yamamoto Y, Watanabe E, Stein PK, Watkins LL, Blumenthal JA, Carney RM. Increased non-Gaussianity of heart rate variability predicts cardiac mortality after an acute myocardial infarction. Front Physiol. 2011;2:article 65.
2. Taleb NN. The black swan: the impact of the highly improbable. New York: Random House; 2007.
3. Sornette D. Dragon kings, black swans and the prediction of crises. Int J Terraspace Sci Eng. 2009;2:2.
4. West BJ. Homeostasis and Gauss statistics: barriers to understanding natural variability. J Eval Clin Pract. 2010;16:403.

5. Gupta HM, Campanha JR, Chavorette FR. Power law distribution in education: effect of economical, teaching, and study conditions in university entrance examination. Int J Mod Phys. 2004;14:449.
6. de Sola Price DJ. Little science, big science... and beyond. New York: Columbia University Press; 1967.
7. Philippe P, Garcia MR, West BJ. Evidence of "essential uncertainty" in emergency-ward length of stay. Fractals. 2004;12:197.
8. West D, West BJ. Physiologic time: a hypothesis. Phys Life Rev. 2013;10:210.
9. Osorio I, Frei MG, Sornette D, Milton J, Lai Y-C. Epiletic seizures, quakes of the brain? Phys Rev E. 2010;82:021919.
10. Davies PM, Jackson DD, Kagan YY. The longer it has been since the last earthquake, the longer the expected time till the next? Bull Seismol Soc Am. 1989;79:1439.
11. Sornette D, Konpoff L. The paradox of the expected time until the next earthquake. Bull Seismol Soc Am. 1997;87:789.
12. Huillet T, Raynaud H. On rare and extreme events. Chaos Solitons Fractals. 2001;12:823.
13. West BJ. Fractal physiology and chaos in medicine. New Jersey: World Scientific; 2013.
14. West BJ. A mathematics for medicine: the network effect. Front Physiol; Fractal Physiol. 2014;5:456. doi: 10.3389/fphys.2014.00456

Chapter 8
Monitoring Variability and Complexity at the Bedside

Andrew J.E. Seely, Kimberley D. Newman, and Christophe Herry

8.1 Uncertainty and Emergence

"Uncertainty" is the ongoing realization that we cannot predict the future, and "surprise" reminds us lest we forget. Uncertainty is undeniable in everyday experiences, and is particularly evident when providing care to patients. While medical science appropriately seeks knowledge, certainty, and prediction, it is also beneficial to our care, research, communication, and management to accept the simple fact that infinite knowledge of the present cannot predict the future, namely there is intrinsic irreducible uncertainty [1]. Similarly, the very defining feature of complex systems is emergence, namely infinite knowledge of the parts of a complex system in isolation cannot explain the systemic properties. Accepting both uncertainty and emergence compels one to try to evaluate the system as a whole, and to track its properties continuously over time, in order to better evaluate system state, trajectory, and warning of impending change.

The clinical problem we are addressing in general terms is that of unacceptable clinical uncertainty in vulnerable patients; for example, uncertainty regarding diagnosis and prognosis of critical illness, or uncertainty regarding predicting extubation outcomes (i.e. removal of endotracheal tube), all resulting in increased mortality and cost [2–6]. To address this clinical uncertainty, researchers have pioneered methods to analyse waveforms, including analysing the degree and

A.J.E. Seely (✉)
Thoracic Surgery & Critical Care Medicine, Associate Professor, University of Ottawa and Scientist, Ottawa Hospital Research Institute, Ottawa Hospital - General Campus, 501 Smyth Road, Box 708, Ottawa, ON, Canada K1H 8L6
e-mail: aseely@ohri.ca

K.D. Newman • C. Herry
Ottawa Hospital Research Institute, 501 Smyth Road, Box 708, Ottawa, ON, Canada K1H 8L6
e-mail: knewman@ohri.ca; cherry@ohri.ca

J.P. Sturmberg (ed.), *The Value of Systems and Complexity Sciences for Healthcare*, DOI 10.1007/978-3-319-26221-5_8

variation of inter-beat and inter-breath interval time-series over intervals-in-time, termed variability analysis, and demonstrated that altered HRV and RRV are unequivocally present in association with and prognostic of critical illness (e.g. sepsis [7–15], organ failure [16–18], and extubation failure [19]). Monitoring and displaying risk of deterioration based on HRV in neonates lowers mortality by 20 % [20]. With these promising advances and published assertions of the potential of variability monitoring [21–29], much research is focussed on applying this research to the bedside.

8.2 What is Variability?

Variability analysis characterizes the patterns of fluctuations with the time-series of a biologic signal (e.g. time series of inter-beat or inter-breath time intervals). In a variety of clinical illness states (e.g. sepsis [7, 10, 30, 31], myocardial infarction [32]), it has been demonstrated that patterns of variability are altered (i.e. reduced degree and complexity of variation) and that the degree of alteration correlates with the severity of illness [33, 34]. The degree and character of this fluctuation can be measured mathematically in several complementary domains of variability. Over 100 techniques of variability analysis have been utilized in the medical literature. While many are correlated, each technique provides a unique perspective. No single technique offers a definitive characterization, and investigators agree a plurality of techniques offers the most complete evaluation [29, 34, 35].

The physiologic interpretation of variability is closely tied to the measures of variability themselves. There are several inter-related theories proposed to explain loss of degree and complexity of variability associated with illness. For example, altered high and low frequency variation is associated with autonomic modulation [36–39], decreased adaptability is thought to be associated with reduction of overall variation [40], decreased organ coupling [41] is thought to contribute to "decomplexification" of systems leading to a loss of complexity measured by multi-scale entropy [25, 29], and finally, entropy production has been linked to the origin and function of self-similar scale-invariant (fractal) variation [42]. Building from these advances, a unified physiologic understanding of the physiology and pathophysiology of variability remains pending.

8.3 Monitoring Multi-Organ Variability

We hypothesize that continuous variability monitoring in the ICU can provide improved ability to predict clinical improvement or deterioration (i.e. detect clinical trajectory) potentially leading to real-time prognostication in this critical care setting. Thus, we developed continuous individualized multi-organ variability analysis (CIMVA^{TM}) software to evaluate HRV and RRV continuously over time. The set-up and process for harvesting patient waveform data are shown in Fig. 8.1. Indeed

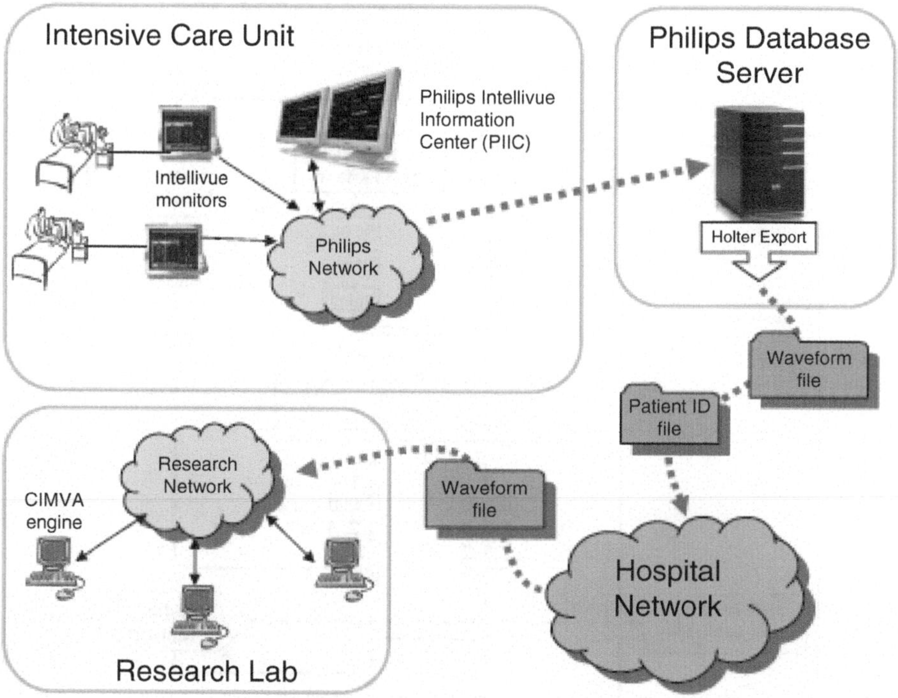

Fig. 8.1 Overview of data harvest set-up and process

a number of different methods are slowly but increasingly available to harvest waveform data from devices, monitors, and ventilators, which is the input into the CIMVA^{TM} software.

When the de-identified waveform data arrive at the research file server after the data harvest process, HRV and RRV analyses are performed for each patient using the CIMVA^{TM} software engine. CIMVA^{TM} is currently implemented in Matlab (The Mathworks, Natick, Massachusetts), and data processing occurs on a standard PC (2 GB RAM, 2.20 GHz processor speed). The data processing steps for both the two principal waveforms studied to date, namely electrocardiogram (ECG) and capnography (etCO^2) waveform data are shown in Fig. 8.2. Automated cleaning and measurement of signal quality and suitability for variability analysis is first performed, evaluating waveform quality, time-series quality, and non-stationarity. Variability measures are calculated using sliding windows of 5-min duration, with 50 % overlap (2.5 min) between adjacent windows. This results in a complete set of variability and data quality measures every 2.5 min. The output from the CIMVA^{TM} data processing engine is a matrix consisting of rows representing every input window (e.g. every 2.5 min) and columns for all measures representing signal quality and all variability measures. The variability measures calculated by

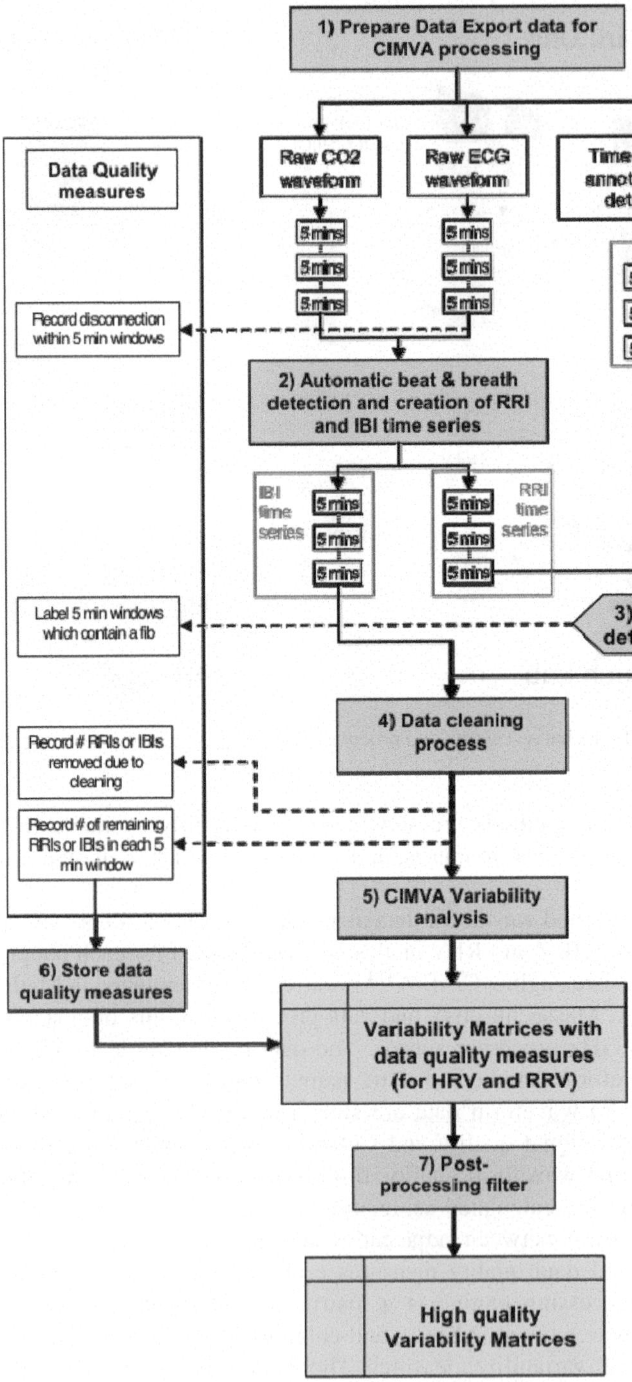

Fig. 8.2 The CIMVA™ data processing steps for both ECG and CO^2 waveform data

CIMVA^{TM} have been verified against surrogate data sets with known properties and, where possible, third-party software [e.g., Kubios HRV (University of Eastern Finland) and Physionet].

8.4 Monitoring Variability and Sepsis

Monitoring HRV to provide early warning of infection is the first bedside application of variability analysis we evaluated and remains ongoing. Early diagnosis of sepsis enables timely resuscitation, administration of antibiotics and prevents subsequent morbidity and mortality. Clinical approaches relying on point-in-time analysis of vital signs or lab values are often insensitive, non-specific, and late diagnostic markers of sepsis. HRV has been documented to be both altered in the presence of sepsis and correlated with its severity [7, 10, 30, 31]. In this study, we hypothesized that by continuously tracking individual patient HRV over time in patients as they develop sepsis, we would demonstrate reduced HRV in association with the onset of sepsis [7]. We monitored heart rate continuously in adult bone marrow transplant (BMT) patients beginning a day before their BMT and continuing until recovery or withdrawal ($n = 21$; 4 could not complete Holter monitoring; total 1264 days monitored). We characterized HRV continuously over time with a panel of time, frequency, complexity, and scale-invariant domain techniques. We defined baseline HRV as mean variability for the first 24 h of monitoring and studied individual and population average percentage change (from baseline) over time in diverse HRV metrics, in comparison with the time of clinical diagnosis and treatment of sepsis (defined as systemic inflammatory response syndrome along with clinically suspected infection requiring treatment). Of the 17 patients who completed the study, 14 patients developed sepsis requiring antibiotic therapy, whereas 3 did not. On average, for 12 out of 14 infected patients, a significant (25 %) reduction prior to the clinical diagnosis and treatment of sepsis was observed in multiple measures of HRV, including standard deviation, root mean square successive difference, sample and multi-scale entropy, fast Fourier transform, de-trended fluctuation analysis, and wavelet variability metrics. For infected patients ($n = 14$), wavelet HRV demonstrated a 25 % drop from baseline 35 h prior to sepsis on average, while in the three non-infected patients, all measures, except root mean square successive difference and entropy, showed no significant reduction [7].

In further analysis, we developed a procedure to integrate multiple measures of HRV into a composite measure for the tracking of sepsis development [10]. A comprehensive panel ($N = 92$) of variability measures was calculated for 5 min-windows throughout the period of monitoring (1264 days). Variability measures underwent filtering and two steps of data reduction with the objective of enhancing the information related to the greatest degree of change. The proposed composite measure was capable of tracking the development of sepsis in 12 out of 14 patients. Simulating a real-time monitoring setting, the sum of the energy over the very low

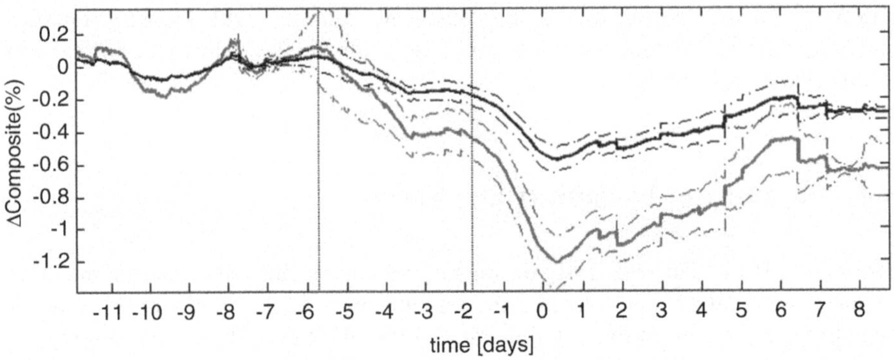

Fig. 8.3 Average composite measure of variability. In the *lower line* is the composite HRV measure; whereas for comparison, the above line is a single HRV metric (de-trended fluctuation analysis area under the curve), after admission condition normalization. The *continuous lines* represent the average value of the time series across the population, and the *dashed lines* represent plus or minus the standard error of the mean. The *two vertical dotted lines* highlight when, on average, the composite variability started to drop

frequency range of the composite measure was used to classify the probability of developing sepsis. Figure 8.3 reveals the higher sensitivity of the composite to sepsis development compared to the sensitivity of a single HRV measure. In fact the composite revealed information about the onset of sepsis about 60 h (median value) before sepsis diagnosis. In a real monitoring setting this quicker detection time might be associated with increased efficacy of the treatment of sepsis; however, this hypothesis remains to be evaluated.

8.5 Monitoring Variability and Organ Failure

Continuous individualized monitoring has the potential to be useful in identifying the progression or regression of a disease process. We conducted a study to evaluate the utility of using continuous HRV and RRV monitoring for (a) tracking daily organ dysfunction in critically ill patients and (b) identifying patterns of variability changes during onset of shock and resolution of respiratory failure [18]. Thirty-three critically ill patients experiencing respiratory and/or cardiac failure underwent continuous recording of their ECG and capnogram (CO^2) waveforms from admission or intubation until discharge (maximum 14 days). HRV and RRV were computed in 5-min overlapping windows, using CIMVA™ software and multiple organ dysfunction scores were recorded daily. HRV and RRV trajectories were characterized during onset of shock and resolution of respiratory failure. Both HRV and RRV decreased with increasing severity of multiple organ dysfunction scores for a variety of variability metrics. A decline in several measures of HRV and no decline in RRV were observed before onset of shock ($n = 6$). In contrast, during resolution of respiratory failure, an increase in RRV was observed in patients who successfully passed extubation ($n = 12$), with no change in RRV in those who subsequently failed extubation ($n = 2$). The results of this study suggest there may be trends of decreasing HRV (with onset of shock) and increasing RRV (with resolution of respiratory failure), which are supported by an association between reduced HRV and RRV and increasing organ dysfunction in critically ill patients. However, despite these population trends, we have nonetheless found it challenging to track individual patient variability as a marker of severity of illness in individual patients as numerous stressors (e.g. pain, anxiety, delirium, bedside interventions) also may transiently decrease HRV. In adult heterogeneous patients, the use of monitoring variability as a marker of illness severity required further.

In the ICU finding the appropriate level of sedation is controversial and remains a daily challenge for clinicians. We conducted a study using CIMVA™ to determine whether sedation reduces HRV and RRV in critically ill patients and whether the extent of reduction depends on degree of organ dysfunction [16]. In 33 critically ill adult patients experiencing respiratory and/or cardiac failure, ECG and end-tidal capnography waveform capture were initiated from admission or intubation, respectively, and continued to intensive care unit discharge or a maximum of 14 days. All patient days with a sedation interruption (defined as cessation of a continuous infusion of sedation agent) were identified. Mean HRV and RRV were computed over two periods: 4 h directly prior to the sedation interruption, and the duration of sedation interruption (median: 1 h 45 mins, interquartile range: 4 h 15 mins or max 4 h). Variability before and during sedation interruption was compared and analysed across multiple organ dysfunction syndrome levels and sedative types. Our results suggest that both HRV and RRV increased during sedation interruption ($p < 0.05$ for coefficient of variation). Patients with low and medium multiple organ dysfunction syndrome experienced greater increase in HRV during sedation interruption ($p < 0.05$ for coefficient of variation), compared to patients with high multiple organ dysfunction syndrome, who failed to mount a significant increase in HRV when sedation was stopped. Similarly, sedation interruption led to increased RRV for low multiple organ dysfunction syndrome patients ($p < 0.05$ for SD), but in contrast, a further deterioration in RRV occurred in the high multiple organ dysfunction syndrome patients. These results suggest that interruption of sedation allows for uncovering a greater restoration of HRV and RRV in patients with low organ failure. The further reduction in RRV during the elimination of sedation in patients with high multiple organ dysfunction syndrome suggests a differential response and benefit from sedation interruption, and merits further investigation. As reduced variability correlates with severity of illness, and need for sedation depends on organ failure, variability monitoring may offer a dynamic measure of a variable response to the benefit, timing, and duration of sedation interruption.

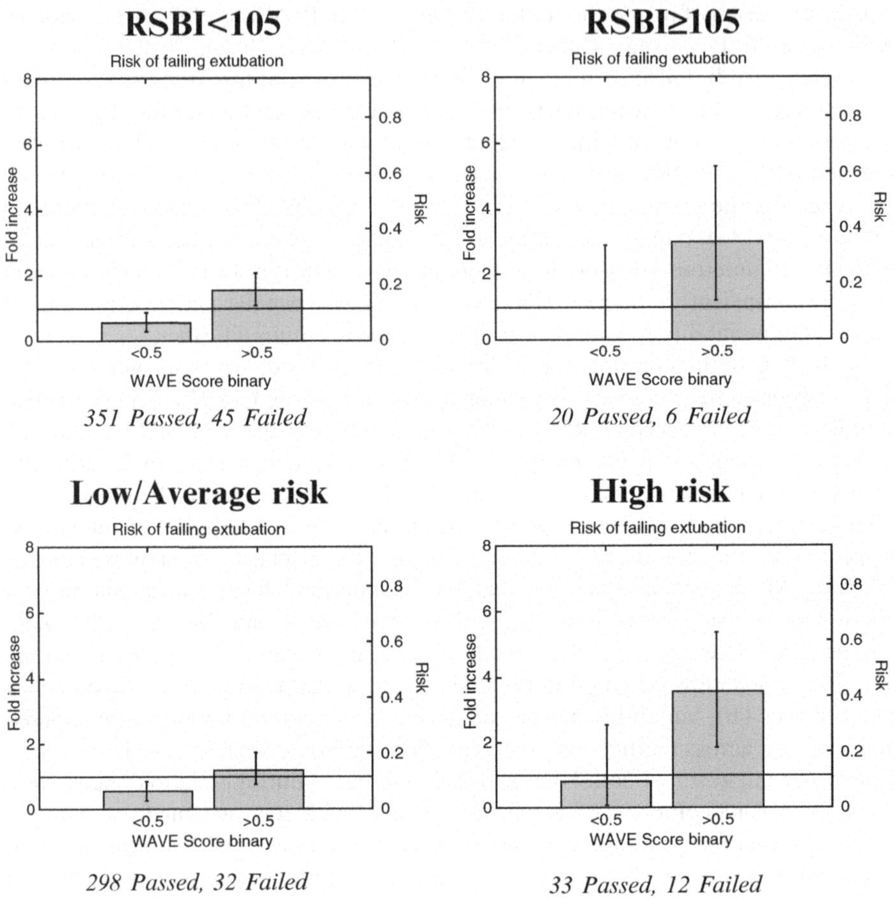

Fig. 8.4 WAVE score, RSBI and clinical impression. These figures show how the risk/fold increase in risk of failing extubation associated with positive WAVE score (i.e. above 0.5) increases with increasing RSBI during SBT (*above*), or the clinical impression of the physician at the end of the SBT (*below*). The risk is defined as the number of patients who failed divided by the total number of patients in a given group (e.g. above 0.5). The fold increase in risk is the risk divided by the average risk of failure of the dataset (∼12 %). There are 396 patients with low RSBI (45 Failed, 351 Passed), and 26 patients with high RSBI (6 Failed, 20 Passed), while 12 Passed had no RSBI reported. There is no statistically significant difference between the number of Failed and Passed that had no RSBI reported (p-value = 0.2, chi-squared test for proportions). There are 330 patients with low/average risk of failure (32 Failed, 298 Passed), and 45 with high risk of failure (12 Failed, 33 Passed), while 7 Failed and 52 Passed have no perceived risk of failure reported. There is no statistically significant difference between the number of Failed and Passed that had no perceived risk of failure reported (p-value = 0.98, chi-squared test for proportions)

8.6 Monitoring Variability and Extubation

Prolonged ventilation and failed extubation are associated with increased harm and cost. The added value of HRV and RRV during spontaneous breathing trials (SBTs) to predict extubation failure remains unknown. We enrolled 721 patients in a multi-center (12 sites), prospective, observational study, evaluating clinical estimates of risk of extubation failure, physiologic measures recorded during SBTs, HRV and RRV recorded before and during the last SBT prior to extubation, and extubation outcomes [19]. Two hundred and eighty-seven patients were excluded because of protocol or technical violations, or poor data quality. Measures of variability (97 HRV, 82 RRV) were calculated from ECG and capnography waveforms followed by automated cleaning and variability analysis using CIMVA^{TM} software. Repeated randomized sub-sampling with training, validation, and testing were used to derive and compare predictive models. Of 434 patients with high quality data, 51 (12 %) failed extubation. Two HRV and eight RRV measures showed statistically significant association with extubation failure ($P < 0.0041$, 5 % false discovery rate). An ensemble average of five univariate logistic regression models using RRV during SBT, yielding a probability of extubation failure (called WAVE score), demonstrated optimal predictive capacity. With repeated random sub-sampling and testing, the model showed mean receiver operating characteristic area under the curve (ROC AUC) of 0.69, higher than heart rate (0.51), rapid shallow breathing index (RSBI: 0.61), and respiratory rate (0.63). After deriving a WAVE model based on all data, training-set performance demonstrated that the model increased its predictive power when applied to patients conventionally considered high risk: a WAVE Score > 0.5 in patients with RSBI > 105 and perceived high-risk of failure yielded a fold increase in risk of extubation failure of 3.0 [95 % confidence interval (CI) 1.2 to 5.2] and 3.5 (95 % CI 1.9 to 5.4), respectively (see Fig. 8.4). The results demonstrate that altered HRV and RRV during the last SBT prior to extubation are significantly associated with extubation failure, and a predictive model derived from RRV during SBT provides added prognostic accuracy in predicting extubation failure, with improved accuracy when combined with clinical impression or RSBI, when compared to physiological variables used in clinical practice, particularly in high risk patients. This model requires validation in an independent cohort to verify its generalizability, and a randomized trial to assess its clinical utility.

8.7 What is the Meaning of Altered Variability?

Over the last three decades, methods to analyse the patterns of variation of physiologic data collected as a series over time have undergone marked development with increasingly sophisticated means to uncover clinically valuable information. For example, using time domain measures (e.g. standard deviation), frequency domain (e.g. power spectra), and non-linear measures such as irregularity or complexity analysis (e.g. sample entropy) and scale-invariant analyses (e.g. Power Law or De-trended Fluctuation analyses), numerous studies have demonstrated that both ageing and illness are associated with reduced overall HRV, reduced irregularity, and altered scale-invariant variation [43–54]. These techniques, as well as many others [55–57], form a tool-kit [58] to enable mathematical analysis and characterization of variability suitable for clinical application.

The development of this tool-kit has been paralleled by the search for the meaning and significance of characteristic patterns of variation in health, as well their alteration in illness. For example, since Sayers [38] and Akselrod [37] introduced the frequency domain measures of HRV the measurement of HRV has been closely related to modulation of the autonomic nervous system (ANS). In addition, since Pincus introduced approximate entropy in 1991 as a measure of irregularity and information [59–62], followed by Sample Entropy by Richman and Moorman [63], and Multi-Scale entropy by Costa et al. [64], investigators have repeatedly observed a reduction in the "complexity" (here defined as degree of irregularity across time scales) of time-series of heart rate in heart disease and ageing; this led to the hypothesis put forth by Goldberger and colleagues [25–27, 29] that illness and ageing were characterized by "decomplexification". Lastly, based upon mathematical modelling in non-linear dynamics, Godin and Buchman introduced the hypothesis of uncoupling of biologic oscillators as a cause of organ failure and loss of variability in association with organ failure [41]. The inter-relationship between different theories is unknown, and the simple question of what is the number of independent dimensions to variability remains unknown. To explore this question, we hypothesize that there is at least two independent but related dimensions to variability, namely degree of variation and complexity of variation.

8.8 Meaning of Degree of Variability?

Others and we have hypothesized that the degree of variation relates to the adaptability of a system. The association of degree of variability and adaptability of the system is discussed in a work by West, "Where Medicine went wrong" [65]. We interpret physiologic adaptability as the ability to augment work if required. Our human biologic system is constantly doing work, manifest by every cardiac and respiratory cycle, muscle activity, and more, which varies continuously, for example during exercise (augmented work output) or sleep (decrease work output). The capacity to augment work relates to the relative difference between the current level of work, and the maximal possible work. It is clear that this concept of physiologic adaptability would be developed through Darwinian evolution.

We have hypothesized that the *overall degree of variation reflects adaptability of the system, which is proportional to the ratio of the maximal work possible* (W_{max}) *divided by resting work output* (W_{rest})*, i.e.,* W_{max}/W_{rest} [42]. For the whole body under physiologic conditions, work relates to oxygen consumption, and W_{max}/W_{rest} may be estimated by maximal oxygen consumption (VO_{2max}) divided by resting oxygen consumption (VO_2). Either decreased W_{max} or increased W_{rest} both represent decreased capacity to adapt to increasing demands. Heart failure and muscular weakness are examples of decreased W_{max} whereas obstructive lung disease and thyrotoxicosis are examples of increased W_{rest}. If the magnitude of fluctuations is a measure of adaptability, it should decrease as W_{max}/W_{rest} decreases. In heart failure and chronic obstructive lung disease this is the case; variability of heart rate and respiratory rate are, respectively, decreased in these diseases. A variation of this hypothesis appears in asthma when the variability to the impedance to the flow of air in and out of the lung is increased. In keeping with this hypothesis, this may be due to an augmentation of W_{max}, indeed to a greater extent than W_{rest}. Last, we briefly address the changes in variability associated with sleep and exercise. According to our hypothesis, sleep is characterized by decreased oxygen consumption (no change in maximal) and therefore decreases in variability (e.g. HRV and RRV). This could easily be evaluated in a sleep lab with continuous monitoring of oxygen consumption and cardiopulmonary variability. In contrast, exercise is characterized by an increase in baseline oxygen consumption, with no change in maximal oxygen consumption, and therefore a progressive reduction in variability occurs until a minimum is reached at maximal oxygen consumption. However, repeated exercise will augment maximal work output and decrease resting output, improving variability measured at rest. Thus, as a first dimension of information contained within patterns of variation, we hypothesize that overall variation of heart and respiratory rate reflects an evolutionarily optimized ratio of resting work to maximal work.

8.9 Meaning of Complexity of Variability?

Complexity of variation appears to be entirely distinct from the degree of variation. The patterns of low to high frequency variation, the degree of information or irregularity, and the scale-invariant self-similarity present within heart and respiratory rate time-series are distinct mathematically and theoretically from the total amount of variation, measured with standard deviation or total power. Inspired from the principle of maximum entropy production within non-equilibrium thermodynamics, we hypothesize the following: within a far-from equilibrium complex system's limits (scale) and boundary conditions, *scale-invariant self-similarity (i.e. fractal variability), structure and connectivity of complex dissipative systems develop as self-organizing event, spontaneously occurring to enable optimal dissipation of energy gradients and maximal entropy production* [42]. In fact, the spontaneous development of so many spatial fractal dissipative structures (e.g. trees, river deltas, lightning, pulmonary anatomy, hurricanes, etc.) and temporal fractal dissipative structures (e.g. solar flares, earthquakes, cardiopulmonary variability etc.) in nature may be precisely because those structures offer the most efficient means for their systems to dissipate energy gradients, consume free energy and produce entropy. We have found an association between increased fractal dimension of central nervous system anatomical structures and increased entropy production, estimated with degree of oxygen metabolism [66]. Mathematical theory and models are required to prove or disprove this hypothesis. As the origins of variability are explored theoretically, experimentally monitoring variation in health and disease will continue to help elucidate the aetiology and pathophysiology of variability, as well as determine its clinical utility.

8.10 Summary

Complex systems have properties that depend on the integrity of the whole, which emerge from the innumerable, dynamic non-linear interactions of the elements of the system. The host response to sepsis, shock or trauma, which involves inflammatory, coagulation, endocrine, metabolic, and end-organ interactions, pathways and feedback loops, is a complex system [67]. Uncertainty regarding diagnosis and prognosis of critical illness leads to worse patient outcomes, including higher mortality rates and increased costs of care [2, 3]. To address this clinical uncertainty in vulnerable patients, researchers have pioneered methods to analyse the degree and variation of inter-beat and inter-breath interval time-series over intervals-in-time, termed variability analysis, and demonstrated that altered HRV and RRV are associated with and prognostic of critical illness. We have initiated the investigation of the potential clinical value of monitoring variability with respect to early warning of sepsis [7–15], prognostication of organ failure and the impact of sedation [16–18], and improved prediction of extubation failure [19]. The bedside application of variability monitoring remains an exciting voyage of theoretical, clinical, and technological research.

Conflict of Interest

Andrew Seely is Founder and Chief Science Officer of Therapeutic Monitoring Systems (TMS); TMS aims to commercialize patent-protected applications of multiorgan variability monitoring to provide variability-directed clinical decision support at the bedside to improve care for patients at risk for or with existing critical illness. Other authors have no relevant conflict of interest to disclose.

References

1. Seely AJ. Embracing the certainty of uncertainty: implications for health care and research. Perspect Biol Med. 2013;56(1):65–77.
2. Luce JM, Rubenfeld GD. Can health care costs be reduced by limiting intensive care at the end of life? Am J Respir Crit Care Med. 2002;165(6):750–4.

3. Detsky AS, Stricker SC, Mulley AG, Thibault GE. Prognosis, survival,and the expenditure of hospital resources for patients in an intensive care unit. N Engl J Med. 1981;305:667–72.
4. Esteban A, Alia I, Tobin MJ, Gil A, Gordo F, Vallverdu I, et al. Effect of spontaneous breathing trial duration on outcome of attempts to discontinue mechanical ventilation. Spanish lung failure collaborative group. Am J Respir Crit Care Med. 1999;159(2):512–8.
5. Esteban A, Frutos F, Tobin MJ, Alia I, Solsona JF, Valverdu I, et al. A comparison of four methods of weaning patients from mechanical ventilation. Spanish Lung Failure Collaborative Group. N Engl J Med. 1995;332(6):345–50.
6. Yang KL, Tobin MJ. A prospective study of indexes predicting the outcome of trials of weaning from mechanical ventilation. N Engl J Med. 1991;324(21):1445–50 [see comment].
7. Ahmad S, Ramsay T, Huebsch L, Flanagan S, McDiarmid S, Batkin I, et al. Continuous multi-parameter heart rate variability analysis heralds onset of sepsis in adults. PLoS One. 2009;4(8):e6642.
8. Ahmad S, Tejuja A, Newman KD, Zarychanski R, Seely AJ. Clinical review: a review and analysis of heart rate variability and the diagnosis and prognosis of infection. Crit Care. 2009;13(6):232.
9. Seely AJ. Heart rate variability and infection: diagnosis, prognosis, and prediction. J Crit Care. 2006;21(3):286–9.
10. Bravi A, Green G, Longtin A, Seely AJ. Monitoring and identification of sepsis development through a composite measure of heart rate variability. PLoS One. 2012;7(9):e45666.
11. Barnaby D, Ferrick K, Kaplan DT, Shah S, Bijur P, Gallagher EJ. Heart rate variability in emergency department patients with sepsis. Acad Emerg Med. 2002;9(7):661–70.
12. Chen WL, Kuo CD. Characteristics of heart rate variability can predict impending septic shock in emergency department patients with sepsis. Acad Emerg Med. 2007;14(5):392–7.
13. Garrard CS, Kontoyannis DA, Piepoli M. Spectral analysis of heart rate variability in the sepsis syndrome. Clin Auton Res. 1993;3(1):5–13.
14. Goldstein B, Fiser DH, Kelly MM, Mickelsen D, Ruttimann U, Pollack MM. Decomplexification in critical illness and injury: relationship between heart rate variability, severity of illness, and outcome. Crit Care Med. 1998;26(2):352–7.
15. Pontet J, Contreras P, Curbelo A, Medina J, Noveri S, Bentancourt S, et al. Heart rate variability as early marker of multiple organ dysfunction syndrome in septic patients. J Crit Care. 2003;18(3):156–63.
16. Bradley BD, Green G, Ramsay T, Seely AJ. Impact of sedation and organ failure on continuous heart and respiratory rate variability monitoring in critically ill patients: a pilot study. Crit Care Med. 2013;41(2):433–44.
17. Arnold R, Green G, Bravi A, Hollenberg S, Seely A. Impaired heart rate variability predicts clinical deterioration and progressive organ failure in emergency department sepsis patients. Crit Care. 2012;16(Suppl1):P37.
18. Green GC, Bradley B, Bravi A, Seely AJ. Continuous multiorgan variability analysis to track severity of organ failure in critically ill patients. J Crit Care. 2013;28(5):879.e1–11.
19. Seely AJ, Bravi A, Herry C, Green G, Longtin A, Ramsay T, et al. Do heart and respiratory rate variability improve prediction of extubation outcomes in critically ill patients? Crit Care. 2014;18(2):R65.
20. Moorman JR, Carlo WA, Kattwinkel J, Schelonka RL, Porcelli PJ, Navarrete CT, et al. Mortality reduction by heart rate characteristic monitoring in very low birth weight neonates: a randomized trial. J Pediatr. 2011;159(6):900–6.e1.
21. Seely AJ, Christou NV. Multiple organ dysfunction syndrome: exploring the paradigm of complex nonlinear systems. Crit Care Med. 2000;28(7):2193–200.
22. Buchman TG. Nonlinear dynamics, complex systems, and the pathobiology of critical illness. Curr Opin Crit Care. 2004;10(5):378–82.
23. Buchman TG, Cobb JP, Lapedes AS, Kepler TB. Complex systems analysis: a tool for shock research. Shock. 2001;16(4):248–51.
24. Buchman TG, Stein PK, Goldstein B. Heart rate variability in critical illness and critical care. Curr Opin Crit Care. 2002;8(4):311–5.

25. Goldberger AL. Non-linear dynamics for clinicians: chaos theory, fractals, and complexity at the bedside. Lancet. 1996;347(9011):1312–4.
26. Goldberger AL. Fractal variability versus pathologic periodicity: complexity loss and stereotypy in disease. Perspect Biol Med. 1997;40(4):543–61.
27. Goldberger AL. Nonlinear dynamics, fractals, and chaos theory: implications for neuroautonomic heart rate control in health and disease. In: Bolis CL, Licinio J, editors. The autonomic nervous system. Geneva: World Health Organization; 1999.
28. Goldberger AL, Amaral LA, Hausdorff JM, Ivanov P, Peng CK, Stanley HE. Fractal dynamics in physiology: alterations with disease and aging. Proc Natl Acad Sci U S A. 2002;99(Suppl 1):2466–72.
29. Goldberger AL, Peng CK, Lipsitz LA. What is physiologic complexity and how does it change with aging and disease? Neurobiol Aging. 2002;23(1):23–6.
30. Rello J, Ollendorf DA, Oster G, Vera-Llonch M, Bellm L, Redman R, et al. Epidemiology and outcomes of ventilator-associated pneumonia in a large US database. Chest. 2002;122(6):2115–21 [see comment].
31. Buchan CA, Bravi A, Seely AJ. Variability analysis and the diagnosis, management, and treatment of sepsis. Curr Infect Dis Rep. 2012;14(5):512–21. doi: 10.1007/s11908-012-0282-4.
32. Odemuyiwa O, Malik M, Farrell T, Bashir Y, Poloniecki J, Camm J. Comparison of the predictive characteristics of heart rate variability index and left ventricular ejection fraction for all-cause mortality, arrhythmic events and sudden death after acute myocardial infarction. Am J Cardiol. 1991;68(5):434–9.
33. Seely AJ, Macklem PT. Complex systems and the technology of variability analysis. Crit Care. 2004;8(6):R367–84.
34. Bravi A, Longtin A, Seely AJ. Review and classification of variability analysis techniques with clinical applications. Biomed Eng Online. 2011;10:90.
35. Bravi A, Herry C, Townsend D, Green G, Ramsay T, Longtin A, et al. Towards the identification of independent measures of heart rate variability. J Crit Care. 2013;28:e16.
36. Frey U, Silverman M, Barabasi AL, Suki B. Irregularities and power law distributions in the breathing pattern in preterm and term infants. J Appl Physiol. 1998;85(3):789–97.
37. Akselrod S, Gordon D, Ubel FA, Shannon DC, Berger AC, Cohen RJ. Power spectrum analysis of heart rate fluctuation: a quantitative probe of beat-to-beat cardiovascular control. Science. 1981;213(4504):220–2.
38. Sayers BM. Analysis of heart rate variability. Ergonomics. 1973;16(1):17–32.
39. Huston JM, Tracey KJ. The pulse of inflammation: heart rate variability, the cholinergic anti-inflammatory pathway and implications for therapy. J Intern Med. 2011;269(1):45–53.
40. Morris JA, Jr., Norris PR, Ozdas A, Waitman LR, Harrell FE, Jr., Williams AE, et al. Reduced heart rate variability: an indicator of cardiac uncoupling and diminished physiologic reserve in 1,425 trauma patients. J Trauma. 2006;60(6):1165–73 (Discussion 73–74).
41. Godin PJ, Buchman TG. Uncoupling of biological oscillators: a complementary hypothesis concerning the pathogenesis of multiple organ dysfunction syndrome. Critical Care Med. 1996;24(7):1107–16 [see comments].
42. Seely AJ, Macklem P. Fractal variability: an emergent property of complex dissipative systems. Chaos. 2012;22(1):013108.
43. Seely AJ, Macklem PT. Complex systems and the technology of variability analysis. Crit Care. 2004;8(6):R367–84.
44. Axelrod S, Lishner M, Oz O, Bernheim J, Ravid M. Spectral analysis of fluctuations in heart rate: an objective evaluation of autonomic nervous control in chronic renal failure. Nephron. 1987;45(3):202–6.
45. Bonaduce D, Petretta M, Marciano F, Vicario ML, Apicella C, Rao MA, et al. Independent and incremental prognostic value of heart rate variability in patients with chronic heart failure. Am Heart J. 1999;138(2 Pt 1):273–84.
46. Guzzetti S, Mezzetti S, Magatelli R, Porta A, De Angelis G, Rovelli G, et al. Linear and non-linear 24 h heart rate variability in chronic heart failure. Auton Neurosci. 2000;86(1–2):114–9.

47. Guzzetti S, Piccaluga E, Casati R, Cerutti S, Lombardi F, Pagani M, et al. Sympathetic predominance in essential hypertension: a study employing spectral analysis of heart rate variability. J Hypertens. 1988;6(9):711–7.
48. Huang J, Sopher SM, Leatham E, Redwood S, Camm AJ, Kaski JC. Heart rate variability depression in patients with unstable angina. Am Heart J. 1995;130(4):772–9.
49. Lishner M, Akselrod S, Avi VM, Oz O, Divon M, Ravid M. Spectral analysis of heart rate fluctuations. A non-invasive, sensitive method for the early diagnosis of autonomic neuropathy in diabetes mellitus. Journal of the autonomic nervous system. 1987;19(2):119–25.
50. Mussalo H, Vanninen E, Ikaheimo R, Laitinen T, Laakso M, Lansimies E, et al. Heart rate variability and its determinants in patients with severe or mild essential hypertension. Clin Physiol. 2001;21(5):594–604.
51. Pardo Y, Merz CN, Paul-Labrador M, Velasquez I, Gottdiener JS, Kop WJ, et al. Heart rate variability reproducibility and stability using commercially available equipment in coronary artery disease with daily life myocardial ischemia. Am J Cardiol. 1996;78(8):866–70.
52. Poulsen SH, Jensen SE, Moller JE, Egstrup K. Prognostic value of left ventricular diastolic function and association with heart rate variability after a first acute myocardial infarction. Heart (British Cardiac Society). 2001;86(4):376–80.
53. van Boven AJ, Jukema JW, Haaksma J, Zwinderman AH, Crijns HJ, Lie KI. Depressed heart rate variability is associated with events in patients with stable coronary artery disease and preserved left ventricular function. REGRESS Study Group. Am Heart J. 1998;135(4):571–6.
54. van de Borne P, Montano N, Pagani M, Oren R, Somers VK. Absence of low-frequency variability of sympathetic nerve activity in severe heart failure. Circulation. 1997;95(6):1449–54.
55. Costa M, Goldberger AL, Peng CK. Multiscale entropy analysis of complex physiologic time series. Phys Rev Lett. 2002;89(6):068102.
56. Glass L, Kaplan D. Time series analysis of complex dynamics in physiology and medicine. Med Prog Technol. 1993;19(3):115–28.
57. Stanley HE, Amaral LA, Goldberger AL, Havlin S, Ivanov P, Peng CK. Statistical physics and physiology: monofractal and multifractal approaches. Physica A. 1999;270(1–2):309–24.
58. Goldberger AL, Amaral LA, Glass L, Hausdorff JM, Ivanov PC, Mark RG, et al. PhysioBank, PhysioToolkit, and PhysioNet: components of a new research resource for complex physiologic signals. Circulation. 2000;101(23):E215–R220.
59. Pincus SM. Approximate entropy as a measure of system complexity. Proc Natl Acad Sci U S A. 1991;88(6):2297–301.
60. Pincus SM, Goldberger AL. Physiological time-series analysis: what does regularity quantify? Am J Physiol. 1994;266(4 Pt 2):H1643–56.
61. Pincus S, Singer BH. Randomness and degrees of irregularity. Proc Natl Acad Sci U S A. 1996;93(5):2083–8.
62. Pincus SM. Assessing serial irregularity and its implications for health. Ann N Y Acad Sci. 2001;954:245–67.
63. Richman JS, Moorman JR. Physiological time-series analysis using approximate entropy and sample entropy. Am J Physiol Heart Circ Physiol. 2000;278(6):H2039–49.
64. Costa M, Goldberger AL, Peng CK. Multiscale entropy to distinguish physiologic and synthetic RR time series. Comput Cardiol. 2002;29:137–140.
65. West BJ, editor. Where medicine went wrong: rediscovering the path to complexity. London: World Scientific Publishing Co; 2006.
66. Seely A, Newman KD, Herry C. Fractal structure and entropy production within the central nervous system. 2014;16(8): 4497–520.
67. Seely AJ, Christou NV. Multiple organ dysfunction syndrome: exploring the paradigm of complex nonlinear systems. Crit Care Med. 2000;28(7):2193–2200.

Chapter 9
Heterogeneity Mediated System Complexity: The Ultimate Challenge for Studying Common and Complex Diseases

Henry H. Heng, Steven D. Horne, Joshua B. Stevens, Batoul Y. Abdallah, Guo Liu, Saroj K. Chowdhury, Steven W. Bremer, Kezhong Zhang, and Christine J. Ye

9.1 Introduction

One of the key features of the complex biological system, which differs from some non-life complex systems, is the high degree of heterogeneity at multiple levels [1–4]. Through our studies on the genomic landscape of cancer and its evolutionary dynamics, we have realized that system heterogeneity plays an essential role both in normal cellular function and cancer evolution [5, 6]. Different types of heterogeneity interact with each other, and genome level heterogeneity represents a determining factor in macro-cellular evolution [7–9]. Importantly, while it is hard to study, heterogeneity provides system robustness, the capability of adaptation, and balances the dynamic relationship between genotype and environments to ensure the consistent phenotype. Furthermore, we have illustrated the existence of new types of inheritance including "system inheritance" and "fuzzy inheritance", which are essential to understanding the genome level and cell population level dynamics.

H.H. Heng (✉) • S.D. Horne • J.B. Stevens • B.Y. Abdallah • G. Liu • S.W. Bremer • K. Zhang
Department of Pathology, Karmanos Cancer Institute, Center for Molecular Medicine and Genetics, Wayne State University School of Medicine, 3226 Scott Hall, 540 E. Canfield, Detroit, MI, USA
e-mail: hheng@med.wayne.edu; shorn@med.wayne.edu; Joshua.b.stevens@gmail.com; jstevens@med.wayne.edu; babdalla@med.wayne.edu; gliu@med.wayne.edu; sbre-mer@med.wayne.edu

S.K. Chowdhury
Research Department, VA John Dingell Medical Center, 4646 John R. Street, Detroit, MI 48201, USA
e-mail: Saroj.chowdhury@va.gov

C.J. Ye
The Division of Hematology/Oncology, University of Michigan Comprehensive Cancer Center, 1500 E Medical Center Dr., Ann Arbor, MI 48109, USA
e-mail: jchrisye@med.umich.edu

J.P. Sturmberg (ed.), *The Value of Systems and Complexity Sciences for Healthcare*, DOI 10.1007/978-3-319-26221-5_9

Together, the stress-increased system heterogeneity and its evolutionary dynamics offer the general basis for many common and complex diseases. In this synthesis piece, we will discuss the concept that heterogeneity represents a level of complexity and propose a general *genomic* model explaining the diverse causes and symptoms for many common and complex diseases. Such understanding will be essential for future medical research.

9.1.1 Re-evaluating the Biological Meaning of Heterogeneity

While bio-heterogeneity is nothing new to biologists, the overwhelming degree of genetic and non-genetic heterogeneity revealed by current—omics technologies is still a surprise to many. Traditionally, the genetic heterogeneity has been considered as insignificant genetic "noise", and often observed stochastic chromosomal aberrations have been ignored as the attention has been focused on commonly shared genetic aberrations [10, 11]. In fact, the goal of the majority of current molecular research is to identify the "pattern" within the "noise".

In recent years, increased reports have revealed the importance of the non-specificity or low specificity of biological systems. Examples include: an individual protein can have a large number of lower affinity substrates; many proteins lack a fixed high order structure; a given gene can function in ways that are both beneficial and harmful for cancer cell growth; some well-known biochemical pathways can be rewired; the promotion of cell death can also lead to cell growth; individual cells can adversely respond under the same treatment and the methylation status can be opposite within the same cell population. To put these surprises together, it is clear that the seemingly stochastic phenomena are based on system heterogeneity and its heterogeneous response to both physiological and pathological stresses.

The next question is why is there so much heterogeneity in bio-systems? Specifically, why do "normal" individuals display so many gene mutations (according to the personal genome project, each individual on average has over 300 gene mutations), and why are there so many genetic and epigenetic variations including non-clonal chromosome aberrations (NCCAs), splicing forms and non-coding RNAs? Why is a proportion of proteins immediately degraded after synthesis? Why is so much waste possibly caused by low-specificity? Are bio-processes, in essence, optimal in terms of specificity and efficiency?

The answer is that heterogeneity represents a new layer of complexity essential for bio-adaptation. Evolution focuses not only on the specificity and efficiency of a bio-process, but also its adaptive ability in response to continuously changing environments. Increased heterogeneity can lower efficiency, but is important for adaptation and ultimately for survival under extreme conditions. It seems that traditional molecular biology has overemphasized bio-specificity at molecular levels but overlooked the heterogeneity-mediated bio-complexity. The following syntheses are useful to understanding the value of genetic heterogeneity.

9.1.1.1 Genotype Heterogeneity Maintains the Phenotype Within a Dynamic Environment

The relationship between phenotype and genotype is expressed as:

$$\text{Phenotype} = \text{Genotype} + \text{Environment}$$

Such relationship should apply to the somatic cell level if most diseases have a cellular basis. After all, it is not the germ line cell that directly contributes to the somatic cellular phenotype. Since the environment is constantly changing, to maintain certain phenotypes (such as different physiological features), the energy as well as genotype need to be adjusted accordingly. According to our hypothesis, to bring back the status of the stress-induced dynamics in normal physiological situations, only energy is needed to restore the system. When the stress is higher than the system can tolerate, some epigenetic changes or even gene mutations will occur to retrieve the stable status. Further stress could then lead to the increase of genome level heterogeneity. As the genotype of a given individual is fixed through the germ line, somatic cellular plasticity beyond the normal range is essential. If multiple levels of genetic and non-genetic heterogeneity were not available at the cellular level, it would be hard to achieve such needed adjustment when the system is under high stress.

9.1.1.2 Heterogeneity Provides Necessary Variation for Somatic Cell Evolution

It is increasingly accepted that many diseases such as cancer represent a somatic cell evolutionary process [12–15]. As heterogeneity mediated variation is the key for evolution, the multiple levels of genetic and non-genetic heterogeneity become the precondition for cancer initiation and progression [3]. Interestingly, since cancer evolution can be divided into two phases (genome replacement dominated punctuated phase and gene/epigene mutation accumulation stepwise phase), and genome reorganization is the driving force for macro-cellular evolution, genome level heterogeneity often can overpower lower level heterogeneity. Since cancer evolution is mainly based on the genome, the stochastic genome alteration can be used to explain different gene mutations and epigene dysfunctions. Such relationship also can be explained by the multiple level landscape model as well as the concept of the evolutionary mechanism of cancer [7, 8]. The evolutionary mechanism of cancer is equal to the collection of all molecular mechanisms. While the general mechanism can be explained by (1) stress, (2) cellular population diversity and (3) genome alteration and evolutionary selection, the molecular mechanisms can be extremely diverse. The current cancer genome sequencing project has amply demonstrated this point.

This general relationship not only explains why focusing on individual molecular mechanisms of cancer is limited, as there are so many "roads" that can lead to cancer, but also explains why identifying any specific changes that occur early in the process is of little value because once the *genome* begins to change, the previous triggering factor is no longer controlling the process, and "the genie cannot be put back in the bottle". In a sense, each molecular mechanism can lead to cancer, but the key is the triggering of *genome* alterations and the formation of dominant new systems with new *genomes*.

It should be noted that the cellular evolution framework could apply to many other diseases. Increased evidence has linked the altered *genome* to many common and complex diseases like autism, Alzheimer's disease, rheumatoid arthritis, osteoarthritis and other inflammatory joint diseases [16–18]. We and others have also detected elevated *genome alterations* from Gulf War Illness and chronic fatigue syndrome patients, as other examples [18–20].

9.1.1.3 Stress Induced Heterogeneity: The Evolutionary Trade-Off

Traditionally, both stress and stress-induced heterogeneity have been considered negative factors [21]. This point can be illustrated by the stress and disease connection, such as the stress–cancer connection [8, 9]. It is clear that the induced heterogeneity favours cancer evolution, and it is essential for many other diseases. Thus, it would seem that induced heterogeneity is harmful for normal cells. With more evidence demonstrating the importance of stress induced heterogeneity in the immune and metabolic systems, it becomes obvious that stress is necessary for many biological processes such as the developmental process. B cell lymphopoiesis requires endoplasmic reticulum or ER stress [22], and the homing of tissue-specific stem cells needs hypoxic stress. In addition, the induced heterogeneity also can be beneficial for short-term adaptation [21, 23]. Under stress, the overall system dynamics are elevated, leading to an increase of multiple levels of genetic and non-genetic heterogeneity, which can promote cellular function at least in the short term. Evidence suggests that stochastic hepatic aneuploidy can promote adaptation to liver injury [24, 25], and increased NCCAs can be detected from various tissues of aged individuals/populations. Based on these observations, we hypothesized that, to maintain normal tissue function under stress (including ageing), variation can be essential for functional composition, as altered genomes/genes can provide additional functions. However, the elevated heterogeneity can also further damage the system and result in long-term harm, as the heterogeneity itself can function as a new stress to the system [7, 26]. In other words, the stress induced cellular heterogeneity in fact represents an evolutionary trade-off (Fig. 9.1) [21].

One example of the trade-off of *genome heterogeneity* is hepatocyte polyploidy and aneuploidy status and its potential linkage to cancer. It was illustrated that newborn mice liver cells display less genomic heterogeneity, as the karyotypes displayed the normal 40 chromosomes. With exposure of environmental challenges, hepatocyte polyploidy and aneuploidy increases, along with potential adaptive function. It is known that the polyploidy aneuploidy status is also linked to cancer potential [27, 28], so the price to pay for metabolic adaptation later on is increased cancer risk. Another example is the age individuals display elevated risk of various

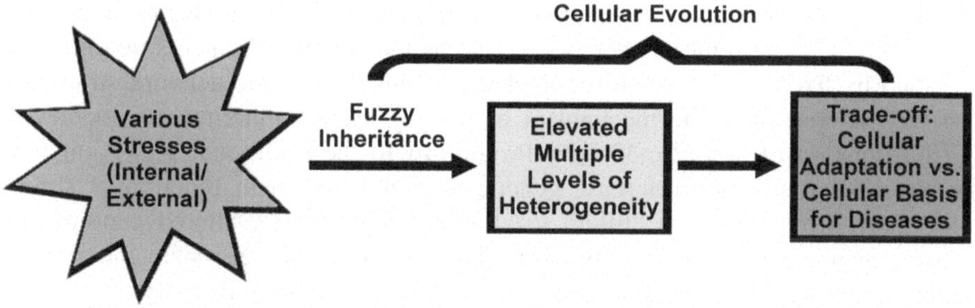

Fig. 9.1 The relationship between stress, fuzzy inheritance and the evolutionary trade-off. Cells are constantly exposed to a wide variety of external and internal stress. In order to adapt and survive in response to these stresses, the cell must display plasticity at multiple genetic levels (e.g. genome, gene, epigene). Fuzzy inheritance maintains these multiple levels of heterogeneity, which are elevated in response to stress. The result is an evolutionary trade-off, where on the one hand, cellular adaptation to the stress event is achieved. On the other hand, elevated heterogeneity could increase the likelihood of disease onset

cancers. In addition to mechanisms associated with reduced system stability, such as shortened telomeres of somatic cells and lower efficiency of various repair systems, the cellular system has to work harder for functional compensation, which can increase further error. More importantly, to achieve functional compensation, cellular systems must increase heterogeneity so that the altered genomes/genes/epigenes can fulfill the function better than the original genetic/non-genetic landscape. However, the altered genomic landscape can increase the likelihood of other diseases in the longer term, especially when these alterations become dominant, which rebalance the cellular populations.

9.1.2 How to Achieve the Multiple Levels of Genetic/Non-genetic Heterogeneity?

There are many levels of cellular heterogeneity. In this manuscript, we will only discuss genetic and epigenetic (one type of non-genetic) heterogeneity. Even though new evidence has revealed the high level of gene mutation heterogeneity and epigenetic heterogeneity through single cell based analyses, the mechanisms leading to such heterogeneity are unclear. For example, there are many de novo gene mutations in cancer cells (many of them are not inherited from previous cellular populations), and for the methylation status, neighbouring cells can have drastically different patterns. Nevertheless, such high level heterogeneity cannot be simply explained by classic gene-mediated inheritance that faithfully passes between cellular generations due to the extremely low rates of mutation.

In fact, the traditional definition of gene mediated inheritance is problematic, as it only accounts for the "parts inheritance" but it lacks a real blueprint which is coded in the "system inheritance" [5, 19]. We have pointed out that the gene mediated parts inheritance cannot code for the interactive relationship among all genes, and the system inheritance is decoded by the *genome* (the genomic topology reflected by fixed karyotype in the nucleus, as this defines the network structure) [16, 29]. Interestingly, the mechanism of passing system inheritance is achieved by the function of sex [26, 30–32]. In contrast to the traditional viewpoint that the function of sex is to increase genetic variation, the main function of sex is now realized to serve as a "filter" to eliminate significantly altered genomes to preserve genome identity. It is possible that sex can preserve system inheritance while promoting the secondary benefit of creating gene (parts) diversity.

While the establishment of the relationship between parts inheritance and system inheritance is highly significant to understand the real genotype, it cannot explain the high level of heterogeneity observed in different somatic organs or tissue types. Based on the observation that different tissues display different frequencies of chromosomal changes, it seems that a new type of inheritance exists to ensure the passing of heterogeneity among somatic cells, which might not exist in the germ line cell. But what is the mechanism? By tracing the system inheritance of an individual cancer cell, we observed that, when the genome is highly unstable, the mother cell cannot pass the same system inheritance or karyotype to the daughter cell. What has been passed is not the same system inheritance, but altered system inheritance. Further comparison of the cell populations revealed that a single cell can generate a population with the similar degree of heterogeneity of the parent population. In other words, the heterogeneity of the parent population can be passed down through a single cell. We name such inheritance that links the individual cell to the degree of heterogeneity of cellular population "fuzzy inheritance" or "inherited heterogeneity". In contrast, "inherited homogeneity" should be equivalent to "system inheritance".

Even though we only demonstrated fuzzy inheritance at the genome level, it is readily applicable to the gene and epigene levels. The key to understanding the fuzzy inheritance at these lower genetic and epigenetic levels is to understand the degree of heterogeneity passed rather than fixed types of genetic/non-genetic alterations. For example, when examining DNA methylation, the fuzzy inheritance is defined by the overall degree of methylation of the genome rather than status of specific loci. In other words, the degree of overall epigenetic dynamics is inherited, but the locus (or loci) that achieves such dynamics is flexible, or fuzzy, and dependent on the stochastic interaction with changing cellular environments. Together, the multiple levels of fuzzy inheritance nicely explain the difference between genotype of the germ line and the genotype of the somatic cells. Due to the requirement of the cellular response to various stresses for survival or adaptation, the somatic genome has to display genetic and epigenetic plasticity, and this key strategy is achieved through maintaining the multiple levels of heterogeneity. Specifically, the heterogeneity at gene, epigene and genome levels is reflected as de novo gene mutations, methylation patterns and NCCAs, respectively. Interestingly, the germ line genome has the capability to pass on fuzzy inheritance only at a limited degree, and is often associated with genetic instability.

9.1.3 The Importance of Heterogeneity in Somatic Cell Evolution

Evolutionary medicine is attracting more attention, as many common and complex diseases are the result of cellular evolutionary processes [13, 21, 33], and the limitations of current molecular medicine are associated with the ignorance of evolutionary principles. For somatic cell evolution to be successful, inheritable variation is required. It is thus logical to integrate system inheritance and fuzzy inheritance into the equation of cellular evolution. In particular, inheritance represents a key element of evolution, and different types of inheritance need to be linked to different patterns of somatic cell evolution. For example, based on cancer evolutionary studies, somatic cell evolution can be divided into two phases, and genome replacement often dominates in the punctuated macro-evolutionary phase, where system inheritance is altered. The punctuated phase has also been linked to pathological changes where the physiological change often involves the stepwise phase of evolution (Fig. 9.2) [7, 8, 33, 34].

It is worth pointing out that each case of cancer represents a successful run of cancer evolution, and different genetic and non-genetic aberrations can contribute to this process. However, due to the large number of factors that can contribute to this process, each of them representing very low penetration in the patient population, none of them can function as a unifying magic target for cancer. This situation applies to many other complex diseases.

Furthermore, since the cellular evolutionary process is highly dynamic, the environmental stress- and time factor-mediated heterogeneity is highly unpredictable when combined with the large number of genetic elements. It is extremely

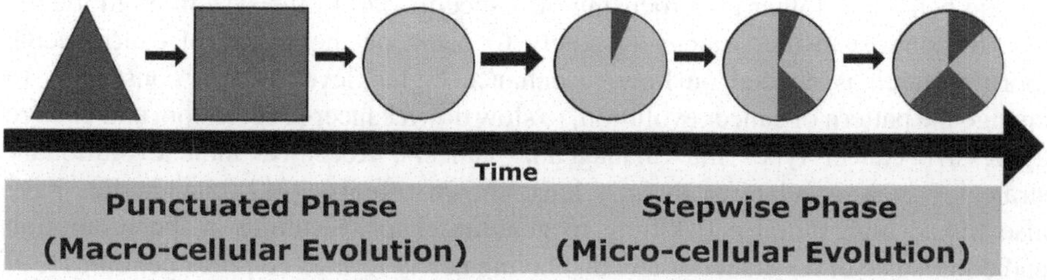

Fig. 9.2 Stochastic model of genome-mediated cancer evolution. Cancer evolution is divided into two distinct evolutionary phases, the punctuated stochastic phase (or macro-evolutionary phase) and the stepwise gradual phase (or micro-evolutionary phase). Punctuated phases are marked by extreme heterogeneity and rapid genome changes, represented by genome system changes over time, with each shape representing a unique genome system. Following selection pressure, a genome system survives (*circle*). In contrast to genomes in the punctuated phase, this genome system in the stepwise phase remains relatively stable over time, although it does acquire low-level changes (represented by pie piece changes) including gene mutations, epigenetic alterations and/or small traceable genome-level alterations that aid in adaptation. Thus, the stepwise phase is mainly associated with system stability and micro-cellular evolution. Only one run of the NCCA/CCA cycle is presented

challenging to treat complex diseases only based on specific molecular mechanisms, as there is no linear causation between these specific mechanisms and the outcomes of the evolutionary process. On the other hand, it is possible to study the evolutionary potential of the disease by monitoring the system's behaviour. One example of how this can be achieved is through measuring the overall degree of heterogeneity and system stability. The complexity of the disease can therefore be simplified [29]. For example, the complex issue of predicting tumorigenicity can simply be achieved by measuring the degree of NCCAs [35]. Similarly, the potential of drug resistance can be judged by both the degree of NCCAs and the degree of karyotype complexity, as the chaotic genome can often be linked to punctuated evolution-mediated drug resistance [36, 37]. The identification of the role of heterogeneity in multiple inheritances, especially in system inheritance and fuzzy inheritance that is responsible for inherited heterogeneity, also can explain why many phenotypic traits cannot be linked to specific genes, and why the missing inheritability of diseases is hard to identify by focusing on genes.

9.2 Implications of Using Heterogeneity Mediated System Complexity to Understand Human Diseases

For cancer treatment, knowing that most of the molecular genetic and non-genetic pathways are moving targets is essential. Even though it might be possible to identify temporarily dominant pathways or gene mutations in an individual patient, soon after the targeting approach is applied to treat the patient, the genetic landscape changes, ultimately making the specific treatment off-target. To deal with pathway heterogeneity and heterogeneous responses to the treatment, monitoring the overall system behaviour rather than focusing on a specific part of the system might be the key. In contrast to the strategy of solely focusing on the killing of cancer cells, more research is needed on how to enhance higher level system constraints to change the pattern of cancer evolution, to slow down cancer progression, and change aggressive cancer types into manageable cancers. Recently, some evolutionary strategies such as adaptive therapy have shown promise [38]. Our studies have also linked high initial cell killing to genome chaos, resulting in the promotion and dominance of resistant outliers displaying newly formed complex genomes [39] (Horne et al., unpublished data).

Another important implication is to provide the conceptual framework to understand the common mechanism(s) of many common and complex diseases. Based on the traditional concept of the genotype and phenotype relationship, decades of effort have been focused on identifying common genetic markers for many common diseases. Despite the genome wide association studies based on large numbers of samples, few useful markers have been identified. On the other hand, for cancer, too many genetic factors have been linked. In light of this extreme spectrum, the genome scanning approach has not worked. Now, with the understanding of system inheritance and fuzzy inheritance or inherited heterogeneity at the somatic cell level, and with the consideration that heterogeneity is the key factor of somatic cell evolution, it is understandable that most of the individual genetic factors will not be identifiable by averaging patient populations. Furthermore, attention needs to be paid to the separation of the germ line and somatic cell genetic profiles, as the latter involve cellular evolution and display tissue/organ and timing specificity.

The essential step is to link the various genetic and environmental factors to stress induced multiple levels of heterogeneity. As the unstable genome can have both adaptive benefits and long-term potential for many diseases, which can be illustrated by the altered genomes or genes that can be linked to various pathways, it will stochastically involve different pathways that lead to the different symptoms. Given the fact that multiple levels of heterogeneity can be detected in many common and complex diseases including autism, Alzheimer's disease and other common diseases such as rheumatoid arthritis and osteoarthritis [17, 18, 40–43], there is an urgent need to study this issue.

By synthesizing (1), the diverse stresses that can be associated with the initiation of different complex diseases/illnesses; (2), cellular evolution where both system recovery and disease progression can occur as a result of genome instability-mediated changes and (3), the understanding that the unstable genome can be linked to diverse molecular pathways and generate an array of phenotypes (Fig. 9.3), we propose a model of common and complex diseases/illnesses in the light of stress, induced instability, adaptation and evolutionary trade-off. This model can be modified to fit different diseases or illness conditions (Fig. 9.4).

We recently have applied this model for studying gulf war illness (GWI). GWI is an illness affecting 25–30 % of Gulf War Veterans [44]. The complex aetiology of GWI makes defining the illness in order to diagnose it difficult. A few years back, the medical community denied acceptance of GWI as a real illness due to the diverse "causative factors" as well as symptoms. According to the traditional definition of an illness/disease, a causative agent and defined symptoms should be identifiable in all affected patients. If these are not found, it is said that there is no solid medical evidence to back up claims of an illness or disease. It should be noted that, in contrast to infectious diseases, many common and complex diseases display diverse factors/symptoms.

While individual studies have illustrated discrete biological or pathological links to GWI, based on our experience in cancer research, it is likely that most of the identified mechanisms will not withstand the rigours of validation due to the highly diverse patient population. Like most common and complex diseases or illnesses, the impacted parts often differ within the patient population, which is the reason why it has been hard to identify a common linkage in the first place.

Interestingly, however, most of these individual mechanisms can be linked to *genome instability*. To illustrate this point, we examined the genome instability by comparing the degree of stochastic chromosomal alterations from short-term lymphocytes culture of GWI patients. Multiple colour spectral karyotyping and other molecular cytogenetic methods were applied [45, 46], and various karyotype

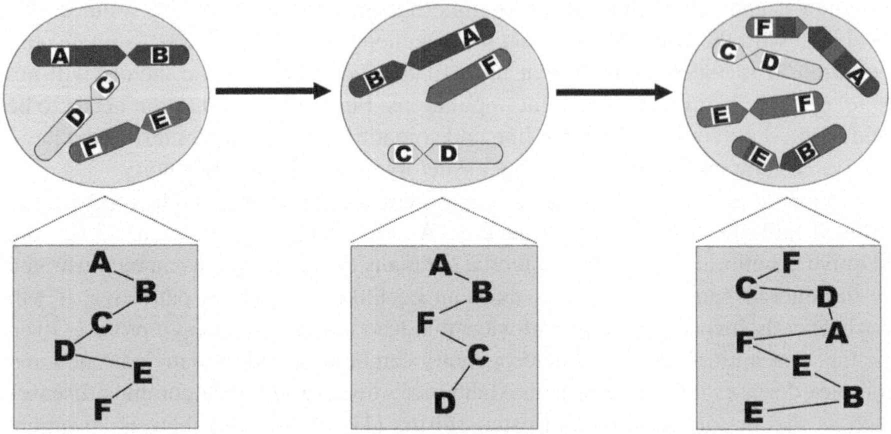

Fig. 9.3 The relationship between genome topology alteration and resulting genetic network reorganization. Different chromosomes are designated by colour (*red*, *yellow*, *blue*) and drawn within the nucleus, representing the genome, and genes are designated A, B, C, D, E, F within the chromosomes. Corresponding protein networks are illustrated by the relationships between proteins A, B, C, D, E, F. Genome topology alteration represented by numerical (e.g. aneuploidy) and/or structural aberrations (e.g. translocations) directly affect the three-dimensional topological relationship between genes which change the overall genetic network structure. This results in drastic systemic changes beyond the influence of genetic and/or epigenetic alterations that may concurrently occur. As a consequence, the corresponding protein network changes are shown by altered relationships between proteins (Color figure online)

abnormalities were observed from GWI patients [18, 19, 47]. Following examination of 25 patients and 25 controls, we demonstrated that genome instability is indeed significantly elevated in GWI patients (manuscript in preparation).

Our GWI research fully supports the general model of how cellular stress can destabilize the genome, and how unstable genomes can stochastically impact different molecular pathways and lead to different symptoms (Fig. 9.4). From the mechanistic point of view, the process of GWI can be divided into three phases: (1) The initial phase. Diverse, extremely high stresses incurred during the Gulf War damage cellular systems. Many war factors such as depleted uranium (DU), nerve gas, pesticides, insect repellents, anti-nerve agent pills and Kuwaiti oil fires can all be potentially linked to GWI (also see Fig. 9.1). (2) The cellular/system evolution phase. Many individuals recover from stress during this phase, however, in those that cannot recover from the initial damage, the *genome* will be destabilized, triggering further cellular evolution. This phase is essential for intervention. Increasing a patient's overall health should reduce stochastic chromosomal aberrations and illness symptoms. (3) The illness phase. In this stage, the altered genome can impact different cellular mechanisms leading to diverse symptoms (also see Fig. 9.3). For impacted pathways, elevated genome instability, mitochondrial dysfunction, impaired immune function, brain white matter pattern changes (reduced neurogenesis, partial neuron loss and mild inflammation in the hippocampus) can be detected.

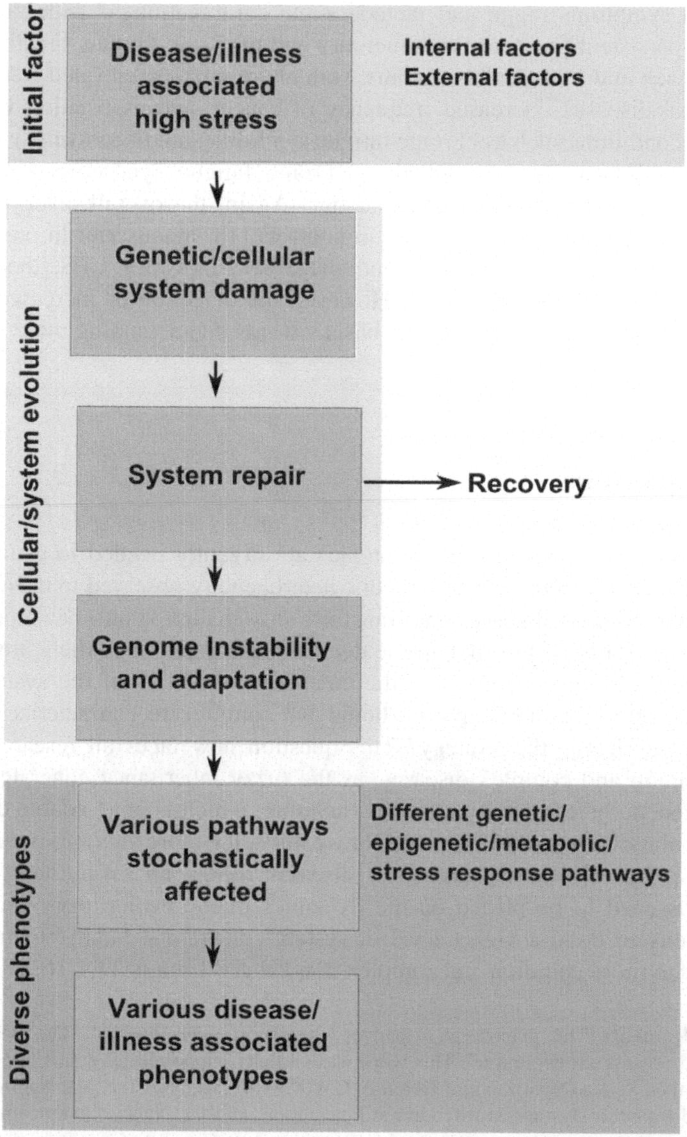

Fig. 9.4 The general model of cellular evolution of common and complex diseases/illnesses. There are three key stages from initial stress to phenotype: (1) Stress induced stochastic genetic/epigenetic changes through the fuzzy inheritance (also see Fig. 9.1). (2) Cellular evolution of multiple cycles of macro-and micro-evolution (also see Fig. 9.2), and (3) Emergent new genome defined systems display specific molecular pathways coupled with different symptoms (also see Fig. 9.3)

The broad symptoms range and include some combination of widespread pain, headache, persistent problems with memory and thinking, fatigue, breathing problems, stomach and intestinal symptoms, skin abnormalities, elevated frequency of neurological diseases, increased frequency of cancer, and association with often idiopathic conditions such as chronic fatigue syndrome and fibromyalgia [44].

Similar analyses can be applied to chronic fatigue syndrome (CFS) study. We have recently analysed 15 CFS patients. Again, the overall level of *genome instability* is significantly higher than in controls [18, manuscript in preparation]. Due to the lack of understanding and diagnostic tools for CFS, there is still doubt in the field about this illness. However, the detection of increased genome heterogeneity in CFS will provide the basis towards understanding more about this condition.

9.3 Conclusions

In conclusion, new concepts and strategies are urgently needed to deal with the multiple levels of genetic and non-genetic heterogeneity observed in most common and complex diseases/illnesses and transform this challenge into new opportunity. If it is less useful to understand all the details of the parts when there are so many of them, and the understanding of the emergent properties of the system is not directly dissectible by these parts, should we continue to characterize the parts or should we change the strategy? This question now faces all researchers who study common and complex diseases, as the fuzzy inheritance generated genetic and non-genetic heterogeneity are overwhelming, which is unavoidable during the cellular evolutionary process. The further we mine, the more alterations will appear. In contrast, by considering that most diseases follow an evolutionary process, new efforts need to be placed on the dynamics of the evolutionary process and heterogeneity to build a higher level of system constraints. Such thinking should be applied to more common and complex non-cancer diseases [15, 16, 18, 47].

Acknowledgements This manuscript is part of a series of studies entitled "The mechanism of somatic and organismal evolution". This work was partially supported by grants to Henry Heng from the United States Department of Defense (GW093028), SeeDNA Inc., the National Chronic Fatigue and Immune Dysfunction Syndrome Foundation, and the Nancy Taylor Foundation for Chronic Diseases.

References

1. Davidoff F. Heterogeneity is not always noise: lessons from improvement. JAMA. 2009;302(23):2580–86.
2. Heng HH. The conflict between complex systems and reductionism. JAMA. 2008;300(13):1580–81.

3. Heng HH, et al. Genetic and epigenetic heterogeneity in cancer: a genome-centric perspective. J Cell Physiol. 2009;220(3):538–47.
4. Heppner GH. Tumor heterogeneity. Cancer Res. 1984;44(6):2259–65.
5. Heng HH. The genome-centric concept: resynthesis of evolutionary theory. BioEssays. 2009;31(5): 512–25.
6. Ye CJ, et al. The dynamics of cancer chromosomes and genomes. Cytogenet Genome Res. 2007; 118(2–4):237–46.
7. Heng HH, et al. Chromosomal instability (CIN): what it is and why it is crucial to cancer evolution. Cancer Metastasis Rev. 2013;32(3–4):325–40.
8. Heng HH, et al. Evolutionary mechanisms and diversity in cancer. Adv Cancer Res. 2011;112:217–53.
9. Heng HH, et al. The evolutionary mechanism of cancer. J Cell Biochem. 2010;109(6):1072–84.
10. Heng HH, et al. Cancer progression by non-clonal chromosome aberrations. J Cell Biochem. 2006;98(6):1424–35.
11. Heng HH, et al. Clonal and non-clonal chromosome aberrations and genome variation and aberration. Genome. 2006;49(3):195–204.
12. Heng HH. Cancer genome sequencing: the challenges ahead. Bioessays. 2007;29(8):783–94.
13. Nesse RM. How is Darwinian medicine useful? West J Med. 2001;174(5):358–60.
14. Podlaha O, et al. Evolution of the cancer genome. Trends Genet. 2012;28(4):155–63.
15. Heng HH. Debating cancer: the paradox in cancer research. Singapore: World Scientific Publishing Company; 2015.
16. Heng HH. Missing heritability and stochastic genome alterations. Nat Rev Genet. 2010;11(11):813.
17. Yurov YB, et al. X chromosome aneuploidy in the Alzheimer's disease brain. Mol Cytogenet. 2014;7(1):20.
18. Heng HH, et al. Karyotype heterogeneity and unclassified chromosomal abnormalities. Cytogenet Genome Res. 2013;139(3):144–57.
19. Heng HH, et al. Decoding the genome beyond sequencing: the new phase of genomic research. Genomics. 2011;98(4):242–52.
20. Wahab MA, et al. Elevated chromosome translocation frequencies in New Zealand nuclear test veterans. Cytogenet Genome Res. 2008;121(2):79–87.
21. Horne SD, Chowdhury SK, Heng HH. Stress, genomic adaptation, and the evolutionary trade-off. Front Genet. 2014;5:92.
22. Zhang K, et al. The unfolded protein response sensor IRE1alpha is required at 2 distinct steps in B cell lymphopoiesis. J Clin Invest. 2005;115(2):268–81.
23. Astolfi PA, Salamini F, Sgaramella V. Are we genomic mosaics? Variations of the genome of somatic cells can contribute to diversify our phenotypes. Curr Genomics. 2010;11(6):379–86.
24. Duncan AW. Aneuploidy, polyploidy and ploidy reversal in the liver. Semin Cell Dev Biol. 2013;24(4):347–56.
25. Duncan AW, et al. Aneuploidy as a mechanism for stress-induced liver adaptation. J Clin Invest. 2012; 122(9):3307–15.
26. Horne SD, et al. Genome constraint through sexual reproduction: application of 4D-Genomics in reproductive biology. Syst Biol Reprod Med. 2013;59(3):124–30.
27. Dewhurst SM, et al. Tolerance of whole-genome doubling propagates chromosomal instability and accelerates cancer genome evolution. Cancer Discov. 2014;4(2):175–85.
28. Duesberg P, et al. The chromosomal basis of cancer. Cell Oncol. 2005;27(5–6):293–318.
29. Heng HH. Bio-complexity: challenging reductionism. In: Sturmberg JP, Martin CM, editors. Handbook on systems and complexity in health. New York: Springer; 2013. p. 193–208.
30. Gorelick R, Heng HH. Sex reduces genetic variation: a multidisciplinary review. Evolution. 2011;65(4):1088–98.
31. Heng HH. Elimination of altered karyotypes by sexual reproduction preserves species identity. Genome. 2007;50(5):517–24.
32. Wilkins AS, Holliday R. The evolution of meiosis from mitosis. Genetics. 2009;181(1):3–12.

33. Horne SD, Pollick SA, Heng HH. Evolutionary mechanism unifies the hallmarks of cancer. Int J Cancer 2015;136(9):2012–21.
34. Heng HH, et al. Stochastic cancer progression driven by non-clonal chromosome aberrations. J Cell Physiol. 2006;208(2):461–72.
35. Ye CJ, et al. Genome based cell population heterogeneity promotes tumorigenicity: the evolutionary mechanism of cancer. J Cell Physiol. 2009;219(2):288–300.
36. Heng HH. Karyotypic Chaos, A form of non-clonal chromosome aberrations, plays a key role for cancer progression and drug resistance. In: FASEB: nuclear structure and cancer. Saxtons River, Vermont: Vermont Academy; 2007.
37. Heng HH, et al. Genetic and epigenetic heterogeneity in cancer: the ultimate challenge for drug therapy. Curr Drug Targets. 2010;11(10):1304–16.
38. Gatenby RA, et al. Adaptive therapy. Cancer Res. 2009;69(11):4894–903.
39. Liu G, et al. Genome chaos: survival strategy during crisis. Cell Cycle. 2014;13(4):528–37.
40. Xu J, et al. Molecular cytogenetics of autism. Curr Genomics. 2004;5(4):347–64.
41. Iourov IY, Vorsanova SG, Yurov YB. Chromosomal mosaicism goes global. Mol Cytogenet. 2008;1:26.
42. Kinne RW, et al. Mosaic chromosomal aberrations in synovial fibroblasts of patients with rheumatoid arthritis, osteoarthritis, and other inflammatory joint diseases. Arthritis Res. 2001;3(5):319–30.
43. Heng HH, Stevens JB, Liu G, Bremer SW, Ye CJ. Imaging genome abnormalities in cancer research. Cell Chromosome. 2004;3:1.
44. Research Advisory Committee on Gulf War Veterans' Illnesses, Gulf War Illness and the Health of Gulf War Veterans: Research Update and Recommendations. Boston: U.S. Government Printing Office; 2009–2013, 2014.
45. Ye CJ, Stevens JB, Liu G, Ye KJ, Yang F, Bremer SW, Heng HH. Combined multicolor-FISH and immunostaining. Cytogenet Genome Res. 2006;114(3–4):227–34.
46. Stevens JB, Liu G, Bremer SW, Ye KJ, Xu W, Xu J, Sun Y, Wu GS, Savasan S, Krawetz SA, Ye CJ, Heng HH. Mitotic cell death by chromosome fragmentation. Cancer Res. 2007;67(16):7686–94.
47. Heng HH. The contribution of genomic heterogeneity. Preface Cytogenet Genome Res. 2013;139(3):141–43

Chapter 10
Multimorbidity: Through a Glass Darkly

Carmel M. Martin

10.1 What is Multimorbidity from a Clinico-Epidemiological Perspective?

A scoping of contemporary literature demonstrates ongoing debates about definitions, however multimorbidity implies multiple diseases (syndromes, or conditions?) in one individual where there is no index disease or condition [1]. Co-morbidity was described by Feinstein [2] as concurrent chronic diseases or complications accompanying an index disease [1]. Multimorbidity in its current form appears to encompass previous terminology such as chronicity, chronic illness and chronic disease.

Multimorbidity, however defined, reflects patterns that challenge recent traditions in healthcare, where single disease-based guidelines or organ specialisms were the cornerstone of medical practice. It is now recognised that more than one disease and one organ system, multiple providers and polypharmacy have become the mean (or mode) for people over 60 years of age.

Multimorbidity is an emerging "catch-all" term to reflect the breakdown of the current model of single diseases. There is debate about whether it is an entity in its own right or a phenomenon of accentuated ageing, while it is demonstrably a research and clinical phenomenon constructed by our current medical models. Despite debates about the definition of multimorbidity there is a burgeoning

C.M. Martin (✉)
Department of Public Health and Primary Care, Trinity College,
College Green, 34/72 Lorimer Terrace, Kelvin Grove, Brisbane Qld 4059, Dublin 2, Ireland
e-mail: carmelmarymartin@gmail.com

J.P. Sturmberg (ed.), *The Value of Systems and Complexity Sciences for Healthcare*, DOI 10.1007/978-3-319-26221-5_10

literature, that is small yet parallel to the much larger literature base of co-morbidity research. A synthesis of patterns of multimorbidity is difficult because multimorbidity is not commonly defined prospectively within a common framework across studies, and there is no universally agreed definition.

Patterns of multimorbidity identified in the literature appear to reflect patterns, such as the following [3]:

1. cardiovascular/metabolic disorders [prevalence female: 30 %; male: 39 %],
2. anxiety/depression/somatoform disorders and pain [prevalence female: 34 %; male: 22 %],
3. neuropsychiatric disorders [prevalence female: 6 %; male: 0.8 %].

Patterns vary considerably across studies[4, 5], altogether 50 % of female and 48 % of male persons maybe assigned to at least one multimorbidity pattern [6], and percentages increase with age.

This literature indicates that however defined, multimorbidity is generally, but not necessarily, associated with patterns of worse outcomes in clinical, cohort and population studies [7]. While cross-sectional clinically based studies indicate worse outcomes and more complicated consultations with multimorbidity [8, 9], longitudinal studies paint a somewhat different picture where singles diseases, or disability or frailty may have a greater impact on outcomes than multimorbidity [7, 10]. Other longitudinal studies have identified that the evolution of disease and multimorbidity, disability and frailty are non-linear with a range of different patterns [11, 12]. Multimorbidity was associated with lower socioeconomic status (inverse care law) and there was an interaction with frailty and disability [13]. Social stress and deprivation appear to cause or promote multiple chronic diseases [13, 14]. The literature has attempted to tease out the impact of disease diagnoses in epidemiological studies. McDaid et al., for example, argue from their studies that diseases have additive effects on outcomes such as mortality and quality of life [7]. In contrast in older cohorts non-linearity and complicated interactions among diseases rather than a simple linear additive impact of single conditions have been demonstrated. Some studies suggest that disability and frailty rather than the diagnoses implicated in multimorbidity had the greatest impact on poor outcomes [10, 15]. In fact, in older cohorts, many individuals appear to demonstrate "adaptation" to chronic diseases and remain in "good health" despite multiple diagnoses. Better outcomes than expected may be due to artefact; older or more frequent attenders having more exposure to tests and resulting in medical diagnoses applied to health states that are not necessarily important to the individual's well-being [16]. On the other hand, patients' knowledge that they have a certain clinical condition changes their subjective assessment of quality of life in the related domain—the social construction of chronic illness—and tempts doctors to initiated additional treatments—highlighting the risk for iatrogenesis [17].

10.1.1 The Centrality of Diagnosis and the Challenges it Brings

Overall, disease diagnosis is integral to the theory of multimorbidity and is central to the work of its definitional dilemmas [18]. Some health services researchers also view the *process* of making the diagnosis central to the subsequent construction of a patient's illness. In addition diagnosis represents the time and location whereby medical professionals and others determine the existence and legitimacy of the condition [21].

The centrality of the diagnosis and the skills of differential diagnosis are the key focus in medical education and clinical practice. In the prevailing paradigm of medicine, disease, including multimorbidity, is thought of in anatomical terms. Hence clinical and therapeutic guidelines are organ- (e.g. neurology, ophthalmology, nephrology, cardiology, endocrinology, etc.) and condition-specific (hypertension, diabetes, asthma).

10.1.2 What Impact Does This Have on Practice?

A meta-analysis of studies that improve outcomes in multimorbidity indicates that improving functioning and addressing common risk factors for deterioration may be most helpful [12]. Psychosocial support is another important component of management [18]. Yet consultation recordings in busy practices indicate multimorbidity of all types are mostly managed according to "guidelines" related to each of the diagnosed diseases, with little attention given to prevention, promotion and associated psychosocial issues [19].

Most health professionals and managers were trained to analyse health problems according to a deterministic disease model that associates a cause (*aetiology* [20]) with an effect (*illness* [21]) and that requires specific interventions (*treatment*). Evidence-based medicine relies in large part on such a model, as does epidemiology, which seeks to establish causal links between exposures and their effects on individuals or populations. These approaches have been extremely effective in many types of problem such as the technologies of hip replacement and cataract surgery, but their limitations are apparent in multimorbidity where treating one disease may inadvertently compromise another condition with polypharmacy and treatments causing further iatrogenic illness. A major example of applying linear thinking to complex problems that has failed in the UK quality and outcomes framework (QOF). Payment for treating blood pressure, blood glucose and lipids and depression (major risk factors for cardiovascular disease and stroke) and cancer early detection to targets (and achieving those targets relatively equally across practices in different socio-economic settings) did not result in lowered disease rates or deaths [22]. Equality of targets and the use of exceptions opened up some of the complexities and inequities of linear pay for performance which "does not reward the additional work required in deprived areas and contributes to a continuation of the inverse care law ... data collected prevent examination of most complex process or treatment measures" [23].

Multimorbidity highlights the problems of reductive disease specialisms with increasing development of "new" diseases and possible iatrogenesis. While the medical industrial complex constructs its work units and profits around disease, many have recognised multimorbidity as a complex phenomenon that requires a generalist approach. This position has been advocated for by primary care and other generalist frameworks such as gerontology and social care for more than 50 years.

10.2 The Emerging Paradigm of Systems Medicine

Systems medicine is an inter-disciplinary field of study that looks at the dynamic systems of the human body as part of an integrated whole, incorporating biochemical, physiological and environment interactions that sustain life. Systems medicine draws on theories from systems science, systems biology and social systems when developing a comprehensive approach that considers complex interactions within the human body to promote an individual's health in light of their genomics, behaviour and the external environment [24]. Psycho-Neuro-Immunology and allostasis also relate to systems in health and health care, although not necessarily under the umbrella term systems medicine [25]. Understanding systems medicine reflects the evolution of systems biology approaches from molecular biology. Biology, including ecology, developmental biology and immunology, has been involved in biological systems. Genomics as dynamic systems have further challenged the prevailing linear molecular biology approaches. Scientific understanding and biotechnological applications are increasingly being constructed as systems building on transformations within systems biology. Nevertheless, despite the name systems biology there remain divergences between fixed structural non-linear approaches and the real world dynamics of how genes behave. This is exemplified in the ongoing focus of the industry on discoveries about the nature of genetic material, structural characterisation of macromolecules and later developments in recombinant and high-throughput technologies versus developments building on non-equilibrium mathematical theory in the 1940s, the increased knowledge of biochemical pathways and feedback controls and the recognition of networks in biology [26].

The clinical classification or construct of multi-morbidity relates to the process of diagnosis with some (yet to be determined or locally determined) combination or permutation of diagnostic nosology [27, 28]. Purportedly based upon molecular biology, and its structural classifications as its basic scientific discipline, diagnostic nosology assumes disease to be fully accounted for by deviations from the norm of measurable biological (somatic) variables [29]. However there is little reference in the molecular biology, systems biology and multi-morbidity literature, and even in the co-morbidity literature to the underlying biological and social systems and their implications for the phenotypes of diseases, illness, frailty and disability that constitute multimorbidity [30].

10.2.1 The Emerging Literature on Systems Medicine

A recent literature scoping in Pub Med reveals the very small overlap between systems biology and systems medicine, psycho-neurology and multimorbidity. Even with the inclusion of co-morbidity there is a <<1 % overlap in the literature.

Seven *multimorbidity* papers also cross-referenced the terms "*networks or systems*". There were no papers of any kind cross-linking with the terms "*social construction and diagnosis and multimorbidity*" (Fig. 10.1). Clearly thus far there have been no published attempts to understand multimorbidity from its biological roots, despite a seminal paper from the NIH calling for such a connection[1] [25].

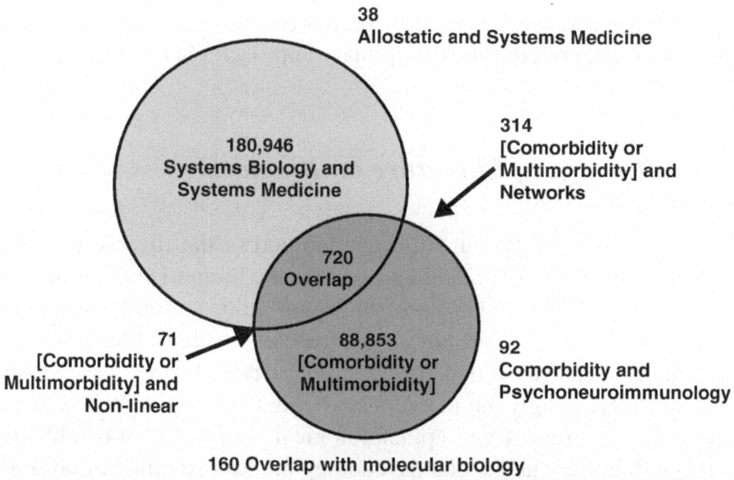

Fig. 10.1 Overlap using raw counts of articles from PubMed searches based on search terms ["Systems Biology" and "Systems Medicine"] with ["Co-morbidity or Multimorbidity"] as the main search with on overlap of 720 articles. Other bibliometrics were "Systems Medicine" and "Allostatic load"; there were no overlaps between "Multimorbidity" and "Networks", "Psycho-Neuro-Immunology", or "Systems Medicine and Systems Biology" with very little overlap between the joint terms ["Co-morbidity or Multimorbidity"] and Non-linear, Molecular Biology and Psycho-Neuro-Immunology

[1]Relative to co-morbidity and multimorbidity indicators, three measurement issues were cited: (1) Limitations in functional status. The degree of independence or difficulty in basic and instrumental activities of daily living should be considered for inclusion in all co-morbidity evaluations. (2) Severity levels of co-morbidity and multimorbidity should address additive and multiplicative

Surprisingly there are no papers looking at the "*processes* of diagnosis" and "the creation of morbidity", while there are only four papers on "*iatrogenesis* and multi-morbidity" and 215 papers on "*iatrogenesis* and co-morbidity and multimorbidity" literature. While there is a significant overlap between coping, multimorbidity and co-morbidity literatures, there are very few studies looking at the social construction or evolution of the diagnosis and its taxonomic underpinning in multimorbidity or co-morbidity [31].

There is almost no overlap between systems biology and systems medicine and multimorbidity; in fact, systems medicine focuses almost exclusively on single diseases such as diabetes, reducing the disease into 12 subtypes based on phenotypes and the phenomena associated with them. The task then is to identify biomarkers for each subtype [32]. Multimorbidity in clinical research is constructed of additive counts of different diseases, although there is recognition of heterogeneity of evolution of such patterns [33]. In contrast, the emphasis in systems medicine literature is on the development of technologies to sample and identify biomarkers is a major activity of the field at present [34–36]. The ageing and frailty literature [34], the population health social determinants literature [37] and the Psycho-Neuro-Immunology literature [38, 39], as examples, take a holistic approach beyond disease and often reference individual experiences and self-rated health [40, 41]. They argue for an integrated trans-disciplinary approach [41].

10.2.2 The Emerging Literature on Biomarkers

There is major commonality, but little overlap across the diverse biomarker and biometric literatures. Figure 10.2 indicates where the biomarkers literature overlaps with other literatures. The diagnosis of multimorbidity is highly dependent upon common biomarkers, e.g. blood glucose, C-reactive protein, blood lipids, etc. as well as biometrics such as blood pressure, heart rate, heart rate variability and respiratory rate. Increasingly, biomarkers are being used to predict worse outcomes in multimorbidity in clinical and epidemiological studies [42–44], although links with social epidemiology and social psychology are less common at present. While biomarkers provide major opportunities to better understand multimorbidity and target interventions, there is also a risk that they will perpetuate disease reductionism with dividing diseases into smaller and smaller phenotypes with greater and greater fragmentation of care.

---

relationships. (3) Although biologic and physical responses within individuals are major foci of treatment and care, they are not disconnected from social and psychological events and changes occurring in older patients' lives.

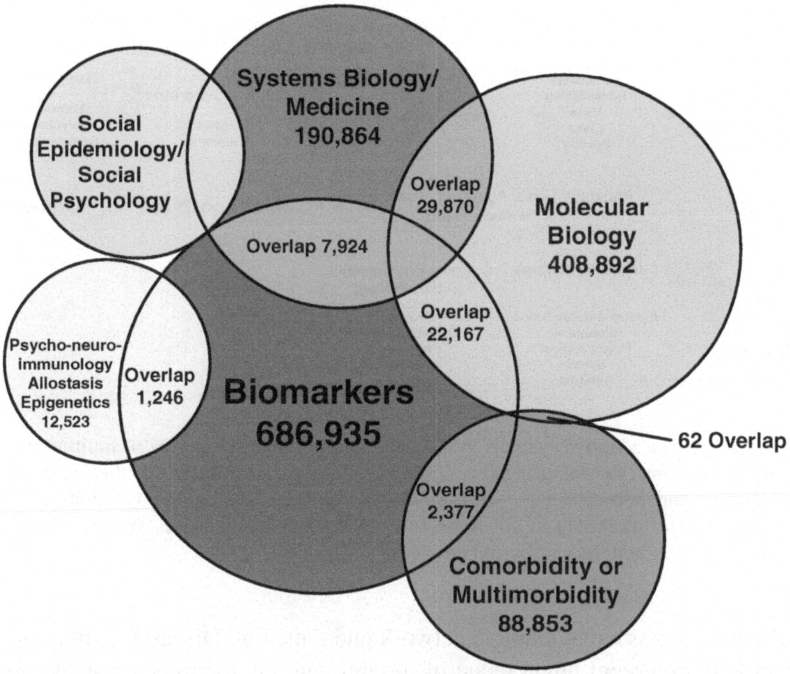

Fig. 10.2 Overlap using raw counts of articles from PubMed searches based on search terms ["Biomarkers"] and ["Systems Biology" and "Systems Medicine"], ["Co-morbidity or Multimorbidity"], ["Molecular Biology"] as the main search with an overlap of 720 articles. Other bibliometrics were "Systems Medicine" and "Allostatic load"; there were no overlaps between "Multimorbidity" and "Networks", "Psycho-Neuro-Immunology" or "Systems Medicine and Systems Biology" with very little overlap between the joint terms ["Co-morbidity or Multimorbidity"] and ["Non-linear, Molecular Biology and Psycho-Neuro-Immunology"]

10.3 An Integrative Model from a Complex Adaptive Health Systems Perspective

Multimorbidity is the expression of dynamic physiological and pathophysiological and psychosocial processes within a discrete individual within their socio-cultural and living environment (Fig. 10.3). The term complexity is ubiquitous in multimorbidity, yet it is generally used in the lay sense of complicated but linear, rather than embracing the dynamics of a complex system [45].

Thus, thinking about the body as a complex adaptive system (CAS) has opened the way of understanding its function in terms of interdependent relationships, i.e., the body functions as a network structure and evolves in an emergent fashion. Internal (bio-psychological) and external (social-environmental) perturbations to an individual's networks that exceed homoeostatic ranges alter feedback relationships, and result in—a usually slow—co-evolution towards multimorbidity, generally accompanying ageing processes.

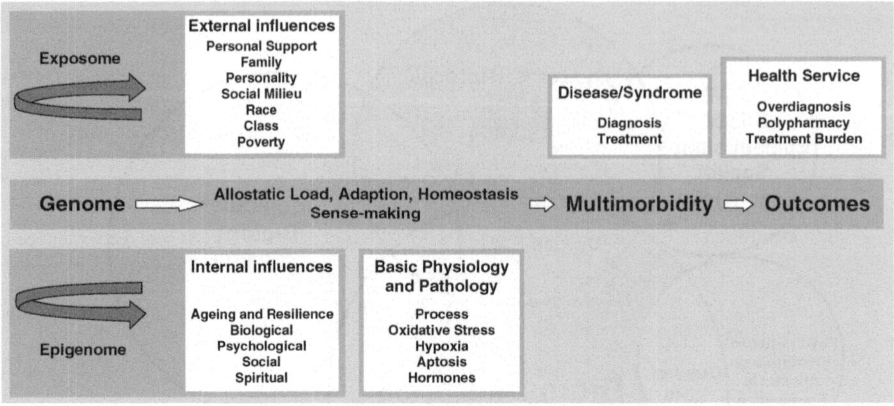

Fig. 10.3 A complex adaptive systems view of the non-linear development of multimorbidity in an individual trajectory, incorporating genetics, epigenetics, exposures that constitute the allostatic load, adaptation and homoeostasis, sense-making in the individuals health system and socio-cultural context. Multimorbidity in this sense encompasses chronic diseases, frailty, disability and poor quality of life as both processes and outcomes

Multimorbidity is a maladaptive network phenomenon. Diseases, syndromes and symptoms are emergent phenomena of the intricate interactions between complex genomic, proteomic and metabolomic networks within the complex dynamic environmental context and the individual's intimate and wider social networks. These networks at the level of the health system are socially constructed by the medical industrial complex [46, 47].

Phenomena that "stress" the immune function resulting in the modulation of inflammatory responses may ultimately lead to *distress and disease*. Tackling stress, immune function and biopsychosocial root causes of *distress and disease* is a disruptive shift and a big challenge for traditional practice with its focus on managing an individual's care according to narrowly based disease guidelines.

A *personal trajectory and life course approach* is arguably the way forward to achieve personalised effective healthcare [48, 49]. This would entail integrating research from biological, behavioural and social science disciplines, and recognising health as a dynamic process throughout the lifespan. Only then can healthcare enable the optimisation of individual and population health trajectories.

Currently the rapid advances in systems biology, systems medicine and technology research are not connected with the burgeoning literature on multimorbidity and co-morbidity. This chapter highlights the need for trans-disciplinary approaches to address social, psychological, biological and genetic influences on multimorbidity, to reduce health disparities, and to better understand the whole of systems approach to chronic illness and optimising health.

A vision for the future to transform the care of people with multi-morbidity involves moving from "discreet disease" to "system dynamics medicine" models, integrating advances in emerging systems knowledge and therapies, technology and informatics that enable individuals and populations. Burgeoning opportunities exist to transcend from fragmented silos of knowledge and reductionistic care into integrated systems embracing biomarkers, clinical care and population health networks.

References

1. International Research Community on Multimorbidity. The definition of multimorbidity: looking for a consensus. http://crmcspl-blog.recherche.usherbrooke.ca/2014. Cited Accessed 3 Oct 2014.
2. Feinstein A. The pre-therapeutic classification of co-morbidity in chronic disease. J Chronic Dis. 1970;23(7):455–68.
3. Valderas JM, Starfield B, Sibbald B, Salisbury C, Roland M. Defining comorbidity: implications for understanding health and health services. Ann Fam Med. 2009;7(4):357–63.
4. Prados-Torres A, Calderón-Larrañaga A, Hancco-Saavedra J, Poblador-Plou B, van den Akker M. Multimorbidity patterns: a systematic review. J Clin Epidemiol. 2014;67(3):254–66.
5. France E, Wyke S, Gunn J, Mair F, McLean G, Mercer S. Multimorbidity in primary care: a systematic review of prospective cohort studies. Br J Gen Pract. 2012;62(597):e297–307.
6. Britt H, Harrison C, Miller G, Knox S. Prevalence and patterns of multimorbidity in Australia. Med J Aust. 2008;189:72–77.
7. McDaid O, Hanly MJ, Richardson K, Kee F, Kenny RA, Savva GM. The effect of multiple chronic conditions on self-rated health, disability and quality of life among the older populations of Northern Ireland and the Republic of Ireland: a comparison of two nationally representative cross-sectional surveys. BMJ Open. 2013;3(6):e002571.
8. Harrison C, Britt H, Miller G, Henderson J. Examining different measures of multimorbidity, using a large prospective cross-sectional study in Australian general practice. BMJ Open. 2014;4(7):e004694.
9. Violán C, Foguet-Boreu Q, Roso-Llorach A, Rodriguez-Blanco T, Pons-Vigués M, Pujol-Ribera E, Muñoz-Pérez M and Valderas J. Burden of multimorbidity, socioeconomic status and use of health services across stages of life in urban areas: a cross-sectional study. BMC Public Health. 2014;14:530.
10. Marengoni A, von Strauss E, Rizzuto D, Winblad B, Fratiglioni L. The impact of chronic multimorbidity and disability on functional decline and survival in elderly persons. A community-based, longitudinal study. J Intern Med. 2009;265(2):288–95.
11. Lappenschaar M, Hommersom A, Lucas PJ. Probabilistic causal models of multimorbidity concepts. AMIA Annu Symp Proc. 2012;2012:475–84.
12. Smith SM, Soubhi H, Fortin M, Hudon C, O'Dowd T. Managing patients with multimorbidity: systematic review of interventions in primary care and community settings. Br Med J. 2012;345:e5205.
13. Barnett K, Mercer S, Norbury M, Watt G, Wyke S, Guthrie B. Epidemiology of multi-morbidity and implications for health care, research and medical education: a cross-sectional study. Lancet. 2012;380(9836):37–43.
14. Mercer S. Multimorbidity and the inverse care law in primary care. Br Med J. 2012;344:e4152.
15. Galenkamp H, Braam AW, Huisman M, Deeg DJ. Somatic multimorbidity and self-rated health in the older population. J Gerontol B Psychol Sci Soc Sci. 2011;66(3):380–86.
16. Nobrega TC, Jaluul O, Machado AN, Paschoal SM, Jacob Filho W. Quality of life and multimorbidity of elderly outpatients. Clinics (Sao Paulo). 2009;64(1):45–50.
17. Martin CM, Peterson C. The social construction of chronicity–a key to understanding chronic care transformations. J Eval Clin Pract. 2009;15(3):578–85.

18. Bayliss EA, Ellis JL, Steiner JF. Seniors' self-reported multimorbidity captured biopsychosocial factors not incorporated into two other data-based morbidity measures. J Clin Epidemiol. 2009;62(5):550–7.
19. Martin CM. The care of chronic illness in general practice. Ph.D. Thesis. Canberra: Australian National University; 1998.
20. Kline TJ, Willness C, Ghali WA. Predicting patient complaints in hospital settings. Qual Saf Health Care. 2008;17(5):346–50.
21. Voorham J, Denig P. Groningen initiative to analyse type 2 diabetes treatment. Computerized extraction of information on the quality of diabetes care from free text in electronic patient records of general practitioners. J Am Med Inform Assoc. 2007;14(3):349–54.
22. Kontopantelis E, Springate DA, Ashworth M, Webb RT, Buchan IE, Doran T. Investigating the relationship between quality of primary care and premature mortality in England: a spatial whole-population study. Br Med J. 2015;350:h904.
23. McLean G, Sutton M, Guthrie B. Deprivation and quality of primary care services: evidence for persistence of the inverse care law from the UK Quality and Outcomes Framework. J Epidemiol Community Health. 2006;60(11):917–22.
24. Federoff HJ, Gostin LO. Evolving from reductionism to holism: is there a future for systems medicine? JAMA. 2009;302(9):994–6.
25. Juster RP, McEwen BS, Lupien SJ. Allostatic load biomarkers of chronic stress and impact on health and cognition. Neurosci Biobehav Rev. 2010;35(1):2–16.
26. Westerhoff HV, Palsson BO. The evolution of molecular biology into systems biology. Nat Biotechnol. 2004;22(10):1249–52.
27. Martin CM, Peterson C. The social construction of chronicity - a key to understanding chronic care transformations. J Eval Clin Pract. 2009;15(3):578–85.
28. Armstrong D. The emancipation of biographical medicine. Soc Sci Med. 1979;13:1–8.
29. Engel GL. The biopsychosocial model and the education of health professionals. Gen Hosp Psychiatry. 1979;1(2):156–65.
30. Yancik R, Ershler W, Satariano W, Hazzard W, Cohen HJ, Ferrucci L. Report of the National Institute on aging task force on comorbidity. J Gerontol A Biol Sci Med Sci. 2007;62(3): 275–80.
31. Sturmberg JP, Martin CM. Diagnosis - the limiting focus of taxonomy. J Eval Clin Pract. 2015. http://dx.doi.org/10.1111/jep.12113. Accessed 21 Dec 2015 [online version 2014].
32. van der Heijden MJ, Schroen Y. Global advances in health and medicine through systems biology: an example from the Netherlands. Global Adv Health Med. 2012;1(4):92–3.
33. Strauss VY, Jones PW, Kadam UT, Jordan KP. Distinct trajectories of multimorbidity in primary care were identified using latent class growth analysis. J Clin Epidemiol. 2014;67(10):1163–71.
34. Baylis D, Bartlett DB, Syddall HE, Ntani G, Gale CR, Cooper C, et al. Immune-endocrine biomarkers as predictors of frailty and mortality: a 10-year longitudinal study in community-dwelling older people. Age (Dordr.) 2013;35(3):963–71.
35. Förhécz Z, Gombos T, Borgulya G, Pozsonyi Z, Prohászka Z, Jánoskuti L. Red cell distribution width in heart failure: prediction of clinical events and relationship with markers of ineffective erythropoiesis, inflammation, renal function, and nutritional state. Am. Heart J 2009;158(4):659–66.
36. Peters S, Janssen H-G, Vivó-Truyols G. Trend analysis of time-series data: a novel method for untargeted metabolite discovery. Anal Chim Acta. 2010;663(1):98–104.
37. Cole SW. Social regulation of human gene expression: mechanisms and implications for public health. Am J Public Health. 2013;103 Suppl 1:S84–92.
38. Christian LM, Glaser R, Porter K, Malarkey WB, Beversdorf D, Kiecolt-Glaser JK. Poorer self-rated health is associated with elevated inflammatory markers among older adults. Psychoneuroendocrinology. 2011;36(10):1495–1504.
39. Jylhä M, Volpato S, Guralnik J. Self-rated health showed a graded association with frequently used biomarkers in a large population sample. J Clin Epidemiol. 2006;59:465–71.

40. Juster RP, Marin MF, Sindi S, Nair NP, Ng YK, Pruessner JC, Lupien SJ. Allostatic load associations to acute, 3-year and 6-year prospective depressive symptoms in healthy older adults. Physiol Cehavior. 2011;104(2):360–64.
41. Picard M, Juster R, Sabiston C. Is the whole greater than the sum of the parts? Self-rated health and transdisciplinarity. Health. 2013;5:24–30.
42. Salanitro AH, Ritchie CS, Hovater M, Roth DL, Sawyer P, Locher JL, et al. Inflammatory biomarkers as predictors of hospitalization and death in community-dwelling older adults. Arch Gerontol Geriatr. 2012;54(3):e387–91.
43. Vanfleteren LE, Spruit MA, Groenen M, Gaffron S, van Empel VP, Bruijnzeel PL, Rutten EP, Op't Roodt J, Wouters EF, Franssen FM. Clusters of comorbidities based on validated objective measurements and systemic inflammation in patients with chronic obstructive pulmonary disease. Am J Respir Crit Care Med. 2013;187(7):728–35.
44. Melis R, Marengoni A, Angleman S, Fratiglioni L. Incidence and predictors of multimorbidity in the elderly: a population-based longitudinal study. PloS One. 2014;9(7):e103120.
45. Kurtz C, Snowden D. The new dynamics of strategy: Sense-making in a complex and complicated world. IBM Syst J. 2003;42(3):462–83.
46. Morgan WK. Letter: Medical-industrial complex. Lancet. 1974;1(7847):96.
47. Relman AS. The new medical-industrial complex. N Engl J Med. 1980;303(17):963–70.
48. Halfon N, Larson K, Lu M, Tullis E, Russ S. Lifecourse health development: past, present and future. Matern Child Health J. 2014;18(2):344–65.
49. Martin CM, Vogel C, Grady D, Zarabzadeh A, Hederman L, Kellett J, et al. Implementation of complex adaptive chronic care: the Patient Journey Record system (PaJR). J Eval Clin Pract. 2012;18(6):1226–34.

Chapter 11
Viewing Mental Health Through the Lens of Complexity Science

David A. Katerndahl

Traditional views of mental disorders depend upon a mechanistic model which assumes that you can study the parts and thereby understand the whole person. Such approaches assume a linear view, in which you apply a treatment and get a predictable response. Current concepts of classification and treatment of mental disorders are based upon a paradigm (derived from research in mental health settings) that symptoms can be clustered into discrete diagnostic groups and assumes predictability of response. Because patients seeking care from mental health professionals have more severe symptomatology, more impairment, more psychiatric co-morbidity, and a worse disease course but less medical co-morbidity than those in primary care settings [1, 2], we should expect that the dynamics of their symptoms may differ as well. If mental disorders are, contrary to current assumptions, non-linear phenomena (in which the input or magnitude of the intervention is not proportional to the output or response) in primary care patients, then a categorical system of diagnosis may be a "poor fit" for these patients and recognition by rigid criteria would suffer because such phenomena are unpredictable in their dynamics and course. Similarly, disorders with non-linear dynamics would not respond predictably to targeted, single-agent interventions and thus practice guidelines may not hold the same usefulness among primary care patients as they would among those in mental health settings displaying linear dynamics.

In this chapter, we will look at mental illness from a complexity science standpoint, noting that non-linear dynamics may be especially relevant to mentally ill patients seen in primary care settings. Focusing on affective disorders, we will

---

D.A. Katerndahl (✉)
Family & Community Medicine, University of Texas Health Science Center at San Antonio, 7703 Floyd Curl Drive, San Antonio, TX, USA
e-mail: katerndahl@uthscsa.edu

J.P. Sturmberg (ed.), *The Value of Systems and Complexity Sciences for Healthcare*, DOI 10.1007/978-3-319-26221-5_11

examine the evidence for the importance of dynamics in mental disorders. Finally, we will re-conceptualize affective disorders from a non-linear perspective and identify the clinical implications of such a perspective if it is borne out.

11.1 Complexity Science in Mental Health

There is a growing realization that "health" is defined by its non-linearity [3]; conversely, illness is associated with loss of variability. Thomasson and Pezard [4] suggest that mental health and psychopathology need to be viewed on a continuum with mental disorders representing bifurcations in mood dynamics. The exact nature of the mood dynamics observed may depend upon the severity of illness, the presence of resources, and social interactions. The fact that mental illness can be controlled but not cured suggests a dynamical disease [5]. Furthermore, when a disorder varies without an obvious cause, it suggests non-linearity resulting from a complex interaction between endogenous and environmental factors [6]. Dynamics assessment has been applied to mood variability in specific disorders. For example, attempts to control problematic thoughts and emotions among patients with generalized anxiety disorder and personality disorders may produce non-linear dynamics [7]. In addition, non-linear dynamics has been suggested as a framework for understanding change in families [8] and family interactions [9]. Recently, Katerndahl et al. [10] found that intimate partner violence demonstrates non-linearity over time for most violent relationships. Both Ehlers [11] and Guastello [12] have extolled the value of non-linear modelling in mental illness.

Even simple systems can display non-linear patterns depending upon their constraints, resources, and interconnections [13]. Non-linear systems can change their behavior and dynamics, moving from randomness to chaos to periodicity based on the state of the system, decreasing the number of possible values of the system as non-linearity decreases. An emerging belief is that, when systems are using healthy, non-linear dynamics, they exhibit adaptability and are resistant to external stressors that might disrupt these healthy dynamics. However, when these systems transition into periodicity due to illness, they become predictable and amenable to intervention, permitting physicians to treat them effectively and hopefully restore the healthy, non-linear dynamics. These considerations then suggest that, even though extreme variability may be detrimental within an illness (such as diabetes) [14], overall non-linearity may be critical to health and well-being. This transition from healthy non-linear dynamics to unhealthy linear dynamics can be understood by realizing that non-linear systems can display a variety of dynamics, depending upon their resources and constraints, interconnectedness, and feedback. But, as the number of chronic medical problems increases, the patient's resourcefulness, flexibility, and adaptability (and, hence, non-linearity) may decrease, leading to linear dynamics and poor overall health, and suggesting that non-linearity may be particularly important in settings that provide care for patients with chronic medical problems (e.g., primary care). As Fig. 11.1 shows, if we view phenomena

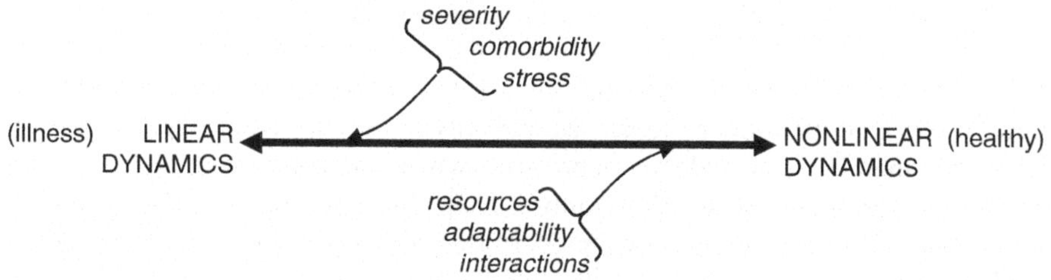

Fig. 11.1 Effects of resources and constraints upon dynamics

as a continuum from linear to non-linear dynamics, the constraining nature of disease severity, co-morbidity, and chronic stress would be expected to suppress health trends towards non-linearity, thus leading to linear dynamics. Recovery from anxiety states, for example, occurs at different rates, and depends upon co-morbidity and disease severity [15]. On the other hand, social interaction and availability of resources with resultant adaptability should encourage the development of non-linear dynamics. Kendler et al. [16] found that familial environment determined symptom expression in major depression. Fone et al. [17] found that poor mental health was associated with low community cohesion and income deprivation. Thus, the dynamics we observe in anxiety and depression may depend upon the severity of their mental illness, chronic stress levels, and co-morbidity as well as social connectedness and support.

11.1.1 Dynamics and Mental Illness

Understanding the dynamics of a system begins with the study of its variability over time. Recently, mental health research has studied the dynamics and variability (usually, standard deviation across time) of autonomic-related measures such as heart rate, blood pressure and respiration, neurological measures such as brain waves, and, ultimately, mood in a variety of patient groups. Although some of these measures may appear to have little to do with mental illness, many in fact correlate with mood or outcomes. Thus, several affective disorders in general demonstrate decreased variability in heart rate and mood compared with healthy individuals, and such loss of variability may be associated with poorer clinical outcomes. Taken a step further, the degree of non-linearity in dynamics has been evaluated in several mental disorders as well.

Recently, investigators have applied measures of non-linearity and non-linear pattern recognition to the study of mental illness. Non-linearity has been measured using approximate entropy (APEN) and Lyapunov exponent (LE). In addition, the identification of attractors within time series has been sought. Finally, the recognition of particular dynamic patterns (i.e., chaos) has been attempted in time series of mood levels.

APEN is an information-based measure and estimates the lack of regularity in time series [18]. Patients with panic disorder have increased respiratory rate APEN compared with controls [19, 20] and, in fact, paroxetine lowers this APEN [21]. Brain wave activity among depressed patients shows a reduced pre-treatment APEN for their first episode of depression when compared with those having recurrent depression and healthy controls [22]. Although the respiratory APEN among panic disorder patients does not correlate with anxiety severity [20], APEN of EEG measures does correlate with mood and response to treatment [23], and mood APEN correlates with happiness ratings among healthy controls [24]. Thus, APEN measures can distinguish mentally healthy from those who are ill and may correspond to clinical outcomes.

LE, a measure of sensitivity to minor differences in starting points, has also been used in mental health research. For example, LLE of QT intervals is lower in controls than patients with panic disorder or major depression [25] and LE is lower for heart rate but higher for blood pressure in those with panic disorder [26, 27]. Children with anxiety disorders [28] or panic disorder have a lower LE for heart rate than controls [29]. Similarly, LE of respiratory measures is increased in panic disorder [19] and paroxetine lowers these LEs [21]. Based on EEG activity, Bob et al. [30] found increased LEs in most adults with panic disorder and controls when asked to recall a stressful memory. In addition, SSRIs have been found to increase LE, improving OCD and normalizing hyperactivity in the striatum [31]. Healthy individuals uniformly display positive LEs in mood variability [32]. Increased LE in EEG activity correlates with anxiety levels [30], while LE of mood correlates positively with hypomania and negatively with anhedonia scores in healthy individuals [32]. As with APEN, LE measures can distinguish healthy from mentally ill individuals and some LEs may have clinical significance.

Although few studies have attempted to study attractors, depression patterns in bipolar patients suggest that attractors may be important. Few patients (15 %) had an attractor in the healthy symptom range; the majority either had two attractors (35 %) or an unstable pattern (28 %) [33]. Correlation dimension (a measure of the strength of attractors) correlated with pleasant affect (and inversely with anhedonia) among healthy controls [32]. Overall, EEG complexity appears to be reduced in patients with depression [22, 34]; white matter connectivity is increased among patients with panic disorder and connectivity correlates with panic severity [35]. Thus, unstable attractors or strong attractors may be associated with mental disorders.

Whether looking at heart rate variability, brain wave activity, or mood change, healthy individuals differ from those with mental disorders in the degree of non-linearity observed. Overall, studies of HRV demonstrate similar patterns despite the time-scale, suggesting a high degree of interdependence in heart rate [36]. As a result, healthy individuals exhibit more chaotic patterns in heart rate but less chaotic patterns in QT variability than those with mental illness [25], and low-dimensional chaos in mood variability as well [32, 37]. Woyshville et al. [38] found more mood interdependence in patients with affective instability, and Hall et al. [39] found circadian and ultradian patterns of mood variability in both depressed and normal patients. In fact, depressed individuals displayed patterns of combined periodicity and chaos in mood variability [37, 40], while controls displayed these patterns for both heart rate and mood variability [36, 41].

11.1.2 Examining Mood Dynamics Among Primary Care Patients with Affective Disorders

To explore the relationship between the dynamics of symptoms of anxiety and depression in patients with newly diagnosed major depressive episode or panic disorder, we enrolled five primary care patients each with either panic disorder, major depressive episode or neither disorder. They were asked to record their hourly levels of anxiety and depression using visual analog scales for 1 month. The resultant time series were analyzed using time series analysis, state space grid analysis, and differential structural equation modelling.

11.1.2.1 Dynamic Patterns of Anxiety/Depression

Healthy patients with neither major depression nor panic disorder demonstrated chaotic patterns in hourly mood variability overlaying a linear (circadian) pattern, possibly related to diurnal cortisol levels (see Fig. 11.2a). For example, the healthy 51-year-old female clerk reported a circadian pattern of mood (depression) variation underlying chaotic hourly variation. However, mentally ill patients may lose one or both of these dynamical components. For example, Fig. 11.2b shows the variability in anxiety levels of a 46-year-old male patient with panic disorder who retained his linear diurnal but lost the embedded hourly chaotic pattern, instead displaying more linear-on-linear dynamics. His low level of education (less than high school diploma), lack of employment, and low income further reduced his resources and adaptability, encouraging linear dynamics. On the other hand, Fig. 11.2c shows the variability in hourly levels of depression in a 48-year-old female patient with major depressive episode and bronchitis; while the hourly chaotic pattern was still seen, the linear circadian pattern was lost. Although unemployed, her college education may have allowed her to maintain her adaptive chaotic pattern even though she has lost her circadian cortisol levels. Hence, patients with major depression may lose their circadian baseline while patients with panic disorder may lose their overlying chaos [41].

In general, non-linearity in mood correlates with mental health and positive clinical outcomes. This non-linearity may result from the combination of the predictability of periodic circadian dynamics with the responsive minute-to-minute chaotic dynamics. Mental illness may represent an uncoupling of this combined periodicity–chaos with selective alteration of one or both components, leading to an overall reduction in non-linearity of mood.

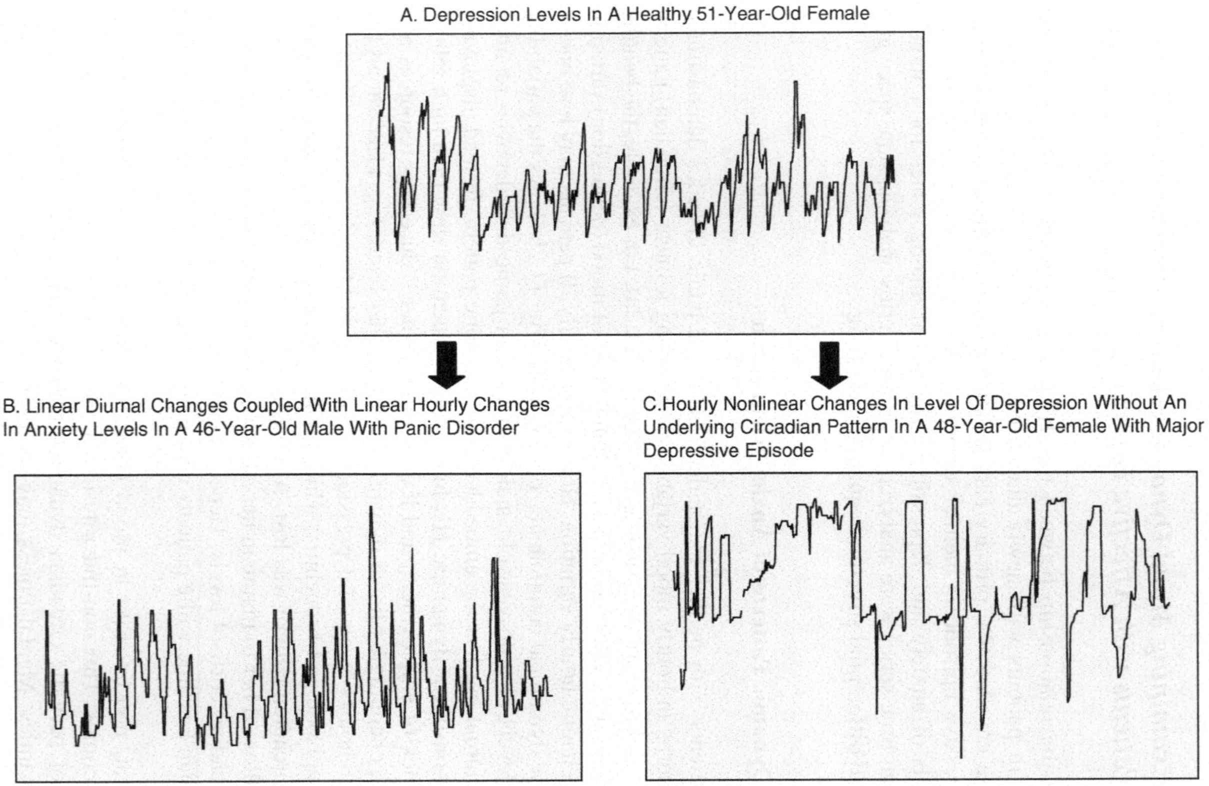

Fig. 11.2 Hourly variability in level of anxiety/depression among subjects. (**a**) Depression levels in a healthy 51-year-old female; (**b**) Linear diurnal changes coupled with linear hourly changes in anxiety levels in a 46-year-old male with panic disorder; (**c**) Hourly non-linear changes in level of depression without an underlying circadian pattern in a 48-year-old female with major depressive episode

11.1.2.2 Dynamic Co-variability of Anxiety and Depression

In addition to patterns of variation for a particular mood (e.g., anxiety), emotional state may reflect the constellation of patterns of various moods combined. In addition, symptom levels of anxiety and depression typically are highly correlated in cross-sectional studies. Yet, lagged correlations in time series are often non-significant [15]. In our study, anxiety and depression were highly correlated in healthy individuals [42], suggesting that healthy individuals may perceive these moods as nonspecific distress [43]. However, anxiety and depression were less-correlated in patients with either major depression or panic disorder, suggesting that such patients perceive these moods as distinct. In addition, while healthy controls reported few, highly stable anxiety–depression configurations (attractors), such attractors were highly unstable in patients with major depression [42]. For example, Fig. 11.3 shows the instability over a 4-week period of the preferred

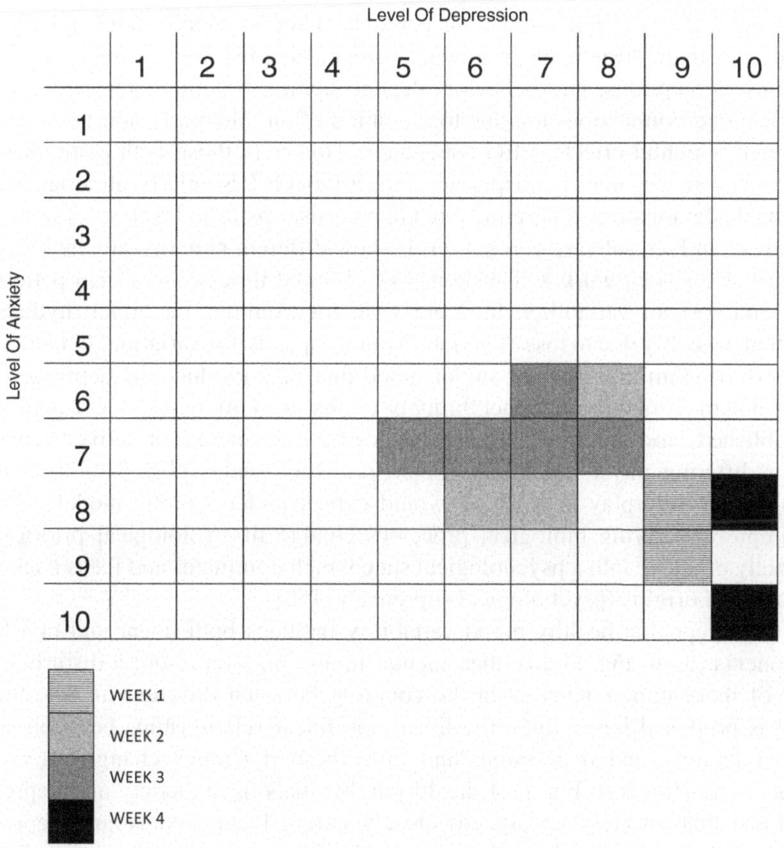

Fig. 11.3 Evolving preferred anxiety–depression states over a 4-week period in a 52-year-old female with major depressive episode and multiple medical problems

anxiety–depression mood configurations for a 52-year-old female patient with major depressive episode, asthma, hypertension, and reflux esophagitis taking six medications. Not only did these preferred configurations change week-to-week, but at times they split into more than one configuration, further emphasizing mood instability. Furthermore, while anxiety and depression levels are interdependent over time in patients with major depression, panic disorder and controls, the accelerations in these moods were the most interdependent [44].

Thus, the degree of coupling between symptoms of anxiety and depression may be an important measure of co-variability. If tightly linked, then we may observe few, but stable recurrent emotional states. If loosely coupled, we may observe many, transiently stable emotional states.

11.2 Imperative for Change

Emotional state is a reflection of a person's inherent mood coupled with their response to their current environment. Toro et al. [45] suggest that cognitions, emotions, perceptions, and behaviors depend upon CNS interconnectedness, and that these interconnections are due to the union of an inherently non-linear system with environmental effects. EEG coherence is lower in those with panic disorder, reflecting decreased inter-hemispheric connectivity [46]. Similarly, although healthy individuals demonstrate a baseline circadian cortisol pattern, levels of cortisol vary with stress. In fact, salivary cortisol levels show different patterns, affected by more than just stress (i.e., work, exhaustion) [47]. Mental illness alters such patterns of mood and cortisol variability. In depression, for example, circadian rhythms are disrupted, possibly due to loss of variability and capacity for variation. In fact, it may be this dysrhythmia in cortisol and/or mood that may produce the depressed state due to either an underlying vulnerability or to mis-attribution [48]. Once depression is established, non-linearity may be enhanced due to increased cortisol reactivity [49] or differing physiological and behavioral time-scales [22]. This biological–psychological interplay is what we would expect under a biotic model in which the simple underlying biological processes change first (biological priority) but ultimately organize into a psychological state which dominates and feeds back upon its biological origins (psychological supremacy) [50].

If we accept that healthy mood variability includes both linear and non-linear components (as in Fig. 11.2a), then mental illness may represent a disturbance in either of these components or in the coupling between different moods. Such a model is proposed based upon the linear-non-linear relationships between symptoms of anxiety and depression, and how these dynamics change as severity increases. As shown in Fig. 11.4, healthy individuals have anxiety and depressive symptoms that strongly covary. So closely coupled are anxiety and depressive symptoms that they may be indistinguishable. Patterns of variation of individual moods (i.e., anxiety levels) have both linear and non-linear components. As the severity of mental illness increases, sub-threshold disorders manifest themselves

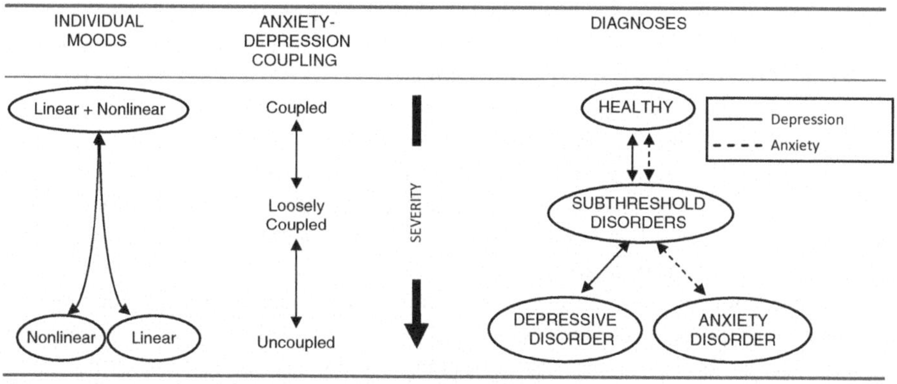

Fig. 11.4 Proposed model of changing dynamical relationships between anxiety and depression

with loosely coupled anxiety and depression levels; patients can begin to distinguish anxiety and depression from general distress. As distinct disorders emerge, the healthy linear–non-linear individual patterns change; people with depressive disorders lose the linear component to their depressive symptoms as their diurnal cortisol cycle is disrupted (see Fig. 11.2b), while those with anxiety disorders lose their non-linear component (with its minute-to-minute adaptability) to their anxiety symptoms (see Fig. 11.4). At this point, anxiety symptoms clearly differ from depressive symptoms, vary in different patterns, and are independent of each other (see Fig. 11.2c).

Such a dynamical paradigm would carry important clinical implications. First, if diagnostic differences are shown to be more dependent upon differences in dynamics and co-variability rather than disease severity, a non-linear approach could lead to a revision in diagnostic approaches and the classification of mental disorders. Just as linear and non-linear measures in HRV may discriminate between different diagnostic populations [51], such measures applied to mood variability may also have important diagnostic applications [6]. Classification of patients into diagnostic categories may reflect bifurcation points in brain activity [34] or establishment of dysfunctional CNS interconnections [45]. Better understanding of mood dynamics, and the relationship between anxiety and depression may help explain the problems of lack of recognition and treatment adequacy observed in primary care settings.

Second, as mentioned above, measures of non-linearity correlate with clinical outcomes. In healthy populations, non-linear measures correlate with levels of happiness, anhedonia, and hypomania. This suggests that assessment of mood variability via patient-completed mood diaries may have diagnostic and prognostic utility. Recent studies suggest that, as catastrophic events approach, dynamics signs (increased variability and lagged autocorrelations) are sent [52]. Glenn et al. [53] found that APEN of daily mood measurements was higher among bipolar patients who experienced an episode of either mania or depression than those who remained euthymic. In addition, the fact that mood variability patterns are self-similar no matter what the time-scale may be, demonstrating the scale-free power law of interdependence, suggests that non-linearity measures of mood variability could be obtained via in-office computer assessment over a few minutes [32] to be used for diagnostic and prognostic purposes. In fact, because HRV may correlate with clinical outcomes, cardiac monitoring among patients with mental illness may also have clinical applications for following treatment response.

Finally, assessment of non-linear dynamics may have treatment implications, especially at the individual patient level [54]. Although antidepressants, resources, and social interaction may work via their effect on dynamics [48], non-linearity may explain poor treatment response to traditional approaches, limiting the benefits of "cookbook" practice guidelines; management plans will need to be tailored to patients. Hence, initial assessment of dynamics and co-variability may imply that, in those patients displaying non-linear dynamics, standard single-agent approaches will probably not help. Such non-linearity in treatment response is supported by the importance of chronotherapy (timed dosing based on biological rhythms); drug efficacy often varies with the time-of-day [55, 56]. Finally, demonstrating non-linearity and co-variability would attest to the presence of a complex system at work, and suggest novel interventions. Interventions targeting dynamics may have applications here; treatments (such as anti-control interventions) would focus on changing the dynamic pattern (i.e., from periodicity to chaos) rather than on symptom levels [6, 57]. Small but well-timed pulse interventions may be successful in altering dynamics without affecting mood extremes, but yielding improved outcomes [6]. In addition, if non-linear dynamics are found, then multifaceted, whole patient approaches may be more successful than single-agent interventions.

But these implications are based upon the construct that a non-linear, dynamical basis for classification and treatment of mental disorders is more parsimonious than the current linear, symptom level model. However, such a paradigm shift is far from proven. Instead, we are left with many questions. What are the determinants of linear and non-linear dynamics in mood variability? What is the optimal time-frame over which to measure such dynamics? What constitutes an attractor in mood variability? How should co-variability in moods be measured? Before we can begin to address these issues, we need basic, large-scale investigations of patients with affective disorders of varying severity from various clinical settings. Measuring mood levels hourly over an extended period of time, such investigation would need to compare the validity of classification based upon DSM criteria versus classification based on dynamical group in terms of its prognosis, co-morbidity, health-related disability, and treatment response. In addition, data from such patients could be used to determine their co-variability using linear and non-linear measures (such as cross-correlation and cross-APEN) to determine their relative impact compared with DSM classification on clinical outcomes. Such investigations could begin to assess whether a non-linear, dynamical framework may provide us with a new, yet rewarding, perspective for understanding the emergence and evolution of mental illness. Only if these non-linear, dynamical approaches can better predict observations and outcomes will this complex systems perspective supplant the entrenched linear, reductionist paradigm.

11.3 Conclusion

A non-linear perspective of mental disorders may be particularly relevant to understanding mental disorders, especially in primary care settings. There is growing evidence that non-linearity of a variety of parameters (from heart rate to mood) may be relevant to our understanding of what constitutes mental health and illness. Monitoring of daily anxiety/depression levels among psychiatric patients demonstrates non-linearity, attractors, and covariation. If true, then non-linear dynamics may have important clinical implications for classification of mental disorders, identification of novel treatments, and monitoring of response. For this reason, a dynamical systems approach has been advocated for psychiatrists and psychologists alike [54], but such advice may be of particular importance to primary care physicians.

References

1. Klinkman M, Schwenk T, Coyne J. Depression in primary care-more like asthma than appendicitis. Can J Psychiatry. 1997;42:966–73.
2. Wells KB, Burnam A, Camp P. Severity of depression in prepaid and fee-for-service general medical and mental health specialty practices. Med Care. 1995;33:350–64.
3. Albrecht G, Freeman S, Higginbotham N. Complexity and human health. Cult Med Psychiatry. 1998;22(1):55–92.
4. Thomasson N, Pezard L. Dynamical systems and depression. Acta Biotheor. 1999;47:209–18.
5. Belair J, Glass L, van der Heiden U, Milton J, editors. Dynamical disease: mathematical analysis of human illness. Woodbury, NY: American Institute of Physics; 1995.
6. Heath RA. Complexity and mental health. In: Holt TA, editor. Complexity for clinicians. Abingdon: Radcliffe; 2004.
7. Warren K, Sprott JC, Hawkins RC. Spirit is willing. Nonlinear Dynamics Psychol Life Sci. 2002;6:55–70.
8. Koopmans M. Chaos theory and the problem of change in family systems. Nonlinear Dynamics Psychol Life Sci. 1998;2:133–48.
9. Pincus D. A framework and methodology for the study of nonlinear, self-organizing family dynamics. Nonlinear Dynamics Psychol Life Sci. 2001;5:139–73.
10. Katerndahl DA, Burge SK, Ferrer RL, Becho J, Wood R. Dynamics of violence. J Eval Clin Pract. 2014;20:695–702.
11. Ehlers CL. Chaos and complexity. Arch Gen Psychiatry. 1995;52:960–4.
12. Guastello SJ. Nonlinear dynamics in psychology. Discret Dyn Nat Soc. 2001;6:11–29.
13. Morrison F. Art of modeling dynamic systems. New York: Wiley; 1991.
14. Hirsch IB, Brownlee M. Should minimal blood glucose variability become the gold standard of glycemic control? J Diabetes Complicat. 2005;19:178–81.
15. De Vries MW, Dijkman-Caes CIM, Delespaul PAEG. Sampling of experience. In: Maser JD, Cloninger CR, editors. Comorbidity of mood and anxiety disorders. Washington, DC: American Psychiatric Association; 1990.
16. Kendler KS, Neale MC, Kessler RC, Heath AC, Eaves LJ. Familial influences on the clinical characteristics of major depression. Acta Psychiatr Scand. 2007;86:371–8.
17. Fone D, Dunstan F, Lloyd K, Williams G, Watkins J, Palmer S. Does social cohesion modify the association between area income deprivation and mental health? Int J Epidemiol. 2007;36:1–8. doi:10.1093/ije/dym004.

18. Pincus SM. Approximate entropy as a measure of irregularity for psychiatric serial metrics. Bipolar Disord. 2006;8:430–40.
19. Yeragani VK, Radhakrishna RKO, Tancer M, Uhde T. Nonlinear measures of respiration. Neuropsychobiology. 2002;46:111–20.
20. Caldirola D, Bellodi L, Caumo A, Migliarese G, Perna G. Approximate entropy of respiratory patterns in panic disorder. Am J Psychiatry. 2004;161:79–87.
21. Yeragani VK, Rao R, Tancer M, Uhde T. Paroxetine decreases irregularity of linear and nonlinear measures of respiration in patients with panic disorder. Neuropsychobiology. 2004;49:53–7.
22. Pezard L, Nandrino JL, Renault B, El Massioui F, Allilaire JF, Muller J, et al. Depression as a dynamical disease. Biol Psychiatry. 1996;39:991–9.
23. Thomasson N, Pezard L, Allilaire JF, Renault B, Martinerie J. Nonlinear EEG changes associated with clinical improvement in depressed patients. Nonlinear Dynamics Psychol Life Sci. 2000;4:203–18.
24. Yeragani VK, Pohl R, Mallavarapu M, Balon R. Approximate entropy of symptoms of mood. Bipolar Disord. 2003;5:279–86.
25. Yeragani VK, Rao KAR. Nonlinear measures of QT interval series. Psychiatry Res. 2003;117:177–90.
26. Rao RKA, Yeragani VK. Decreased chaos and increased nonlinearity of heart rate time series in patients with panic disorder. Auton Neurosc. 2001;88:99–108.
27. Yeragani VK, Mallavarapu M, Radhakrishna RKA, Tech M, Tancer M, Uhde T. Linear and nonlinear measures of blood pressure variability. Depress Anx. 2004;19:85–95.
28. Yeragani VK, Rao KAR, Pohl R, Jampala VC, Balon R. Heart rate and QT variability in children with anxiety disorders. Depress Anx. 2001;13:72–7.
29. Srinivasan K, Ashok MV, Vaz M, Yeragani VK. Decreased chaos of heart rate time series in children of patients with panic disorder. Depress Anx. 2002;15:159–67.
30. Bob P, Kukleta M, Riecansky I, Susta M, Kukumberg P, Jagla F. Chaotic EEG patterns during recall of stressful memory related to panic attack. Physiol Res. 2006;55(1):S113-9.
31. Kubota S, Sakai K. Relationship between obsessive-compulsive disorder and chaos. Med Hypotheses. 2002;59:16–23.
32. Schuldberg D, Gottlieb J. Dynamics and correlates of microscopic changes in affect. Nonlinear Dynamics Psychol Life Sci. 2002;6:231–57.
33. Johnson SL, Nowak A. Dynamical patterns in bipolar depression. Personal Soc Psychol Rev. 2002;6:380–7.
34. Sarbadhikari SN, Chakrabarty K. Chaos in the brain. Med Eng Phys. 2001;23:445–55.
35. Han DH, Renshaw PF, Dager SR, Chung A, Hwang J, Daniels MA, et al. Altered cingulated white matter connectivity in panic disorder patients. J Psychiatr Res. 2008;42:399–407.
36. Cecen AA, Erkal C. Long march: from monofractals to endogenous multifractality in heart rate variability analysis. Nonlinear Dynamics Psychol Life Sci. 2009;13:181–206.
37. Combs A, Winkle M, Daley C. Chaotic systems analysis of rhythms in feeling states. Psychol Record. 1994;44:359–68.
38. Woyshville MJ, Lackamp JM, Eisengart JA, Gilliland JAM. On the meaning and measurement of affective instability. Biol Psychiatry. 1999;45:261–9.
39. Hall DP Jr., Sing HC, Romanoski AJ. Identification and characterization of greater mood variance in depression. Am J Psychiatry. 1991;148:1341–5.
40. Heiby EM, Pagano IS, Blaine DD, Nelson K. Modeling unipolar depression as a chaotic process. Psychol Assess. 2003;15(3):426–34.
41. Katerndahl D, Ferrer R, Best R, Wang CP. Dynamic patterns in mood among newly-diagnosed patients with major depressive episode, panic disorder, and normal controls. Prim Care Comp J Clin Psychiatry. 2007;9(3):183–7.
42. Katerndahl D, Wang CP. Dynamic co-variation of symptoms of anxiety and depression among newly-diagnosed patients with major depressive episode, panic disorder and controls. Nonlinear Dynamics Psychol Life Sci. 2007;11(3):349–65.

43. Barlow DH, Campbell LA. Mixed anxiety-depression and its implications for models of mood and anxiety disorders. Compr Psychiatry. 2000;41(suppl. 1):55–60.
44. Katerndahl DA. Power laws in covariability of anxiety and depression among newly-diagnosed primary care patients with major depressive disorder, panic disorder and controls. J Eval Clin Pract. 2009;15:565–70.
45. Toro MG, Ruiz JS, Talavera JA, Blanco C. Chaos theories and therapeutic commonalities among depression, Parkinson's disease, and cardiac arrhythmias. Compr Psychiatry. 1999;40:238–44.
46. Hanaoka A, Kikuchi M, Komuro R, Oka H, Kidani T, Ichikawa S. EEG coherence analysis in never-medicated patients with panic disorder. Clin EEG Neurosc. 2005;36:42–8.
47. Dahlgren A, Akerstedt T, Kecklund G. Individual differences in the diurnal cortisol response to stress. Chronobiol Int. 2004;21:913–22.
48. Healy D, Williams JMG. Dysrhythmia, dysphoria, and depression. Psychol Bull. 1988;103:163–78.
49. Sussman EJ, Dorn LD, Inoff-Germain G, Nottelmann ED, Chrousos GP. Cortisol reactivity, distress behavior, and behavioral and psychological problems in young adolescents. J Res Adoles. 1997;7:81–105.
50. Sabelli HC. Bios: a study of creation. New Jersey: World Scientific; 2005.
51. Yeragani VK, Nadella R, Hinze B, Yeragani S, Jampala VC. Nonlinear measures of heart period variability. Depress Anx. 2000;12:67–77.
52. Scheffer M, Bascompte J, Brock WA, Brovkin V, Carpenter SR, Dakos V, et al. Early-warning signals for critical transitions. Nature. 2009;461:53–9.
53. Glenn T, Whybrow PC, Rasgon N, Grof P, Alda M, Baethge C, Bauer M. Approximate entropy of self-reported mood prior to episodes in bipolar disorder. Bipolar Disord. 2006;8:424–9.
54. Tschacher W. Dynamics of psychosocial crises. J Nerv Ment Dis. 1996;184:172–9.
55. Nagayama H. Influences of biological rhythms on the effects of psychotropic drugs. Psychosom Med. 1999;6:618–29.
56. Kraft M, Martin RJ. Chronobiology and chronotherapy in medicine. Disease-A-Month 1995;41:503–75.
57. Christini D, Collins J, Linsay P. Experimental control of high dimensional chaos. Phys Rev E. 1996;54:4824–7.

Chapter 12
Quantitatively Demonstrating the Complex Nature of Intimate Partner Violence

David A. Katerndahl, Sandra Burge, Robert Ferrer, Johanna Becho, and Robert Wood

Intimate partner violence (IPV) is a multi-dimensional problem [1], which depends upon cultural, oppression, historical, and situational constructs [2]. A commonly applied model, family systems theory (FST), describes family processes including family communication and conflict, cohesion, and adaptability. According to this perspective, due to the wealth of family interdependencies, simple cause-and-effect mechanisms rarely apply. In addition, family systems are hierarchical with individuals nested within couples nested within households nested within communities. Marital interaction is therefore often a product of more than the issues inherent to the couple. Thus, FST includes many of the concepts that define complexity science: interacting agents that create a system whose properties feed back to influence the agents [3].

Using complexity science as an overarching framework, this study sought to describe the daily phenomenon of IPV. It sought to better understand the mechanisms of violence and its outcomes. Ultimately, the goal was to promote theoretical and practical understanding of IPV, and point to future interventions and investigations.

12.1 Studying Partner Violence

We studied violence dynamics by collecting data longitudinally on day-to-day events within abusive relationships [4]. This study recruited 200 adult women from six primary care clinics during routine office visits. Women who reported being

D.A. Katerndahl (✉) • S. Burge • R. Ferrer • J. Becho • R. Wood
Family & Community Medicine, University of Texas Health Science Center at San Antonio, 7703 Floyd Curl Drive, San Antonio, TX 78229, USA
e-mail: katerndahl@uthscsa.edu; burge@uthscsa.edu; ferrerr@uthscsa.edu; becho@uthscsa.edu; wood@uthscsa.edu

J.P. Sturmberg (ed.), *The Value of Systems and Complexity Sciences for Healthcare*, DOI 10.1007/978-3-319-26221-5_12

abused within the past month but did not intend to leave the relationship completed a daily telephone survey using interactive verbal response (IVR) every day for 12 weeks. IVR questions addressed the previous day's level of violence, arguments, hassles, distress, marital harmony, emotional upset concerning violence, life events, husband's and wife's alcohol intake, and forgiveness. Women completed baseline and end-of-study quantitative assessments of attitudinal and clinical outcomes.

Participants provided 9618 daily assessments with women reporting abuse on 39 % of days. On average, the violence had occurred 5.5 (±6.5 SD) years, beginning at 32.6 (±11.3 SD) years of age. Women were in relationships for 9.6 (±8.9 SD) years; most often (43 %), these were common law marriages and quite dysfunctional. Husbands used a variety of behaviours to control their wives. On average, there was a 4.0-year (±6.6 SD) lag between the onset of the relationship and the onset of violence with 39 % of women reporting that the violence did not begin for at least 2 years into the relationship. Similarly, while half of women reported the onset of violence prior to marriage, 26 % reported that it only began after 2 years of marriage.

Violence dynamics was often non-linear with unclear causality. Alcohol–violence attractors were evident and, ultimately, violence dynamics was important to both attitudinal and clinical outcomes.

12.2 IPV Dynamics and Predictions

IPV varies non-linearly, Umberson et al. [5] found that non-violent men were more emotionally reactive to relationship dynamics and stress than their violent counterparts. Ristock [6] found a theme of shifting power dynamics in violent lesbian relationships. These studies suggest that patterns of violence may have both predictable and unpredictable components: predictable in the perpetrator's lack of emotional reaction to relationship dynamics and stress, but unpredictable in the shifting power dynamics within the relationship. The dynamics of help-seeking may also be non-linear, Chang et al. [7] found that women moved through stages-of-change in a non-linear fashion, influenced by internal and external factors, until a "turning point" was reached, which enabled them to progress. Hence, the dynamics of IPV and help-seeking appears to have both linear and non-linear components.

Although there are many theories concerning causes of IPV, only three behavioural models speak to the dynamics of IPV, each suggesting a different dynamical pattern. The Cycle Theory of Violence [8] states that battered women are not constantly or randomly abused. Instead, *battering appears to recur in cycles* (see Fig. 12.1a). Under the cycle theory, the three phases yield a cyclic or periodic pattern. Although the period would vary among couples due to variable phase length, the constellation of constraints and history would keep the periodicity fairly constant. Periodic systems are predictable and respond predictably to interventions, and are often described as "deterministic" (predictable over the long-term). Although little research on FST [9] speaks to IPV, the extant research

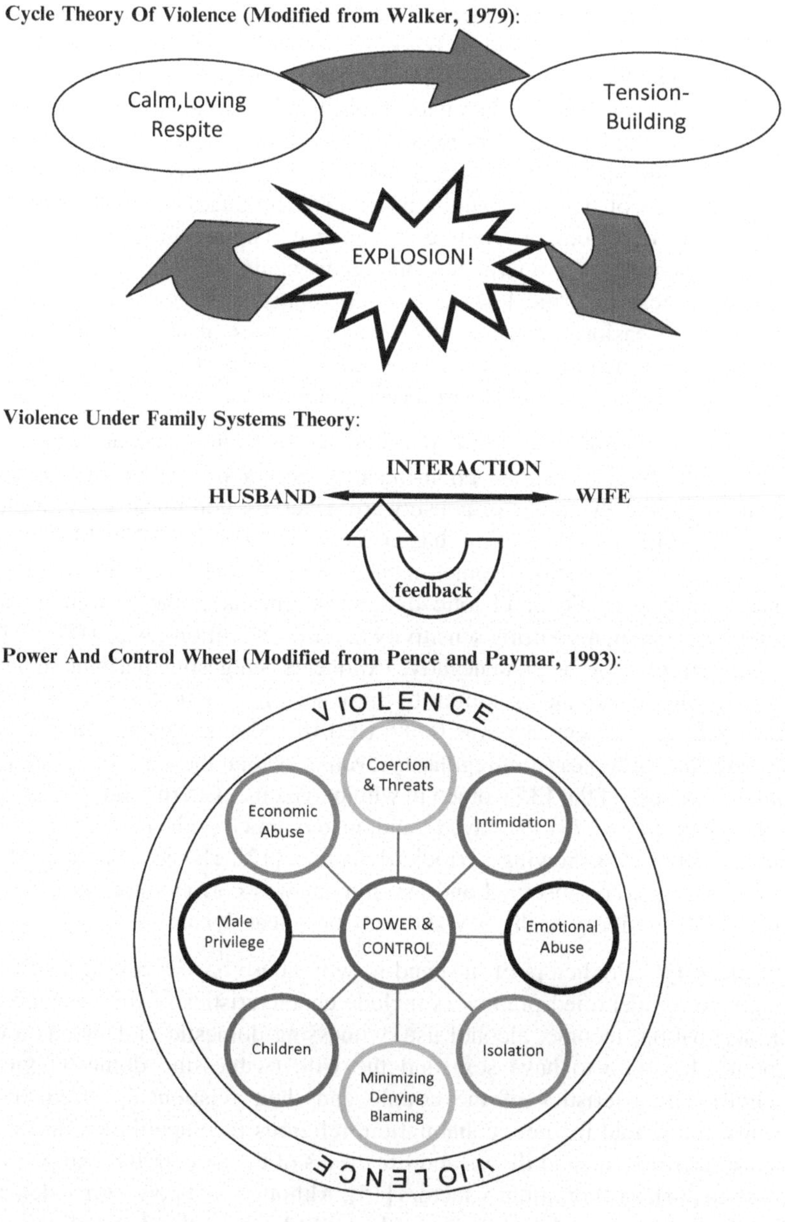

Fig. 12.1 Three theories of violence dynamics (adapted from [10])

focuses on wife *battering as an ongoing interaction pattern* resistant to change (see Fig. 12.1b). Under the systems theory, violence depends on variable feedback loops between victim and batterer, theoretically yielding a chaotic pattern. Chaotic systems are unpredictable over the long-term and do not respond predictably to interventions; yet, chaotic systems can be deterministic over the immediate short-term. Finally, the Power and Control Wheel Theory [10] posits that violence is used to control people's behaviour Here, *abuse is a constant force* in battered women's lives (see Fig. 12.1c). Abusive behaviours used by men to control their partners include: coercion and threats, intimidation, emotional abuse, isolation, denying, blaming or minimizing the violence, using the children, evoking male privilege, and economic control. The constant threat of abuse produces constant stress within the relationship, occasionally erupting in violence. The use of multiple strategies for control resembles the interdependent components with varying predilection to respond, typical of critical systems under constant stress. These conditions would lead to occasional random violent catastrophes of varying intensity and the dynamics of criticality, common in complex systems. Thus, these systems are unpredictable in behaviour and in response to intervention.

Dynamics Description Prior pilot research suggests that violence varies non-linearly [11]. All three measures of non-linearity used in the current study suggested that, as a group, the dynamics of abuse were generally non-linear LZ complexity, measuring algorithmic complexity, had a mean of 1.035 (±0.225 SD). The LZ complexity statistics for most women measured above the levels for standardized time series with periodic or chaotic dynamics. Similarly, the overall mean for Lyapunov's exponent, measuring sensitivity to initial conditions, was 0.041 (±0.328 SD). Although some women had negative exponents, suggesting periodic dynamics, most had Lyapunov exponents similar to those seen in chaotic time series. Finally, the mean approximate entropy was 0.686 (±0.187 SD), suggesting non-linearity. All approximate entropies (non-regularity) were less than those of the standardized random time series. Of the 135 women in whom dynamic patterns could be assigned, more than half ($n = 79$) displayed random dynamics with 40 (30 %) showing chaotic and 16 (12 %) showing periodic dynamics [12]. Hence, although all three dynamic patterns were observed and assignment was corroborated by supporting data, overall the majority of the IPV showed non-linear dynamics.

IPV "Causality" Predictors of husband-to-wife abuse have received much attention. Commonly identified predictors include characteristics of the husband (education, occupation, income, alcohol use, witnessing domestic violence as a child, and forcing his wife to have sex) and the wife (witnessing domestic violence as a child), characteristics of the couple and their relationship (frequency of arguments, household income, cohabitation, religious incompatibility, and marital dissatisfaction) [13], mental illness and life events of the perpetrator, and pregnancy in the victim [14], and community factors [15]. Although we know a great deal about risk factors for abusive relationships, we know little about the detailed day-to-day patterns of abuse and their triggers.

To evaluate immediate, prior-day and prior-week triggers of violent events, we examined same-day IVR correlates as well as vector autoregressive (VAR) models with husband-perpetrated violence as the dependent variable [16]. With the exception of the wife's alcohol intake, all of the same-day factors correlated with violence; only closeness was inversely related (see Table 12.1). However,

Table 12.1 Results of vector auto-regressions and same-day correlates pooled across subjects (adapted from [16])

Predictors of Man's violence	Same-day correlates (r)	Prior-day predictors (b[SE])
Violence		
Man's	–	0.09 (0.01)*
Woman's	0.679*	0.01 (0.02)
Hassles	0.450*	0.01 (0.00)*
Frequency of arguments	0.705*	0.01 (0.01)
Alcohol consumption		
Woman's	0.170	0.01 (0.01)
Man's	0.427*	−0.01 (0.00)*
Level of stress	0.551*	0.01 (0.01)
Sense of marital closeness	−0.435*	−0.02 (0.01)*
Degree of emotional upset	0.720*	0.07 (0.02)*
Forgiveness		
Sought	0.483*	0.02 (0.04)
Given	0.368*	0.03 (0.04)

* $p \leq 0.05$

because we cannot determine whether these assessments reflect conditions prior or subsequent to the violence, we cannot make causal statements. All factors were significant ($p \leq 0.0000$) in the prior-week analysis, suggesting that all factors during the prior week contribute to a violent event today. The strongest causal statements involve prior-day factors. In this analysis, four prior-day factors contributed to index-day violence: First, husband-perpetrated violence yesterday increased the risk of violence today; violence perpetuated violence. Second, hassles and emotional upset also contribute, perhaps suggesting that these factors serve to "charge" the environment. Finally, lack of closeness (perhaps due to the emotional upset) made violence more likely.

The complete prior-day VAR matrix appears in Table 12.2. Although husband-perpetrated violence may be triggered by his prior violence as well as hassles, emotional upset, and lack of closeness, wife-perpetrated violence depends upon her prior violence and alcohol intake. Second, while seven factors were associated with subsequent arguments, prior arguments were only a risk for future arguments. Conversely, the wife's forgiveness was associated with seven different subsequent non-violence factors. Finally, all but two factors (wife's alcohol intake, husband seeking forgiveness) showed feed-forward effects.

Hence, while all prior-week and most same-day factors were associated with current violent events and most showed feed-forward dynamics, only some factors seemed to trigger violence the following day; closeness and emotional upset were circularly causal with violence.

IPV-Alcohol "Attractors" The perpetrator's alcohol intake is often cited as a trigger of IPV. Meta-analyses have found consistent links between male alcohol

Table 12.2 Prior-day predictors in vector auto-regressions [b(SE)] (adapted from [16])

Outcomes	Violence		Alcohol intake		Forgiveness						
Predictor	Man's	Woman's	Hassles	Arguments	Woman's	Man's	Stress	Closeness	Upset	Sought	Given
Violence											
Man's	0.09 (0.01)*	0.00 (0.01)	0.03 (0.02)	0.02 (0.01)*	−0.01 (0.01)	0.00 (0.01)	0.01 (0.01)	−0.02 (0.01)*	0.02 (0.01)*	0.00 (0.00)	0.01 (0.00)*
Woman's	0.01 (0.02)	0.04 (0.01)*	0.07 (0.03)*	0.04 (0.01)*	0.01 (0.01)	−0.01 (0.01)	0.01 (0.02)	0.01 (0.01)	0.04 (0.01)*	0.00 (0.00)	.00 (0.00)
Hassles	0.01 (0.00)*	0.00 (0.00)	0.32 (0.01)*	0.01 (0.00)*	0.00 (0.00)	0.00 (0.00)	0.03 (0.01)*	0.00 (0.00)	0.01 (0.00)*	0.00 (0.00)	0.00 (0.00)
Arguments	0.01 (0.01)	0.01 (0.01)	0.03 (0.04)	0.07 (0.02)*	0.00 (0.01)	−0.01 (0.01)	−0.01 (0.02)	0.00 (0.01)	0.00 (0.01)	0.00 (0.00)	0.00 (0.01)
Alcohol Intake											
Woman's	0.01 (0.01)	0.02 (0.00)*	−0.04 (0.02)*	0.00 (0.01)	0.00 (0.01)	−0.01 (0.01)	−0.01 (0.02)	0.00 (0.01)	0.00 (0.01)	0.00 (0.00)	0.00 (0.00)
Man's	−0.01 (0.00)	0.00 (0.00)	−0.01 (0.01)	0.00 (0.00)	0.02 (0.00)*	0.12 (0.01)*	−0.01 (0.01)	0.00 (0.00)	0.01 (0.00)*	0.00 (0.00)	0.00 (0.00)

Stress	0.01 (0.01)	0.00 (0.00)	0.06 (0.02)*	0.01 (0.01)	0.00 (0.00)	0.01 (0.01)	0.18 (0.01)*	−0.01 (0.01)	0.01 (0.01)	0.00 (0.00)	0.00 (0.00)
Closeness	−0.02 (0.01)*	0.00 (0.01)	0.02 (0.03)	−0.04 (0.01)*	0.00 (0.01)	−0.01 (0.01)	0.00 (0.02)	0.21 (0.01)*	−0.02 (0.01)	0.00 (0.00)	0.00 (0.00)
Upset	0.07 (0.02)*	0.01 (0.01)	−0.05 (0.04)	0.04 (0.01)*	−0.01 (0.01)	0.02 (0.01)*	0.02 (0.02)	0.01 (0.01)	0.08 (0.02)*	0.01 (0.00)*	0.01 (0.00)*
Forgiveness											
Sought	0.02 (0.04)	0.04 (0.03)	0.04 (0.10)	0.01 (0.04)	−0.04 (0.02)*	0.04 (0.02)*	0.06 (0.05)	−0.02 (0.03)	0.08 (0.04)*	0.03 (0.02)	0.03 (0.01)*
Given	0.03 (0.04)	0.03 (0.02)	0.00 (0.12)	−0.09 (0.04)*	−0.05 (0.02)*	0.04 (0.02)*	−0.17 (0.06)*	0.06 (0.03)*	−0.04 (0.04)	0.06 (0.01)*	0.09 (0.02)*

* $p \leq 0.05$

intake and male-perpetrated IPV [13, 17] as well as female alcohol intake and female-perpetrated IPV [17]. However, it remains unclear whether the relationship between perpetrator's alcohol intake and IPV is causal [18] and whether the relationship is continuous or dependent upon a threshold level of alcohol consumption [19]. Also, the alcohol–violence link may only exist for particular subgroups [20]. Understanding longitudinal patterns across days may clarify the relationship.

Thus, husbands' alcohol intake and violent behaviours are interrelated, but in complex ways. In the current study, his prior-week and same-day alcohol intake were predictive of violence today, yet prior-day alcohol intake was not. These findings were independent of underlying violence dynamics. But his prior-day alcohol intake may trigger her drinking. In fact, among the women, their alcohol intake and violence were circularly causal.

Prior study suggested the presence of 3-day IPV patterns [21]. Using orbital decomposition to identify multi-day patterns between violence and alcohol intake in the current study suggested that, although patterns were observed across 5, 7, and 9 days, these were generally just extensions of 4-day patterns [22, 23]. Frequency and level of male-perpetrated violence diminished as the level of female-perpetrated violence decreases. Consecutive days of male-perpetrated, moderate-level violence were common. Heavy alcohol intake by the husband was under-represented in days involving verbal abuse only but over-represented in consecutive days of such abuse. Husband's alcohol intake preceded his verbal abuse and a sequence of husband-perpetrated verbal abuse followed by mutual abuse followed by wife-perpetrated verbal abuse was noted; no patterns involved heavy alcohol intake by the wife. In addition, within dynamic patterns, unique multi-day attractors were observed. While periodic dynamics often involved heavy alcohol intake by the husband or mutual moderate–severe violence, random dynamics uniquely involved mutual verbal abuse with husband's alcohol intake on same or different days as well as husband-perpetrated moderate–severe violence with or without husband-perpetrated minor violence. Chaotic dynamics uniquely involved a variety of combinations from wife-perpetrated minor violence alone to combinations of husband's heavy alcohol intake with or without husband-perpetrated minor violence, mutual verbal abuse, and husband-perpetrated verbal abuse with or without husband's heavy alcohol intake. Hence, there was evidence for multi-day, alcohol–violence attractors, but wife's alcohol was not involved. Although most multi-day patterns involving more than four consecutive days are simply extensions of 4-day patterns, some unique 5-day patterns were seen.

12.3 Understanding IPV as a Complex Adaptive System: Outcomes

In addition to acute injuries [24], battered women have a high prevalence of chronic health problems. They have higher health care utilization than other women, visiting physicians twice as often, incurring costs that are 2.5 times higher [25]. Common complaints include insomnia, fatigue, gastrointestinal symptoms, premenstrual symptoms, chronic pain, and anaemia [26]. Battered women experience more negative pregnancy outcomes [27]. Victimization is associated with negative health behaviours such as eating disorders, substance abuse, and risk for sexually transmitted diseases and HIV [26]. Psychologically, victims of violence, compared to non-victims, have more difficulty coping with anger or aggression, have lower self-esteem, and are less able to trust others [28] as well as elevations on depression, anger, confusion, fearfulness, paranoia, and social introversion scales [29]. More than half had significant elevation on a chemical abuse index [29] and abused women are at high-risk for suicide [30]. Several investigators have diagnosed high rates of post-traumatic stress disorder (PTSD) among samples of battered women and the severity of the symptoms correlated with severity and the recency of the violence [31].

In the current study, we measured attitudinal and behavioural (appraisal, coping, hope, social support) as well as clinical (symptomatology, readiness-for-change, health care utilization, functional status) outcomes [32]. Table 12.3 presents the results of the regression analyses for the attitudinal/behavioural outcomes after controlling for demographic and background characteristics. For three outcomes (positive appraisal, negative coping and hope/support), the degree of violence non-linearity (ApEn and Lyapunov exponent) contributed significantly to the models beyond violence frequency and episode severity. On the other hand, Table 12.4 demonstrates that for none of the clinical outcomes did violence non-linearity

Table 12.3 Regression analyses of violence versus attitudinal/behavioural outcomes [β (p)] (adapted from [32])

Predictors	Coping		Appraisal		Hope & Support
	Positive	Negative	Positive	Negative	
Husband's violence					
Frequency			−0.205 (0.027)		
Episode severity					−0.180 (0.086)
Non-linearity					
– Approximate entropy			0.232 (0.009)		−0.280 (0.009)
– LZ Complexity					
– Lyapunov exponent		0.226 (0.014)	0.179 (0.038)		
Model					
F (*p*-value)	1.98 (0.140)	4.49	6.44 (0.000)	0.079 (0.971)	4.23 (0.001)
Adjusted R^2	0.039	0.197	0.259	−0.027	0.232

Adjusted for age, socioeconomic status, race/ethnicity (Hispanic), and childhood, mental health and relationship variables

Table 12.4 Regression analyses of violence versus attitudinal/behavioural outcomes [β (p)] (adapted from [32])

Predictors	Symptoms & functioning	Medical utilization	Readiness for change	Social symptoms & mental health utilization
Attitudinal/behavioural outcomes				
Appraised importance			0.187	 (0.057)
Seeks support for emotional reasons				−0.387 (0.000)
Hope				−0.230 (0.011)
Total support				−0.271 (0.011)
Husband's violence				
Frequency				−0.151 (0.080)
Episode severity				
Non-linearity				
– Approximate entropy				
– LZ complexity				
– Lyapunov exponent				
Model				
F (*p*-value)	23.41 (0.000)	5.62 (0.000)	4.91 (0.000)	8.83 (0.000)
Adjusted R^2	0.671	0.157	0.240	0.445

Adjusted for age, socioeconomic status, race/ethnicity (Hispanic), and childhood, mental health and relationship variables

contribute; the only violence variable that was significant in any model was violence frequency, which was inversely related to social symptoms/mental health utilization. To evaluate whether the non-linearity-outcome relationships were curvilinear with a mid-range optimal level of non-linearity, each regression model was rerun with three "optimal" non-linearity estimates added. Optimal approximate entropy was positively related to both symptoms and functioning ($\beta = 0.092$, $p = 0.077$) and readiness-for-change ($\beta = 0.167, p = 0.033$). However, the non-linearity of outcomes raises the possibility that some IPV outcomes may depend upon cusp catastrophe modelling (CCM). In fact, three of the nine CCMs accounted for more outcome variance than did linear models. With violence non-linearity serving as the bifurcation variable, both positive and negative coping as well as readiness-for-change were best modelled using CCM [33]. Thus, not only did violence non-linearity contribute significantly to models of outcomes, but it also served as a bifurcation variable, distorting the relationship between violence severity and outcomes. Hence, violence dynamics was important to outcomes, often more important than violence frequency or severity.

12.4 Imperative for Change

If we accept that the dynamical patterns do indeed reflect the behavioural models as proposed, then no one model was supported by the data. How can this be explained? First, IPV may be a dynamical disorder, a disorder defined by its dynamics alone and not by theoretical explanations [34]. However, if we believe in the dynamics–model linkage proposed, then no ***one*** model explains ***all*** IPV. Thus, a second possibility is that IPV is a mixture of violent relationships in which any of the three models may explain the violence. IPV is then a conglomeration of violent relationships and not a single population. A third possibility is that the violence dynamics and its drivers evolve over time. Perhaps the violent relationship begins in chaos, emerging from FST, but as the husband grows in his desire for control, the Power and Control Wheel becomes prominent and the dynamics reflects randomness. After years of such control, the relationship moves into periodicity and the cycle of violence because his control is so ingrained that only rare, periodic violent reinforcement is needed to maintain control. The final possibility is that current theories are wrong; either we need a new "umbrella" theory that incorporates the current models or we need a completely new theoretical approach to understanding violence. Experience suggests that the incorporation of non-linear dynamical systems theory into existing theories can create a "meta-theory" that recognizes the value of temporal dynamics in explaining the "local" theories [35]. Thus, consideration of dynamics may clarify relationships among the theories or lead to development of a new theory.

IPV Understanding Violence is a "complex" phenomenon. First, IPV demonstrates non-linear dynamics; not only do most of the non-linearity measures fall within the chaos-random range, but only 12 % of dynamic patterns were periodic in nature. In addition, such IPV dynamics is important to patient outcomes. While non-linearity is independently predictive of attitudinal/behavioural outcomes (appraisal, coping, hope, support), optimal non-linearity is predictive of clinical outcomes (symptomatology, functional status, readiness-for-change). In fact, non-linearity can act as a bifurcation variable, distorting the relationship between violence severity, and coping and readiness-for-change. Hence, not only is IPV non-linear, but that non-linearity is relevant to outcomes. Second, IPV is complex because it is dependent upon multiple, interdependent factors. In fact, most of the same-day and all of the prior-week factors were important to the occurrence of violent acts, and these factors were themselves interdependent. Third, prior-day factors show that IPV and its predictors are circularly causal. Most of these factors show feed-forward characteristics, and marital closeness and emotional upset were circularly causal with husband-perpetrated violence. Finally, orbital decomposition found evidence for the presence of multi-day attractors around husband's alcohol use. Not only is there recurrent daily abuse and husband–wife violence interdependence, but multi-day patterns between husband's verbal abuse and alcohol intake as well as husband's alcohol-induced violence and wife's violent responses were seen. As a complex phenomenon, IPV demands a new framework, a non-linear perspective, for understanding. Old linear explanations are doomed to fail. In addition, the complex nature of IPV should alter our expectations for outcomes and help-seeking. Not only should non-linear patterns be expected, but the fact that coping and readiness-for-change behave catastrophically suggests that we should anticipate sudden changes in both with only small changes in triggers or circumstances. Once understood, IPV's complex nature requires that interventions reflect its complexity.

IPV Intervention Intervention in complex phenomena is difficult and often unpredictable. Simple interventions are unlikely to succeed with all patients. The exception to this may be a mindfulness intervention.

However, if intervention is possible, the complex nature of IPV suggests that intervention would be most effective if individualized. First, VAR approaches could identify high-risk situations ***prior*** to violent events, enabling a woman to either intervene to avert violence or remove herself from the situation. Second, if we can identify the particular violence dynamics at work, we may be able to tailor interventions to the dynamic pattern or attempt to ***change*** the dynamic pattern to one more amenable to intervention. Thus, periodic dynamics may be the most predictably responsive pattern to both intervention and identification of triggers. In chaotic patterns, however, interventions may need to be appropriately timed to be effective and attractors may need to be modified by reinforcing positive attractors and/or nudging negative attractors in positive directions. Random patterns should be the most difficult in which to intervene; in fact, the only appropriate intervention may be to end the relationship. If intervention in random patterns is attempted, multi-faceted interventions or introducing new agents into the relationship may be the only logical approaches.

The alternative to dynamics-specific interventions may be to attempt to modify the dynamic pattern, typically either from chaos-to-periodicity to improve predictability or from periodicity-to-chaos to improve adaptability while minimizing violence frequency and episode severity. Control and anti-control interventions may work [36], involving periodic perturbations through personal contacts or use of resources.

Finally, focusing specifically on the relationship between husband-perpetrated violence and alcohol intake, we observed complex, multi-day patterns. While a variety of factors can lower the threshold for violence, alcohol may serve to promote violence through several mechanisms. Not only could alcohol abstinence increase an addicted husband's irritability, thus serving as a stressor that might provoke violence, but alcohol intake could also decrease sensitivity to his threshold for violence, making it more likely to be crossed. In addition, her alcohol intake may decrease her sense of risk and lead/keep her into high-risk situations. Thus, alcohol intake may serve to inhibit mindfulness in both spouses, and thereby facilitate violence. While intervention must again be tailored to the individual relationship, education about this alcohol–violence linkage may facilitate mindfulness. However, the presence of multi-day alcohol–violence attractors could enable a woman to intervene early in the sequence. For example, although she may have no control over her partner's behaviour, by refraining from consuming alcohol herself or responding to his verbal abuse, she may be able to reduce the subsequent days of violence.

In conclusion, the complex nature of IPV emphasizes the difficulty in intervention. It forces us to recognize the lack of predictability, the futility of global approaches and the need for tailored, perhaps timed, interventions. Knowing the dynamics of the violence and incorporating mindfulness may be important to the development of IPV interventions.

12.5 Future IPV Research

The lack of consistent theoretical support suggests a need for more research. The observation that all of the prior-week factors were significantly related to violent events testifies to their relevance to IPV research. Complex dynamics is an understudied, yet important, framework for understanding violence and its intervention. However, this raises the need for a simple way of identifying violence dynamics. Although daily assessments over extended periods of time using online or mobile phone apps would be possible, this would still require considerable time. The complex, non-linear patterns of actions taken by women emphasize the specific need to better understand how women in violent relationships make decisions concerning seeking help, taking legal action, and/or leaving the relationship. In addition, because prior research has included mainly men legally required to attend perpetrator groups and women in shelters, future studies should include women experiencing moderate–severe violence who remain in the relationship and violent men. Until these research needs are addressed, our understanding of IPV will continue to lag and our theoretical frameworks will not be grounded in evidence. Without such understanding and theoretical underpinning, interventions will remain rudimentary and largely ineffective.

Acknowledgements This study was funded by the National Science Foundation (#0826812). We wish to thank Stephanie Mitchell, Kelli Giacomini, Robert Mesec, and Wilson Pace at the University of Colorado, Department of Family Medicine for their invaluable assistance.

References

1. Weaver TL, Resnick H. Toward developing complex multivariate models for examining the intimate partner violence-physical health relationship. J Interpers Violence. 1994;19(11): 1342–9.
2. Lindhorst T, Tajima E. Reconceptualizing and operationalizing context in survey research on intimate partner violence. J Interpers Violence. 2008;23(3):362–88.

3. Whitchurch GG, Constantine LL. Systems theory. In: Boss PG, Doherty WJ, LaRossa R, Schumm WR, Steinmetz SK, editors. Sourcebook of family theories and methods. New York: Plenum Press; 1993.
4. Burge SK, Becho J, Ferrer RL, Wood RC, Talamantes M, Katerndahl DA. Safely examining complex dynamics of intimate partner violence. Fam Syst Health. 2014;32(3):259–70.
5. Umberson D, Anderson KL, Williams K, Chen MD. Relationship dynamics, emotion state, and domestic violence. J Marriage Fam. 2003;65(1):233–47.
6. Ristock JL. Exploring dynamics of abusive lesbian relationships. Am J Community Psychol. 2003;31(3–4):329–41.
7. Chang JC, Dado D, Ashton S, Hawker L, Cluss PA, Buranosky R, Scholle SH. Understanding behavior change for women experiencing intimate partner violence. Patient Educ Couns. 2006;62(3):330–9.
8. Walker LE. The battered woman. New York: Harper & Row; 1979.
9. Giles-Sims J. Wife battering: a systems theory approach. New York: Guilford Press; 1983.
10. Pence E, Paymar M. Education groups for men who batter. New York: Springer Publishing Company; 1993.
11. Katerndahl D, Burge S, Ferrer R, Becho J, Wood R. Complex dynamics in intimate partner violence. Prim Care Comp J Clin Psychiatry. 2010;12(4):e1–12.
12. Katerndahl DA, Burge SK, Ferrer RL, Becho J, Wood R. Dynamics of violence. J Eval Clin Pract. 2014;20(5):695–702.
13. Hotaling GR, Sugarman DB. An analysis of risk markers in husband to wife violence: the current state of knowledge. Violence Vict. 1986;1(2):101–24.
14. Schumacher JA, Feldbau-Kohn S, Slep AMS, Heyman RE. Risk factors for male-to-female partner physical abuse. Aggress Violent Behav. 2001;6(2–3):281–352.
15. Capaldi DM, Knoble NB, Shortt JW, Kim HK. Systematic review of risk factors for intimate partner violence. Partner Abuse. 2012;3(2):231–80.
16. Katerndahl DA, Burge SK, Ferrer RL, Becho J, Wood R. Webs of causation in violent relationships. J Eval Clin Pract. 2014;20(5):703–10.
17. Foran HM, O'Leary KD. Alcohol and intimate partner violence. Clin Psychology Rev. 2008;28(7):1222–34.
18. Graham K, Plant M, Plant M. Alcohol gender and partner aggression. Addict Res Theory. 2004;12(4):385–401.
19. O'Leary KD, Schumacher JA. Association between alcohol use and intimate partner violence. Addict Behav. 2003;28(9):1575–85.
20. Cunradi CB, Ames GM, Duke M. Relationship of alcohol problems to the risk of unidirectional and bidirectional intimate partner violence among a sample of blue-collar couples. Violence Vict. 2011;26(2):147–158.
21. Katerndahl D, Ferrer R, Burge S, Becho J, Wood R. Recurrent patterns of daily intimate partner violence and environment. Nonlinear Dynamics Psychol Life Sci. 2010;14(4):511–24.
22. Katerndahl DA, Burge SK, Ferrer RL, Becho J, Wood R. Multi-day recurrences of intimate partner violence and alcohol intake across dynamic patterns of violence. J Eval Clin Pract. 2014; 20(5):711–8.
23. Katerndahl D, Burge S, Ferrer R, Becho J, Wood R. Recurrent multi-day patterns of intimate partner violence and alcohol intake in violent relationships. Nonlinear Dynamics Psychol Life Sci. 2015;19(1):41–63.
24. United States Department of Justice. Violence between intimates. Bureau of Justice Statistics: Selected Findings (NCJ-149259). Washington, DC; 1994.
25. Koss MP, Woodruff WJ, Koss PG. Relation of criminal victimization to health perceptions among women medical patients. J Consult Clin Psychol. 1990;58(2):147–52.
26. Koss MP, Heslet L. Somatic consequences of violence against women. Arch Fam Med. 1992;1:53–9.
27. Helton AS, McFarlane J, Anderson ET. Battered and pregnant: a prevalence study. Am J Public Health. 1987;77(10):1337–9

28. Carmen EH, Rieker PP, Mills T. Victims of violence and psychiatric illness. Am J Psychiatry. 1984;141(3):378–83
29. Rosewater LB. Battered or schizophrenic? Psychological tests can't tell. In: Yllo K, Bograd M, editors. Feminist Perspectives on Wife Abuse. Newbury Park: Sage Publications; 1988
30. Bergman B, Brismar B. A 5-year followup study of 117 battered women. Am J Public Health. 1991;81:1486–9
31. Astin MC, Lawrence KJ, Foy DW. Posttraumatic stress disorder among battered women: risk and resiliency factors. Violence Vict. 1993;8(1):17–28
32. Katerndahl DA, Burge SK, Ferrer RL, Becho J, Wood R. Do violence dynamics matter? J Eval Clin Pract. 2014;20:719–27
33. Katerndahl D, Burge S, Ferrer R, Becho J, Wood R. Effects of violence nonlinearity upon outcomes in violent relationships. Presented at the annual conference of the Society for Chaos Theory in Psychology and Life Sciences. Baltimore; 2012
34. Heath RA. Complexity and mental health. In: Holt TA, editors. Complexity For Clinicians. Abingdon: Radcliffe Publishing; 2004
35. Guastello S. A crisis in replication, or a replication of a crisis? SCTPLS Newsl. 2014;21(3):9–16
36. Christini DJ, Stein KM, Markowitz SM, Mittal S, Slotwiner DJ, Scheiner MA, Iwai S, Lerman BB. Nonlinear-dynamical arrhythmia control in humans. Proc Natl Acad Sci. 2001;98:5827–32

Chapter 13
Depression: Not Just a Top–Down Phenomenon

Jeanette M. Bennett and Joachim P. Sturmberg

Depression can be characterized as a state of mental and physical lethargy in which sufferers report irritability, lack of focus, little or no motivation, lack of interest in previously enjoyed activities, sleep and appetite disturbances, hopelessness, and desired social isolation [1]. It is the second leading of cause of disability worldwide and #1 in the United States of America (USA). In the USA, there is an estimated $83 billion in economic burden due to depression yearly; 31 % direct medical costs, 7 % suicide-related mortality costs, and 62 % workplace associated costs [2]. While the economic costs to society are staggering, the personal cost of depression to the individual and on one's social network is dramatic.

If untreated, depression can result in substantial impairment in daily functioning. Depression, even at subclinical levels, can lead to substance use and/or abuse, failed or abusive relationships, or loss of employment. Children exposed to depressed parent(s) have an increased likelihood of developing depression [3]; thus, unmanaged depression has cross-generational consequences. Using a multi-disciplinary lens, depression is associated with behavioural, biological, psychological, environmental, and genetic risk factors.

J.M. Bennett (✉)
Ph.D. Program in Health Psychology, The University of North Carolina at Charlotte,Charlotte, NC, USA

Department of Psychology, The University of North Carolina at Charlotte, 9201 University City Blvd, Charlotte, NC, USA
e-mail: jeanette.bennett@uncc.edu; jbenne70@uncc.edu

J.P. Sturmberg
School of Medicine and Public Health, Faculty of Health and Medicine, The University of Newcastle, PO Box 3010, Wamberal, NSW 2260, Australia
e-mail: jp.sturmberg@gmail.com

J.P. Sturmberg (ed.), *The Value of Systems and Complexity Sciences for Healthcare*, DOI 10.1007/978-3-319-26221-5_13

13.1 Physiological Underpinnings

Depression can occur independently of psychological or physical disease; however, it frequently complicates chronic physical conditions such as cardiovascular disease, diabetes, and cancer [4, 5] and traumatic emotional experiences, suggesting that poor physical health, disrupted physiological functioning, and unresolved emotional experiences and depression may have shared underlying mechanisms.

13.1.1 Neurotransmitter Imbalance

In clinical practice, depression is commonly treated as a neurotransmitter imbalance where patients are prescribed medications to increase the presence of catecholamine neurotransmitters in the brain [6]. For example, monoamine oxidase inhibitors, tricyclic antidepressants, and a variety of reuptake inhibitors including selective serotonin, serotonin-norepinephrine, and dopamine-norepinephrine, are thought to elevate serotonin, dopamine, and norepinephrine in the brain and effectively reduce depressive symptoms.

Medications offer the perception of a quick or easy fix which many patients demand, especially in the USA. However, research pioneered by Dr. Irving Kirsch and colleagues [7] suggest that placebos are just as effective as antidepressants for patients with mild to moderate depression (85–90 % of the population) without their negative side effects.[1] In fact, the small benefit provided by antidepressants over the placebo may still have to do with the placebo effect; the negative side effects that patients had may have led to an increased perceived benefit because they knew they were on the drug and not placebo [8]. Due to the ineffectiveness of antidepressants over placebo, and their potential to result in an increase in suicidal/homicidal thought especially early in treatment (FDA-blackbox warning, its strongest available measure short of withdrawing a drug from the market), the neurotransmitter imbalance theory as the cause for depression is largely challenged and at times referred to as a myth [8].

---

[1] What Do These Findings Mean?
These findings suggest that, compared with placebo, the new-generation antidepressants do not produce clinically significant improvements in depression in patients who initially have mild to moderate depression, but show significant effects only in the most severely depressed patients. The findings also show that the effect for these patients seems to be due to decreased responsiveness to placebo, rather than increased responsiveness to medication. Given these results, the researchers conclude that there is little reason to prescribe new-generation antidepressant medications to any but the most severely depressed patients unless alternative treatments have been ineffective. In addition, the finding that extremely depressed patients are less responsive to placebo than less severely depressed patients but have similar responses to antidepressants is a potentially important insight into how patients with depression respond to antidepressants and placebos that should be investigated further (http://journals.plos.org/plosmedicine/article?id=10.1371/journal.pmed.0050045).

Yet, in the severe and/or treatment-resistant depression, lithium and atypical antipsychotics can augment antidepressant effects of selective serotonin reuptake inhibitors [9]. In addition, repetitive transcranial magnetic stimulation of the right prefrontal cortex and deep brain stimulation[2] of white matter tracts near subgenual cingulate gyrus or of the subcallosal cingulate gyrus and nucleus accumbens (independently) mitigate depressive symptoms [10–13]. Taken together, neurobiological dysfunction governs severe depression, but these tools only reliably and effectively help a small portion (10–15 %) of those dealing with depression. Thus, for the vast majority of patients with depression, the underlying mechanism(s) of their symptoms may not be brain abnormalities as observed in those with severe depression; time to go beyond the brain.

13.1.2 Disruption of Homoeostatic Hormones

According to the Diagnostic and Statistical Manual of Mental Disorders 5th edition [1], an individual can be labelled with major depressive disorder if for 2 weeks, they have felt five of the nine following symptoms nearly every day; depressed mood/irritable, decreased interest or pleasure, significant weight/appetite change, disordered sleep, change in activity, fatigue, guilt/worthlessness, decreased concentration, or suicidal thoughts. The major problem with this "definitional symptom" list is that the symptoms can be an exceedingly common occurrence even in healthy people, and they are often caused by a variety of different stimuli related to stress (e.g., diagnosis with a serious medical condition, grief, job loss, relocation, etc.).

The human body consists of a series of complex organ systems that interact and attempt to maintain homoeostasis via regulatory hormonal pathways. The neuroendocrine arousal systems are the most widely studied in connection with stress-related diseases, including sympathetic nervous system (SNS) activation leading to norepinephrine and epinephrine release, and stimulation of the hypothalamic–pituitary–adrenal (HPA) axis resulting in the secretion of hormones including corticotropin releasing hormone (CRH), adrenocorticotropin hormone (ACTH), and cortisol [14].

Cortisol mobilizes energy, catalyses protein breakdown, and stimulates the cardiovascular system to ensure oxygen and nutrient supplies to skeletal muscles and the brain. Cortisol naturally peaks 30–45 min post-waking, has an accelerated decline through lunch time, and then slowly declines the remaining time an individual remains awake. This diurnal rhythm varies significantly within a person as

[2]Andres Lozano: Parkinson's, depression and the switch that might turn them off. January 2013 at TEDxCaltech
http://www.ted.com/talks/andres_lozano_parkinson_s_depression_and_the_switch_that_might_turn_them_off?language=en.

between people, but does show dyadic synchrony [15]. Due to cortisol's energizing effects, it also is released in response to a stressor. Following the perception of a stressor, the body responds by activating the fight-or-flight SNS and the slower, but longer lasting, HPA axis that remains active until cortisol levels are elevated to provide negative feedback to the brain shutting down the system [16].

Dysregulation of the stress response systems has been associated with depression including, SNS hyperactivity, abnormal diurnal cortisol rhythmicity, and maladaptive cortisol response to stress [14]. For example, depressed individuals have an elevated cortisol response to waking and higher cortisol at bedtime compared to healthy controls [17]. In addition, those who are depressed exhibit an exaggerated hormonal (i.e., CRH and cortisol) response to stress compared to non-depressed controls [17]. This prolonged excessive cortisol production and exposure may be the result of neurons in the hippocampus and hypothalamus reducing their sensitivity to cortisol. However, the type of depression plays a critical role in the underlying biological profile [14, 17].

Melancholic depression,[3] or the 'typical' depressive profile, is connected to hyperactivity of stress response systems including elevated norepinephrine, CRH, and cortisol. Atypical depression presents behaviourally and hormonally as the antithesis of melancholic depression; the HPA axis is hypoactive [14] and may contribute to elevated systemic inflammation found in patients with this form of depression [17] (Fig. 13.1).

13.1.3 Excessive Inflammation

Proinflammatory cytokines can produce sickness behaviour or depression-like symptoms including low mood, fatigue, and psycho-motor slowing in otherwise healthy volunteers [18–20]. Thus, the relationship between depression and inflammation has been and continues to be examined thoroughly.

---

[3]History: 50 years ago, clinical depression was either endogenous (melancholic) or reactive (neurotic). Endogenous depression was a categorical biological condition with a low lifetime prevalence (1–2 %). By contrast, reactive depression was exogenous—induced by stressful events affecting a vulnerable personality. (Parker, G. Is depression overdiagnosed. BMJ, 2007;335:328.)
DSM-IV criteria:

- Anhedonia (the inability to find pleasure in positive things) and
- Lack of mood reactivity (i.e., mood does not improve in response to positive events) and at least three of the following:
- Depression that is subjectively different from grief or loss
- Severe weight loss or loss of appetite
- Psycho-motor agitation or retardation
- Early morning awakening
- Guilt that is excessive
- Worse mood in the morning

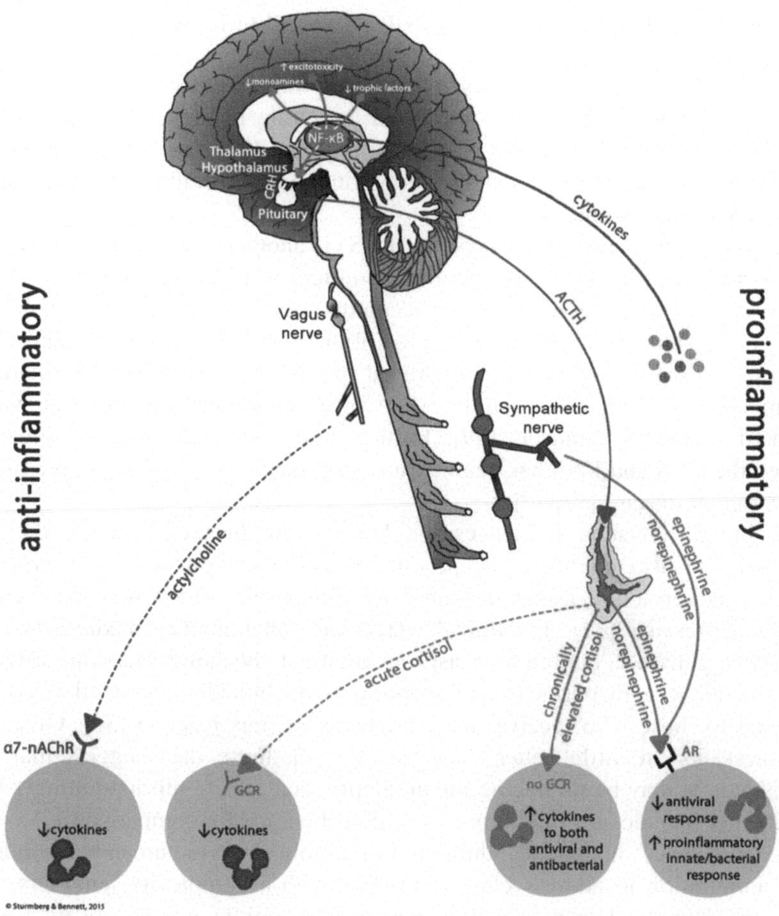

Fig. 13.1 Schematic review of communication between the arousal/stress systems and immune cells during acute and chronic arousal situations. Acute stimulation of the stress systems results in a short-lived innate/antibacterial immune response that diminishes following resolution of the stressor and activation of the parasympathetic nervous system (PNS) during recovery. Chronic stress leads to unregulated cytokine production due to protracted sympathetic activation, down-regulation of the glucocorticoid receptor, and persistent PNS withdrawal. Excessive inflammation stimulates the stress systems and induces sickness behaviour. Dashed lines indicate inhibitory or anti-inflammatory effects and solid lines indicate activating or proinflammatory effects. *α7-nAChR*: alpha 7-nicotinic acetylcholinergic receptor, *ACTH*: adrenocorticotropin hormone, *AR*: adrenergic receptor, *CRH*: corticotropin releasing hormone, *GCR*: glucocorticoid receptor

Both syndromal depression and self-reported depressive symptoms are associated with elevated proinflammatory mediators including IL-1, IL-6, and CRP [21–24]. In addition, as depressive symptoms worsen, inflammatory markers increase; supporting a dose response relationship between depression and systemic inflammation [24, 25]. One mechanism underlying this relationship may be related to the dysregulated stress reactivity observed in those who are depressed. For example, individuals who are depressed exhibit decreased sensitivity to glucocorticoids' anti-inflammatory effects as well as greater NF-κB activity compared to those who are non-depressed; resulting in higher IL-6 and TNF-α levels [26, 27]. Thus, excessive NF-κB activity and decreased responsiveness to glucocorticoids may enhance and sustain production of proinflammatory cytokines in individuals with depression.

The parasympathetic nervous system (PNS) is another potent anti-inflammatory mechanism. Acetylcholine, the neurotransmitter of PNS, can decrease NF-κB activity via nicotinic acetylcholinergic receptors; resulting in reduced immune cell activity [28]. Thus, the excessive activation of the SNS observed in individuals who are depressed occurs to chronic withdrawal of PNS activity, leading to increased inflammation. Indeed, PNS activity was lower in clinically depressed women compared to healthy controls [29]. Furthermore, the cardiovascular imbalance between the SNS and PNS has been a purported mechanism linking depression to cardiovascular disease [17, 30].

The immune system influences the brain. Cytokines can initiate the HPA axis; they can also modulate the production and metabolism of neurotransmitters such as serotonin, dopamine, and norepinephrine which may play critical roles in depression [31]. In clinical trials, anti-inflammatory medications such as cyclooxygenase-2 inhibitor or aspirin augment the antidepressants effect of serotonin and norepinephrine reuptake inhibitors in clinically depressed individuals compared to those who receive the antidepressant plus placebo [32]. Given that antidepressants are little better than placebo [8], these data suggest that anti-inflammatories may be producing the antidepressant effect—disappointingly these trials did not include anti-inflammatory or placebo arms for comparison.

Recent advances in understanding gut microbiota's role in human behaviour add more ammunition to address chronic disease with a complexity lens. Drs. John Cryan and Timothy Dinan [33] illustrate the connections among gut microbiota, excessive inflammation, and mood; resulting in the emergence of the microbiota–gut–brain axis theory. Although this field is in its infancy, the wide use of antibiotics and antibacterial solutions may also play a significant role in the brain and its behavioural output. Taken together, multi-system dysregulation underlies the heterogeneous experience of depression; suggesting that an understanding of complexity must be applied to successfully help patients with any form of depression.

13.1.4 Co-Morbidity

Chronic physical diseases and depression are often linked—either one is a risk factor for developing the other. Physiological dysregulation of one organ system (e.g., psychological stress, insulin resistance, hypertension, etc.) strains the rest of the body; resulting in adaptations that might not be "healthy" or positive, but allows the person to survive in this distressed state, as known as allostasis or allostatic load, a theory linking stress to disease popularized by Bruce McEwen, Ph.D. [34].

The acute medical response to a physical or emotional disorder is to treat the immediate system perturbation. For example, if a patient has hypercholesterolaemia, a statin is prescribed to reduce their cholesterol, the primary outcome. However, studies now show that statins have significant anti-inflammatory effects [35]; suggesting that statins may influence a reduction in depressive symptoms that are caused by elevated systemic inflammation. Thus, examining the untoward effects of pharmacological treatment for a chronic physical disease might enable us to understand all the mechanisms actually driving this two-way communication between the brain and the periphery.

13.2 Psychosocial Environment

Individuals do not function in isolation. Health psychologists view an individual through a biopsychosocial lens. To fully understand a person's health, one must consider biological (e.g., genetics, gender, etc.) and physical symptoms, but also psychological and social factors concurrent with physical health and major life events in the present or past. The first physical chronic disease that launched the field of health psychology was cardiovascular disease. Initially, Type A personality, defined as competitive, intense, anxious, and hostile, was linked to an increase incidence of cardiac events—eventually narrowed down to trait hostility [36]. This foreign concept that personality could impact physical health evolved into the examination of individual differences among health outcomes.

Today, when examining the factors that influence depression, health psychologists look at multiple levels including the individual, family, social networks (e.g., work, religious groups, etc.), ethnicity/culture, and even the national and global forces that might be at work. Perceived socioeconomic status (SES) reliably explains health disparities; in a dose-dependent manner, lower SES is associated with greater incidences of depression, cardiovascular disease, diabetes, and dysregulated immune and neuroendocrine function in comparison to higher SES [37–39]. In addition to and often confounded with SES, depression can be explained via individual differences in health behaviours such as tobacco smoking, poor diet, and reduced physical activity, and psychosocial factors like childhood trauma, social isolation, interpersonal stressors, violence, and workplace stress [17]. These factors can impact genomic expression including neurotransmitter production and release, neuroendocrine regulatory pathways, inter- and intracellular metabolism, and the immune system [40, 41]—bringing the depression and chronic disease relationship full circle.

Culturally, those diagnosed with depression are marginalized and often the victim of externalized and internalized stigma [42]. Society and close social networks will explicitly or implicitly tell depressed individuals that they just need to "pull it together" and "stop being so sensitive". However, stigma and ignorant understanding of depression increase psychological stress, thus activating the very biological systems underlying the development of depression. Given the strong link between depression and the dysregulated biological systems, we need to use this knowledge to change the general population's perception of mental health and diagnosis. If people understand that what drives depression also advances the development of chronic physical conditions like cardiovascular disease or Type 2 diabetes, then acceptance and early treatment of depression may help avoid the serious escalation that can occur if the brain's perception is left unchecked.

13.3 Predisposed to Depression?

Drs. Raison and Miller [43] suggest that our immune systems have developed a strong inflammatory bias aimed to enhance survival chances in constantly changing, thus challenging, physical environment. This predisposed inflammatory bias, once a positive adaptation, is no longer required in an environment where technological advances have minimized external microbial and existential threat levels. Our inability to counterbalance the proinflammatory bias now appears to be our undoing, as our brains are "unnecessarily" primed to detect and perceive stress and our immune cells efficiently produce inflammatory messengers—releasing a hormonal cascade that taxes multiple organ systems disrupting homeostasis.

Sedentary lifestyles, ample access to calorie-dense foods, and uncontrolled psychological stress amplify our predisposition towards excessive inflammation. For example, inflammation acutely rises to physical exercise; however, individuals who are physically active have lower systemic inflammation than those who are sedentary [16]. Many of the factors that influence inflammation are also independently related to depression [17]. To break the depression–inflammation cycle, there must be a point that interventions and preventative care can target. Luckily, people have control over many of the inflammatory inducing factors including physical inactivity, obesity, anxiety, diet, exercise, tobacco smoking, social support, and sleep. Thus, it is imperative that physicians and the medical/health field as a whole address behaviour because medications cannot solve our complex diseases.

13.4 Imperative for the Twenty-First Century

The transition from a solely symptom focused treatment plan to one that incorporates understanding of the psychosocial components of disease is essential—the most prevalent causes of morbidity and mortality have changed, thus adaptation is necessary. The incorporation of a health psychologist or other health behaviour specialists as an active member in a patient's care team will add the expertise necessary to improve patient outcomes. Similar to physicians, health psychologists and other behavioural health experts may specialize in a specific population such as psycho-oncology or they may work with a broad population much like a general practitioner educating people on stress management tools. Given the dysregulation of multiple systems, medication alone cannot solve our health problems over the long haul. Primary care must expand to include treatment associated with health behaviour change (i.e., exercise, diet, sleep, etc.) and stress management. Finally, increasing awareness to the imbricate causes of mental and physical health disorders may reduce/diminish stigma and increase pursuit of behavioural health services.

References

1. Association AP. The diagnostic and statistical manual of mental disorders, Fifth edition: DSM-5. Arlington, VA: American Psychiatric Association; 2013.
2. Greenberg PE, Kessler RC, Birnbaum HG, Leong SA, Lowe SW, Berglund PA. The economic burden of depression in the United States: how did it change between 1990 and 2000? J Clin Psychiatry. 2003;64(12):1465–75.
3. Biederman J, Faraone SV, Hirshfeld-Becker DR, Friedman D, Robin JA, Rosenbaum JF. Patterns of psychopathology and dysfunction in high-risk children of parents with panic disorder and major depression. Am J Psychiatry. 2001;158(1):49–57.
4. Musselman DL, Evans DL, Nemeroff CB. The relationship of depression to cardiovascular disease: epidemiology, biology, and treatment. Arch Gen Psychiatry. 1998;55(7):580–92.
5. Massie MJ. Prevalence of depression in patients with cancer. J Natl Cancer Inst Monogr. 2004;2004(32):57–71.
6. Advokat C, Comaty J, Julien R. A primer of drug action: a comprehensive guide to the actions, uses, and side effects of psychoactive drugs. 13th ed. New York, NY: Worth Publishers; 2014.
7. Kirsch I, Deacon BJ, Huedo-Medina TB, Scoboria A, Moore TJ, Johnson BT. Initial severity and antidepressant benefits: a meta-analysis of data submitted to the Food and Drug Administration. Plos Med. 2008;5(2):e45.
8. Kirsch I. The emperor's new drugs: medication and placebo in the treatment of depression. In: Benedetti F, Enck P, Frisaldi E, Schedlowski M, editors. Placebo. Handbook of experimental pharmacology, vol. 225. Berlin/Heidelberg: Springer; 2014. p. 291–303.
9. Edwards S, Hamilton V, Nherera L, Trevor N. Lithium or an atypical antipsychotic drug in the management of treatment-resistant depression: a systematic review and economic evaluation. Health Technol Assess. 2013;17:1–90.
10. Fitzgerald PB, Benitez J, de Castella A, Daskalakis ZJ, Brown TL, Kulkarni J. A randomized, controlled trial of sequential bilateral repetitive transcranial magnetic stimulation for treatment-resistant depression. Am J Psychiatry. 2006;163(1):88–94.
11. Lozano AM, Mayberg HS, Giacobbe P, Hamani C, Craddock RC, Kennedy SH. Subcallosal cingulate gyrus deep brain stimulation for treatment-resistant depression. Biol Psychiatry. 2008;64(6):461–7.
12. Mayberg HS, Lozano AM, Voon V, McNeely HE, Seminowicz D, Hamani C, et al. Deep brain stimulation for treatment-resistant depression. Neuron. 2005;45(5):651–60.
13. Bewernick BH, Hurlemann R, Matusch A, Kayser S, Grubert C, Hadrysiewicz B, et al. Nucleus accumbens deep brain stimulation decreases ratings of depression and anxiety in treatment-resistant depression. Biol Psychiatry. 2010;67(2):110–6.
14. Gold P, Chrousos G. Organization of the stress system and its dysregulation in melancholic and atypical depression: high vs low CRH/NE states. Mol Psychiatry. 2002;7(3):254–75.
15. Liu S, Rovine MJ, Cousino Klein L, Almeida DM. Synchrony of diurnal cortisol pattern in couples. J Fam Psychol. 2013;27(4):579.

16. Bennett JM, Gillie BL, Lindgren ME, Fagundes CP, Kiecolt-Glaser JK. Inflammation through a psychoneuroimmunological lens. In: Handbook of systems and complexity in health. New York: Springer; 2013. p. 279–99.
17. Penninx BW, Milaneschi Y, Lamers F, Vogelzangs N. Understanding the somatic consequences of depression: biological mechanisms and the role of depression symptom profile. BMC Med. 2013;11(1):129.
18. Reichenberg A, Yirmiya R, Schuld A, Kraus T, Haack M, Morag A, et al. Cytokine-associated emotional and cognitive disturbances in humans. Arch Gen Psychiatry. 2001;58(5):445–52.
19. Bryclon L, Harrison NA, Walker C, Steptoe A, Critchley HD. Peripheral inflammation is associated with altered substantia nigra activity and psychomotor slowing in humans. Biol Psychiatry. 2008;63(11):1022–9.
20. Dantzer R. Cytokine-induced sickness behavior: where do we stand? Brain Behav Immun. 2001;15(1):7–24.
21. Maes M, Meltzer HY, Bosmans E, Bergmans R, Vandoolaeghe E, Ranjan R, et al. Increased plasma-concentrations of interleukin-6, soluble interleukin-6, soluble interleukin-2 and transferrin receptor in major depression. J Affect Disord. 1995;34(4):301–9.
22. Bremmer MA, Beekman AT, Deeg DJ, Penninx BW, Dik MG, Hack CE, et al. Inflammatory markers in late-life depression: results from a population-based study. J Affect Disord. 2008;106(3):249–55.
23. Lesperance F, Frasure-Smith N, Theroux P, Irwin M. The association between major depression and levels of soluble intercellular adhesion molecule 1, interleukin-6, and C-reactive protein in patients with recent acute coronary syndromes. Am J Psychiatry. 2004;161(2):271–7.
24. Suarez EC, Krishnan RR, Lewis JG. The relation of severity of depressive symptoms to monocyte-associated proinflammatory cytokines and chemokines in apparently healthy men. Psychosom Med. 2003;65(3):362–8.
25. Glaser R, Robles TF, Sheridan J, Malarkey WB, Kiecolt-Glaser JK. Mild depressive symptoms are associated with amplified and prolonged inflammatory responses after influenza virus vaccination in older adults. Arch Gen Psychiatry. 2003;60(10):1009–14.
26. Pace TWW, Mletzko TC, Alagbe O, Musselman DL, Nemeroff CB, Miller AH, et al. Increased stress-induced inflammatory responses in male patients with major depression and increased early life stress. Am J Psychiatry. 2006;163(9):1630–2.
27. Miller GE, Rohleder N, Stetler C, Kirschbaum C. Clinical depression and regulation of the inflammatory response during acute stress. Psychosom Med. 2005;67(5):679–87.
28. Tracey KJ. Physiology and immunology of the cholinergic antiinflammatory pathway. J Clin Invest. 2007;117(2):289–96.
29. Holsen LM, Lee J-H, Spaeth SB, Ogden LA, Klibanski A, Whitfield-Gabrieli S, et al. Brain hypoactivation, autonomic nervous system dysregulation, and gonadal hormones in depression: a preliminary study. Neurosci Lett. 2012;514(1):57–61.
30. Abboud FM, Harwani SC, Chapleau MW. Autonomic neural regulation of the immune system: implications for hypertension and cardiovascular disease. Hypertension. 2012;59(4):755–62.
31. Anisman H, Merali Z, Hayley S. Neurotransmitter, peptide and cytokine processes in relation to depressive disorder: comorbidity between depression and neurodegenerative disorders. Prog Neurobiol. 2008;85(1):1–74.
32. Raison CL, Miller AH. Is depression an inflammatory disorder? Curr Psychiatry Rep. 2011;13(6):467–75.
33. Cryan JF, Dinan TG. Mind-altering microorganisms: the impact of the gut microbiota on brain and behaviour. Nat Rev Neurosci. 2012;13(10):701–12.
34. McEwen BS, Stellar E. Stress and the individual: mechanisms leading to disease. Arch Intern Med. 1993;153:2093–101.
35. Tousoulis D, Psarros C, Demosthenous M, Patel R, Antoniades C, Stefanadis C. Innate and adaptive inflammation as a therapeutic target in vascular disease: the emerging role of statins. J Am Coll Cardiol. 2014;63(23):2491–502.
36. Suls J, Wan CK. The relationship between trait hostility and cardiovascular reactivity: a quantitative review and analysis. Psychophysiology. 1993;30:615–26.

37. McEwen BS, Gianaros PJ. Central role of the brain in stress and adaptation: links to socioeconomic status, health, and disease. In: Adler NE, Stewart J, editors. Biology of disadvantage: socioeconomic status and health. Annals of the New York academy of sciences, vol. 1186. Malden: Wiley-Blackwell; 2010. p. 190–222.
38. Stowe RP, Peek MK, Perez NA, Yetman DL, Cutchin MP, Goodwin JS. Herpesvirus reactivation and socioeconomic position: a community-based study. J Epidemiol Community Health. 2010;64(8):666–71.
39. Adler N, Rehkopf D. US disparities in health: descriptions, causes, and mechanisms. Annu Rev Public Health. 2008;29(1):235.
40. Cole SW. Human Social Genomics. PLoS Genet. 2014;10(8):e1004601.
41. Picard M, Juster RP, McEwen BS. Mitochondrial allostatic load puts the 'gluc' back in glucocorticoids. Nat Rev Endocrinol. 2014;10(5):303–10.
42. Barney LJ, Griffiths KM, Jorm AF, Christensen H. Stigma about depression and its impact on help-seeking intentions. Aust N Z J Psychiatry. 2006;40(1):51–4.
43. Raison CL, Miller AH. The evolutionary significance of depression in pathogen host defense (PATHOS-D). Mol Psychiatry. 2013;18(1):15–37.

Part II
Complexity and the Healthcare System Ethics, Organisation Policy, and Politics

Many of the pragmatic issues facing healthcare professionals, managers and policy makers are inherently complex, and usually cannot be resolved with *simple and straightforward* approaches. We know that most of us somehow just muddle through and often *get away with it*, but this approach is also fraud with danger and has resulted in some spectacular failures. Are there better ways to handle these issues? The contributions in the 2nd part of the *Proceedings* wrestle with the complex in healthcare with a focus on ethics, evidence, healthcare and health systems organisation and the messy domains of policy and politics.

It is hoped that some readers will be encouraged to explore complexity science approach in their area of interest and present their insights at the next meeting in 2016.

Chapter 14
Ethical Complexities in Systems Healthcare: What Care and for Whom?

Kevin T. FitzGerald

"Medicine for the 21st century must broaden its understanding and appreciation of health and disease while extending its practices to embrace the dynamics of complex adaptive systems integral to much of the disease processes and for patients' adaptive responses to their disease and its management [1]". This statement by Joachim Sturmberg captures much of the impetus and goals of this volume, and yet at the same time raises several fundamental ethical issues. What is the basis of this obligation ("must") to broaden the understanding and appreciation of health and disease? Who will inform medicine as to this new understanding and how will this informing group be chosen? How much and what kind of input will patients have regarding the assessment of their adaptive responses to their diseases and disease management? These are some of the questions that arise from this move towards *Systems and Complexity Sciences in Healthcare*, and, hence, they are the focus of this chapter, which attempts to clarify and elucidate these questions as well as propose directions for how best to address these coming challenges.

One often used scheme for describing the goals of this movement towards Systems and Complexity Sciences in Healthcare is called P4 medicine [2]. The P4 refers to the four fundamental improvements that this type of medical advance is purported to bring. Medicine will become more *p*redictive, *p*reventive, *p*articipatory, and *p*ersonal. These four goals are fairly straightforward with regard to the terms that are used to describe the goals. By collecting, analysing and integrating large amounts of healthcare data from around the world, healthcare professionals will be able to: (1) become more focused on the individual *person*, including

K.T. FitzGerald (✉)
Center for Clinical Bioethics, Georgetown University, 37th and O Streets, N.W., Washington, DC 20057, USA

Department of Oncology, Georgetown University Medical Center, Georgetown University, Box 571200, Washington, DC 20057, USA
e-mail: Kevin.FitzGerald@georgetown.edu; ktf3@georgetown.edu

J.P. Sturmberg (ed.), *The Value of Systems and Complexity Sciences for Healthcare*, DOI 10.1007/978-3-319-26221-5_14

that individual's unique health situation (genetics, epigenetics, family history, environment, lifestyle, diet, etc.), (2) *predict* each individual's healthcare risks and, hence, (3) be better able to *prevent* the onset of illness and disease through (4) the increased *participation* of that individual in making lifestyle changes that will significantly reduce the risk of disease, as well as its duration and intensity. However, though the goals may appear fairly straightforward, there are imposing challenges to accomplishing these goals as many of the proponents of this new approach to healthcare acknowledge.

> The challenge in bringing P4 medicine to patients and consumers is twofold: first, inventing the strategies and technologies that will enable P4 medicine and second, dealing with the impact of P4 medicine on society - including key ethical, social, legal, regulatory, and economic issues. Managing the societal problems will pose the most significant challenges. Strategic partnerships of a variety of types will be necessary to bring P4 medicine to patients [2].

The fundamental ethical issues raised by *Systems and Complexity Sciences in Healthcare*, stated above, fall squarely into this area of most significant societal challenges identified by these P4 medicine proponents. How then to begin to more precisely delineate and address these challenges?

In September 2007, the U.S. Department of Health and Human Services (DHHS), under the direction of Secretary Michael Levitt, announced a major public policy shift in the direction of P4 medicine by rolling out its new program: "Personalized Health Care: Opportunities, Pathways, Resources [3]". This program was to use the latest developments in genomics, health information technology, and clinical evidence/delivery to provide, "The right treatment for the right person at the right time [3, p. 12]".

Why unquestionably a laudable goal for the program, one could rightly and readily ask the question, "but had not all patients come to healthcare professionals before this new program expecting that what they received would be the right treatment for them at that particular time?" If so, then why the fanfare regarding the delivery of what had always been a patient's expectation? The answer to that question was presented at the very beginning of this report, in Secretary Levitt's Forward, wherein he states that while healthcare has not been very good at delivering this standard of care up to that point in time the promise of Personalized Healthcare is that we can now achieve it [3, p. 1]. Secretary Levitt gave a clear example of why healthcare had failed in the past to deliver the precise care patients expect in the Forward to the second report released by DHHS in November, 2008, "Personalized Health Care: Pioneers, Partnerships, Progress."

> It remains common medical practice to follow a trial-and-error process for finding the right diagnosis, the right treatment and the right pharmaceutical dosage for each patient. Even our definitions of diseases remain rooted in 18th and 19th century terms. We refer to asthma, but there are many varieties of asthma. From a treatment perspective, they are actually different diseases, yet we are barely at the cusp of being able to identify them accurately and provide the right treatment at the first encounter. We refer to colon cancer, but this term is really a surrogate for five different known diseases. We refer to breast cancer, but in reality there is no such single disease - rather, cancers of different kinds may arise in breast tissue. From a treatment perspective, the notion of treating "breast cancer," as

> opposed to a cancer that arises from dysfunction in a particular gene-based mechanism, is already outdated. One result is that most women who are treated with dangerous, painful and expensive chemotherapies are receiving treatments that are actually ineffective for their condition [4, p. 9].

The conclusion, reached in both of these reports, is that in too many instances what healthcare is delivering is not in line with patients' expectations regarding either precision or efficacy. Patients are not receiving the right treatment at the right time, and much of this situation is due to a mismatch between the desires for what patients want healthcare to deliver, and what healthcare actually does deliver. While it is the hope and goal of *Personalized Healthcare*, by embracing complexity and systems medicine, to improve dramatically upon this problematic situation, one must also acknowledge that the early results of this new approach may well be to make it more evident just how far healthcare is from delivering the right treatment for the right person at the right time. Hence, the first crucial step to addressing the societal challenges of healthcare in the twenty-first century will be to communicate more clearly and comprehensively just how much recent research is indicating we do not yet understand about the complexities of health and disease, and how far we are from delivering timely, effective treatments for each and every patient.

One major obstacle to communicating clearly the actual state of global healthcare is the difficulty in integrating the apparently amazing biomedical advances that are reported almost daily in the mass media into the larger healthcare reality of too many patients receiving ineffective and even harmful treatments. Part of this difficulty resides in the fact that some of these amazing research results are actually challenging and changing traditional concepts of health and disease, as was stated in the 2008 DHHS report. One recent discovery provides a good example of how surprising, and challenging, new findings can be to our traditional concepts of health and disease.

For over 20 years a group of people from Ecuador, who were all related and who all suffered from a metabolic disorder called Laron Syndrome that significantly stunted their growth (most are less that 4′6″ tall), were carefully studied by researchers both to find the cause of their condition and a possible treatment. In 2011, the researchers published their findings which did uncover the genetic basis for their shared condition, along with some remarkable additional features of their "disease" which revealed how apparently simple genetic differences can result in extremely complex and confounding balances between health and disease in human beings. What the researchers discovered was that the same genetic change in the growth hormone receptor (GHR) gene (primarily a single DNA base change from an adenosine to a guanine) resulted not only in the clinically identified deleterious phenotypic differences among this group (e.g. short stature), but also an amazing reduction in the risk of acquiring either cancer or type 2 diabetes [5]. In fact, among the members of the group studied none exhibited type 2 diabetes or malignant tumours while the control group to whom they were compared showed a 5 % rate of type 2 diabetes and a 17 % rate for cancer. Considering the fact that both cancer and type 2 diabetes are recognized as two of the most significant diseases we face globally in the twenty-first century, one could easily ask the question as to which

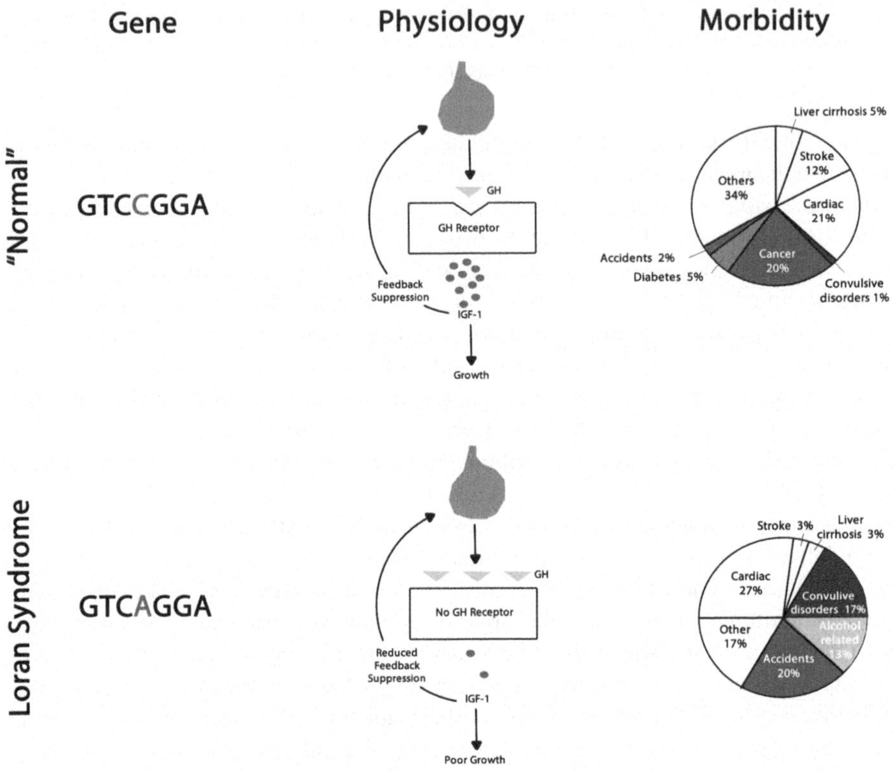

Fig. 14.1 "Normal"—who shall decide?

group in the study should have been identified as the "healthy" control group and which the "diseased" group being studied? This question about the health status of the people with Laron Syndrome is made all the more challenging when one notes that approximately one third of the deaths in this group are due to social/behavioural causes (accidents and alcohol) that are likely exacerbated by their difficulties fitting in with "normal" human society (Fig. 14.1). In a society geared towards their physiology, one could reasonably speculate that their average lifespan might in fact exceed that of their "healthy, normal" neighbors.

Obviously such a finding stimulated additional inquiry and research, which led the authors of a later review article to conclude, "Numerous studies suggest that GH deficiency early in life is beneficial for healthy ageing with likely mechanisms including reduction in cancer incidence and improved stress resistance ...." Yet at the same time, "GH is essential for growth, reproductive fitness, and providing optimal tissue function through life, but at the cost of increased neoplastic disease later in life. [6, p. 308]" This insight into the role of the GHR gene in human biology reveals a balance between health and disease that is built into the very genetic fabric of our human nature. This intrinsic balance will become an ever increasing challenge for healthcare as research uncovers more and more of the intricate biological complexity behind our experience of health and illness. Not only we will be challenged by such genetic complexity, but we will have to address the magnified complexity that will come from combining such complex genetic information with information regarding how our genetic make-up interacts with our environment, our diet, and our lifestyles.

All this complexity will be found in each and every individual patient, as we all have our own genetic and behavioural balances that shape our health and our disease risk. How then will healthcare institutions grounded in complex and systems biology balance the diverse, and potentially conflicting, healthcare needs of entire communities and populations?

For example, over the past several decades clinical experience has shown that if healthcare professionals take a group of patients who have all been diagnosed with the same disease, and treat them all with the same medication, the group will experience four different types of health outcomes: (1) some will benefit in the way that was intended by the healthcare professional treating them, and also have no significant undesired side effects; (2) some will benefit, but also experience significant harmful side effects; (3) some will not benefit, but will experience significant harms; and (4) some will not experience any real benefit or harm from the treatment [7]. The goal of Personalized Healthcare is, of course, to move all of these patients into the group where all benefit and experience no harmful side effects. This goal is to be accomplished by identifying the factors that cause certain individuals to sort to one group or another (these factors could be genetic, epigenetic, environmental, lifestyle, etc., or a combination of some or all of these). Then, drugs or other treatments can be selected that will be tailored to the specific factors of each patient to maximize the desired benefits and minimize the harms (Fig. 14.2).

Many ethical issues arise at this point, including concerns regarding the development and availability of all these precision drugs and treatments for all the different types of patients we will discover there are. How will all these precision treatments be developed, and how will they be made available/affordable to the relatively small groups of individuals who might need each precisely tailored treatment? Also, what if the best treatment is to effect a lifestyle change the patient is not eager, or even willing, to undertake? While these issues are indeed formidable, they are also part of our past and current healthcare terrain, and are being taken into account in the extensive discussions surrounding *Personalized Healthcare*. The hope is that each will be effectively addressed with a combination of advancing technology and prudent healthcare policy.

But what are we to do about the issues that will come as a surprise as a result of our complexity and systems biology research—such as the people in Ecuador with Laron Syndrome? How, and who, decides if it is better to be of abnormally short stature and experience the harms of growth hormone deficiencies in order to avoid the scourges of cancer and type 2 diabetes, or to be more like the vast majority of people who have "normal" levels of growth hormone activity and more average risks of cancer and type 2 diabetes? In response, one can always argue that ultimately

Fig. 14.2 The challenges for P4 medicine

research and technology will find a way around dilemmas such as these, but that response does not address the reality of this issue today or guarantee any solutions in the near, or even distant, future. Hence, do we treat children with Laron Syndrome to make them more like us; do we treat all other children to inhibit their growth hormone pathways to address the increasing health problems of cancer and type 2 diabetes, or do we just leave it to individuals to sort out what disease risks they want to run and which they wish to reduce or avoid? Is this last option really healthcare? Is it really the goal of *Personalized Healthcare*, employing the techniques and technology of complexity and systems biology, just to create more and more options for patients to choose from with regard to what diseases they are willing to risk getting and which they wish to try to avoid? If the goal is to maximize everyone's health, how will that health be defined and delineated, and by whom? One might respond to this line of questioning by arguing that the Laron Syndrome case is an extreme one, and that it is not representative of the healthcare challenges the vast majority of people will face. Such a response misses the point of this chapter. Though indeed an extreme example, the Laron Syndrome case does reveal the tensions that can arise when healthcare decisions regarding different physiological states are mixed in with strong personal or cultural values or goals. This tension is already a part of our healthcare landscape in the discussion and debates around a variety of conditions which involve genetic differences that result in significant phenotypic differences, e.g. the issue of deafness and the Deaf community.

While many people may identify deafness as a disease, to be avoided, treated, and/or cured, this physiological condition has been recognized by the United Nations as the defining feature of a culture that deserves protection and support [8]. In addition, some members of the Deaf community argue that attempts to treat and cure this condition, such as cochlear implants, are akin to genocide as they seek to end the existence of the community itself [9]. While the justifications and ramifications of this claim continue to generate debate and discussion [9], the underlying tension of defining such physiological differences as diseases or instances of human diversity is much more broadly applicable. Add to that tension the increasing biological evidence that every human being is a genomic mix of both "good" and "bad" traits, and one can begin to see how cases such as Laron Syndrome, where the balance of good and bad traits is relatively dramatic, help reveal the challenges ahead as we attempt to integrate the complexities of systems biology into our healthcare decision-making processes.

How, then, will the goals of Systems and Complexity Sciences in Healthcare be defined, and by whom? If this new approach to medicine is to truly benefit everyone, then does it not make sense that everyone needs to have the opportunity to contribute to the delineation and definition of this new understanding of health and disease, especially since everyone has some genetic features that are considered to be health risks? How else will those working to bring about this change of direction in healthcare know which way to go with all the new and surprising information that will be generated by the research supporting this new understanding?

This need for broad public engagement (not merely public education) in order to develop successfully this new approach to healthcare has already been recognized by individual scholars, community groups, and national committees. Again in the U.S. DHHS, the Secretary's Advisory Committee for Genetics, Health and Society (SACGHS) identified this need for public engagement in several of its recommendations in its March 2007 report: "Policy Issues Associated with Undertaking a New Large U.S. Population Cohort Study of Genes, Environment, and Disease [10]".

In chapter Three of this report, "Policy Issues Associated with a New Large Population Study of Genes, Environment, and Common Diseases", the Committee articulated "a single overarching policy recommendation" that should guide the actions of the DHHS Secretary in implementing the broad population studies that will be a key part of the new approach to healthcare:

> As part of the process for determining whether to undertake such a large-scale research project, the HHS Secretary should initiate a thorough consideration of the full range of policy issues outlined in this report. The HHS Secretary should consult and engage the full range of potential partners for such a project during this decisionmaking process, including the public at large, the full scientific community, a wide spectrum of Government agencies and policymakers, and the private sector [10, p. 23].

What the Committee was emphasizing with this overarching recommendation was the recognition that none of the other many recommendations in the report would be useful or successful if this broad public engagement were not undertaken, for both public guidance and public commitment would be necessary for this new approach to healthcare to achieve its purported goods and goals.

This insight into the need for extensive public engagement has been spreading across the genomic medicine landscape. On the website of the *National Human Genome Research Institute* at the *National Institutes of Health* there are statements recognizing the necessity of both public participation and public engagement in clinical research if healthcare is to advance in good clinical decision-making and good research methodology, as well as in the development of new technologies [11].

Proponents of *Systems and Complexity Sciences in Healthcare* will do well to join this movement to integrate public engagement into the development of this new approach to medicine. The questions and concerns raised at the beginning of, and throughout, this chapter can only be addressed well if the public is thoroughly engaged in all aspects of the development and expansion of *Systems and Complexity Healthcare*. Answers to the issues of who is healthy and what is health are as dependent on social and cultural values and goods as they are on biology and technology. Decisions determining how new technologies and treatments will be applied, and to whom, will require a strong sense of public understanding and goals in addition to the traditional requirement of well-informed consents, because the healthcare of the twenty-first century will contextualize individual patient decisions within the larger healthcare needs and goals of society—as is already the case in the public health arena with regard to issues such as limiting public smoking and the development of public programs encouraging healthier behaviours.

If *Systems and Complexity Sciences in Healthcare* does indeed bring more surprises and challenges such as the case of Laron Syndrome, then an engaged and invested public will be both the best defence against abuse of any new knowledge or technology, and the best insurance of broad participation in programs that will help everyone move towards the right treatments at the right time. Though such an extensive public engagement will itself be challenging, one might justifiably presume that proponents of *Systems and Complexity Sciences* should not be daunted by the complexities of a system of broad and continual public involvement in the development of healthcare that truly brings healing and care to each and all.

References

1. http://complexityandhealth.georgetown.edu/agenda/. Accessed 9 Feb 2015. 2014.
2. Price ND, Edelman LB, Lee I, Yoo H, Hwang D, Carlson G, Galas DJ, Heath JR, Hood L. Systems biology and systems medicine, Chap. 5. In: Ginsburg G, Willard H, editors. Genomic and personalized medicine: from principles to practice. 2nd ed, vol.1. Waltham, MA: Academic; 2013. pp. 60–72. doi:10.1016/B978-0-12-382227-7.00005-7
3. United States Department of Health and Human Services Report. Personalized health care: opportunities, pathways, resources. 2007. http://www.genome.gov/Pages/Policy/PersonalizedMedicine/DHHSReportPersonalizedHealth.pdf. Accessed 9 Feb 2015.
4. United States Department of Health and Human Services Report. Personalized health care: pioneers, partnerships, progress. 2008. https://www3.marshfieldclinic.org/proxy///mcrf-visitors-wgi-phcreport.1.pdf. Accessed 9 Feb 2015.
5. Guevara-Aguirre J, Balasubramanian P, Guevara-Aguirre M, Wei M, Madia F, Cheng CW, Hwang D, Martin-Montalvo A, Saavedra J, Ingles S, de Cabo R, Cohen P, Longo VD. Growth hormone receptor deficiency is associated with a major reduction in pro-aging signaling, cancer, and diabetes in humans . Sci Transl Med. 2011;3(70):70ra13. doi:10.1126/scitranslmed.3001845.
6. Perry JK, Liu DX, Wu ZS, Zhu T, Lobie PE. Growth hormone and cancer: an update on progress. Curr Opin Endocrinol Diabetes and Obes. 2013;20(4):307–13. doi:10.1097/MED.0b013e328363183a.
7. Piquette-Miller M, Grant DM. The art and science of personalized medicine. Clin Pharmacol Ther. 2007;81(3):311–5. doi:10.1038/sj.clpt.6100130.
8. United Nations Convention of the Rights of Persons with Disabilities. http://www.un.org/disabilities/convention/conventionfull.shtml. Accessed 9 Feb 2015. 2006.

9. Sparrow R. Defending deaf culture: the case of cochlear implants. J Political Philos. 2005;13(2):135–52. doi:10.1111/j.1467-9760.2005.00217.x.
10. United States Department of Health and Human Services Report. Policy issues associated with undertaking a new large U.S. population cohort study of genes, environment, and disease. March 2007. http://osp.od.nih.gov/sites/default/files/SACGHS_LPS_report.pdf. Accessed 9 Feb 2015.
11. www.genome.gov/27530874, last reviewed March 2012, and last accessed December 2015.

Chapter 15
Systematic Reviews: Beyond Cochrane to Complexity

Frances Griffiths and Jane Goudge

This paper considers the systematic review of empirical research literature as a research method in itself, and how it can be used for understanding our complex world. We consider two different approaches to such reviews used within the health domain. First we consider the contribution of Cochrane reviews to developing new knowledge and their limitation in the face of our complex world, considering particularly the issue of evaluating complex health interventions. We then outline the realist approach to literature reviews identifying the commonalities and differences with the Cochrane approach and how they can be complimentary. Finally we consider the role of realist reviews undertaken comparatively across very different contexts, such as low and high income countries and how this can suggest areas where research is likely to lead to new knowledge.

15.1 Cochrane Reviews for Evaluating Health Interventions

Systematic reviews that follow the Cochrane process aim to evaluate health interventions. The Cochrane Collaboration provides a rigorous and transparent process for such reviews, and has established high standards for the process of systematic reviewing [1]. This is of importance for informing clinical practice and

F. Griffiths (✉)
Social Science and Systems in Health Research Unit, Division of Health Sciences, Warwick Medical School, University of Warwick, Gibbet Hill Road, Coventry CV4 7AL, UK
e-mail: F.E.Griffiths@warwick.ac.uk

J. Goudge
Centre for Health Policy, School of Public Health, University of the Witwatersrand, 1 Jan Smuts Avenue, Johannesburg, Braamfontein 2000, South Africa
e-mail: jane.goudge@wits.ac.za

J.P. Sturmberg (ed.), *The Value of Systems and Complexity Sciences for Healthcare*, DOI 10.1007/978-3-319-26221-5_15

health care provision decisions. As the volume of research evidence has increased research teams are also undertaking such rigorous reviews before proposing new research. Cochrane reviews are well known in the health domain. However, it is important to remember that other disciplines also have rigorous approaches to the use of published evidence as research data, all be it using different approaches. In the discipline of history, great care is taken to understand the provenance and audience of published work. Sociologists will often start with an established theory and use evidence to develop it further, and use the process of publishing and receiving critique to add rigour to the research. Research that is rigorous has a clear methodology that reflects a particular epistemology and ontology. It has a clear aim and a pre-specified research question. The research question will include an indication of the boundary of its reach, for example, limiting the research to people with stage 1 breast cancer; to adults with hypertension in sub-Saharan Africa; or to obese adults in high income countries. Rigorous research includes processes for checking that all relevant data has been included and for checking the quality of that data. It can be argued that rigorous research is also repeatable by others leading to similar results, particularly experimental research. However, as our bio-social world is continually changing any repeated research and its context will be somewhat different to the original and so will not actually be the same. We discuss further this issue of change over time and between contexts in the next section where we consider Cochrane reviews of complex interventions.

15.2 Cochrane Reviews and Complex Interventions

Many health care interventions are considered complex interventions and they are commonly evaluated within a randomised controlled trial—an experimental study design [2]. A complex intervention can be described as having a number of component parts, there is interaction between at least some of the component parts and there is interaction with the context [3]. The context includes the people, the place and the politics including relationships, organisational structures and economic resources. The intervention, intervention recipients and context change over time [4]. An example of such a complex intervention is an intervention for back pain based on cognitive behavioural approaches delivered to patients in a group over six weekly sessions. The intervention includes teaching about exercise, pacing, fear avoidance and pain management [5]. Another example is an intervention being evaluated in rural South Africa, designed to improve medication compliance among those with hypertension with the aim of improving the blood pressure control of these people. Currently only 9 % of people with hypertension have their blood pressure under control in this locality. The intervention includes nurse and community health worker training as well as additional community health worker resource.

There is concern even among Cochrane reviewers about how to systematically review studies that evaluate complex interventions [6]. The concern is that for a Cochrane review the interventions included in the review need to be, as far as possible, the same. However, the interaction within a complex intervention and interaction with the context result in changes to the intervention, so even if the intention is for an intervention to be the same, in different evaluations done at different times and in different places, it will be different. A discussion by Shepperd et al. [6] suggests two different approaches to this conundrum. The first is to attempt a full description of the complex interventions drawing on as much supplementary evidence as possible so the reviewers can be clear the extent of difference between interventions. There is, however, an epistemological problem with this. If something is complex, a full description of it will be as complex as the thing itself. This issue was well rehearsed by the early twentieth century sociologist Gabriel Tarde [7] and has been reiterated by more recent philosophers such as Paul Cilliers [8]. We have to abstract, that is, leave aside detail to try to get to the key aspects of the intervention. This is the second approach suggested by Shepperd et al. [6], that is, to clarify the key components of the complex intervention, i.e. how is the intervention meant to work. We can then include in the review interventions that have similar key components. An example of this approach is a review of the use of computer reminders for physicians. It was specified that the computer reminder had to be directly related to the specific patient based on their clinical notes (for example, reminding the physician the patient was due a blood test or needed their blood pressure checked as the previous measurement was high) and visible to the physician at the same time as they encountered the patient so the physician had the possibility of responding to the reminder while with the patient [9].

The Cochrane approach to reviewing evaluations of complex interventions where the key components are similar, can give us an indication as to whether these interventions tend to work, accepting that in some contexts they may not work at all and in others they may work well. As a result, the overall mean effect tends to be small. However, this can be very useful for informing policy about the provision of interventions, particularly for a country such as the UK where we have one giant health care organisation which is relatively homogeneous when compared with health care systems in other countries. If an intervention tends to work in the UK, then it is probably worth the UK NHS investing resource to provide it. In a country such as South Africa, with very different health care systems for different sectors of the population, a review is likely to inform only certain sectors of the health care system. In the next section we consider a different approach to reviewing research evidence that addresses this issue of transferability of evidence review results to different contexts.

15.3 Complex Interventions and Realist Reviews

The evaluation of complex interventions can be undertaken using a very different approach, the realist approach [10–13]. This recognises the complexity of interventions—the interaction of different components within the intervention, the interaction with the context and that the intervention and context will change over time. Recognising this, a realist review sets out to find out what works for whom, where, when and why? At the start of a realist review the review team considers how an intervention is meant to work. So, for example, the electronic reminders for physicians described above were meant to work by providing a timely reminder, that is, when there is opportunity for action, prompting the physician to read the reminder and decide whether or not to take the opportunity for action. There is interaction between what is provided to the physician as a resource (the reminder) and the reasoning and decision making of the physician [14]. The next step in the review is to look for evidence to support the idea that this mechanism of action will work in the relevant context. This evidence need not be within the health literature. For evidence that timely reminders work the review team might go to psychology or organisation science. If there is evidence suggesting that the intervention (the timely reminders) will lead to the required outcome (physician undertakes the action), then we consider, in what contexts this mechanism will work. Again this might not be evidence from the health literature but from research on work practices. For example, fatigue affects performance so timely reminders may not work at the end of a working day. Feeling overwhelmed with work affects performance so timely reminders may not work if there are too many of them or there are other work priorities. This then provides the evidence about how the context affects whether the intervention (the timely reminders) will result in the outcome (physician takes action). In different contexts the mechanism of action of the intervention will be different as the interaction between the intervention and the individual physician is different.

When undertaking a realist review it is necessary to know about the contexts in which the intervention is used. Sufficient data about the context may be available in published literature and policy documents. However, in some situations it is necessary to go and find out about specific contexts by talking to people who know them through key informant interviews, and direct observation of the context. This allows us to identify what it is about the context that might enable or prevent the intervention bringing about the desired outcome and then where necessary backing this up with evidence from the literature. Understanding the theories underpinning the intervention and the interaction between the intervention and the person engaging with the intervention helps focus this data collection on aspects of the context most likely to impact on whether or not the intervention has its desired outcome.

The realist review seems very different from a Cochrane review of complex interventions but there are commonalities. Both recognise complexity. Both include the identification of what the intervention is intended to do. Both recognise the importance of context. Rigour is equally important in both. In the next section we consider the issue of context and transferability for both Cochrane and realist reviews.

15.4 Context and Transferability

Our aim with research is to produce new knowledge, so we understand more about how the world functions than we did before undertaking the research. The world is constantly changing and the tools we have to study the world are constantly changing, and we continue with research to understand the world as it changes. However, if it is clear how some aspect of the world functions, then we do not have to undertake research—although sometimes we do so when someone in power demands further evidence before being prepared to change. We are alerted to the need for research when we notice a difference or change and the processes underlying this difference or change are not obvious. We then undertake research to try to clarify what is happening but is not obvious. By comparing lots of instances of similar things happening, we develop theory—a conceptualisation of what seem to be a recurring pattern of how things work in the world.

Although the world is constantly changing there are many ways in which the world works that remain very similar over time—and are similar across different contexts—at least over recent historical time and known human contexts. An example is the social phenomenon of stigma [15]—this manifests itself in different ways in different contexts and has different outcomes, but it is recognisably the same.

As discussed earlier, when undertaking a Cochrane review, the reach of the review is pre-defined, usually as part of the research question and additionally in the inclusion and exclusion criteria. Sometimes the reach of the review is implicit—for example, the review of computer physician reminders discussed earlier did not have to specify that low income countries were excluded as there were no studies from low income countries as physicians and computerised medical records are rare in this setting. Specifying the reach of the review limits the variation in context in which the randomised controlled trials included in the review have taken place. When a policy maker or clinician wants to use the results of a Cochrane review, they have to consider whether the trials included in the review were undertaken in populations and contexts sufficiently similar to their health care context for the results to be applicable. For complex interventions it is unlikely that they will have a similar effect internationally, across very different health care systems. Thus for very different contexts such as low and high income countries, different Cochrane reviews are needed.

Complex interventions are considered by a Cochrane reviewer to be made up of components in contrast to the realist reviewer's concern with mechanisms of action of the intervention. With well-designed interventions, each component will have been developed based on theory about how it should work but in the process of becoming a component it takes on aspects of its context. For example, in the back pain intervention described earlier, psychological theory about fear avoidance was used but the component was teaching the group about how to tackle fear that led them to avoid movement. In a different context, the theory might be developed into a different component. For example, in a rural area with poor public transport the intervention might be delivered via telephone to individuals in their homes. Embedded within the components of complex interventions are theory or assumptions about how the person engaging with the intervention will interact with it. As discussed earlier, the intervention and the interaction between intervention and user is what constitutes the mechanism of action and is what a realist review seeks to understand. There are mechanisms that are likely to be similar across different contexts, for example, the social processes of stigma interacting with treatments for certain health conditions, where the latter varies by context. So across different contexts the outcome from provision of treatment for a health condition will vary depending on the role of stigma in the interaction between treatment and treatment recipient. In a realist review this influence of context on mechanism and outcome is clarified.

15.5 The Complementarity of Cochrane Reviews and Realist Reviews

We have outlined above the role of Cochrane reviews in synthesising evidence of outcome from experimental evaluations of somewhat similar interventions in somewhat similar contexts and populations. In contrast a realist review synthesises evidence on how particular mechanisms in particular contexts lead to outcome. Both are interested in outcome. Both draw on theory but in different ways. A Cochrane review includes evidence from evaluations of interventions where often the intervention has been developed from theory. A realist review draws directly on theory to identify the types of evidence needed for the review. These similarities are illustrated in Fig. 15.1. Realist reviews have other roles in relation to Cochrane reviews. A realist review can suggest whether an RCT is needed in a specific context. There are contexts where it is obvious that something will not work so an RCT is not needed—for example, the use of an intervention requiring stable electricity supply in a context where this is not available. There are contexts where it is obvious that something will work and an RCT is not needed—such as tele-consultations for follow-up appointments for chronic illness in rural Scotland, where the losses from using tele-consultations are outweighed by gains from not having to travel large distances. Realist reviews can guide Cochrane reviewers as to which interventions have similar mechanisms of action, remembering that there may be a number of mechanisms of action at play for any one intervention. It can also guide Cochrane reviews about the appropriate reach of a review. For example, there may be theory and empirical evidence that an intervention is unlikely to work in a particular age group or population group (see Fig. 15.1).

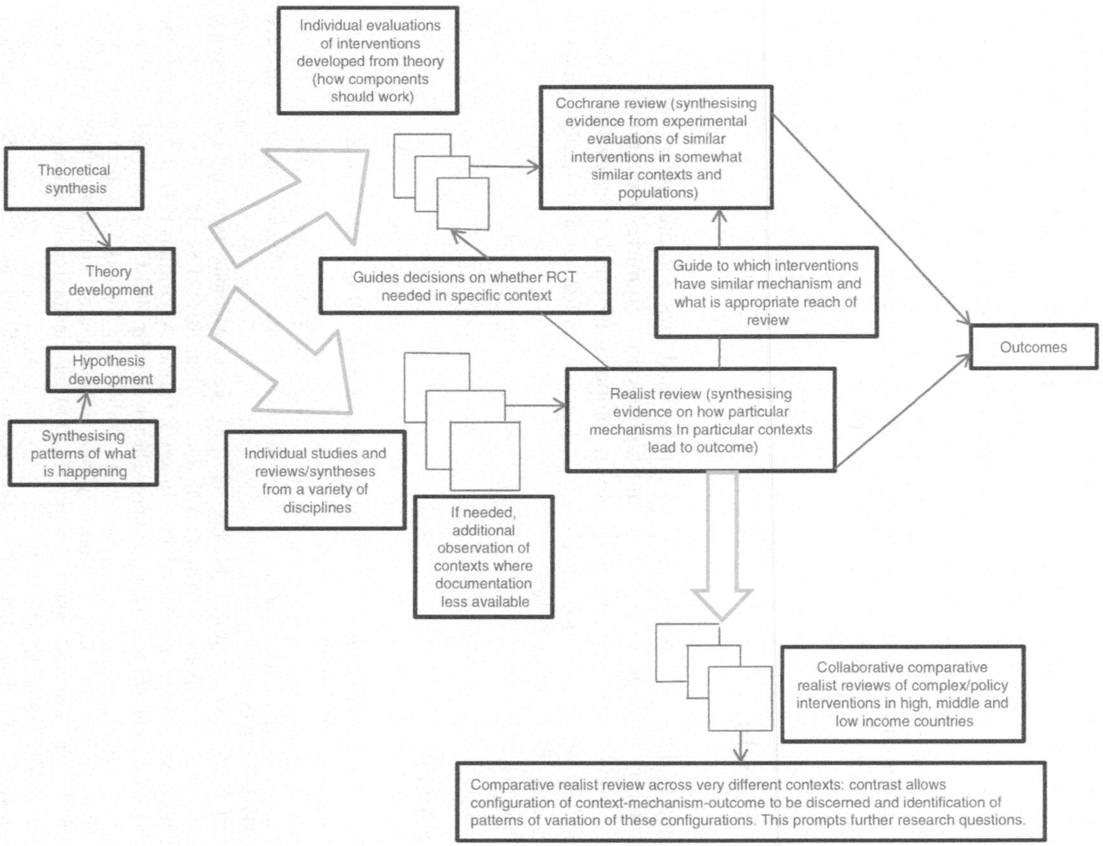

Fig. 15.1 Complementarity of Cochrane reviews and realist reviews and the role of international comparison between high, middle and low income countries

15.6 International Comparison and Realist Review

Contexts can vary hugely, such as the contrast between the context of health care delivery in low, middle and high income countries. As we have discussed the mechanism of action of an intervention will be different depending on the context, resulting in different outcomes. Configurations of context–mechanism–outcome can be difficult to discern where an intervention is truly complex [14]. However, comparison of realist reviews from very different contexts could provide sufficient contrast to allow us to discern these more easily. This would allow us to then identify patterns of variation in the configurations of context–mechanism–outcome. Sometimes such variation will have an obvious cause such as poor roads leading to late presentation of obstetric emergencies. Sometimes the variation will not be so obvious and require further research to understand.

15.7 Conclusion

Cochrane reviews and realist reviews can be used in a complimentary ways. For very different settings such as low and high income countries Cochrane reviews have to be undertaken separately. However, comparison of realist reviews from these different settings has the potential to suggest new areas for research likely to lead to the creation of new knowledge.

References

1. The Cochrane Collaboration. The Cochrane Collaboration; 2014. Available from: http://www.cochrane.org/. 20 Oct 2014
2. Craig P, Dieppe P, Macintyre S, Michie S, Nazareth I, Petticrew M. Developing and evaluating complex interventions: the new Medical Research Council guidance. Br Med J. 2008;337:a1655
3. Bonell C, Fletcher A, Morton M, Lorenc T, Moore L. Methods don't make assumptions, researchers do: a response to Marchal et al. Soc Sci Med. 2013;94:81–2
4. Campbell NC, Murray E, Darbyshire J, Emery J, Farmer A, Griffiths F, et al. Designing and evaluating complex interventions to improve health care. Br Med J. 2007;334(7591):455–9
5. Lamb S, Lall R, Hansen Z, Castelnuovo E, Withers EJ, Nichols V, et al. A multicentred randomised controlled trial of a primary care-based cognitive behavioural programme for low back pain. The Back Skills Training (BeST) trial. Health Technol Assess (Winchester, England). 2010;14(41):1–253, iii–iv
6. Shepperd S, Lewin S, Straus S, Clarke M, Eccles MP, et al. Can We Systematically Review Studies That Evaluate Complex Interventions? PLoS Med. 2009;6(8):e1000086. doi: 10.1371/journal.pmed.1000086
7. Barry A, Thrift N. Gabriel Tarde: imitation, invention and economy. Econ Soc. 2007;36(4):509–25
8. Cilliers P. Complexity and postmodernism. New York: Routledge; 1998

9. Holt T, Thorogood M, Griffiths F. Changing clinical practice through patient specific reminders available at the time of the clinical encounter: systematic review and meta-analysis. J Gen Intern Med. 2012;27(8):974–84
10. Rycroft-Malone J, McCormack B, Hutchinson A, DeCorby K, Bucknall T, Kent B, et al. Realist synthesis: illustrating the method for implementation research. Implement Sci. 2012;7(1):33
11. Pawson R, Tilley N. Realistic evaluation. London: Sage; 1997
12. Pawson R, Greenhalgh T, Harvey G, Walshe K. Realist review: a new method of systematic review designed for complex policy interventions. J Health Serv Res Policy. 2005;1:21–34
13. Pawson R. The science of evaluation: a realist manifesto. London: Sage; 2013
14. Marchal B, Westhorp G, Wong G, Van Belle S, Greenhalgh T, Kegels G, et al. Realist RCTs of complex interventions—an oxymoron. Soc Sci Med. 2013;94:124–8
15. Goffman E. Stigma: notes on the management of spoiled identity. New York: Simon and Schuster; 1963

Chapter 16
Agent-Based Modelling of Organizational Performance

Russell S. Gonnering and David Logan

All models are wrong ... but some are useful. George E.P. Box, 1976 [1]

Improving performance is important in any organization, particularly in healthcare organizations. While most efforts are directed at altering proxy process indicators of "quality", improving such proxy indicators may have little effect on improving outcomes [2]. Process tools may help deal with "complicated" process-driven problems. However, rather than responding to reductionist expert knowledge, "complex" problems exhibit emergent order where agents and the system co-evolve and starting point and path dependency take on added importance [3–5]. In a Complex Adaptive System (CAS), agent-based models allow investigation into the emergent order and co-evolution of agents and systems that are key to understanding the movement of such a system over time [6].

If the tool to investigate a CAS in agent-based modelling, what are the principal parameters to study when investigating performance? Both Csikszentmihaly [7] and Sawyer [8] described the emergent property of creativity in human group dynamics as essential to the increase in performance [9]. Logan and co-workers conducted a 10-year study into organizations and found that "Organizational Culture" was the primary determinant of performance. While the term "Organizational Culture" has been described with many meanings, they used "the pattern of adaptation based upon shared history, values, purpose and future". Their research showed a linear

R.S. Gonnering (✉)
Medical College of Wisconsin, 1780 San Fernando Drive, Elm Grove, WI 53122, USA
e-mail: rsgonnering1@me.com

D. Logan
Marshall School of Business, The University of Southern California,
3670 Trousdale Parkway, Los Angeles, CA 90089, USA

CultureSync, 2211 Corinth Avenue, Suite 310, Los Angeles, CA 90064, USA
e-mail: logan@culturesync.net; david.logan@marshall.usc.edu

J.P. Sturmberg (ed.), *The Value of Systems and Complexity Sciences for Healthcare*, DOI 10.1007/978-3-319-26221-5_16

advance of an organization along five stages of culture, with a non-linear increase in performance at each transition. Most organizations, and virtually all healthcare organizations in their study, were locked at an intermediate Stage 3 culture where the tag-line was "I'm great . . . and by the way, you aren't".

16.1 Prior Investigations

To investigate the utility of using agent-based models to study performance, we first developed a NetLogo^{TM}[10] model to show that culture spread as a meme through an organization [11]. In this model, a hypothetical organization consisting of 2 executives, 4 managers and 25 workers exchanges "culture" (positively or negatively, depending upon their relative differences in individual culture and organizational hierarchy) as they moved through time and space. We confirmed that Organizational Culture did indeed spread as a meme and that its spread was influenced by starting point, internal and external pressures and path-dependent elements.

We then amplified upon that model to investigate the interrelationships of Organizational Culture, Organizational Values, Intellectual Capital and Organizational Performance [12]. We found that the model mirrored the real-world findings of Logan et al.: Without intervention, Organizational Culture stabilized at a Stage 3 level and Organizational Performance advanced very slowly and with linear dynamics. By introducing "triading" whereby structural holes were closed in the network structure of the organization, the probability the Organizational Culture could advance beyond Stage 3 to Stage 4 was increased. At that point, a phase-transition was seen with non-linear improvement in Organizational Performance. In addition, sensitive dependence on initial conditions was seen, as small differences in starting point had large differences in outcome.

We also chose to utilize a scaling model similar to the allometric scaling model for biologic variables popularized by West and Brown [13]. Our reasoning was that Intellectual Capital plays a role in the organization similar to mass in the organism. While super-linear scaling is seen in cities [14], corporations "die" where cities usually do not. The sub-linear scaling seen in biologic entities seems to hold true with corporations.

16.2 The Current Model

The model presented is yet a further refinement of these prior two. It consists of:

- A starting point of 2 executives, 4 managers and 25 workers.
- Sliders allow a stochastic assignment of values within a range for: individual culture, core values, purpose, breadth of knowledge, depth of knowledge and "perspective". The new variable, perspective, was added in order to allow for diversity of viewpoint separate from core values [15].

- At start up, additional variables for education and disenchantment are stochastically assigned to the agents. These are randomly advanced and when a threshold is reached, small increments of culture are either added or subtracted from the agent's fund. In addition, the agent's knowledge is increased when the education threshold is reached. The variables are then reset.
- The agents move in time and space, exchanging culture and knowledge based upon the formula described in the previous model [12]. Direction of heading and step-length can be controlled by sliders to vary clustering based upon similar core values (Nearest-Neighbour or Random Network) and either random or Lévy step-length.
- At pre-set levels of Organizational Culture, "triading" can be introduced among a percentage of the agents. This has the effect of increasing the clustering coefficient of the network and creating a "Small World"-type network.
- As the Organizational Culture level advances, additional agents can be added ("growth" of the organization) or, at an even higher level a "merger" can occur with another organization of similar Organizational Culture. The number of agents is, however, capped at 100 to fit the "tribal" model of Logan et al. [9] above.
- As the Organizational Culture reaches high Stage 4, variance in core values and purpose is reduced, coinciding with what was found by Logan et al. [9].
- The model runs for 200 ticks, or until no agents are left. At each tick the following are calculated: Organizational Culture, Intellectual Capital, Variances in Core Values, Purpose and Perspective and Organizational Performance.
- The allometric scaling equation, $y = kx^{\alpha}$ is used to calculate Organizational Performance (the main outcome parameter) where y is Organizational Performance, k is a complex constant made up of Organizational Culture, variance of Core Values, Purpose and Perspective, x is Intellectual Capital (Organizational Knowledge × Variance of Organizational Knowledge) and α is .75.

It is important to understand that the "tribe" is the productive unit of any organization. It is not the section, or the department, the work group or even the designated "team". The tribe is a collection of individuals bound together by "vital intangibles" chief of which are shared core values and purpose. These vital intangibles are joined together in service of a cause. A given organization is composed of a "tribe of tribes", with their relationships within and among the tribes determining the performance.

Logan and associates found five stages of culture in the organizations they studied, and applied a tag-line to each (Table 16.1). The degree to which that collection of individuals is bound and the cause served is the essence of the culture. This produces a pattern of adaptation based upon the shared core values and purpose, history and future. It is tacit, and not explicit. It is emergent and not imposed. It is communicated primarily through language, and that language is both descriptive and prescriptive. *Changing language can change a culture.*

A vivid example of the power of language to help transform a culture is the experience of Southcentral Foundation (SCF) in Alaska. Through their "Nuka"

Table 16.1 Cultural map

Cultural stage	%	Behaviour	Relationships	Language
5	2	Innocent wonderment	True creative team	"Life is great"
4	22	Tribal pride	Stable partnership	"We are great and *they* aren't"
3	49	Lone worrier	Personal domination	"I'm great (and *you* are not)"
2	25	Apathetic victim	Separate	"My life sucks"
1	2	Undermining	Alienated	"Life sucks"

The five stages of culture, from Logan et al. [9]

system of care, they transformed a dysfunctional healthcare system into one that won a 2011 Malcolm Baldrige National Quality Award. Simple changes in language, such as changing "patients" into "owner-customers" transformed the culture of both the health professionals and those who before had been merely passive recipients of care [16]. The emergent result was a massive non-linear improvement in performance of all involved.

In our model, we wanted to capture an initial range of shared core values and purpose, as well as a means to use increasing returns to increase the degree to which those "vital intangibles" are shared as the culture advances. Our constant in the allometric scaling equation includes the variance of Core Values and Purpose as negative parameters. As the Organizational Culture reaches a mid Stage 4, when agents meet to exchange culture and knowledge, they also begin to decrease their differences in Core Values and Purpose, mimicking the transformation from "I'm Great" to "We're Great" language found in the real world. With each interaction, the overall variance of those two parameters gradually decreases and the constant therefore increases.

While shared Core Values and Purpose are essential to advance Organizational Culture and improve Organizational Performance, it is imperative to retain a level of diversity that provides the engine for innovation. The agents retain their own level of perspective, and the variance of that continues to act as a positive variable in the scaling constant.

16.3 Results

The model was run at baseline parameters for 1200 ticks. This resulted in an asymptotic limit of Organizational Culture to a low Stage 3 level and a linear rise in performance based upon the increasing fund of Intellectual Capital as the organization progressed in its life course. Altering the starting point whereby all two executives and all four managers began with a Stage 4 level of individual culture did not allow the organization to reach a Stage 4 culture as a whole. When four

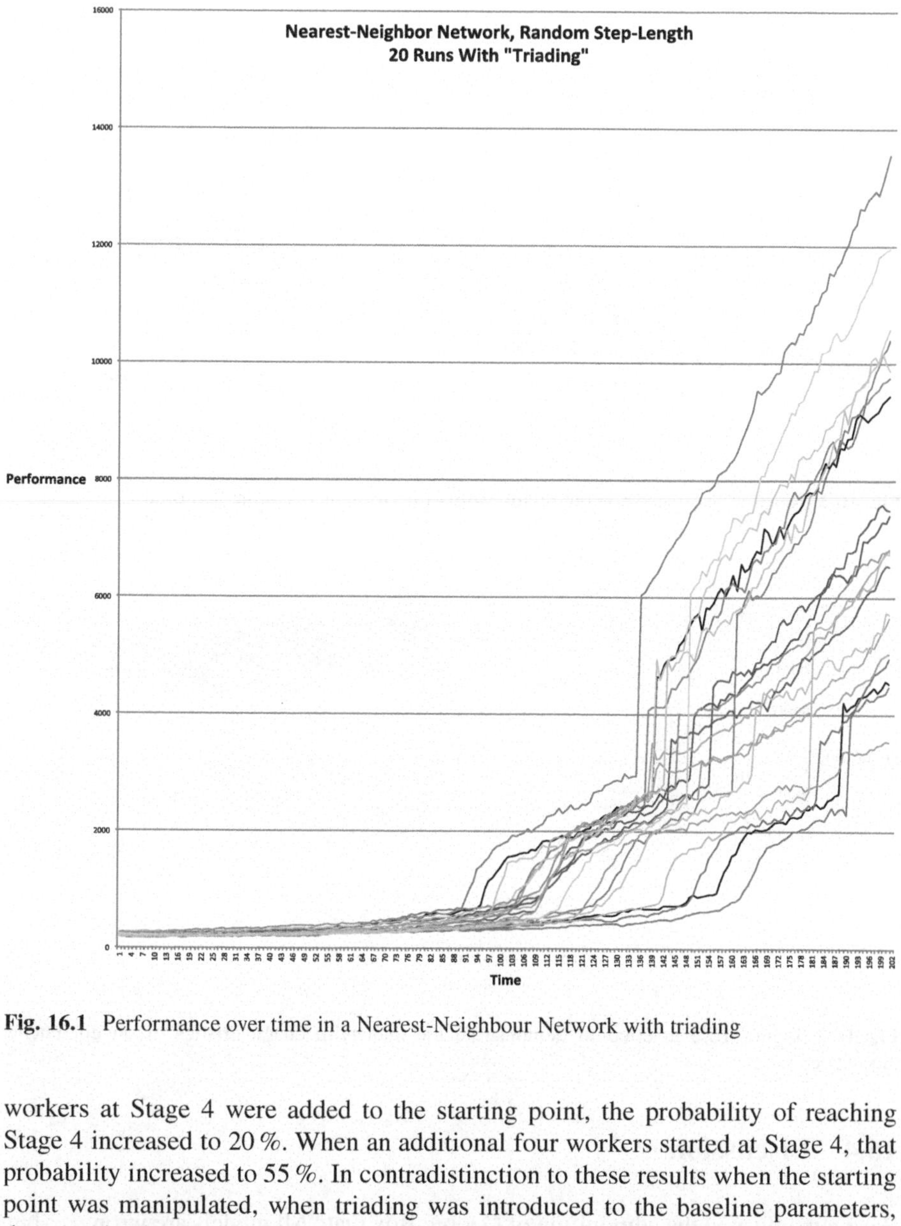

Fig. 16.1 Performance over time in a Nearest-Neighbour Network with triading

workers at Stage 4 were added to the starting point, the probability of reaching Stage 4 increased to 20 %. When an additional four workers started at Stage 4, that probability increased to 55 %. In contradistinction to these results when the starting point was manipulated, when triading was introduced to the baseline parameters, the organization had a 95 % chance of reaching Stage 4 (Fig. 16.1).

The impact upon Organizational Performance can best be understood by Fig. 16.2. Without triading, there is a slow climb up a gentle ridge of performance. The climb is linear and not very exciting. However, when triading is introduced, a rapid transition from the ridge to the "mesas" and "spires" of Organizational Performance can be enjoyed.

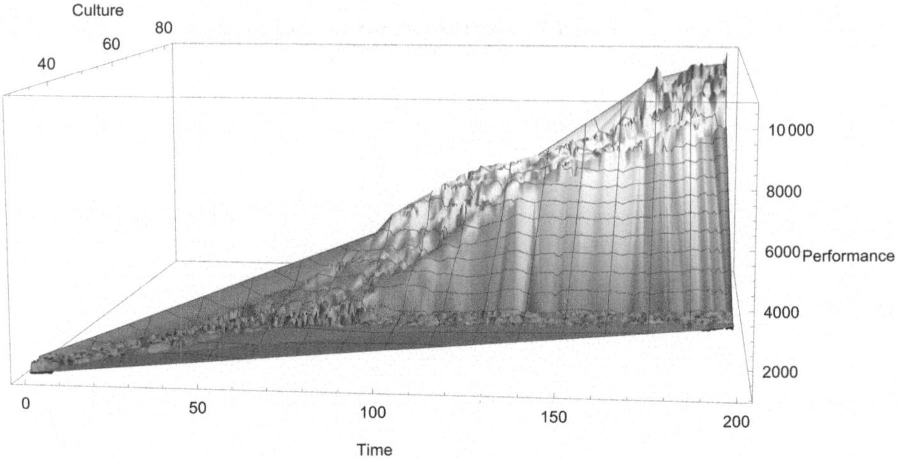

Fig. 16.2 Response surface showing relationship of performance, culture and time

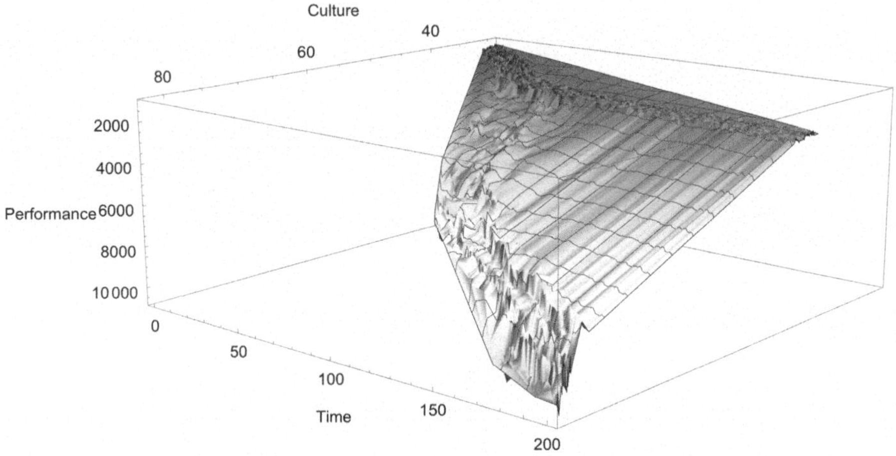

Fig. 16.3 Figure 16.2 inverted to demonstrate the data with characteristics of an epigenetic landscape

16.4 Discussion

We again return to the admonition of George Box that "All models are wrong . . . but some are useful". Likewise, we wish to heed the caution of Werner and McNutt to resist the temptation to put too much faith in measures. However, we feel agent-based modelling in general, and this model in particular, has significant advantages when attempting to study performance parameters in healthcare organizations.

If our "Performance Mountain" of Fig. 16.2 is inverted to produce Fig. 16.3, we see a response surface very reminiscent of an epigenetic landscape [17]. Perhaps in this instance it should be called an "epimimetic" landscape. Instead of climbing a mountain, we now can appreciate that introducing techniques to advance a culture, such as "triading", causes the performance "marble" to roll into creodes that lead to corresponding levels of performance. As the underlying cultural memes that create the performance response curve are activated or suppressed, we can visualize the linear advance of an organization's culture but the corresponding non-linear, path-dependent course of its performance.

We feel there is a direct link between Organizational Culture and the ability to understand emergence and the impact of Complexity Science, particularly in healthcare. Imagine a tapestry hanging free in a gallery. Viewing the tapestry from the back, one is confronted with a maze of knots and cords. It is all very *complicated.* A Stage 3 organization sees the complications and attempts to catalogue, analyse and optimize each of them. A Stage 4 organization walks around to the other side and sees the beautiful image.

One imperative for healthcare in the twenty-first century is to reach into our quiver of capability arrows to pick the tools and concepts from outside our own professional experience and adapt them to new uses. The answer to the challenges to healthcare now and in the future will be transcendent. If the answers were not transcendent, they would have been recognized already! It is our hope that tools such as agent-based modelling will be added to training of healthcare professionals so that "complexity thinking" can be routinely employed in their armamentarium of ideas. We want to appreciate the image, not dwell on the knots!

References

1. Box GEP. Science and statistics. J Am Stat Assoc. 1976;71:791–9
2. Werner RM, McNutt R. A new strategy to improve quality: rewarding actions rather than measures. J Am Med Assoc. 2009;301:1375–7
3. Rittel HWJ, Webber MM. Dilemmas in a general theory of planning. Policy Sci 1973;4:155–69
4. Snowden D, Boone ME. A leader's framework for decision making. Harv Bus Rev 2007;85:68–76
5. Gonnering R. The seductive allure of "best practices": improved outcome is a delicate dance between structure and process. E:CO. 2012;13:104–11
6. Epstein JM. Agent-based computational models and generative social science. Complexity. 1999;4:41–60
7. Csikszentmihaly M. Creativity: flow and the psychology of discovery and invention. New York: Harper Perennial; 1996
8. Sawyer RK. Group genius: the creative power of collaboration. New York: Basic Books; 2007
9. Logan D, King J, Fischer-Wright H. Tribal leadership: leveraging natural groups to build a thriving organization. New York: Harper Business; 2011
10. Wilensky U. NetLogo [computer software]. Evanston, IL: Center for Connected Learning and Computer-Based Modeling, Northwestern University. http://ccl.northwestern.edu/netlogo/
11. Gonnering R. Modeling the spread of a "cultural meme" through an organization. Annual Meeting, Computational Social Science Society of the Americas; 2012 Sep; Santa Fe, NM. http://computationalsocialscience.org/wp-content/uploads/2012/09/Gonnering2012.pdf
12. Gonnering RS, Logan D. Modeling the interrelationship of organizational culture, values, intellectual capital and productivity: the influence of "Triad Formation" and starting point. Annual Meeting of the Computational Social Science Society of the Americas; 2013 Aug; Santa Fe, NM

13. West GB, Brown JH. The origin of allometric scaling laws in biology from genomes to ecosystems: towards a quantitative unifying theory of biological structure and organization. J Exp Biol. 2005;208:1575–92
14. Bettencourt LMA. The origins of scaling in cities. Science 2013;340:1438–41
15. Page SE. Diversity and complexity. Princeton, NJ: Princeton University Press; 2011
16. Blash L, Dower C, Chapman S. Southcentral Foundation: Update 2014, Research Brief, Center for the Health Professions at the University of California at San Francisco, September. http://futurehealth.ucsf.edu/LinkClick.aspx?fileticket=s8HWM5LlluY%3D&tabid=161 (2014). Accessed 19 Nov 2014
17. Paaby AB, Rockman MV. Cryptic genetic variation: evolution's hidden substrate. Nat Rev Genet. 2014;15:247–58

Chapter 17
Leading the Emergency Department as a Complex Adaptive System

Paola Camorlinga and Sergio Camorlinga

Healthcare is a convoluted system with a large number of opportunities and challenges. No matter what administrative task is performed, interdependencies of people, resources and processes are everywhere. Many times services provided are not achievable as originally expected. Due to the business complexity, it is often difficult to identify what is the cause of the inefficiency. Performance metrics can be defined and measured without having a good understanding of the factors that generated those metrics. This has an impact on the value of health systems interventions because no clear cause of benefit or costs can be associated to the intervention outcomes. Another instance are initiatives to integrate healthcare, which are faced with limited success to reduce costs and bring substantial improvements in healthcare delivery. These are some among many examples where health systems' complexity requires application of a different perspective in its administration and leadership.

The need to apply alternative approaches to the administration and leadership of the healthcare organization has been identified as a key factor to tackle some of the healthcare management challenges [1–4]. Lately these challenges are becoming larger as a result of increase demand for health services, rising costs, and patient needs for the best care delivery [5, 6].

P. Camorlinga
Department of Emergency Medicine, University of British Columbia, Room 3300, 910 West 10th Avenue, Vancouver, BC V5Z 1M9, Canada
e-mail: paola.camorlinga@alumni.ubc.ca

S. Camorlinga (✉)
Department of Applied Computer Science, University of Winnipeg, 3D29 - 515 Portage Avenue, Winnipeg, MB R3B 2E9, Canada
e-mail: s.camorlinga@uwinnipeg.ca

J.P. Sturmberg (ed.), *The Value of Systems and Complexity Sciences for Healthcare*, DOI 10.1007/978-3-319-26221-5_17

Recently the use of Systems and Complexity Sciences has been identified as a viable methodology to understand and manage the challenging health care system from a variety of perspectives including human health, health services, and the health care organization [7, 8]. In short, Systems and Complexity Sciences aim to understand how things are connected with each other, and how these interactions work together. Complex Adaptive Systems (CAS) is a branch of Systems and Complexity Sciences, which is the study of adaptive systems [9]. CAS is an interdisciplinary field that brings a different perspective to help lead healthcare organizations. CAS concepts of non-linearity, interdependencies, adaptability and emergence are applicable to health system administration and provide a relatively novel approach to manage healthcare organizations.

In this chapter, we discuss the identification and application of CAS concepts to the administration and leadership of the health care organization. Four fundamental CAS concepts are discussed to introduce the CAS paradigm and facilitate the assimilation towards the management of the healthcare organization. The Emergency Department (ED) is utilized as a case study to analyse and identify the application of CAS concepts. The ED has become an important component of the health organization as an entry point for a large number of patients into the hospital and provider of primary care [10]. CAS concepts are briefly described in Sect. 17.1, followed by a discussion of the main ED participants in Sect. 17.2. The relationships and information exchanges among these participants create a network of relationships that form an ED system that is responsible to provide health care services. Section 17.3 examines how to position the ED organization to a CAS perspective. The case study facilitates the understanding of CAS concepts and their applicability to other health care organizations and departments. Section 17.4 concludes with some final thoughts on the next steps for the use of CAS on the healthcare organization and how these ideas can be extended beyond the ED organization.

17.1 Complex Adaptive System Concepts

There are several CAS concepts that are relevant to a healthcare organization. The following concepts of non-linearity, interdependencies, adaptability and emergence are briefly described from an organizational perspective. Despite other applicable CAS concepts [11, 12], our approach suggests to begin with these four fundamental concepts and learn about their implications on the organization. This assists the initiation of thinking and managing the healthcare organization from a CAS perspective.

Non-linearity is a widely used term in mathematics to infer a relationship that is not of first degree or linear. For instance, a variable y with a linear relationship to another variable x implies that when the value of x changes, the value of y will proportionally change, i.e. there is a linear change. When there is a non-linear mathematical relationship, then a change in the value of x will generate a change in the value of y that is not proportional. The change in y can be much larger or smaller than the change of x. If we empirically translate the concept of non-linearity to the healthcare organization, it implies that people actions and their relationships among themselves can have large or small impacts on the outcomes of the organization. Sometimes it is desirable to have a large impact when an action is carried out (e.g. a well-intended health system intervention to increase patient safety), but sometimes it is the opposite that is desirable to minimize impact (e.g. when a key staff leaves the organization). A key challenge for leaders is how to identify the actions and relationships within the organization that can have the desirable impact level.

Interdependencies is another critical CAS concept. We all know that we live in a highly connected world where everybody and everything depends on each other to some extent. This has become more apparent with the proliferation of the Internet in the last two decades that has made readily and speedily the access of information. It does not matter what view is utilized: financial, environmental, societal, etc.; we are all connected from a variety of perspectives creating a mesh of interdependencies that are difficult to understand in base of their strengths and effects. Healthcare organization interdependencies exist internally and externally. A hospital is affected by interdependencies with government (e.g. policies), insurance companies (e.g. coverage policies), medical groups (e.g. clinical protocols), vendors (e.g. biomedical technologies), staff (e.g. skills), patients (e.g. pandemics), etc. All these participants carry out actions and relationships that create interdependencies to a variable strength and influence.

Adaptability is particularly relevant to healthcare. Adaptability is defined as the capacity of the organization to change and continue providing services relatively at the same desired level when internal or external conditions vary. For instance, humans frequently adapt to changing conditions. It is common to plan activities, and have those activities change to manage current conditions. At the hospital, every day is different bringing a variety of tasks with diverse needs of care and service. Traditionally the healthcare organization has been adaptable to some extent, for instance, adjusting work-flows to manage changes in service demand and requirements, but meanwhile following standard protocols of care. However, this has recently changed in many health settings because of a variety of factors like increasing demand, resource constraints, limited staff, complex conditions, etc. All these varying conditions expose the adaptability capacity limitation of some organizations. For instance, in Canada we observe a variety of ED wait times across the nation [13] demonstrating how well different settings are adapting when they face varying conditions. For fairness in our discussion, we acknowledge that those varying conditions are not necessarily the same among health settings, hence we can expect different ED wait times across the country.

Emergence is perhaps one of the most important CAS concepts. Emergence is technically defined as the appearance of system properties coming out of the activities and relationships among system components. Intuitively, emergence assists to provide an explanation of how it is possible to achieve properties at a systems level. From a healthcare organizational perspective, actions and relationships carried out among stakeholders produce emergent properties. In the ED case, the activity and

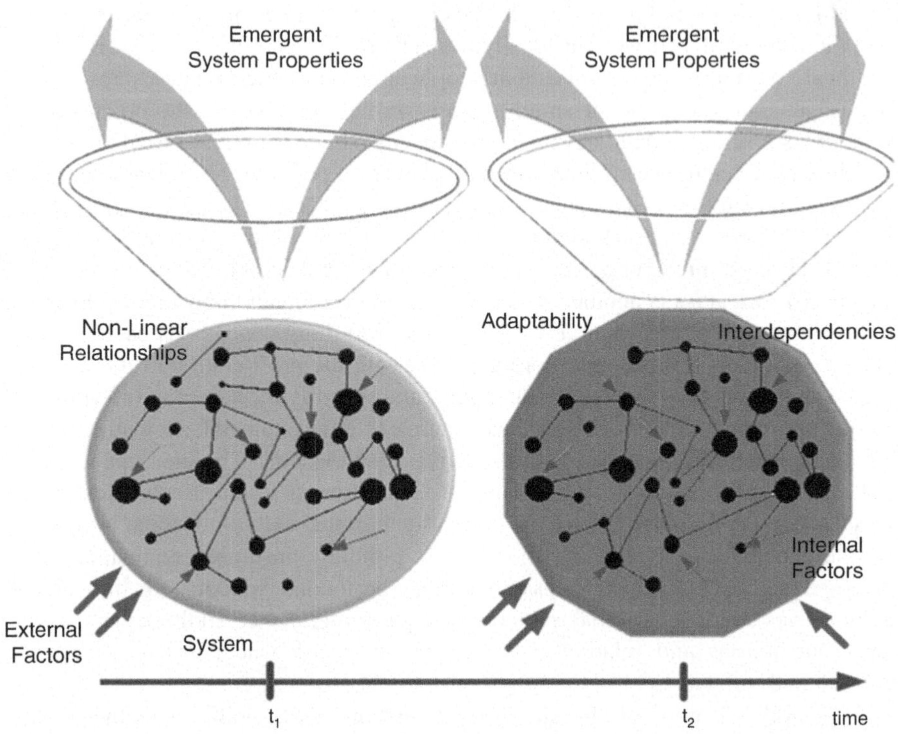

Fig. 17.1 Integration of CAS concepts

relationships among ED participants described in Sect. 17.2 together with internal and external factors give rise to a series of system properties, which are usually measured from a variety of metrics. Samples of ED emergent system properties are ED length of stay, ED re-admission rates, time to physician initial assessment (PIA), number of medical misdiagnosis, etc. It is not an easy task for organizational leaders to properly identify the components that give rise to a given emergent system property. In the ED case, besides participant actions and relationships, external and internal factors like facility type and location, age and sex distribution of patients, and condition severity are some of many factors that can also influence the emergence of the ED system property.

Before applying CAS concepts into the ED case, an understanding of how the four concepts integrate is required. Figure 17.1 outlines a simplified view of how the concepts connect to each other in a given system.

The system under study is located inside the circle of Fig. 17.1 with its components (solid dots) carrying out actions and relationships. These activities produce a mesh of interdependencies and non-linear relationships (solid links among dots). The system exists within a larger ecosystem with external and internal factors (red arrows) influencing the system components thereby their actions and relationships;

and consequently their interdependencies and non-linearities. The set of actions, relationships, interdependencies, and non-linearities generate emergent system properties that characterize the system as an entity (large arrows emerging from the circles). The emergent properties will provide the system the adaptability to internal and external factors that continuously change, i.e. the system view on the right circle (time = t_2) is adapting to new factors and interdependencies, but still providing the same or equivalent emergent system properties as the system view on the left circle (time = t_1).

17.2 The Emergency Department System

ED participants play a variety of roles critical to the success of the ED as a system. The ED is considered a system within a larger system (e.g. a hospital) with its own properties emerging from the actions and relationships of its participants (i.e. components). For instance, ED wait times from the time people arrive until the time they are discharged or admitted to the hospital is a system property that emerges from the actions and relationships of the ED participants. Other ED system properties are defined later in Sect. 17.3. Although there are other system components, in our analysis we consider two main system components for the ED case: human participants and information technology. Human participants' actions form relationships among the participants creating a network that produce the system property of interest (e.g. length of time people spent in ED). Information technology is a component tool that facilitates the communication and information exchange among human participants. Suitable information technology in place can substantially influence how the human participants perform their actions and the relationships they have with other participants, thereby also affecting the ED system properties emerging from it (e.g. ED wait times). Table 17.1 lists ED human participants and briefly outlines their actions and roles. Table 17.2 lists ED information technology.

Human participants roles and actions (Table 17.1) give rise to a rich variety of interactions and scenarios. A representative sample of the set of interactions is listed in Table 17.3. The interactions will create interdependencies among those human participants with non-linear affects. These interactions are influenced by the use of information technology tools (Table 17.2). The influence can impact the interdependency and non-linear effect observed out of a given interaction.

17.3 Applying Complex Adaptive Systems into the Emergency Department

Figure 17.1 is a simplified depiction of reality. A system can be seen from a variety of perspectives. One approach is to have a perspective based on the emergent system

Table 17.1 ED system human participants

Human participant	Main actions performed
Triage nurses	Triage nurses decide the order in which patients are to be evaluated by physicians. Once the patient arrives the triage staff makes a clinical assessment of the patient along with vitals. This ultimately results in the patients being categorized into a triage category. The triage category along with the ED volume will affect the time interval between being seen in triage to being seen by a physician [14]. Registration also occurs simultaneously or in sequence, and the patient's demographic and identifying data is taken down into most commonly an electronic patient tracking system
ED nurses	After the patient is triaged and brought into a room, an ED nurse is assigned to a patient or patients in the assigned area. Depending on ED volume and staffing numbers, nursing staff will take care of varying numbers of patients at one time. The nurse will do re-assessments and monitor the clinical status of patients at regular intervals. Along with this, they also, carry out physician orders (i.e. phlebotomy, IV line placement, administration of fluid and medications). Nurses also provide assistance for procedures performed in the ED, patient education and look after the general comfort of the patients
Attending physicians	Attending physicians in the ED identify the following themes of collaborator, communicator, collection of information, and quality of care along with attending to patients as their main actions. ED physicians begin and end their shift with communicating and collaborating in transfer of information between other ED physician staff. This is an important process as the new oncoming ED staff will then inherit patients that require ongoing care and will need to attend to them along with the new incoming patients. The attending staff collects information through their interactions with other ED staff (i.e. nurses, residents, consultants, etc.) as well as from information technology to obtain key information on the patients they are providing care for. The attending physician teaches and collaborates with the learners they are supervising meanwhile coming up with a patient management plan. Collaboration and communication with other consultants of a variety of specialities through phone calls or in person is also required given the wide range of presenting patient complaints. Overall, it has been shown that most of a physician's time in the ED is spent on multitasking [14]
Learners (teaching hospital setting—residents, medical students)	Learners will evaluate and assess patients to decide on a possible diagnosis and ultimately a plan of management. The learner's responsibility is then to formally present the patient to the attending physician and propose their findings and management plans. Together, the learner and the attending physician devise a final management plan to provide patient care. One of the learner's major roles and challenges is the role of learning. They must look up information when posed with the unknown, receive teaching from their attending staff, and must get accustomed to the environment. The work-flow of the resident closely reflects that of the attending physician

Consultants	ED physicians must collaborate with consultants representing the various disciplines of medicine, transfer information about the patient, and if chosen to be admitted, a transfer of care. Consultants assess patients in the ED and play a role in the patient's management by either choosing to admit them, follow them or by providing advice on care to the ED physician
Desk clerks	The desk clerk manages all clerical duties in the specific area. Usually each treatment area (i.e. major, intermediate, minor) has its own desk clerk. Desk clerk duties include making phone calls for physicians, keeping track of patient flow, and paperwork duties
Technicians (laboratory technicians, radiology technicians)	Technicians are often available throughout the day, and deliver services when called or orders are filled. The ED is highly dependent on the efficiencies of other departments as lab and radiology. Without their services, the physician's management plan is difficult to follow and the efficiency of the ED is negatively impacted [14]
Health care workers	Health care workers move patients around the emergency room, and ensure that rooms are prepared and cleaned between patients
Social workers	Social workers help patients with social issues like housing, financial, and finding other resources that are unique to each patient's needs. Very beneficial during working hours, but often some ED do not have around the clock social workers and often their services are only available during certain times of day

Table 17.2 ED system information technology

Information technology	Main actions performed
Electronic Patient Record (EPR) system—or equivalent	An electronic record system provides retrieval of information on patients, ability to check for laboratory test results, or admission and discharge information. In some hospitals EPR is also used for documentation, consultation, and order input as related to a patient
Drug Program Information Network (DPIN) system—or equivalent	DPIN is an electronic, online, point of sale drug system to support the patient drug management. DPIN system stores, manages, distributes, and provides access to patient medication data
Radiology Information System (RIS)/Picture Archival and Communication System (PACS)—or equivalent	RIS/PACS is an electronic system used by radiology and medical groups to store, manage, distribute, and provide access to radiology reports and imaging
Labs Information System (LIS)—or equivalent	LIS is an electronic system used by laboratory operations and medical groups to store, manage, distribute, and provide access to patient (inpatient, outpatient) laboratory tests processes and results

Table 17.3 ED interaction/scenario sample

Interactions/scenarios
Patients entry into the ED is either through walk-in, Emergency Medical Services (EMS), or transfer from another hospital/area • Patients that are walk-ins are then triaged on entry, and then will be seen based on triage category • Patients coming in through EMS or transfer process are usually pre-triaged either by EMS or by staff doing the transfer
Once patient is within the ED they are provided care from • Nursing staff and are evaluated by either attending physician, resident, and/or medical student through a history and physical exam • Then diagnostic investigations (imaging, laboratory work) are carried out depending on entrance complaint and data gathering carried out by evaluating staff
Consulting services are called/notified if a patient needs to be admitted to a specific service, or if more specific expertise is needed in their specific field. The patient ultimately being admitted to a floor, transferred to a different facility or discharged home with follow-up • Bed availability is often a rate-limiting component of the scenario
House staff use resources (technology and non-technology) for decision making: • clinical information systems that provide access to laboratory information, patient's previous medical history including results of previous investigations (imaging and lab work) and previous physicians and nurses notes • paper charts • telephones to consult services for consults or advice • lab delivery system and imaging • auxiliary forms
At the end of the shift, the attending physician must do "handover" with the new attending physician coming on and his/her team • Shift change is when the majority of information transfer occurs, and the process is usually conducted in either a form of "sit down rounds" or "walk rounds"

property under study. Two system properties are described next as examples of emergence coming out of the actions and relationships active at the ED system. Figure 17.2 shows a sample of the ED time-based system properties and how they relate to each other.

Wait Time for Physician Initial Assessment—Once the patient enters the ED they are initially triaged based on their level of acuity[1] and registered for patient name, demographics, etc. Based on the patient's acuity level, they will be triaged and this will affect the order that they are seen in the ED. Patients with lower CTAS scores (1, 2) are often seen very quickly, versus those with scores of (3–5) may have to wait longer depending on the volume of patients already present at the ED [15]. The triaging designator (usually a nurse triage) plays an important role in

[1]Canadian Emergency Department Triage and Acuity Scale (CTAS) system is the most commonly used triage scoring system in Canada.

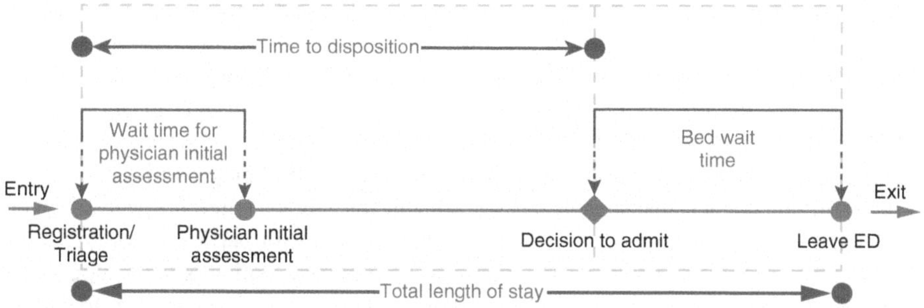

Fig. 17.2 System properties related to wait times

ultimately deciding the order that the patients will be seen, and accuracy is of utmost importance. The time measured here is from initial ED registration/triage to the point when the physician does their initial assessment. In this instance we observe various participants (triage nurses, attending physicians, learners, desk clerks, health care workers, etc.) carrying out actions and relationships with the assistance of information technology tools. All these activities with their interdependencies and non-linear relationships will give rise to the Wait Time for PIA observed at the ED. The ED system adaptability can be observed on scenarios where service demand exists for a large number of patients with a specific acuity (e.g. many patients with low CTAS scores). The ED will be adaptable up to a certain level to the external factor of increase demand of services. At some point of demand, the Wait Time for PIA is affected substantially unless other logistic measures are taken.

Time to Disposition—Disposition in the ED refers to the point in time when the assessment for the patient has been completed and the final plan decided. Disposition is usually either the decision to admit to the hospital or to discharge home with or without follow-up at an outpatient department. The time to disposition includes from the point the patient enters the ED after triage/registration to the point when a final disposition plan is made by the attending physician [16]. During this period of time, history and physical assessments are made by nurses, learners (if at a teaching hospital), and physicians. Diagnostic procedures are ordered which can include laboratory and imaging investigations. As well old patient information is often retrieved through either an electronic medical record or if old documentation not available on electronic system it is often requested from another location. Interventional procedures and treatment are often begun in the ED. All these actions are to eventually be able to make the decision whether the patient will need to be admitted, discharged, or need further re-assessment/second opinion. This system property has a more complex perspective compared to others because more ED participants and tools can take part. Similarly a large number of interdependencies and non-linear relationships exist that contribute to the system property of Time to Disposition.

ED system properties are also affected by external and internal factors (Fig. 17.1). For example, evidence from other studies has shown that system properties are affected by the patient's age, gender, acuity of problem, whether registered through the ambulance or a walk-in, and the time of day that the patient presents [13]. Of course, high acuity patients that present to the ED will have lower wait times to be initially assessed, but studies have shown that they have overall higher total ED Length of Stay (LOS[2]) durations. Similarly, the Canadian Institute for Health Information [13] shows that although patients who end up being admitted vs. their non-admitted counterparts have lower initial wait time assessment, they have longer total ED LOS. It has also been shown that these system properties are variable on the type of ED that is involved. The duration of time that patient's wait appears to vary on geographical location, rural vs. urban, as well as teaching vs. non-teaching hospitals. It has been noted that urban teaching hospitals tend to have higher volume of patients presenting to the ED, and this seems to correlate with a higher number of more acutely ill patients. All these provide evidence of large number of factors (internal, external) besides system participant actions and relationships that contribute to the system properties emerging. In the study of a system from a CAS perspective, many system properties can be examined. For the ED case, some other system properties that may be relevant for the ED administration can include

- Bed wait time[3]
- Number of patients seen per day
- Number of patients discharged, admitted
- Number of patients LWBS (Leave Without Being Seen)
- Number of patient recidivism (patients that frequently visit ED in short durations)
- Number of medical errors per day/week/month/year

17.4 Extending the Use of Complex Adaptive Systems Beyond the Emergency Department

This chapter has focused on understanding the fundamentals of CAS concepts of non-linearity, interdependence, emergence, and adaptability as a method to introduce a CAS perspective in the management and leadership of health systems. The ED has been discussed as an instance to exemplify how the CAS concepts can be applied. The goal is to start building the bridge that facilitates the use of concepts and methodology from Systems and Complexity Sciences into the Health Sciences realm.

In Sciences, a general approach to increase our understanding of the realm is to create models and simulate/experiment their behaviours. Most common methods to

[2]Length of Stay (LOS) is the duration of time that the patient stays within the ED from the point of registration/triage to the moment of disposition and leaving the ED.

[3]Bed wait time begins from the point the disposition plan is to admit a patient to the point the patient leaves the ED to the ward when a bed is available.

carry out the general approach include: laboratory experiments and/or field studies; mathematical formulations; and computer modelling and simulation. Currently, most of the CAS research is done with computer modelling and simulation [17–19]. Mathematics can be quite complex when dealing with large number of system components. Similarly laboratory experiments and/or field studies may not be possible or limited in scope for the same reasons. Instead, computer modelling and simulation provide flexibility and scalability for scenarios and have become a common approach to study CAS.

Creating a proper computer model for the system under study can however be challenging. Critical to the success is to choose the correct participant actions and relationships giving rise to the desired system properties. Understanding and applying the CAS concepts assist to identify the key actions and relationships to create better computer models for the system under study.

Future work will expand this initial study to develop methodology to extend CAS concepts and apply them in building computer models and simulations. The computer models and simulations will help evaluate healthcare interventions, and assist identifying causes and benefits from a holistic perspective. Better healthcare interventions can substantially improve the impact of policies on our health system. Computer modelling and simulation with a CAS perspective can provide an alternative approach to lead and manage health systems in the twenty-first century.

Acknowledgements This work was supported in part by the University of Winnipeg, Department of Applied Computer Science through the Major Research program and the Natural Sciences and Engineering Research Council of Canada through the Discovery Development Grant program, and in part by the University of Manitoba, College of Medicine.

References

1. Fraher EP, Ricketts, TC, Lefebvre A, Newton W. The role of academic health centers and their partners in reconfiguring and retooling the existing workforce to practice in a transformed health system. Acad Med. 2013;88(12):1812–6
2. Clancy GP, Duffy D. Going "All In" to transform the Tulsa community's health and health care workforce. Acad Med. 2013;88(12):1844–8
3. Egger MJ, Day J, Scammon DL, Li Y, Wilson A, Magill MK. Correlation of the care by design primary care practice redesign model and the principles of the patient-centered medical home. J Am Board Fam Med. 2012;25(2):216–23
4. Markov C, Shams I, Ajorlou S. A predictive analytics approach to reducing 30-day avoidable readmissions among patients with heart failure, acute myocardial infarction, pneumonia, or COPD. Health Care Manag Sci. 2015;18(1):19–34
5. Arduino KK. Ripple effects of reform on capital financing. Healthc Financ Manage. 2014; 68(5):62–7
6. Peiró M, Barrubés J, New context and old challenges in the healthcare system. Rev Esp Cardiol (Engl Ed). 2012;65(7):651–5
7. Quinn GR, Le E, Soni K, Berger G, Mak YE, Pierce R. 'Not So Fast!' The complexity of attempting to decrease door-to-floor time for emergency department admissions. Jt Comm J Qual Patient Saf. 2014; 40(1):30–8

8. Sturmberg JP, Martin CM. Complexity in health: an introduction. In: Sturmberg JP, Martin CM, editors. Handbook of systems and complexity in health. New York: Springer; 2013. p. 1–18
9. Gell-Mann M. What is complexity? Complexity. 1995;1(1):16–9
10. Bolton P, Mira M, Sprogis A. Oranges are not the only fruit: the role of emergency departments in providing care to primary care patients. Aust Health Rev. 2000;23(3):132–6
11. Ahmed E, Elgazzar AS, Hegazi AS. An overview of complex adaptive systems. Mansoura J Math 2005;1:1–26
12. Brownlee J. Complex adaptive systems, Swinburne University of Technology, CISL technical report 070302A; March 2007
13. Canadian Institute for Health Information. Understanding emergency department wait times: access to inpatient beds and patient flow. Ottawa: CIHI; 2007
14. Laxmisan A, Hakimzada F, Sayan OR, Green RA, Zhang J, Patel VL. The multitasking clinician: decision-making and cognitive demand during and after team handoffs in emergency care. Int J Med Inform. 2007;76(11–12):801–11
15. Canadian Institute for Health Information. Understanding emergency department wait times: how long do people spend in emergency departments in Ontario? Executive summary; 2007. p. 1–21
16. Canadian Institute for Health Information. Understanding emergency department wait times: who is using emergency departments and how long are they waiting? Ottawa: CIHI; 2005
17. Sturmberg JP, Churilov L, McDonnell G. “Modeling”. In: Sturmberg JP, Martin CM, editors. Handbook of systems and complexity in health. New York: Springer; 2013. p. 81–112
18. Miller JH, Page SE. Complex adaptive systems: an introduction to computational models of social life. Princeton/Oxford: Princeton University Press; 2007
19. Mitchell M. Complexity: a guided tour. Princeton: Princeton University Press; 2009

Chapter 18
The Value of Systems and Complexity Thinking to Enable Change in Adaptive Healthcare Organisations, Supported by Informatics

Beverley S. Ellis

This paper stems from the researcher's interest in the value of complex adaptive systems thinking to explain responses to the challenges faced when a system[1] is perturbed, illustrated by the introduction of a quality improvement programme within the context of two United Kingdom (UK) National Health Service (NHS) Primary Care Organisations (PCOs) whose characteristics are shown in Fig. 18.1.

18.1 The Problem

Towards the end of the twentieth century, concerns about quality in the UK appeared to be widespread and increasing in frequency due to a number of high profile system failures that included The Shipman Inquiry [2]. The UK government argued that the NHS operated within an increasingly competitive world; it had become more demanding, less stable and the consequences of failure immediate. There was a perceived need for a more holistic approach because the NHS was providing variable quality of care to patients and resources were limited. Clinical governance, a quality improvement programme, was introduced described as:

> "A framework through which the NHS organisations are accountable for continuously improving the quality of their services and safeguarding high standards of care by creating an environment in which excellence in clinical care will flourish." [3]

---

[1]The term "system" used throughout this paper follows the definition provided by Plesk [1]—the coming together of parts, their interaction and sense of purpose.

B.S. Ellis (✉)
Health Informatics Team, School of Health Sciences, College of Health and Well-being, University of Central Lancashire (UCLan), Victoria Road, Preston PR1 2HE, UK
e-mail: BSEllis@uclan.ac.uk

J.P. Sturmberg (ed.), *The Value of Systems and Complexity Sciences for Healthcare*, DOI 10.1007/978-3-319-26221-5_18

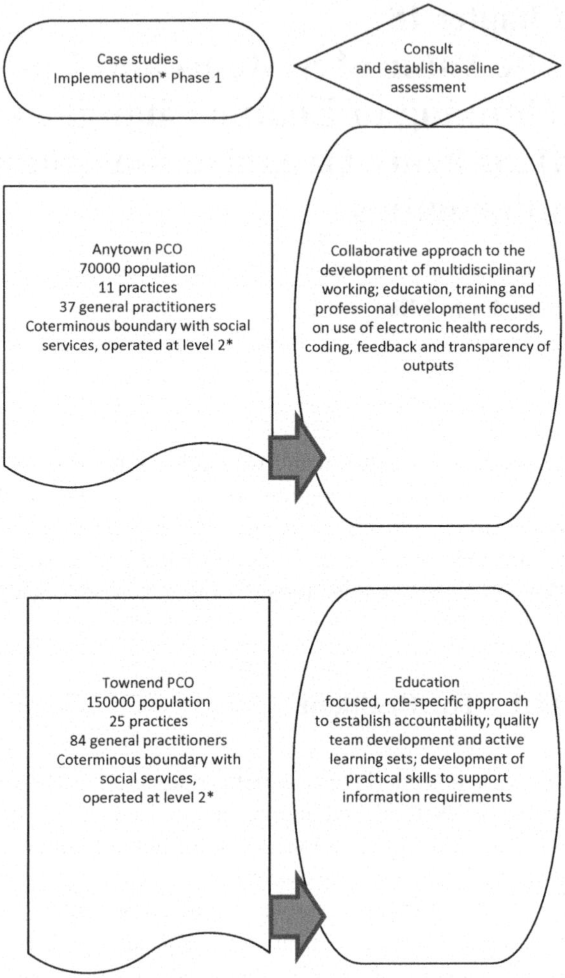

Fig. 18.1 PCO characteristics and context, NHS organisational maturity model ranging from level 1 to level 4

The remit for clinical governance sat amongst other NHS reorganised structures and processes within an organisational maturity model that ranged from levels 1 to 4, (level 1 organisations providing advisory support to Health Authorities, to free standing Trusts at level 4). The "stepped" model designed to support an evolutionary approach at a pace that was to be agreed locally; justified in terms of reducing inequalities, inefficiencies and fragmentation in the quality of service provision, coupled with a need to maintain the NHS in financial balance. Networks were constructed as governance-linked structures forming Primary Care Organisations (PCOs) each serving populations ranging from 50,000 to over 250,000. Explicit within policy was a requirement to develop a "corporate culture" in which governance and quality improvement were to be seen as a shared enterprise "*whereby initiatives would not be implemented in isolation*" [4, p. 244]. In the light of proposals to develop PCOs, a "core" electronic patient record, integrated at the general practice level developed.

18.2 The Actors

Those initially involved in establishing clinical governance arrangements in the two studied PCOs included a board of 13 general practitioners, nurses, general managers and lay representatives in each organisation. Primary healthcare systems include multiple health professionals who often are dispersed across different physical locations.

18.3 The Argument

It is argued that a systems and complexity perspective has important implications to two complementary foci addressed in this paper. The first focus is on demonstrating the value of embedding technological innovation into existing complex adaptive systems such as primary care to support symmetry of information amongst stakeholders.

The second focus is to provide a framework for organisational change management that forms the basis for appropriate educational interventions across health care organisations [5, 6].

18.4 Research Strategy

Longitudinal case studies, based in two North of England NHS PCOs, conducted over 6 years in three phases between 2000 and 2006, traced responses to the implementation and development of clinical governance—a quality improvement programme. The first case study, Anytown, followed a relatively small PCO representing a population of approximately 70,000. The second followed Townend, representing a population of approximately 150,000. The PCOs consist of a mixture of urban, suburban and rural General Practices.

The decision to study the real world phenomenon of responses to governance, using a qualitative case study within a social constructionist ontological perspective, was based on the assumption that it was necessary to consider the meanings attributed to the experience of those involved in implementing and developing quality improvement programmes. In particular, the case study approach provides a "*way of thinking about complex situations which takes the conditions into account*" [7, p. 445]. The methodology includes a review of literature, survey, interviews, participant observer notes and documentation review.

Limitations of the case study methodology include a tendency to provide selected accounts. These are potentially biased and risk trivialising findings. Rooted in specific context, their generalisability to other contexts is limited by the extent to which contexts are similar. Reasonable attempts were made to minimise any bias. For example, multiple data gathering techniques were used that included a postal survey, face-to-face interviews, observation notes and document analysis, conducted within an overall qualitative case study. The diversity of data collection methods used in this study was an attempt to counterbalance the limitations highlighted in one method by strength from alternative techniques. For example, survey, as a method of data collection, allows a limited amount of information to be obtained at a given point in time; which was counterbalanced by the strength of in-depth, face-to-face interviews characterised as flexible, adaptable and associated with rich, illuminating data focused on human narratives, to obtain insight of phenomena and investigate underlying motives that self-administered surveys cannot.

18.5 Findings

18.5.1 Literature: An Overview of Complex Adaptive Systems

A CAS approach is interpreted as a framework that assists in thinking about the nature of primary care that allows consideration of its dynamic beyond the practice, the background of trend towards integrated organisations and federated models of practice [8]. A CAS perspective acknowledges primary care structures and moves towards semi-autonomous networked organisations. Key elements that characterise a CAS, based on the works of Reynolds [9], Kaufman [10] and Gell-Mann [11], include:

- *Multiple components*, which interact with the environment, some may represent different world-views. Such systems are open systems that can be understood by observing, as a participant, and appreciating interrelated relationships, rich interaction, feedback and behaviour amongst components.
- *Self-organising networks*: influence is exercised both by the system on the components and by the components on the system, termed mutual causation. The pervasive nature of non-linear, interlinked interactions can be observed in the patterning of behaviours that emerge in response to change, which cannot be predicted by studying the elements.
- *Co-evolution and adaptation of the system*: there may be no central direction; small inputs may have large effects and vice versa.
- *Complex systems have a history which co-creates the present*: non-linear interactions generate new properties, known as emergent behaviours of the system. Associated principles acknowledge that there is a need to respect ecologies by avoiding disturbance of natural systems with major change, and allowing time for properties to emerge.

Second-order systems based thinking moves away from simple objective observation to understand humans as participants in systems that allows for the flow of energy (motivation, information and innovation), networked interactions, continuous feedback and interdependencies.

Table 18.1 translates the CAS principles to primary care and emphasises its impact on understanding quality improvement programmes.

18.5.2 Clinical Governance

The components of clinical governance are presented in Table 18.2.

To function most effectively the system of managing performance depends on quality improvement, use of electronic health records and shared learning/education supported by informatics. This approach highlights the importance of lifelong learning, and the role of health informatics in actively managing individual performance in a primary care setting.

18.5.3 Electronic Health Records

Informatics is acknowledged as a mechanism to link electronic health record outputs, quality improvement and resources [12]. The use and access to electronic health records is essential in supporting the strategic drive for quality within the context of UK primary care, with its increased focus on multidisciplinary teams to deliver care. Information flows, feedback and co-evolution form the essence of processes in primary care systems; their iterative patterning co-creates coherent behaviours and outcomes. This establishes a service accountable to patients, open to the public and shaped by their perspectives. This has implications to primary care strategists in terms of the empowerment and responsibilities of local communities, which can be thought of as ecosystems that place an emphasis on a holistic "whole system" management perspective. Moreover, thinking from a CAS perspective suggests the benefit of considering both the linear and non-linear features of the system. Approaches incorporated professional self-regulation that built on the skills and strengths of the clinicians. There was considerable variation in the way in which consultation data was captured, recorded and organised, which included free text, coded data and structured data collected using templates. An emphasis on incentivised information sharing led to local consensus on standard coding policies and models of data recording well before it became a national contractual requirement [12]. Investment in informatics, education and training was identified as development priorities in order to embed clinical governance principles in practice, shown in Fig. 18.2.

Table 18.1 Complex adaptive system conceptual framework to understand the implementation of quality improvement initiatives

CAS core elements	CAS properties	CAS properties	Network governance properties	Principles relevant to the governance of quality improvement
Emergent behaviours leading to system adaptation				
Multiple agents, different world-views (based on Gell-Mann [11])	Divergent perceptions—conflicts between underlying ideologies Novel solutions—based on relationships that evolve Interaction builds culture and knowledge	Interdependencies lead to patterns of behaviour and rules Coherent action stems from mutual adjustment based on common values Influence ripples but is not uniform Integrative solutions	Self-assessment, earned autonomy	Accept the democratic principles that contribute to the development of quality improvement programmes and ultimately to the emergence of self-regulated, evolutionary PCs
Self-organisation (based on Kaufman [10])	Rely on simple rules	System of quality improvement can be perturbed, but will respond and self-organise Coordination of multiple knowledge sources	Governance not government Non-hierarchical, based on relations and interdependencies	Observe that there may be no central direction Respect for the pervasive nature of interlinked interactions It is in the patterning of behaviours that emerge that would result in the governance of quality improvement programmes
Co-evolution (based on Kaufman [10])	Agents and whole system goals are likely to be more or less compatible	Through connectivity and the constant exchange of feedback, a system and its environment co evolve, adapting simultaneously Characteristics emerge that support mutual sustainability Consider the timing of perturbations	Based on reciprocal information requirements—systems evolve	Respect for ecologies, avoid disturbing an ecology with major changes Allow time for properties to emerge

Table 18.2 Components of clinical governance (Ellis and Howard [6], based on Nicholls et al. [21])

Patient–public–professional partnership
Clinical effectiveness
Risk management effectiveness
Patient experience
Communication effectiveness
Resource effectiveness
Strategic effectiveness
Learning effectiveness
Systems awareness
Communication
Ownership
Leadership

18.5.4 Education: Through Shared Learning

Initial responses to the implementation of a quality improvement strategy focused on creating safe space, time for stakeholders to meet and bring about mutual adjustment, to support shared learning and establish partnerships, supported by informatics. These patient–public–professional partnerships show a willingness to exchange information about the quality of care. Those involved in this study reported the importance of creating an environment conducive to education and learning to develop this willingness, within a context of stakeholder and inter-professional working. This approach provides a wider perspective for learners, but also highlights the importance of inter-professional cooperation in the development, clinical management and monitoring of health information. Learning models that include "action learning" sets [13] and "learning organisation concepts" [14, 15] were adopted and manifest an understanding of the need for skills and knowledge to be embedded in experience, and allow reflection on that experience to create new meaning and enduring changes in behaviour. One explanation is that shared learning reflects a social world,

- constructed by the perceptions and interests of those involved and the meaning they share, expressed as *"I think it's been quite, I think bringing professionals together is very powerful indeed and I think that's (Clinical Education Society) been very, very good for achieving that and significant numbers turn up regularly."* (Chief Executive, lines 237 ... 238), and
- supported by a perceived need to distribute responsibilities through team development *"I don't think I can fulfil my responsibilities for clinical governance by myself. I think that it* [clinical governance] *is something that is developed as part*

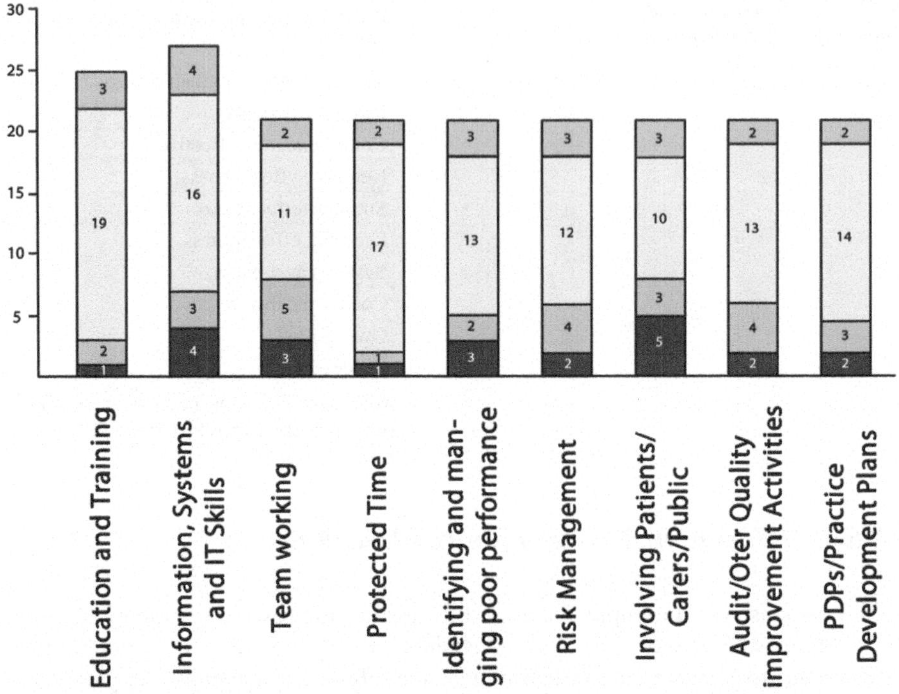

Fig. 18.2 Responses to the need for support of practices in developing aspects of quality improvement (Ellis and Herbert [6]). Reprinted with kind permission of copyright holder @2011 Primary Health Care Specialist Group, British Computer Society

of a team and that it would be impossible to do really without that, and I am quite happy to be part of developing how a team is going to approach that and be part of delivering it in the practice." (GP 4, lines 26 ... 29)

Figure 18.3 shows PCO characteristics and responses to system perturbation.

18.6 Themed Results

The findings reflect the following broad-based themes: mutual adjustment of a plurality of stakeholder perceptions, preferences and priorities; the development of networked information and communication systems, empowered by informatics; an emphasis on education and training to build capacity and capability. Participants reported a need to collaborate with a range of stakeholders that included multi-disciplinary teams. This was found to lead to an evolving learning approach that contributed to the implementation and development of each PCO quality improvement programme, rapid increases in information exchanges and feedback. Preferred

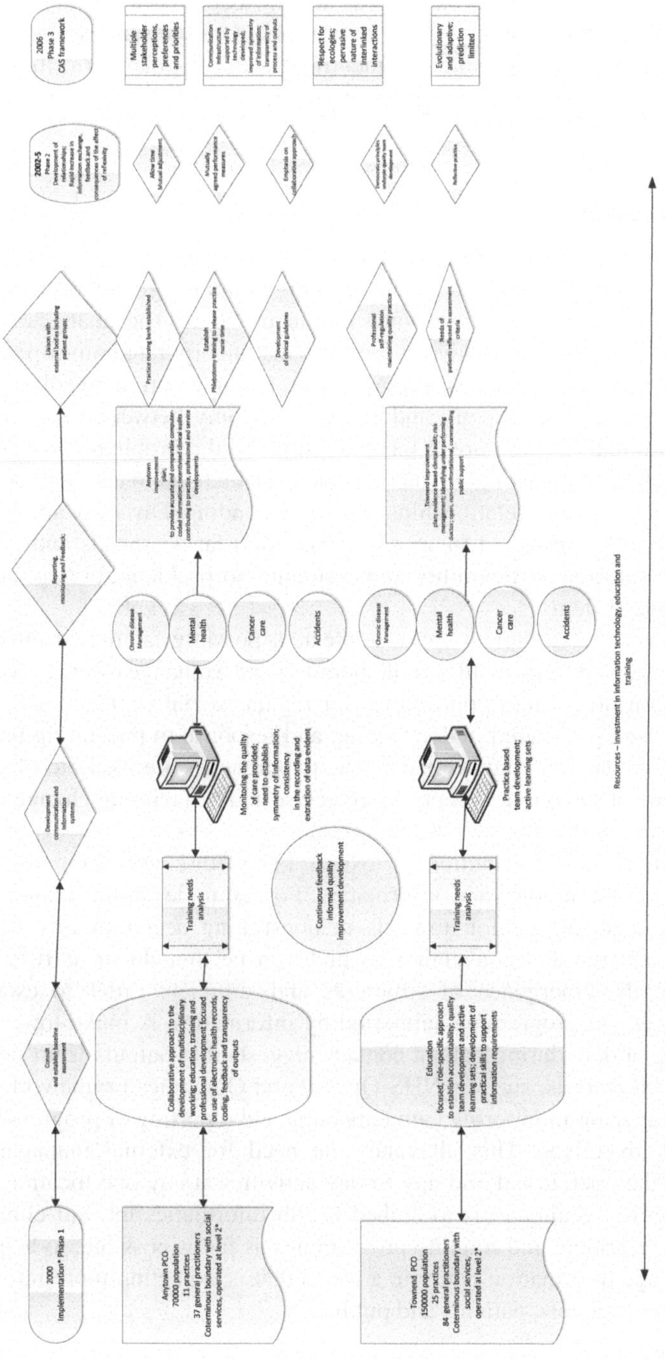

Fig. 18.3 Responses to the need for support of practices in developing aspects of quality improvement

approaches incorporated professional self-regulation that built on the skills and strengths of the clinicians. Informatics was acknowledged as a mechanism to link electronic health record outputs, quality improvement and resources. Investment in informatics, education and training was identified as development priorities in order to embed quality improvement principles in practice.

18.7 Discussion

PCOs in this study behaved as CAS, reaching mutual agreement without the need to impose a particular world-view of the problem. The changes observed were achieved through collaborative approaches that incorporated multi-perspective world-views, local ownership and empowerment. Complex problem solving stimulated both a degree of reciprocity and earned autonomy between those involved. Each PCO community found novel local solutions to the problems brought about by the introduction of clinical governance policies, which led to the development of cooperation, open trusting relationships and understanding. Diversity amongst constituents needs to be protected to accommodate multifarious needs and priorities. This provides a degree of flexibility and resilience to problem solving capability within the whole system.

It is important that sufficient space is created, possibly facilitated through the provision of protected time, to allow collaboration and exchange of ideas. Managers need to focus on providing opportunities for regular social forums, such as team meetings, to develop a shared understanding and response to presenting problems. Top–down command and control management approaches are likely to obscure, or constrict, the novel behaviour that produced action and behavioural change found in working practices within the two PCOs.

The collection and distribution of expert knowledge was supported by an increased use of technology and informatics. For example, initial responses that reflected a strategic orientation towards demonstrating accountability translated into quality standards and conventions, which can be thought of as rules. These in turn led to the emergence of structures and sufficient order to establish a quality improvement programme supported by informatics. A move towards real-time recording of data during patient contact suggests that outputs from integrated electronic health records, such as NHS Quality and Outcomes Framework (QOF), facilitate management monitoring, authenticating and reporting of progress towards organisational objectives. This alleviates the need for external management to interfere with the operational and day-to-day activities at any one location in each PCO. The ongoing challenge is to embed health informatics into all clinical and non-clinical educational and training programmes as far as possible, to help health care staff manage information better in a world that is expecting more information empowered professionals, patients and public.

18.8 Conclusions

The application of the CAS framework provides insight into the emergent, socially constructed nature of the process of implementation where results are unpredictable. Clinical governance emerges from a set of complex interactions, rather than from rational planning. The theme suggests that the effectiveness of individuals may be related to their ability to acquire and learn specific skills and knowledge within available resources. Thinking from a CAS perspective has an important role to play in improving the public's confidence in the delivery and quality of primary healthcare. Informatics complements this role based on the belief that the best decisions are based on the best information that flows throughout networked systems of healthcare to establish symmetry of information, the delivery of information technology enabled change and meet the future information requirements of patients, public and healthcare service.

18.9 Impact and Imperatives

This study has made a significant impact on the development and application of CAS models for technology implementation as well as the development of policy in relation to education and learning to manage health information technology [6, 12, 16]. Outcomes include the implementation of electronic records systems in the UK, supporting diversity in user support organisations, and the author's work with the Royal College of General Practitioners resulting in improved patients' online access to their electronic health records [17–19].

Twenty-first century primary health care systems will increasingly need to distribute responsibilities and encourage professional, patient public partnerships, supported by informatics. One problem for informatics that supports clinical practice is the tension between local specialism "the way we do things round here" and approaches that seek to standardise, recognising that outputs may be of interest to one or more stakeholders, and the need to reduce asymmetry of information. The use of informatics allows individuals and organisations to demonstrate how clinical teams can integrate the use of information and information systems within the broader context of continuous quality improvement. Practical tools such as training need analysis linked to competency frameworks [20] and quality methods are reported to improve system-wide performance (organisational learning), leading to improved patient care and economic benefit [16]. This approach integrates technology throughout care and business processes enabling continual learning through feedback. The motivation for change is explained as a need to facilitate access and delivery of effective quality health care within available resources through continuous feedback supported by electronic records, in response to the challenges brought about by social, economic, technical, political and organisational changes. It is envisaged that the development and use of open source software and "apps" on mobile devices by healthcare professionals, patients and the public will increase and impact on twenty-first century primary health care systems, ensuring flexible and agile solutions designed to meet the health, social and information needs of local, national and global populations. It is suggested that there is a need to increase the tolerance of diversity and failure, noting that levels of achievement can be variable, which will contribute to an environment conducive to innovation.

References

1. Plesk P. Re-designing healthcare with insights from the science of complex adaptive systems, crossing the quality chasm: a new health system for the 21st century. vol. 322. Washington, DC: National Academy of Sciences; 2000. p. 355. www.ihi.org/iomreport
2. The Shipman Inquiry. Presented to parliament by the Secretary of State for Health, September, 2000. Crown Copyright; 2000
3. Department of Health. Clinical Governance: quality in the new NHS, HSC (99) 065. London: Department of Health; 1999a
4. Jackson S. Exploring the possible reasons why the UK Government commended the EFQM excellence model as the framework for delivering governance in the new NHS. Int J Healthc Qual Assur. 1999;12(6–7):244–53
5. Ellis B. Managing governance programmes in primary care: lessons from case studies of the implementation of clinical governance in two primary care trusts [Ph.D.]. UCLan; 2008
6. Ellis B, Howard J. Clinical governance, education and learning to manage health information. Clin Gov: Int J. 2011; 16(4):337–52. Emerald Group Publishing Ltd. Available via: http://dx.doi.org/10.1108/14777271111175378
7. Keen J, Packwood T. Qualitative research: case study evaluation. Br Med J. 1995;311(7002):444–6
8. Ellis B. An overview of complexity theory: understanding primary care as a complex adaptive system. In: Sturmberg JP, Martin C, editors. Handbook on complexity in health. Chap. 29. NY: Springer Science and Business; 2013. ISBN: 978-1-4614-4997-3
9. Reynolds C W. Flocks, Herds and schools: a distributed behaviour model. In: SIGGRAPH '87: Proceedings of the 14th Annual Conference on Computer Graphics and Interactive Techniques. 21(4); 1987. p. 25–34
10. Kaufman SA. Origins of order: self organisation and selection in evolution. Oxford: Oxford University Press; 1993
11. Gell-Mann M. The quark and the jaguar. New York: Freeman; 1994
12. Ellis B. Agreeing a PCG coding policy, BCS healthcare computing, 2001 (Conference Proceedings); 2001
13. Revans R. The origins and growth of action learning. Bromley: Chatwell-Bratt; 1982
14. Argyris C. On organizational learning. Reading: Addison-Wesley; 1999
15. Argyris C, Schön D. Organisational learning: a theory of action perspective. New York: McGraw Hill, 1978
16. Cowley C, Daws L, Ellis B. Health informatics and modernisation: bridging the gap. J Inform Prim Care. 2003;11(4):207–14
17. Royal College of General Practitioners. Patient online access to records roadmap; 2013. Available via http://www.rcgp.org.uk/~/media/Files/CIRC/POA/RCGP-Road-Map.ashx
18. de Lusignan S, Mold F, Sheikh A, Majeed A, Wyatt JC, Quinn T, Cavill M, Gronlund TA, Franco C, Chauhan U, Blakey H, Kataria N, Barker F, Ellis B, Koczan P, Arvanitis TN, McCarthy M, Jones S, Rafi I. Patients' online access to their electronic health records and linked online services: a systematic interpretative review. Br Med J Open 2014;4: e006021. doi:10.1136/bmjopen-2014-006021

19. Mold F, de Lusignan S, Sheikh A, Majeed A, Wyatt JC, Quinn T, Cavill M, Gronlund TA, Franco C, Chauhan U, Blakey H, Kataria N, Barker F, Ellis B, Koczan P, Arvanitis TN, McCarthy M, Jones S, Rafi I. Patients' online access to their electronic health records and linked online services: a systematic review. Br J Gen Pract. 2014. doi:10.3399/bjgp15X683941
20. Gillies A, Howard J. Managing change in process and people: combining a maturity model with a competency-based approach. Total Qual Manag Bus Excell. 2003; 14(7):779–87
21. Nicholls S, Cullen R, O'Neill S, Halligan A. Clinical governance: its origins and its foundations. Clin Perform Qual Health Care. 2000;8(3):172–8

Chapter 19
Using a Team Approach to Address Avoidable Emergency Department Utilization and Re-hospitalizations as Symptoms of Complexity Through Quality Improvement Methodology

Jacqueline Morse, Andrew S. Valeras, Dominic Geffken, Daniel Eubank, A. John Orzano, Douglas Dreffer, Amanda DeCook, and Aimee Burke Valeras

19.1 Introduction

Decreasing inappropriate emergency department (ED) utilization and the rate of re-hospitalizations are two important issues in our current healthcare system. Improvement efforts often focus on the care team's functioning, such as better scheduling processes to increase the same day access and creating communication protocols to improve coordination and information transfer between systems. This paper describes two concurrent Quality Improvement (QI) projects that focused on team learning, rather than team functioning, to drive improvement.

Inappropriate ED utilization and preventable re-hospitalizations are two patterns created within a complex adaptive system (the local healthcare system) and therefore require tools designed to adapt in order to address complexity, rather than processes and protocols designed to address complicated (technical) problems. Team learning in this context goes beyond "single loop" learning, the transmission of information, and even beyond "double loop" learning, changing assumptions and inferences that lead to certain understandings of particular situations. Sustained fundamental change across situations requires "triple loop" learning, transforming the core values, beliefs, and cultural norms that underlie frames (Fig. 19.1) [1].

Changing a complex adaptive system requires either double or triple loop learning, depending on how deeply embedded the values, beliefs, and assumptions are that form individuals' internal rules and the system's organizational patterns. Team learning requires time, opportunity, and facilitation to practice the skills necessary

J. Morse (✉) • A.S. Valeras (✉) • D. Geffken • D. Eubank • A.J. Orzano • D. Dreffer
A. DeCook • A.B. Valeras
Concord Hospital Family Health Center, New Hampshire Dartmouth Family Medicine Residency, 250 Pleasant St., Concord, NH 03301, USA
e-mail: jmorse@crhc.org; asvalera@crhc.org; dgeffken@crhc.org; Eubank.dan@gmail.com; jorzano@crhc.org; ddreffer@crhc.org; adecook@crhc.org; avaleras@crhc.org

J.P. Sturmberg (ed.), *The Value of Systems and Complexity Sciences for Healthcare*, DOI 10.1007/978-3-319-26221-5_19

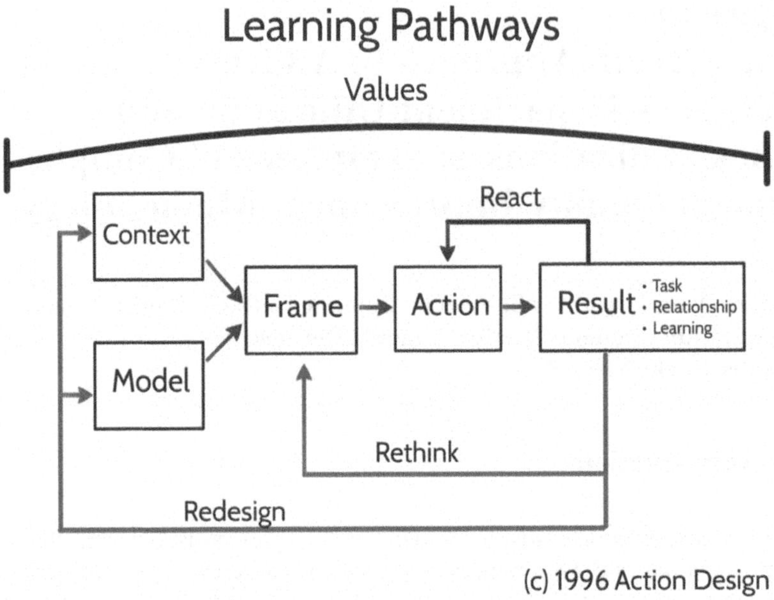

Fig. 19.1 Double/triple loop learning

to be capable of having dialogue and skilled discussion, dealing with conflict, which is seen as inherent to learning, and embracing the value of new attitudes and frames.

These two utilization-focused QI projects attempted double or triple loop learning, as it was necessary to "improve" the equilibria of ER utilization and re-hospitalization rates at Concord Hospital Family Health Center (CHFHC), a community health centre providing care to the under-served and housing family medicine and preventive medicine residencies.

19.2 ED Utilization

The volume of ED use at Concord Hospital (CH) is the highest in the state of New Hampshire. At the beginning of this project, 50 % of ED visits by CHFHC patients were by "high utilizers" (defined as four or more ED visits in a 12-month period). An interdisciplinary improvement team created a registry of "high utilizers" using the EHR and then implemented a Patient Advisory Committee (PAC). First, all 127 patients on the registry were invited to join the PAC, six of whom participated. This group was maintained as the active PAC and was invited to monthly 1.5 h meetings over 6 months, which with their consent, were recorded and transcribed. These transcriptions, as well as transcribed focus groups with the healthcare team, were qualitatively analysed using an iterative process with an open coding method [2] to explore whether double and triple loop learning occurred. Open coding involves marking text excerpts of interest and giving them descriptive labels and then combining these codes to form overarching themes [3]. The entire team reviewed these themes and further refined them. The data were then re-examined, looking for confirming and dis-confirming evidence for identified themes. Any differences in interpretation were resolved through discussion.

The PAC was facilitated to elucidate how CHFHC could improve urgent care delivery, in regards to perception, communication, and relationship with the healthcare team. The information obtained was then relayed to the healthcare team through weekly 20-min briefings, which allowed for discussion and dialogue. The PAC identified utilization of the ED was often due to technical barriers, such as lack of access to CHFHC or nurses sending patients via phone-triage to the ED or communications issues, like not understanding what "triage" means or not understanding the range of urgent care services available at CHFHC. While these barriers were identified, the most often heard theme was a request for healthcare providers to listen to their patients:

> Encourage [team members] to ask questions, because if they don't, you won't tell them what's really going on and they won't know. Also, patients should be encouraged to ask questions.

Eliciting direct patient input from "high utilizers" allowed the healthcare team to understand their patients' decision-making processes in regards to choosing the place of care for their urgent care needs, highlighting both individual and system contributions. This feedback served as the impetus for the transformational learning among the team that eventually changed their patient interactions.

The team started with a simple change: each team member on the telephone explained who they were, and what the triage process was, including details of why the patient might hear silence or typing, and the time frame in which a patient could expect a return call. Two new questions were included in the triage process: *"What worries you most about your symptoms?"* and *"Do you agree with this plan?"* These questions allowed patients to go beyond the biophysical report to how he/she made *sense* of their present health issue or problem [4].

The second team-driven initiative was a general shift to "yes" we have access, rather than "no", including increased access with nurses or providers. The team members described their new mental model of "high utilizers" as:

> Our thinking has shifted to a problem-solving mode. I now see it as a challenge, not a problem, in particular patients with chronic anxiety, or few social supports, or who may not feel heard.

With time, the enthusiasm and empowerment of PAC members grew as they witnessed change. One patient asked, *"Can I ask a question? Is there a piece of paper that says we are on the committee and they're supposed to be nice to us? Is that just a coincidence?"* Another agreed, *"Since I've been going to these meetings, it has been different here."* At the third PAC meeting, one participant said, *"I am seeing what we have done so far in three months here and I have already started seeing changes."*

Table 19.1 Implementation template

Urgent Plan of Care (UPOC) discussion template
1. Symptoms
a. What are the symptoms that typically lead to an ED visit or frequent calls for perceived urgent health care need? (Attractors)
b. What about these symptoms important or worrisome to you? (Internal rules)
c. What has worked for you in the past to address these concerns? (Positive feedback loops)
2. Who is on your team
a. Who knows you best at this practice? (Relationships)
b. Who has been most helpful in addressing your concerns? (Agents)
c. Who outside of this practice is helpful in meeting your urgent care needs? (Embedded systems)
3. Detailed executable plan
a. What do you want to happen when you have an urgent care need? (Anticipatory)
b. How do you want the plan relayed to you? (phone, in person, by whom)
c. When would be a good time to check in with you after addressing your urgent care need?

Members of the PAC joined with members of the healthcare team to develop an "Urgent Plan of Care" (UPOC) as part of a person-centered care plan [5], which meant to serve as a personalized foundation for how CHFHC could provide urgent care (Table 19.1). One team member noted, *"I think the UPOC has helped to identify the why behind their frequent use and address that."* The UPOC was a conversation tool opening up dialogue on a topic that previously had been undiscussable or unrecognized, allowing team members to gain a richer understanding of each individual "high utilizer", in terms of their motivations and needs during a perceived urgent medical issue.

> It helps us have a conversation (could also be considered an intervention) with the patient about their reasons for utilization and their perceptions of our services.

These conversations between patients and teams are an example of team learning. Individual team members did not directly impact patients' choices, but by transforming their interactions and mental model of the patient's situation, a different kind of relationship with patients developed. This new relationship led to a change in patient's perception and behaviour in regards to where to access urgent care, and patients began to identify the team as their "provider", rather than their physician.

> Even though there have been two or three doctors, I still had the same nurses or medical assistants, seeing the same ones. I usually see the same two, and I feel comfortable around both of them. I feel as though I have a healthcare team.

> We have to go through the team before we get to the doctor. (She) is a middle person. Today when I called for a refill, she asked me how I was doing; she remembered. So I think they

know us more than the doctors do. They play a bigger role. They just see and talk to us more by talking about the small things.

They know who I am. They ask questions and write things down. I feel the team knows me because they know the questions to ask. They are the backbones of the doctors.
They know that my grandson died, the depression, knows all that stuff so they treat me like a person, not a mental case.

It is imperative that primary care, facing the indelible challenges of working with patients with complex medical and psychosocial needs, must rely on team-based care to survive in the twenty-first century. Effective and sustainable team-based care is possible only through the ability to build and maintain quality relationships between members and patients.

19.3 Avoidable Re-hospitalization

A team-based approach was taken to embrace the complex care process of hospital discharge. CHFHC's 30-day baseline readmission rate ranged from 13 to 15 % in 2010, a sign that not all patients' post-hospital needs were met. This resulted in discharge summaries being enhanced, standards were implemented around the use of electronic reminders in transfer of information, an outpatient nurse made follow-up calls within 48-h post-discharge, and a weekly team-based group visit was conducted, to ultimately increase the number of successful transitions from hospital to home for patients and thus decrease overall readmission rates.

Recently discharged CHFHC patients were offered a team-based hospital follow-up visit where they met with a medical assistant, nurse, resident, behavioural health (BH) clinician,[1] attending physician, and a pharmacist in a 2-h team-based setting. The group visit provided patients with a bridge from inpatient to outpatient setting by ensuring patients access to care with a scheduled appointment at the time of discharge, enabling patients to review care plans with a physician within days of discharge, providing medication reconciliation, and allowing outpatient BH clinicians to be actively involved in care and assist with psychosocial barriers as the patient transitioned to home. Patients were also invited to raise concerns about their hospitalization, their emotional experience, and their post-hospital needs, so the healthcare team could learn how to best help patients in this unique setting.

[1] A behavioural health clinician is a member of the primary healthcare team, typically with a graduate degree in a behavioural health field (Ph.D. in psychology or Masters of Social Work, Mental Health Counselling, or Marriage and Family Therapy), who serves as a bridge between the biomedical and psychosocial worlds. They work with people with complex illnesses and psychosocial risk factors by providing support, education, and advocacy, as well as crisis intervention, assessment, and brief therapy. They work to reduce fragmentation and duplication of services by helping bridge services and communication between speciality mental health services and primary care [6].

One realization was that recently discharged patients were often still quite ill and slowly recovering, often teetering on the need for legitimate and necessary readmission. Because the level of acuity of patient needs varied so greatly, the team had to learn together to be flexible and adaptable to prevent readmission to the hospital and keep the patient improving in their health status in their own home, while at times also having to acknowledge a patient's declining or unstable status requiring a seamless path to readmission.

A unique aspect of this group visit was the incorporation of the BH clinician into the team. Each patient met with the BH clinician, rather than a meeting prompted by a clearly identified need, as is the case in the traditional outpatient visit. Most patients discharged from hospitalization have many areas of concern beyond their medical condition. While patients had the option to decline, 67 % of patients met with a BH clinician during the team visit and were invited to bring up whatever psychosocial issues they felt were important. Qualitative data analysis [2] revealed that these interactions most frequently focused on accessing resources, on psychosocial stressors, and coping skills, particularly around adjusting to health problems and disability. Patients were provided with solution-focused psychosocial support, such as financial assistance, brief counselling, mental health therapy intakes, and care coordination of resources. The majority of these patients would not have interacted with a BH clinician had they not been seen in the team-based visit, and therefore may have continued struggling with interpersonal relationships, stress management, and other resource needs without accessing formal support and knowing that continued support is available at CHFHC.

Patients described the value of the opportunity to share their hospital experience with both other patients and the healthcare team, through surveys obtained at the end of the visit. The open-ended survey questions were analysed qualitatively and re-emerging themes were identified [2]. Patients felt empowered by the group experience where they were asked open-ended questions about their hospitalization:

> The fact that staff actually wanted feedback - it felt good to voice my issues.
>
> This showed me I was not alone and other people are dealing with chronic illnesses as well.

The healthcare team also learned from patients what they needed most post-hospitalization. Important themes were access to healthcare, having time to express their concerns, and having clear communication about what exactly they needed to do post-discharge. Patients also repeatedly expressed the importance of a whole person approach, with access to resources being an important theme.

> A comfortable setting to ask questions and voice concerns and more overall time to express quality of life with all involved practitioners.
>
> They took the time to talk with me.

This feedback reaffirmed the team-based group approach to the post-discharge hospitalization needs, and highlighted the value of a behavioural health clinical as a central member of the team.

19.4 Reflections

Using a framework of complex adaptive systems, these projects sought to obtain a better understanding of both the patient and the system contributors to the "problem of ED over-utilization and re-hospitalization". The emphasis was to explore the relationships of interactions between the patients and the systems.

The percentage of ED visits by "high utilizers" and the number of visits per week by "high utilizers" were tracked prospectively with data available weekly through billing data. This quantitative measure was tracked longitudinally with Statistical Process Control (SPC) charts (XmR and p) and analysed for statistically significant special cause variation that could be associated temporally with the above interventions. There was a significant reduction in ED utilization among the 127 pre-identified "high utilizers" on this medical team, both in the number of weekly visits and as a percentage of the total ED visits. In the groups at CHFHC that did not hear the direct feedback from the PAC, a similar pattern of decreased utilization was observed but not to the same degree as the intervention group, which may, in part, speak to the cyclical nature of ED utilization, i.e. high utilization likely occurs in waves. The notion that increased ED utilization occurs in waves is reflected anecdotally by providers' observation that patients use the ED during crisis periods in their lives. This is important information in addressing the issue of high utilization; it allows teams to appropriately identify, treat, and prevent future high utilization among those patients more likely to access care at the ED. There was also a statistically significant decrease in the number of visits and percentage of ED visits by a rolling list of current "high utilizers" following the intervention of PAC and UPOC. This data represents all "high utilizers" and was not reproduced in CHFHC control groups. The change reflected in the all "high utilizer" data infers a transformative change in the process, work-flows, patient experience, and culture surrounding the care of this sub-population of patients. This effect is believed to be a direct result of the ongoing dialogue between patients in the PAC, the interdisciplinary improvement team, and the micro-system providing care and thus, the impact of the cultural shift was not limited to the pre-identified "high utilizer" group.

Hospital discharge data was also monitored prospectively through the use of SPC charts, through monthly readmission rates. Quantitative process measures were also collected, monitoring the percent of patients that were discharged from the hospital with a follow-up appointment and the percent that were seen within 7 days of discharge. During the first year of the implementation of the post-hospitalization team-based visit, (2011–2012), 95 patients attended a weekly visit, with a range of 1–10 patients seen per visit. The readmission rate for those who attended the group visit was 13.6 %, which was not different from the overall CHFHC readmission rates. During the second year of the visit (2012–2013), however, 91 patients attended a team-based visit and only 3 were readmitted within 30 days of discharge (rate 3.4 %). The readmission rate for patients that attend this visit continues to be lower than those patients who do not. It is worth considering whether and how the patients that attend the group may for some reason have a different risk for readmission, and how we might be able to learn from their experiences.

19.5 Conclusion

An imperative in twenty-first century health care is to go beyond problem-focused methodologies to address issues embedded in a complex adaptive system. Re-framing ED utilization and re-hospitalization as phenomena of a complex system behaviour, and using complex adaptive systems principles to better understand the relationships inherent in these processes allows for a meaningful and valuable understanding of both issues. With these new understandings, cultural change has been enabled and hopefully embedded in our organization, allowing us to ongoingly support the highly variable complex biomedical needs, but especially social, psychological, and cognitive needs of patients "at risk of utilizing ED and/or being readmitted".

References

1. Argyris C, Schon D. Organisational learning: a theory of action perspective. Reading, MA: Addison Wesley; 1974
2. Crabtree BF, Miller WL. Doing qualitative research: research methods for primary care. Thousand Oaks, CA: Sage; 1999
3. Strauss A., Corbin J. Basics of qualitative research. 2nd ed. Thousand Oaks, CA: Sage; 1998
4. Baird M, Peek CJ, Gunn W, Valeras AS. Working with complexity in integrated health settings. In: Talen M, Valeras AB, editors. Integrating primary care and behavioral health: evaluating the evidence, identifying the essentials. New York, NY: Springer; 2013
5. Council L, Geffken D, Valeras A, Orzano J, Rechisky A, and Anderson S. A medical home: changing the way patients and teams relate through Patient Centered Care Plans. Fam Syst Health 2012; 30(3):190–8
6. Talen M, Valeras A. Integrated behavioral health in primary care: evaluating the evidence, identifying the essentials. New York, NY: Springer; 2013

Chapter 20
Access to Primary Care: A Complex Adaptive Systems Lens on Acuity

Carmel M. Martin and David Emanuel Surate Solaligue

Reducing pressure on emergency departments (ED) and reducing inappropriate hospital admissions and readmissions is a pressing issue international for practice, policy and research [1]. Lack of access to primary care services for acute needs may be a significant factor in the high rate of "unnecessary", or rather inappropriate, use of emergency departments [2], and a reason for deterioration in the state of patients with brittle conditions leading to unnecessary hospitalization.

Our aim is to conduct an exploratory analysis of literature on *access to comprehensive primary care*, operationalized as "scheduling planned ahead" or "unplanned appointments", using a complex adaptive systems (CAS) framework. This paper provides an investigates of competing priorities in PC practices that have the goal of mitigating avoidable emergency hospital utilization within the context of the delivery of comprehensive primary care.

A scoping of PubMed (Medline), Google and other online general search engines, and hand searching of "access" literature using a complex systems framework. The literature on high risk groups and emergency department use related to access to PC were scoped from the provider perspective, and articles were scoped on the themes of CAS. This scoping analysis is limited to countries or settings with general practitioner-type services (GP) or health services which provide integrated primary care services (PC) with "universal access"—such as Accountable Care

---

C.M. Martin (✉)
Department of Public Health and Primary Care, Trinity College Dublin,
College Green, Dublin 2, Ireland, 34/72 Lorimer Terrace, Kelvin Grove, Brisbane Qld 4059
e-mail: carmelmarymartin@gmail.com

D.E.S. Solaligue
Max Plank Institute Bad Nauheim, MBML (Molecular Biology and Medicine of the Lung),
63 Unterhof, Apartment 7712, 32395 Giessen, Hessen, Germany
e-mail: desurate@gmail.com

J.P. Sturmberg (ed.), *The Value of Systems and Complexity Sciences for Healthcare*, DOI 10.1007/978-3-319-26221-5_20

Organizations. References were ordered into a narrative review according to their relevance to the access to "same day" or "planned appointments" in PC yielding 25 relevant papers. Major themes were identified and a synthesis was developed.

20.1 Multiple Dimensions to Access

Primary care (PC), internationally, aims to provide timely access and continuity of care to a comprehensive range of services for most personal health needs (Table 20.1). Interdependent PC dimensions include providing access, continuity, prevention and chronic care, addressing case-mix and social needs. Primary care practice integrates care across primary and hospital-based care and comprises the bulk of health services delivered. Specific interrelationships exist among separate aspects of the structure (accessibility, range of services, identification of the eligible population and continuity), process (utilization and problem recognition) and outcome of care [4].

"First-contact accessibility is the ease with which a person can obtain, needed care (including advice) from the practitioner of choice within a time frame appropriate to the urgency of the problem" [5]. Accessibility-accommodation refers to *"the way primary health care resources are organized to accommodate a wide range of patients' abilities to contact health care clinicians and reach health care services"* [6, 7].

Table 20.1 Comprehensive primary (health) care (adapted from [3])

PC organizations ensure that their practice populations receive: • Rapid management of acute, urgent health problems • Timely provision of non-urgent routine care (including well care and chronic illness management) • Recommended preventive services • Appropriate referral to hospitals and specialist • Follow-up care after hospitalization • Primary biopsychosocial and mental health care • Coordinated care of multimorbidity, disability and frailty • End-of-life care

20.1.1 Patient Access Needs

Looking at PC from a patient perspective—it is important to understand why patients seek PC access. There is considerable heterogeneity in demand for access for acute versus other presentations in primary care. Approximately 20 % of presentations to PC are acute, about 5 % are urgent and 3 % of encounters are referred from PC to ED; 30 % of PC presentations may be "indeterminate"— around 20 % of PC visits in Australia are for undifferentiated conditions [8]. In addition, some people seek ED care, without trying to access PC and bypass the GP gatekeeping role in their personal health journey [9].

20.1.2 Scheduling Studies

A major question is how to supply appointments urgently, conveniently and equitably through the organization by booking and scheduling. Scheduling research has focused on the dynamics of "advanced bookings" versus "same day bookings". Waiting times vary similarly whether the system is "open access" or "pre-booked and triaged", and may vary from 24 h for acute patients to 20 days for routine patients, according to supply and demand. Longer PC waiting times compromise patient satisfaction, health outcomes and are associated with increased emergency room crowding [10]. Five different patterns of scheduling have been identified with four mixed patterns relying on front-line receptionists and triage by health professionals (Table 20.2). On the other hand, advanced ("open") access scheduling aims to deliver patient-driven scheduling instead of prearranged appointments [11]. Matching supply and demand using "advanced access" ensures continuity for vulnerable patients has emerged. Incorporating dynamic modelling with an oversight panel to ensure appropriateness and equity has shown an improvement reducing waiting times from 20 days to 1 day in the Veterans' Administration Health Systems [12]. However "pure open access" trials have not achieved continuity with other unintended consequences in other settings and are only feasible for very large practices [13].

Innovations and adoptions involving agents, processes and system boundaries Increasing demands for PC with greater priority to address acuity have led to innovations. Reallocation of provider roles to improve triage, usually utilizing advanced practice nurses, has not improved access for acuity in trials [1]. The supply of all types of PC personnel is an important determinant of access for acute presentations [14, 15], however, the most important determinant of access, the accommodation for acute or same day care in hours, is physician supply [13]. Conversely, the utilization of advanced practice nurses providing group visits for those with long-term illness, self-management support and individual well care appears to reduce demand for scheduled appointments, freeing up appointments for acute presentations [16]. Care management approaches that involve caring for very

Table 20.2 Appointment systems types in primary care (adapted from Knight [12] and Murray [37])

Types of appointment systems identified:
1. **Open access** (No appointments. Seen by time of arrival with modified queuing systems and some continuity with preferred doctors)
2. **Same day booking** (Appointments allocated on the day for only that day via phone calls each morning)
3. Full appointments (Appointments are booked according to the patient's request. Acute appointments are "squeezed in" by double booking or in lunch times)
4. **Protected acute care** (Practices preserve a number of appointments each day for acute care within their other preferred appointment system)
5. **Advanced access** (Same day appointments—using queuing and systems engineering approaches to redesign the whole practice as a system—balancing supply and demand, reducing backlog, reducing appointment types, developing contingency plans for unusual circumstances, working to adjust demand profiles and increasing the availability of bottleneck resources. Not sustainable if patient demand for appointments is permanently greater than physician capacity to offer appointments)

high risk elderly or seriously ill or socially disadvantaged patients to some extent pre-empts acute presentations, by identifying them in sub-acute or chronic phases [17–21]. After-hours access to primary care services is linked with lower emergency department use and less unmet medical need internationally [22, 23].

Various modelling approaches and predictive analytic models, particularly the combined predictive models, where indicators were extracted at the time of hospital discharge or from PC records, have improved the predictions of who is at very high risk of emergency medical treatment [24]. Nevertheless moderately high risk patients are still high utilizers of PC requiring same day access for urgent problems [25]. Risk is a dynamic and changing phenomenon, and people move between groups (regression to the mean) and away from equilibrium in response to perturbations [26, 27].

The use of Internet and mobile technologies has the potential to be a disruptive innovation which improves both convenience and crisis management in accommodating access [28, 29]. Such technologies may enable patient journeys, from the point of view of trajectory ability, with fluctuating resilience [30]. Articulating acuity can be challenging if the patient's trajectory is unstable and their illness is nonspecific [31, 32].

20.2 A Complex Adaptive Systems Lens

A Complex Adaptive System is one composed of many heterogeneous agents, interacting with each other in subtle or non-linear ways [33]. CAS characteristics include the individuality of each agent, creating heterogeneity, yet interdependences and interconnectedness influenced by external and internal attractors or drivers. In order to address the dynamics of access, there is a need to balance acuity and continuity, case-mix and different types of patient journeys with social pressures including convenience. Relationships among the agents are dynamic and changing, understandable but somewhat unpredictable, yet can include linear or directly predictable relationships. Figure 20.1 describes an overview summary of the complex dynamics of providing access to primary care.

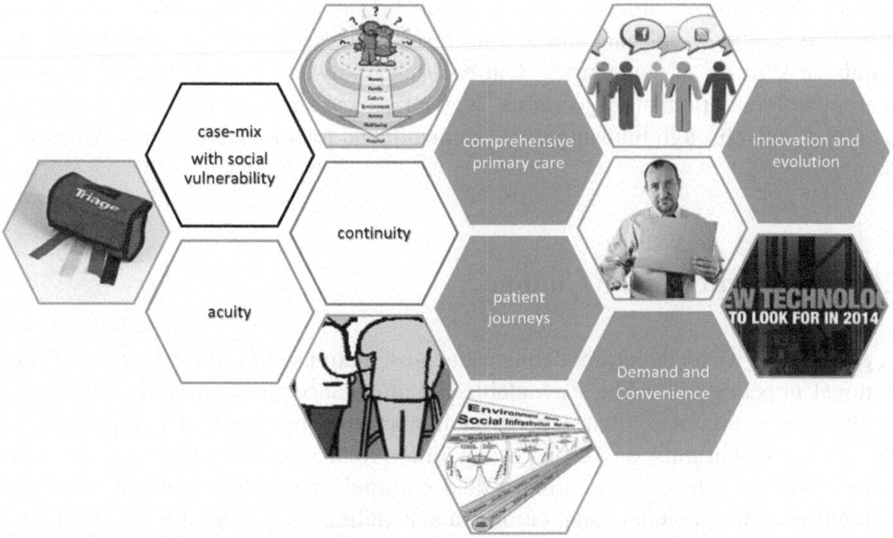

Fig. 20.1 A framework for the complex nature of access to comprehensive primary care with some key elements identified in the literature. Scheduling needs to balance the rapid management of acute, urgent health problems (acuity), continuity and the convenient provision of non-urgent routine care (including well care and chronic illness management) as well as addressing uncertain presentations. Acuity beyond simple or self-assessed report must address the nature of patient journeys expressed through narratives and or informatics systems, and may need to be assessed or triaged by receptionists, nurses and physicians [25]. Continuity [34] and relationship-based care are highly sensitive to case-mix such as Ambulatory Care Visit Groups [35] or other morbidity profiles. Taking account of poor social support, transport, work, child-minding pressures and reduced networks is important. Comprehensive primary health care also includes convenient access to recommended preventive services; referral and follow-up with respect to hospitals and specialist. Demand must be balanced by supply constraints [36] on the appointment system. On the positive end, innovation and evolution of new technologies may mitigate supply and issues and promote more timely access

Routine non-acute appointments can be allocated using "simple", "open access" and/or "rule-based" processes [37]. Complex and chaotic scheduling states are likely to emerge when there are tensions among elements such as acuity of medical need or psychosocial crisis versus long-term continuity needs of those with chronic multimorbid conditions, or versus convenience for routine care and prevention. Success requires continual adaptation to change with the need to self-organize and correct within the boundaries of the system. However unintended consequences will inevitably emerge with system shifts in favour of one PC domain in this case access over others such as continuity or comprehensiveness.

In every system in the papers reviewed there was a need for human sense-making to adjudicate these challenges. Accommodating human sense-making; self-organization, rules-based, modelling and outreach can address acuity by adjusting routine and planned appointments in response to demand. Open systems vary dynamically according to demand on the system; there remains a need for some human arbitration in order to address competing needs and demands in order to prioritize acuity, social and illness trajectories. Excessive external constraint may require a shifting of boundaries. Outreach and non-linear modelling of systems that incorporate patient trajectories as well as case-mix and in-reach through patient portals through innovations in telehealth and telemedicine would extend PC boundaries.

20.3 Imperatives for Change

A greater priority for accommodating acute presentations in PC has become an international imperative to reduce avoidable ED attendances and hospital admissions. Addressing acuity has always been an important component of comprehensive PC. Given constraints on resources, in order to maximize acuity access while minimizing an impact on continuity and comprehensiveness, adaptive changing is required. This includes: adaptations in scheduling and internal work practices; shifting of roles among providers and shifting of the external boundaries of PC practices. The continual refining of the diverse range of mixed scheduling systems with open and planned access to better address potentially serious acute deterioration would encompass integrating human judgement and sense-making for linear and non-linear synergistic, overlapping or competitive priorities. Ongoing innovations in e-health and service models such group visits and care management for vulnerable groups will shift the system boundaries though increasing the modes of access and increased support for very high risk groups. Diversity, adaptation and human sense-making are the key to success in making comprehensive primary care systems fit for purpose.

References

1. Ismail SA, Gibbons DC, Gnani S. Reducing inappropriate accident and emergency department attendances: a systematic review of primary care service interventions. Br J Gen Pract. 2013;63(617):e813–20
2. Cowling TE, Harris MJ, Watt HC, Gibbons DC, Majeed A. Access to general practice and visits to accident and emergency departments in England: cross-sectional analysis of a national patient survey. Br J Gen Pract. 2014;64(624):e434–9
3. Haggerty J, Martin CM. Evaluating primary health care in Canada: the right questions to ask!. Ottawa: Publications Health Canada; 2005
4. Starfield B. Measuring the attainment of primary care. J Med Educ. 1979;54(5):361–9
5. Haggerty JL, Levesque JF, Santor DA, Burge F, Beaulieu C, Bouharaoui F, et al. Accessibility from the patient perspective: comparison of primary healthcare evaluation instruments. Healthcare Policy/Politiques de sante 2011;7(Spec Issue):94–107
6. Haggerty JL, Pineault R, Beaulieu M-D, Brunelle Y, Gauthier J, Goulet F, et al. Practice features associated with patient-reported accessibility, continuity, and coordination of primary health care. Ann Fam Med. 2008;6(2):116–23
7. Starfield B, Shi L, Macinco J. Contribution of primary health care to health systems and health. Milbank Q 2005;83(3):457–502
8. Britt H, Miller GC, Charles J, Henderson J, Bayram C, Pan Y, et al. General practice activity in Australia 2009–10. General practice series no. 27. Cat. no. GEP 27. Canberra: AIHW; 2010
9. Land L, Meredith N. An evaluation of the reasons why patients attend a hospital Emergency Department. Int Emerg Nurs. 2011;21(1):35–41
10. Sampson F, Pickin M, O'Cathain A, Goodall S, Salisbury C. Impact of same-day appointments on patient satisfaction with general practice appointment systems. Br J Gen Pract. 2008;58(554):641–3
11. Mehrotra A, Keehl-Markowitz L, Ayanian JZ. Implementing open-access scheduling of visits in primary care practices: a cautionary tale. Ann Intern Med. 2008;148(12):915–22
12. Schall MW, Duffy T, Krishnamurthy A, Levesque O, Mehta P, Murray M, et al. Improving patient access to the Veterans Health Administration's primary care and specialty clinics. Jt Comm J Qual Saf. 2004;30(8):415–23
13. Ozen A, Balasubramanian H. The impact of case mix on timely access to appointments in a primary care group practice. Health Care Manag Sci. 2013;16(2):101–18
14. Olsen KR, Gyrd-Hansen D, Sorensen TH, Kristensen T, Vedsted P, Street A. Organisational determinants of production and efficiency in general practice: a population-based study. Eur J Health Econ. 2013;14(2):267–76
15. Bankart MJ, Anwar MS, Walker N, Mainous AG, Baker R. Are there enough GPs in England to detect hypertension and maintain access? A cross-sectional study. Br J Gen Pract. 2013;63(610):e339–44
16. Jones KR, Kaewluang N, Lekhak N. Group visits for chronic illness management: implementation challenges and recommendations. Nurs Econ. 2014;32(3):118–34
17. Bower P, Roland M, Campbell J, Mead N. Setting standards based on patients' views on access and continuity: secondary analysis of data from the general practice assessment survey. Br Med J 2003;326(7383):258
18. Sweeney L, Halpert A, Waranoff J. Patient-centered management of complex patients can reduce costs without shortening life. Am J Manag Care 2007;13(2):84–92
19. Wright PN, Tan G, Iliffe S, Lee D. The impact of a new emergency admission avoidance system for older people on length of stay and same-day discharges. Age Ageing 2014;43(1):116–21
20. Department of Health VG, Australia. Hospital Avoidance Reduction Program (HARP); 2009. http://www.health.vic.gov.au/harp/index.htm
21. Lewis GH. "Impactibility Models": identifying the subgroup of high-risk patients most amenable to hospital-avoidance programs. Milbank Q 2010;88(2):240–55

22. O'Malley AS. After-hours access to primary care practices linked with lower emergency department use and less unmet medical need. Health Aff. 2013;32(1):175–83
23. Ng JY, Fatovich DM, Turner VF, Wurmel JA, Skevington SA, Phillips MR. Appropriateness of healthdirect referrals to the emergency department compared with self-referrals and GP referrals. Med J Aust. 2012;197(9):498–502
24. Wennberg D, Siegel M, Darin B, Filipova N, Russell R, Kenney L, et al. Combined predictive model. London: King's Fund Publication; 2006. http://www.kingsfund.org.uk/sites/files/kf/field/field_document/PARR-combined-predictive-model-final-report-dec06.pdf. Accessed 21 Dec 2015
25. Solaligue DES, Martin C, Hederman. L. What weekday? an analysis of planned and unplanned GP visits by older multi-morbid patients in the Patient Journey Record System database. An acuity of GP care utilisation study. J Eval Clin Pract 2014;20(4):522–26
26. Roland M, Abel G. Reducing emergency admissions: are we on the right track? Br Med J 2012;345:e6017
27. Roland M, Dusheiko M, Gravelle H, Parker S. Follow up of people aged 65 and over with a history of emergency admissions: analysis of routine admission data. Br Med J. 2005;330(7486):289–92
28. Rezende EJ, Tavares EC, Alves HJ, dos Santos Ade F, de Melo Mdo C. Teleconsultations in public primary care units of the city of belo horizonte, Brazil: profile of patients and physicians. Telemedicine 2013;19(8):613–18
29. Standing C, Gururajan R, Standing S, Cripps H. Making the most of virtual expertise in telemedicine and telehealth environment. J Organ Comput Electron Commer 2014; 24(2–3):138–56
30. Martin C. Self-rated health—patterns in the journeys of patients with multi-morbidity and frailty. J Eval Clin Pract 2014;20(6):1010–6
31. Martin M, Hin PY, O'Neill D. Acute medical take or subacute-on-chronic medical take? Ir Med J 2004;97(7):212–4
32. Martin C. Do 'complex' non-specific states predict hospital utilization? Patterns in a cohort of 'at risk' patients. North American Primary Care Research Group Conference Paper; 2013. www.napcrg.org
33. Hammond RA. Complex systems modeling for obesity research. Prev Chronic Dis 2009;6(3):A97
34. Bjorkelund C, Maun A, Murante AM, Hoffman K, De Maeseneer J, Farkas-Pall Z. Impact of continuity on quality of primary care: from the perspective of citizens' preferences and multimorbidity—position paper of the European Forum for Primary Care. Qual Prim Care 2013;21(3):193–204
35. Starfield B, Weiner J, Mumford L, Steinwachs D. Ambulatory care groups: a categorization of diagnoses for research and management. Health Serv Res 1991;26(1):53–74
36. Balasubramanian H, Biehl S, Dai L, Muriel A. Dynamic allocation of same-day requests in multi-physician primary care practices in the presence of prescheduled appointments. Health Care Manag Sci 2014;17(1):31–48
37. Murray M, Tantau C. Same-day appointments: exploding the access paradigm. Fam Pract Manag. 2000;7(8):45–50

Chapter 21
"If the Facts Don't Fit the Theory, Change the Theory": Implications for Health System Reform

Joachim P. Sturmberg

> ***I don't blame anybody - they're just doing what makes sense and we have to change what makes sense.*** *Don Berwick*

Current health systems around the world have a predominant focus on diseases and economic imperatives. So it should come as no surprise that they are delivering disease management within an economically constraint environment—reducing or maximising services to meet respective stakeholders' budgetary imperatives. However, despite being the prevailing perspective, there are others who champion a focus on the much broader concept of health and the long-term economic performance of the whole system.

21.1 The *Health Vortex*: Conceptualising a Complex Adaptive Health System

Healthcare systems are remarkably stable, they are structurally open but organisationally closed, i.e. despite the constant flow of activity they retain a stable form, and they do so autonomously through self-organisation based on simple rules. Capra suggested that these characteristics can be best illustrated by a vortex; a vortex requires a central focus that starts the process of self-organising its characteristic shape and behaviour. Disturbing the vortex alters its shape; however, the interconnected organisational behaviours maintain its overall structure and function [1].

The health vortex in Fig. 21.1 illustrates the principle structure of the health system and its various organisational levels—the local service delivery, community health and infrastructure, regional health and infrastructure and the overarching

J.P. Sturmberg (✉)
Department of General Practice, School of Medicine and Public Health, The University of Newcastle, Newcastle, PO Box 3010, Wamberal, NSW 2250, Australia
e-mail: jp.sturmberg@gmail.com

J.P. Sturmberg (ed.), *The Value of Systems and Complexity Sciences for Healthcare*, DOI 10.1007/978-3-319-26221-5_21

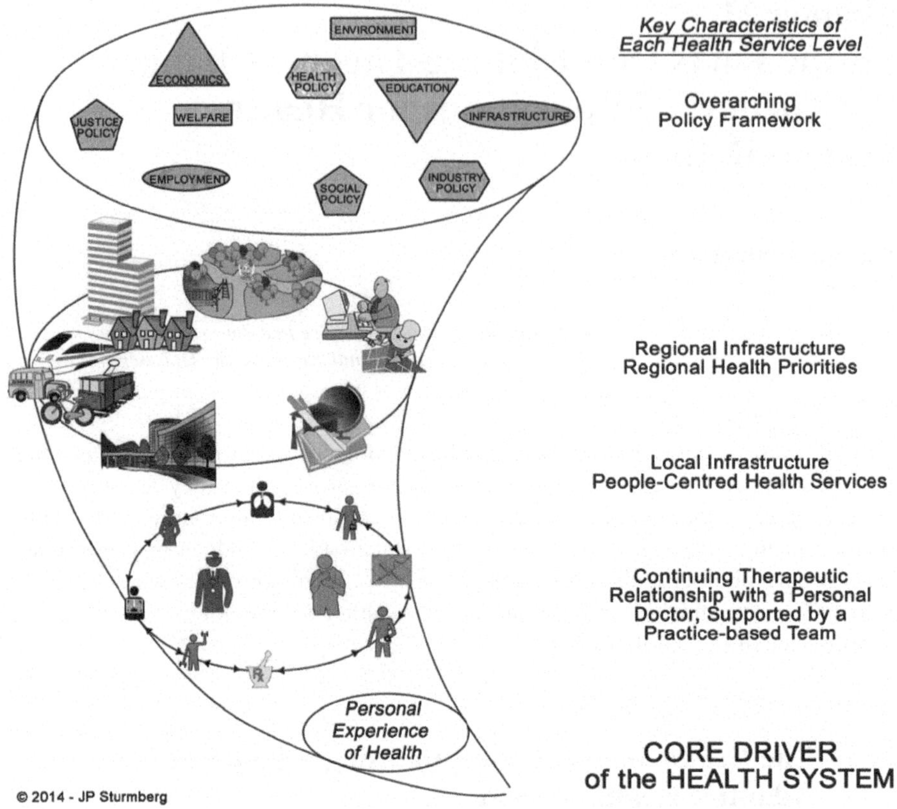

Fig. 21.1 The principles of the healthcare vortex

policy levels. Whilst each of these levels has unique structural and functional characteristics, to work in synergy as "one system" they all have to align around a common focus.

21.1.1 The Role of "Core Values" and "Simple Rules"

Self-organisation underpins the structure and function of any complex adaptive system. Self-organisation depends on two features: *core values* which define a system's focus and purpose, and simple rules (or operating principles) which provide its operational framework. Core values and simple rules provide the freedom as well as the necessary constraints for neighbouring agents to interact. These interactions have system-wide effects which result in the observable behaviour of the system [2, 3].

Core values are those that remain unchanged in a changing world: they do not change in response to market, financial or administrative changes, and sustain the organisation in times of challenge. *Values and ethics* give an organisation its "soul", define what it stands for, how it conducts itself and how it guides the behaviour of its members. As "governing principles" they apply uniformly to all members and all organisational units.
Simple rules are generated when people central to the success of a particular endeavour consider the relationship between the organisation's goals and its *core values.* These reflections enabling the crafting of simple rules or operating principles—usually 3–5, as too few do not provide sufficient boundaries and too many constrict creativity—and define the manner in which the organisation's work should be undertaken [4, 5]. Figure 21.1 compares the *simple rules* of the disease-focused versus the health-focused perspective on organising the health system.

21.1.2 "Fit for Purpose"

System structures and functions emerge in response to a problem; a well-functioning system is one that constantly adapts to the rapidly changing demands in a changing environment to remain *fit for purpose.* In the context of healthcare core aspects of fitness for purpose entail "safe service delivery", "improving the patient's health experience", "maintaining health through self-care" and "minimising harm to health".

Fitness for purpose has to be achieved in a constantly changing environment with diverse perceptions and stakeholders. It can only be accomplished through collaboration across networks of diverse domains of expertise as illustrated schematically in Fig. 21.2. Of note, fitness for purpose requires input from areas that are not normally associated with health achievement, like the building of physical infrastructure or the maintenance of a sustainable environment.

21.2 What Do the Facts Tell Us

Healthcare expenditure and health outcomes show a rather mixed relationship. The USA has the highest healthcare expenditure in the world (17.7 % of GDP; compare: UK spends 9.4 % and Australia 8.9 % of GDP), has a substantial number of people unable to afford healthcare (though this is changing under Obamacare; universal health coverage in the UK and Australia) but achieves some of the worst health outcomes amongst OECD countries (infant mortality, low-birth weight, diabetes incidence, suicide rate, cardiovascular mortality rate and life expectancy [6]).

The evidence also shows that many of the commonly held assumptions about diseases and disease management as well as outcomes-based reward incentives are unfounded.

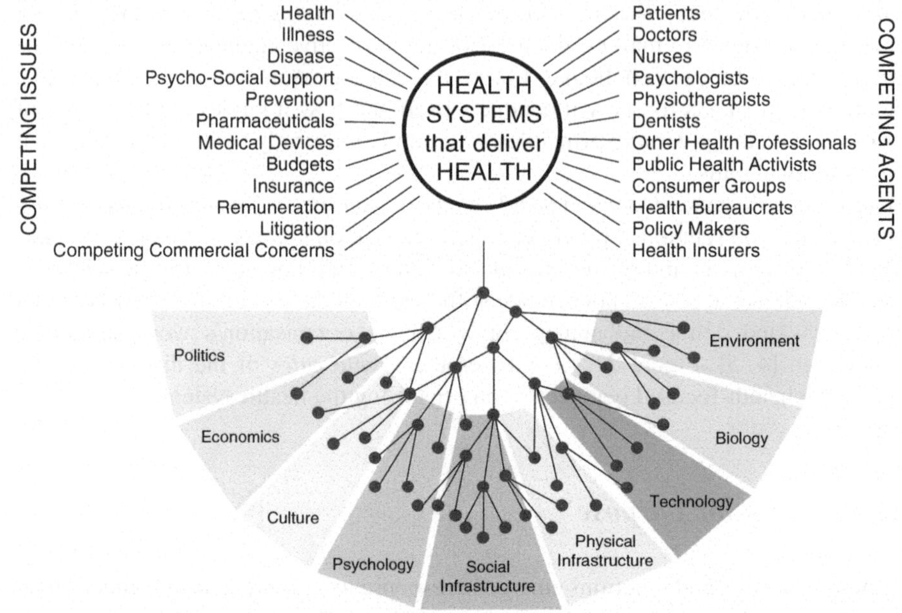

Fig. 21.2 Fitness for purpose results from managing the interconnected features impacting on healthcare

For example, Port [7] re-analysed the Framingham data and had to reject the proposition of a linear—"the lower the better"—blood pressure and mortality relationship; in fact mortality and blood pressure show a non-linear relationship with a threshold behaviour for readings up to 120 + age, only readings higher than that are associated with an exponential increase in risk. The absolute benefit of treating hypertension on total mortality, myocardial infarction, stroke and heart failure is minuscule [8]—total mortality decreases by 2.7 per 1000, myocardial infarction by 3.9 per 1000, stroke by 0.8 per 1000 and heart failure by 2 per 1000 patients—however, adverse effects occur in 66 per 1000.

The treatment of non-insulin dependent diabetes has only a marginal effect on preventing cardiovascular disease over the next 10 years—for a 60-year-old male with uncontrolled diabetes (HbA1c 10 %) and acceptably controlled diabetes (HbA1c 8.5 %) the risk is reduced from 28 and 25, respectively, to 23 for those with good control (HbA1c 7.5 %; within 1 % above "normal") compared to 20 for non-diabetics; the respective figures for a female are 21, 18, 17 and 15 [9]. The lifetime risk for the above of micro-vascular diseases is reduced from 2 to 1 for dialysis and 2 to <0.5 for blindness [10]. The Accord study suggests that aiming for too tight a control of diabetes may be associated with an increase in mortality of 10 per 1000 patients [11].

Population-based screening for cancer or the lowering of "normality" to define "pre-disease" have shown no meaningful **absolute** benefit in terms of either disease specific or population health outcomes [12–14]. However, they result in high numbers of over-diagnoses and unnecessary treatments associated with physical impairments and ongoing negative emotional consequences [15–18].

Improvement initiatives involving pay-for-performance strategies, like the UK "Quality Outcomes Framework", have focused on disease-specific, largely biomedical, markers as surrogate indicators of quality [19, 20]. This approach has resulted in significant shifts in the focus of the consultation away from the patient's concern to the recording of the required markers for payment purposes [19, 21] without having achieved any significant or lasting improvement in patient well-being or population health outcomes [22].

In general terms western health systems' performance can be summarised as follows:

- Limited in scope in terms of patient care, largely focused on the biomedical aspects of conditions and diseases,
- Lacking coordination and integration with the social dimensions of the patient's capacity and capability to cope and manage,
- Service structures that are focused on vertical biomedical service integration to maximise profits, coupled with the constant threat of litigation (practice safe medicine),
- Widespread fee-for-service arrangements that bias health professionals in doing more, again coupled with the constant threat of litigation,
- Health professionals' general lack of awareness of "high-value care",
- Cooperation controlled health service enterprises and health insurance companies with an imperative to maximise shareholder return, and
- An uncoordinated policy approach to healthcare, with many countries still lacking a universal access approach to healthcare, allowing the promotion of disease mongering, failing to coordinate policies that have a negative impact on the interdependent social and environmental dimensions on health, and preferencing resourcing for chronic disease management over prevention.

Table 21.1 provides an—by no means comprehensive—overview of key activities arising from a disease compared to a health-focused approach to health system organisation. While many activities overlap there is a significant difference in emphasis between the two approaches.

21.3 If the Facts Don't Fit the Theory, Change the Theory

How can we understand these differences? They reflect our appreciation of a problem emerging from the overlap of complexity, system effects and ways of reasoning. Reasoning in particular is susceptible to fallibility based on cognitive biases and competing ideas and interests. We favour arguments and actions that support our vested interests and our short-term gains imperatives, even when there is overwhelming evidence to the contrary.

Table 21.1 Key activities arising from a disease compared to a health-focused approach to health system organisation

Outcome domains	Disease/economic focus	Health focus
Patient outcomes		
Consultations	Identify all potential and real disease Management decisions based on relative epidemiological benefit Apply guidelines for each disease	Understand patient's concerns and expectations Management decisions based on absolute benefit considerations Prevention Food and exercise
Continuity of care	Episodic care for acute conditions Chronic disease management	Foster provider continuity for all care Care coordination clinics Community outreach staff Smartphone technology to remind and monitor e-communication with doctors
Social dimension of health and illness	Smoking Alcohol Drugs	Smoking Alcohol Drugs Racial background Social background Occupation Education Competing priorities Isolation Limited mobility Coping skills Housing Nature of environment, e.g. violence Life circumstances
Affordability	Focus on investigations and treatments that maximise profits	Focus on investigations and treatments that are needed
Health outcomes	Disease-specific indicators Poor population health achievements, e.g. obesity, physical activity, less so for smoking	Quality of life Enablement—the ability to cope Level of disability Social functioning

(continued)

Table 21.1 (continued)

Organisational integrity at the service delivery level		
Service integrity	Vertical integration of biomedical domains	Vertical integration of biomedical and support service domains
Community help desks function in clinics	Social care needs	Food and nutrition Violence prevention Community care options like day care, dementia support, falls prevention
Community integration		Local fresh food supply Environmental safety issues Building social capital
Supply chain issues		Green supply chains
Economic performance		
Remuneration	Fee-for-service drives overuse and over-servicing Fee-for-service risks under-use of less costly modalities Fee-for-service is a disincentive to avoid low-value care	Shared-savings contracts Reimbursement for care-coordination Financial incentives to make appropriate referrals to both institution-based and community-based resources Financial incentives to communicate effectively with social workers, community health workers, therapists, counsellors and other service providers
Political priorities		
Financing	Institutionalised sick care system—costs up to 18 % GDP In USA 1/3 of spending is wasteful Payment for procedures Value volume over value 70 % chronic care 4 % prevention	Push money upstream to prevent sickness in the first place Payment for outcomes
Health insurance	For profit insurance, variable restrictions on excluding services based on health status	For profit or mutual insurance, no exclusions based on health status
Access	Variable, ability to pay buys preferential access	Universal access

(continued)

Table 21.1 (continued)

Patient awareness	Fostering fear of disease and disease mongering	Improving health literacy Promotion of positive image of health Patient education about low-value care
Prevention	Limited by industry interests, e.g. food production and fast food restaurants, petro-chemical industry	Food labelling Public transport Healthy housing Building social infrastructure Building healthier physical environments Educational infrastructure and learning support Safe and stable work
Litigation	Unregulated and open ended	Limited in scope Universal care in case of medical mishaps

We have to accept that when confronted with complex problems we are limited by our brain's capacity to simultaneously process more than a few things at a time (on average 7 ± 2)—we are poor in detecting connections between seemingly unconnected objects or facts, and easily anticipating—in particular non-linear—behaviours more than a step or two ahead [23].

The facts are clear—the prevailing activities are not *fit for purpose for a **health-producing** health system*. It is also glaringly obvious that the prevailing actors find it easier to "muddle with the facts" and stick with the current "disease/economic" theory than to change the theory to one that embraces *health*. As Fig. 21.3 illustrates, one easily can identify the competing and conflicting interests at the different levels in the system.

A new theory would place the patient and his health experience [24, 25] at the centre of the health system [4, 5]. Community epidemiology consistently demonstrates that 80 % of the community manage well without health professional intervention, 16 % require solely care from a primary care provider, 3.2 % have a need for disease-specific interventions and only 0.8 % need all the expert interventions and care provided by a tertiary hospital [26, 27].

The hallmark of a patient/person-centred health system is its focus on the *needs of the patient/person* [24, 25, 28–30]. This focus is of pragmatic importance as these needs arise from the patient's perception of his health which is strongly related to his morbidity and mortality [31, 32].

At a biological level we have been able to trace the mechanisms of health and disease through network analysis at the "omics", psycho-neuro-immunology and social network levels. Of critical importance to all is the impact of constant *environmental perturbations*. While genes are *associated* with diseases, many diseases have

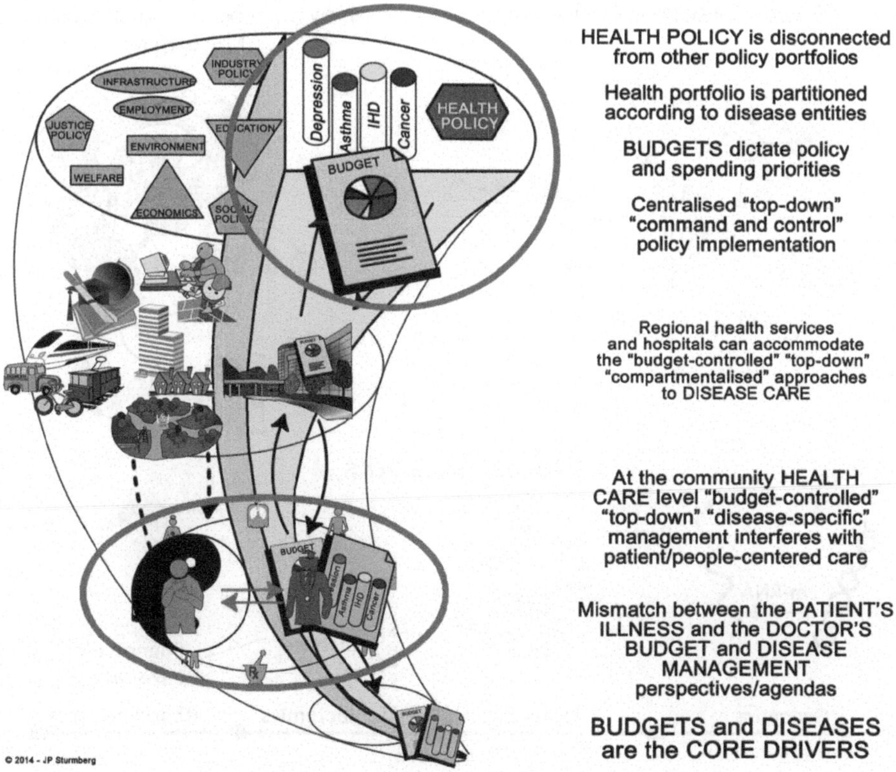

Fig. 21.3 The failings of the current health system configurations

a huge variety of gene associations. The mapping of these genotypic/phenotypic associations has coining the notion of the *diseasome* [33] and the characterisation of *disease networks* [33, 34] as the basis for *personalised network medicine* [35].

The concurrent discoveries in the field of psycho-neuro-immunology have provided important insights in understanding how and why physical, social and emotional experiences are interconnected through feedback loops between the inflammatory mediators and the adreno-cortical and hypothalamic-pituitary-adrenal axis in health, disease and somatisation [36, 37].

Understanding a patient's health and disease as the phenotypic outcome of his highly interconnected network activities from the nano to the macro level means that medical interventions are perturbations of these networks. It is time to accept that we implement healthcare interventions from a *network perturbation perspective*; the desire to cure one disease-specific domain is frequently associated with undesirable and at times catastrophic consequences. In dynamic system interventions *less is often more*! [38, 39] (Fig. 21.4).

A health-focused health system applies the *simple rules* outlined in Table 21.2 as its operating principles for every person at every level of health system organisation.

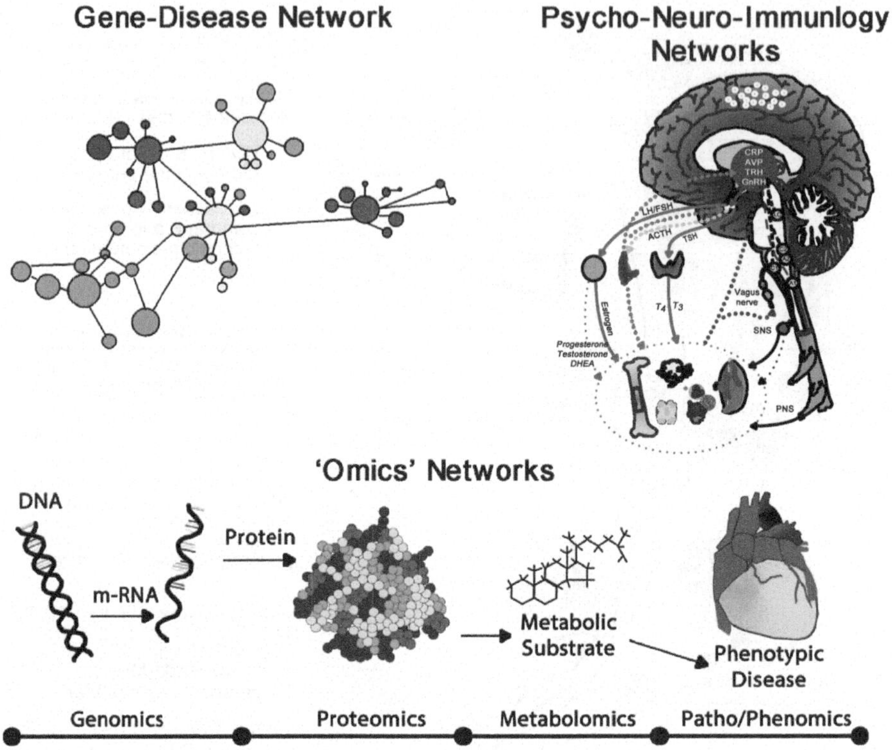

Fig. 21.4 Three networks determining health and disease: gene-disease networks, psycho-neuro-immunology networks and 'omics' networks

Table 21.2 Differences between *simple rules* or operating principles of a disease/economy and a health-focused health system

Disease and economic focus	Health and whole of system economic focus
Meet consumers' disease management demands	Understand the patient's needs
Focus on one disease, limit time and increase throughput	Develop ongoing relationships of trust between patients and their key providers
Follow protocols that standardise service delivery	Consider and understand the patient's context before delving into detail
Market services that maximise profits	Explore the effects of your intended actions on other agents in the system
Integrate service in-house	Consider time delays between actions and outcomes

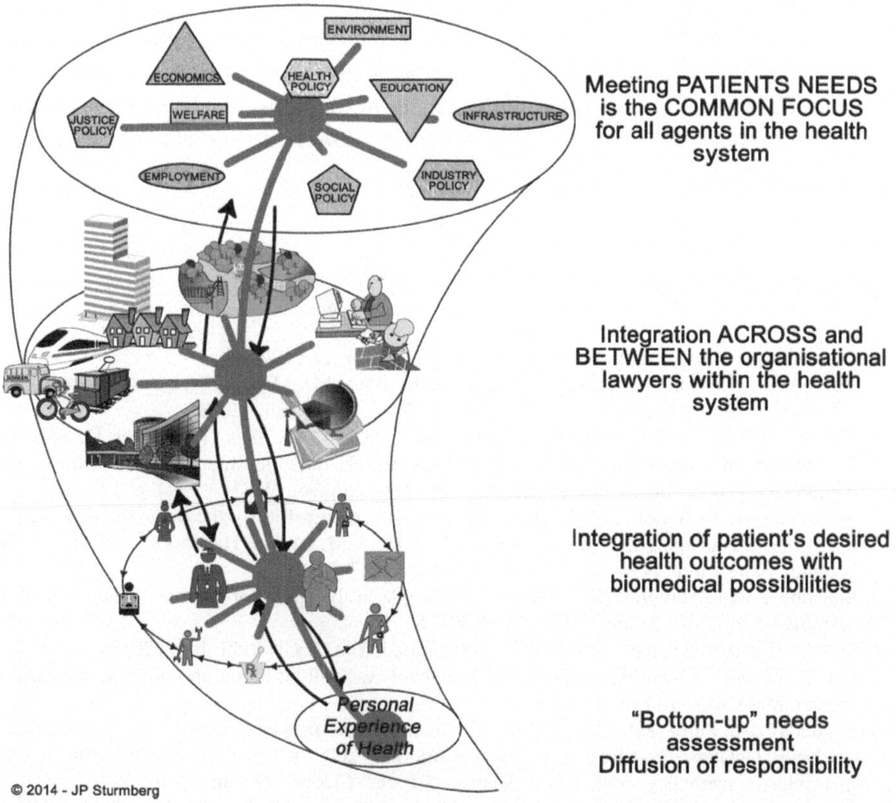

Fig. 21.5 A seamless, fully integrated, coordinated and networked health system model that operates between all levels of care and across all levels of organisation

This will create a seamless, fully integrated, coordinated and networked system between all levels of care and across all levels of organisation (Fig. 21.5). Its benefits include:

- The right care for the right condition in the right place,
- Solving the biomedical as well as the personal, social and environmental issues contributing to poor health experiences,
- Balancing the *person's desired health outcomes* and the provider's application of bio-technical interventions,
- Balancing the *therapeutic alliance* between the provider and patient and the *biomedical intervention* of the provider with the disease,
- Sharing the identification of problems, their potential local solutions and their implementation between the organisational layers of the health system,
- Sharing the financial responsibilities amongst all agents of the systems (patients, providers, service organisations, insurers and policy makers), and
- Maximising the return in *health of the community* for the investment into all domains of the system.

A highly networked environment demands network dynamic approaches and solutions to ever changing conditions. The outlined propositions offer one possible way of doing better, it is our responsibility as health professionals to pursue such progress for the benefits of our patients and our professions—let us all be reminded by William Osler: *"The good physician treats the disease; the great physician treats the patient who has the disease"*.

References

1. Capra F. The web of life. London: Harper Collins Publishers; 1996.
2. Heylighen F. Complexity and self-organization. In: Bates MJ, Maack MN, editors. Encyclopedia of library and information sciences. London: Taylor & Francis; 2008.
3. Gell-Mann M. Complex adaptive systems. In: Cowan GA, Pines D, Meltzer D, editors. Complexity: metaphors, models, and reality, Santa Fe Institute studies in the sciences of complexity. Proceedings Volume XIX. Reading, MA: Addison-Wesley; 1994. p. 17–45.
4. Sturmberg JP, O'Halloran DM, Martin CM. Health care reform - the need for a complex adaptive systems approach. In: Sturmberg JP, Martin CM, editors. Handbook of systems and complexity in health. New York: Springer; 2013. p. 827–53.
5. Sturmberg JP, O'Halloran DM, Martin CM. People at the centre of complex adaptive health systems reform. Med J Aust. 2010;193(8):474–8.
6. OECD. Health at a glance 2013: OECD indicators. Paris: OECD Publishing; 2013.
7. Port S, Demer L, Jennrich R, Walter D, Garfinkel A. Systolic blood pressure and mortality. Lancet. 2000;355(3):175–80.
8. Arguedas JA, Perez MI, Wright JM. Treatment blood pressure targets for hypertension. Cochrane Database Syst Rev. [serial on the Internet] 2009; (3). Available from: http://www.mrw.interscience.wiley.com/cochrane/clsysrev/articles/CD004349/frame.html.
9. Hoerger TJ, Segel JE, Gregg EW, Saaddine JB. Is glycemic control improving in U.S. Adults? Diabetes Care. 2008;31(1):81–6.
10. Vijan S, Hofer TP, Hayward RA. Estimated benefits of glycemic control in microvascular complications in type 2 diabetes. Ann Intern Med. 1997;127(9):788–95.
11. The ACCORD Study Group. Long-term effects of intensive glucose lowering on cardiovascular outcomes. N Engl J Med. 2011;364(9):818–28.
12. Simmons RK, Echouffo-Tcheugui JB, Sharp SJ, Sargeant LA, Williams KM, Prevost AT, et al. Screening for type 2 diabetes and population mortality over 10 years (ADDITION-Cambridge): a cluster-randomised controlled trial. Lancet. 2012;380(9855):1741–8.
13. Schröder FH, Hugosson J, Roobol MJ, Tammela TLJ, Ciatto S, Nelen V, et al. Screening and prostate-cancer mortality in a randomized European study. N Engl J Med. 2009;360(13):1320–8.
14. Esserman L, Shieh Y, Thompson I. Rethinking screening for breast cancer and prostate cancer. JAMA. 2009;302(15):1685–92.
15. Brodersen J, Siersma VD. Long-term psychosocial consequences of false-positive screening mammography. Ann Fam Med. 2013;11(2):106–15.
16. Moynihan R, Doust J, Henry D. Preventing overdiagnosis: how to stop harming the healthy. Br Med J. 2012;344:19–23.
17. Welch HG, Black WC. Overdiagnosis in cancer. J Natl Cancer Inst. 2010;102(9):605–13.
18. Krumholz HM, Lee TH. Redefining quality implications of recent clinical trials. N Engl J Med. 2008;358(24):2537–9.
19. Campbell SM, McDonald R, Lester H. The experience of pay for performance in English family practice: a qualitative study. Ann Fam Med. 2008;6(3):228–34.

20. Mangin D, Toop L. The quality and outcomes framework: what have you done to yourselves? Br J Gen Pract. 2007;57:435–7.
21. McDonald R, Roland M. Pay for performance in primary care in England and California: comparison of unintended consequences. Ann Fam Med. 2009;7(2):121–7.
22. Alshamsan R, Majeed A, Ashworth M, Car J, Millett C. Impact of pay for performance on inequalities in health care: systematic review. J Health Serv Res Policy. 2010;15(3):178–84.
23. Dörner D. The logic of failure: recognizing and avoiding error in complex situations. New York: Metropolitan Books; 1996.
24. Sturmberg JP. The personal nature of health. J Eval Clin Pract. 2009;15(4):766–9.
25. Sturmberg JP. Health: a personal complex-adaptive state. In: Sturmberg JP, Martin CM, editors. Handbook of systems and complexity in health. New York: Springer; 2013. p. 231–42.
26. White K, Williams F, Greenberg B. The ecology of medical care. N Engl J Med. 1961;265(18):885–92.
27. Green L, Fryer G, Yawn B, Lanier D, Dovey S. The ecology of medical care revisited. N Engl J Med. 2001;344(26):2021–5.
28. Searl M, Borgi L, Chemali Z. It is time to talk about people: a human-centered healthcare system. Health Res Policy Syst. 2010;8(1):35.
29. Miles A, Mezzich JE. The care of the patient and the soul of the clinic: person-centered medicine as an emergent model of modern clinical practice. Int J Pers Cent Med. 2011;1(2):207–22.
30. Fuks A, Kreiswirth M, Boudreau D, Sparks T. Narratives, metaphors, and the clinical relationship. Genre. 2011;44(3):301–13.
31. Idler EL, Benyamini Y. Self-rated health and mortality: a review of twenty-seven community studies. J Health Soc Behav. 1997;38(1):21–37.
32. Jylhä M. What is self-rated health and why does it predict mortality? Towards a unified conceptual model. Soc Sci Med. 2009;69(3):307–16.
33. Goh K-I, Cusick ME, Valle D, Childs B, Vidal M, Barabási A-L. The human disease network. Proc Natl Acad Sci. 2007;104(21):8685–90.
34. Loscalzo J, Kohane I, Barabasi A-L. Human disease classification in the postgenomic era: a complex systems approach to human pathobiology. Mol Syst Biol. 2007;3:124.
35. Chan SY, Loscalzo J. The emerging paradigm of network medicine in the study of human disease. Circ Res. 2012;111(3):359–74.
36. Dantzer R, O'Connor JC, Freund GG, Johnson RW, Kelley KW. From inflammation to sickness and depression: when the immune system subjugates the brain. Nat Rev Neurosci. 2008;9(1):46–57.
37. Bennett JM, Gillie BL, Lindgren ME, Fagundes CP, Kiecolt-Glaser JK. Inflammation through a psychoneuroimmunological lens. In: Sturmberg JP, Martin CM, editors. Handbook of systems and complexity in health. New York: Springer 2013. p. 279–99.
38. Sluzki CE. Personal social networks and health: conceptual and clinical implications of their reciprocal impact. Fam Syst Health. 2010;28(1):1–18.
39. American Geriatrics Society Expert Panel on the Care of Older Adults with Multimorbidity. Patient-centered care for older adults with multiple chronic conditions: a stepwise approach from the American Geriatrics Society. J Am Geriatr Soc. 2012;60(10):1957–68.

Appendices

A—Programme
B—Session chairs
C—Award winners
D—Best young researcher awards
E—Organising Committee

J.P. Sturmberg (ed.), *The Value of Systems and Complexity Sciences for Healthcare*, DOI 10.1007/978-3-319-26221-5

Appendix A: Programme

Day 1			
8:00–8:10	Welcome	Howard Federoff	
8:10–8:45	Keynote	Joachim Sturmberg	Returning to holism—an imperative for the twenty first century

Howard Federoff and Joachim Sturmberg

Session 1
Title: **Foundations of Systems Medicine**
Session Chair: Mark Smith

8:45–9:15	Keynote	Howard Federoff	Systems neuromedicine and Alzheimer's disease: detecting preclinical disease
9:15–9:30		Henrik Vogt	Systems medicine—holistic and personalized in a humanistic sense?
9:30–9:45		S. Lee Hong	Complicated vs. complex, disease vs. illness: rethinking diagnosis, therapy, and restoring health
9:45–10:00		Abdulrahman El-Sayed	A system for systems epidemiology: the example of inference from agent-based models
10:15–10:30		Martin Konitzer	Complexity and risk in family medicine's epidemiology. An interdisciplinary approach
10:30–10:45		Sonali Vaid	Complexity science and rabies control. Applying complexity science to understand the spread and mitigation of a public health problem

10:45–11:00		James C. Palmer	The human processual interdependent phenotype: a complexity sciences contribution to the theoretical foundations of systems based medicine
11:00–11:15		Tom Staiger	Anticipation in complex systems: potential implications for improving safety and quality in healthcare
11:15–12:00	Panel discussion		
	Moderator: Howard Federoff		

Martin Konitzer, Hendrik Vogt,James Palmer, Tom Staiger and Howard Federoff

Session 2A
Title: **Disease Complexity—Physiology**
Session Chair: Frances Griffith

01:00–1:30	Keynote	Bruce West	Thinking about complexity for medicine
1:30–2:00	Keynote	Andrew Seely	Monitoring variability and complexity at the bedside
2:00–2:15		Henry Heng	Heterogeneity mediated system complexity: the ultimate challenge for studying common and complex diseases
2:15–2:30		Martin Picard	A bioenergetic origin of disease complexity
2:30–3:00	Panel discussion		
	Moderator: Brian Castellani		

Frances Griffiths, Henry Heng, Andrew Seely and Bruce West

Session 2B
Title: **Disease Complexity—Clinical**
Session Chair: Hakima Amri

3:30–4:00	Keynote	Carmel Martin	Multimorbidity—through a Glass Darkly
4:00–4:15		Brian Castellani	Modeling the temporal dynamics/trajectories of depression
4:15–4:30		David Katerndahl	Viewing mental health through the lens of complexity science
4:30–4:45		David Katerndahl	Quantitatively demonstrating the complex nature of partner violence
4:45–5:00		Jeanette Bennett	Depression: not just a top-down phenomenon
5:00–5:30	Panel discussion		
	Moderator: Joachim Sturmberg		

Poster Session (6:00–7:30pm)
Session Chair: Rene Crichlow

The Complex Nature of Health	
Moderator: Lee Hong	
Robert Eyre	Social networks and health: spreading of depressive symptoms over adolescent friendship networks
William Taylor	A Complexity definition of health
Krithika Bhuvaneshwar	G-Doc plus—the next generation systems medicine platform for precision medicine
Carmel Martin	Taxonomic 'complexity'! complex versus complex adaptive/nonlinear concepts in evaluative primary care research
Henry White	Mapping complex co-morbidities

Technology	
Moderator: Martin Picard	
Frances Griffiths	The potential for digital communication to improve access to UK National Health Service (NHS) general practice by marginalised groups: a realist review
Naiem T Issa	Net-TMFS: novel computational platform for drug discovery and repurposing that integrates systems pharmacology and metabolite signatures
Abhishek Pandey	Reducing the complexity of clinical -omics reporting using the Syapse semantic data platform
Francis Griffiths	Improving health outcomes for young people with long term conditions: the role of digital communication in current and future patient-clinician communication for UK National Health Service (NHS) providers of specialist clinical services: The LYNC study.
Organizational Learning	
Moderator: Paul Plsek	
Rick Botelho	Design health movements: Creating catalytic innovation for transformational leadership development
Andrew S. Valeras	A family medicine curriculum to teach the role of complexity science in healthcare
Nneka Mokwunye	Ethically complicated patients: moving clinical ethics beyond informed consent forms to full systemic integration at a Tertiary Care Hospital
Alan E Zuckerman	Opportunities to use the new sub-specialty of clinical informatics to improve the management of complexity in healthcare
Kath Skinner	Responding to the complexity of a nested system of new paradigms to support the emergence of a new palliative care service in New South Wales (Australia) providing last-days-of-life home support primary healthcare
Gaetano R. Lotrecchiano	Measuring culture change preference in an Academic Medicinal Center Steering Team for Education
Disease Complexity	
Moderator: Markus Thygeson	
Hakima Amri	Parsimony phylogenetics: a systems biology solution to cancer data heterogeneity and complexity
Mary R. Talen	Tackling complexity care: an empanelment process using EHR variables for identifying and medical, system, and patient complexity
Talgat Nurkas	Role of TGF-β induced Epithelial Mesenchymal Transition (EMT) and metabolism in pancreatic ductal adenocarcinoma
Clinical Care	
Moderator: Martin Konitzer	
Jeremiah Altman	Lack of utility of head CT in concussive head injury amongst non-geriatric patients
Abdulrahman M. El-Sayed	Stigma and the etiology of depression among the obese: insights from an agent-based social network model
Sister Grace Miriam (Rachel) Usala	Hyponatremia is associated with increased osteoporosis and bone fractures in a large health system population
Jenna Nicole Ray	Disentangling irritable bowel syndrome interventions: social care, breath training, and mindfulness
Carmel Martin	Assessing primary care: patterns in individuals with high risk health journeys

Health System Development	
Moderator: Holly Lanham	
Sreenivas Rangan Sukumar	Long-tails, power-laws and complexity: what it means to our healthcare system?
Samuel McAleese	Understanding system variation to improve sepsis care at Medstar Health
Syed Azizur Rahman	Unqualified health care providers in rural health care system in Bangladesh: quality of services and effects on maternal and child health
Mallikarjun Shankar	Complementing RCTs: in silico analytics, modeling, and simulation of healthcare
Rutger Ijntema	Success factors within business models for primary health care businesses physical therapy in the Netherlands; systematic review with critical interpretative synthesis.

Day 2
Session 3
Title: **Ethics and Education—The Challenges for Systems-Based Medicine**
Session Chair: Beverley Ellis

8:00–8:30	Keynote	Kevin T. FitzGerald	Ethical complexities issues in systems medicine: what care and for whom?
8:30–9:00	Keynote	Fred Hafferty	Reconceptualizing medical education as a complex adaptive environment: an institutional imperative
9:00–9:15		Stewart Mennin	Uncertainty and praxis in medical education
9:15–9:30		Stewart Mennin	Integration in health professions education as emergence
9:30–9:45		Erick Valdes Meza	Complexity and bioethics in the twenty first century
9:45–10:00		Damjana Rozman	Systems medicine of multifactorial disorders: the approaches of CASyM, the coordinated actions systems medicine in Europe
10:15–10:30		Frances Griffiths	Systematic literature reviews—beyond Cochrane to complexity
	Panel discussion		
	Moderator: Rene Crichlow		

Stewart Mennin, Damjana Rozman, Fred Hafferty, Beverley Ellis and Kevin FitzGerald

Session 4A
Title: **Change in an Adaptive Organization**
Session Chair: Aviad Haramati

11:15–11:30		Shimon Waldfogel	Public reporting: potential for healing the US healthcare system
11:30–11:45		Russell S. Gonnering	Agent-based modeling of organizational performance
11:45–12:00		Sergio Camorlinga	Leading the healthcare organization as a complex adaptive system
12:00–12:15		Beverley Ellis	The value of systems and complexity thinking to enable change in adaptive healthcare organisations, supported by informatics
12:15–12:30		Jacqueline Morse	Addressing avoidable ED utilization and rehospitalizations as symptoms of complexity through a quality improvement methodology

Session 4B
Title: **Change in an Adaptive Organization**
Session Chair: Paul Plsek

1:30–1:45		Carmel Martin	Access to primary care: a complex adaptive systems perspective
1:45–2:00		Yaneer Bar-Yam	Complex systems science and healthcare improvement
2:00–2:15		Joachim Sturmberg	"If the facts don't fit the theory, change the theory." Implications for Health System Reform
2:15–2:30		Lucy Leykum	Manifestations and implications of uncertainty for improving healthcare systems: an analysis of observational and interventional studies grounded in complexity science
2:30–3:00	Keynote	Curt Lindberg & Elizsabeth Ciemins	Implementing change
3:00–3:30	Panel discussion		
	Moderator: Stewart Mennin		

3:30–3:45	Final thoughts and conclusion

Appendix B: Session Chairs

Hakima Amri, PhD
Associate Professor, Department of Biochemistry and Molecular and Cellular Biology, Georgetown University Medical Center;
Co-Director, Complementary and Alternative Medicine Program, Georgetown University.

Beverley Suzanne Ellis, MA, PhD
Principal Lecturer in Health Informatics, School of Health, University of Central Lancashire.

Francis Griffiths, PhD
Professor of Medicine in Society, Warwick Medical School.

Aviad Haramati, PhD
Professor of Physiology, Department Biochemistry and Molecular and Cellular Biology, Georgetown University Medical Center;
Co-Director, Complementary and Alternative Medicine Program, Georgetown University.

Renee Crichlow, MD
Assistant Professor, University of Minnesota North Memorial Hospital Family Medicine Residency Program.

Paul E. Plsek, MS
Mark Hutcheson Chair of Innovation, Virginia Mason Medical Center, Seattle, Washington.

Mark Smith, MD
Director, MedStar Institute for Innovation, Washington DC.

Appendix C: Participants

A	Janice Allen	Barnes Jewish College, Goldfarb School of Nursing
	Jeremy Altman	Georgetown University Medical Center
	Hakima Amri	Georgetown University Medical Center
	David Aron	CWRU/Cleveland VA Medical Center
	Yaneer Bar-Yam	New England Complex Systems Institute
B	Jeanette Bennett	University of North Carolina, Charlotte
	Todd Bentsen	Georgetown University Medical Center
	Krithika Bhuvaneshwar	Georgetown University Medical Center
	Rick Botelho	Retired from the University of Rochester,NY
C	Paola Camorlinga	College of Medicine, University of Manitoba
	Sergio Camorlinga	University of Winnipeg—Canada
	Brian Castellani	Kent State University
	Amrita Cheema	Georgetown University Medical Center
	Elizabeth Ciemins	Partnership for Complex Systems and Healthcare Innovation
	Cathy Coleman	University of San Francisco School of Nursing and Health Professions
	Renee Crichlow	University of Minnesota
	Elliott Crooke	Georgetown University Medical Center
	Lynn Curry	CurryCorp Inc.
D	Evan G. DeRenzo	Center for Ethics, MedStar Washington Hospital Center
	Nicholas Downing	Yale University
E	David Eland	Ohio University Heritage College of Osteopathic Medicine
	Mohammed El-Khatib	Georgetown University Medical Center
	Beverley Ellis	University of Central Lancashire—UK
	Abdulrahman El-Sayed	Columbia University in the City of New York
	Robert Eyre	Centre for Complexity Science, University of Warwick—UK
F	Howard Federoff	Georgetown University
	Kevin FitzGerald	Georgetown University Medical Center

G	Shaun Gleason	Oak Ridge National Laboratory
	Jefferey Goldstein	Adelphi University
	Russell Gonnering	The Medical College of Wisconsin
	Frances Griffiths	Warwick Medical School, UK
H	Fred Hafferty	Mayo Clinic, Rochester MN
	Simeon Hain	Ohio University Heritage College of Osteopathic Medicine
	Aviad Haramati	Georgetown University Medical Center
	Sean Hawkins	Georgetown University Medical Center
	Henry Heng	Wayne State University School of Medicine
	S. Lee Hong	Ohio University
I	Rutger Ijntema	University of Applied Sciences Utrecht—Netherlands
	Naiem Issa	Georgetown University Medical Center
K	Alisa Kang	
	David Katerndahl	University of Texas Health Science Center at San Antonio
	Martin Konitzer	Hannover Medical School Academic Teaching Practice—Germany
L	Joe Lake	Oak Ridge National Laboratory
	Holly Lanham	The University of Texas Health Science Center San Antonio
	Luci Leykum	University of Texas Health Science Center at San Antonio and STVHCS
	Curt Lindberg	Partnership for Complex Systems and Healthcare Innovation
	Kristie Loescher	The University of Texas at Austin
	Gaetano Lotrecchiano	George Washington University
	Michael Lumpkin	Georgetown University Medical Center
	Joseph Lyons	WeiserMazars
M	Lois Macias	St. Joseph Healthcare
	Subha Madhavan	Innovation Center for Biomedical Informatics, Georgetown University
	Kevin Malloy	Institute for Innovation
	Carmel Martin	Trinity College Dublin—Ireland
	Samuel McAleese	Georgetown University Medical Center
	Simon McBride	Australian E-Health Research Centre (CSIRO)—Australia
	Stewart Mennin	Mennin Consulting & Associates—Brazil
	Eric Miller	Ohio University Heritage College of Osteopathic Medicine

	Dave Milzman	Georgetown University School Of Medicine
	Talat Mohammed	Marywood University
	Steve Moore	Georgetown University Medical Center
	Jacqueline Morse	Concord Hospital
N	Atul Nakhasi	Johns Hopkins School of Medicine
	Sinem Nalbantoglu	Georgetown University Medical Center
P	James Palmer	Caldwell Palmer
	Abhi Pandey	Syapse
	Joshua Phillips	Georgetown University Medical Center
	Martin Picard	University of Pennsylvania and Children's Hospital of Philadelphia
	Paul Plsek	MedStar Institute for Innovation
	Eddie Price	Complexity Science Medical Systems—Australia
	Mary Prybylo	St Joseph Healthcare
	Jacqueline Pugh	South Texas Veterans Health Care System (STVHCS)
R	Vivian S. Rambihar	Scarborough Hospital, Toronto—Canada
	Jenna Ray	University of North Carolina, Charlotte
	Damjana Rozman	University of Ljubljana, Faculty of Medicine—Slovenia
S	Andrew Seely	The Ottawa Hospital—Canada
	Mallikarjun Shankar	Oak Ridge National Laboratory
	J. C. Smart	Georgetown University
	Mark Smith	Georgetown University Medical Center
	James Sorace	
	Tom Staiger	University of Washington Medical Center
	Joachim Sturmberg	University of Newcastle—Australia
	Sreenivas Sukumar	Oak Ridge National Laboratory
T	Mary Talen	Northwestern Family Medicine Residency
	Mike Taylor	Johns Hopkins Medicine
	Marcus Thygeson	Blue Shield of California
	Georgia Tourassi	Oak Ridge National Laboratory
U	Rachel Usala	Georgetown University Medical Center

V	Sonali Vaid	University Research Co. LLC
	Erick Valdes Meza	Universidad del Desarrollo—Chile
	Aimee Valeras	NH Dartmouth Family Medicine Residency
	Andrew Valeras	NH Dartmouth Family Medicine Residency
	Douglas Varner	Georgetown University Medical Center
	Sona Vasudevan	Georgetown University Medical Center
	Jo Veltman	Norfolk & Norwich University Hospital
	Henrik Vogt	General Practice Research Unit, Norwegian University of Science and Technology—Norway
W	Shimon Waldfogel	Abington Memorial Hospital
	Shangzi Wang	Georgetown University Medical Center
	Gil Weigand	Oak Ridge National Laboratory
	Louis Weiner	Lombardi Comprehensive Cancer Center
	Peg Weissinger	Georgetown University Medical Center
	Bruce West	Duke University
	Henry White	Brookline Community Mental Health Center
	Vince WinklerPrins	Georgetown University Medical Center
	Lauren Wolkoff	Georgetown University Medical Center
Z	Alan Zuckerman	Georgetown University School of Medicine

Volunteers	
Payal Banerjee	Georgetown University Medical Center
Shuyin (Casey) Chen	Georgetown University Medical Center
Nupur Deshpande	Georgetown University Medical Center
Shreyas Gadre	Georgetown University Medical Center
Celena Gomez	Georgetown University Medical Center
Leslie Hansen	Georgetown University Medical Center
Zachary Heins	Georgetown University Medical Center
Kritika Khurana	Georgetown University Medical Center
Elizabeth Luttner	Georgetown University Medical Center
Shruti Rao	Georgetown University Medical Center
Vikas Soni	Georgetown University Medical Center
Shruthi Sriramkumar	Georgetown University Medical Center
Tony Tan	Georgetown University Medical Center
Bridget Tripp	Georgetown University Medical Center
Johnny (Zheng) Zhuang	Georgetown University Medical Center

Appendix D: Best Young Researcher Awards

Best Oral Presentation

Jacqueline Morse and Andrew Valeras

Jacqueline Morse, Andrew S. Valeras, Dominic Geffken, Aimee Valeras, Dan Eubank and Travis Harker
Addressing avoidable ED utilization and rehospitalizations as symptoms of complexity through a quality improvement methodology

Their research project is described in Chapter 19 of the *Proceedings*.

Best Poster Presentations

Naiem T Issa, Jordan Kruger, Rajarajan Raja,Stephen W Byers and Sivanesan Dakshanamurthy
Net-TMFS: Novel Computational Platform for Drug Discovery and Repurposing that Integrates Systems Pharmacology and Metabolite Signatures

Identification and targeting of disease-related protein targets are important for targeted drug discovery and repurposing. Two significant bottlenecks in the target-based drug discovery process involve: (1) establishing biologically valid drug–target associations, and (2) assessing the physiologic effect of those drug–target interactions at the systems level. Network pharmacology of drugs and metabolites can help overcome these bottlenecks to reduce failures at the early-phase clinical trial level and to further reveal new disease targets and biomarkers through systems biology analytics. Here we present Net-TMFS, a computational drug discovery platform that accurately predicts empirical drug- and metabolite-target (DT/MT) interactions and integrates them into a multi-tiered network analysis. Net-TMFS incorporates information from disease-associated targets, cell signaling pathways, protein molecular functions and protein–protein interactions to enrich predicted DT effects on overall disease pathophysiology. We apply Net-TMFS to cancers and rare diseases to provide examples of the platform's utility. Furthermore, we use Net-TMFS for the novel prediction of MT interactions for cancer-associated metabolites to hypothesize new links between diseases and metabolites. Many Net-TMFS-generated predictions were also validated using existing literature and experimental evidence. In summary, Net-TMFS is a powerful method for sampling a large chemical and protein target space to predict biologically plausible interactions and contextualizing those interactions in systems biology through network analysis for enriched pharmacological and clinical success.

Krithika Bhuvaneshwar, Anas Belouali, Varun Singh, Robert M Johnson, Lei Song, Shruti Rao, Adil Alaoui, Michael A. Harris, Yuriy Gusev and Subha Madhavan
G-DOC *Plus*—the next generation systems medicine platform for precision Medicine

G-DOC *Plus* is an enhanced web platform that uses cloud computing and other advanced computational tools to handle NGS and medical images so that they can be analyzed in the full context of other omics and clinical information. It allows translational science researchers to explore data one sample at a time, as a sub-cohort of samples; or as a population as a whole, providing the user with a 360-degree view of the data. G-DOC *Plus* tools have been leveraged in the cancer and non-cancer realms for hypothesis generation; biomarker detection and multi-omic analysis, in-silico and population genetics analysis; and to explore somatic mutation and breast cancer MRI images. The long-term vision of G-DOC *Plus* is to extend this systems medicine platform to hospital networks to provide clinical decision support using multi-omics and relevant clinical information to support personalized patient care.

Appendix E: Organising Committee

Chairs

Howard Federoff, MD, PhD
Executive Vice President for Health Sciences, Georgetown University Medical Center;
Executive Dean, School of Medicine, Georgetown University.

Joachim Sturmberg, MD, PhD
Associate Professor of General Practice, Department of General Practice, The University of Newcastle, Newcastle, Australia.

Committee Members

Sona Vasudevan, PhD
Associate Professor of Biochemistry and Molecular Biology, Georgetown University;
Education Task Lead, Clinical and Translation Science Awards (CTSA), Georgetown University;
Director, Systems Medicine Graduate Program, Georgetown University.

Brian Castellani, PhD
Professor of Sociology, Kent State University, Kent Ohio, USA;
Head, Complexity in Health Group, Robert S. Morris Health and Science Building, Kent State University at Ashtabula;
Advisory Board Member, Center for Complex Systems Studies, Kalamazoo College, Kalamazoo, MI, USA.

Renee Crichlow, MD
Assistant Professor, University of Minnesota North Memorial Hospital Family Medicine Residency Program.

Elliott Crooke, PhD
Professor and Chair, Department of Biochemistry and Molecular & Cellular Biology;
Senior Associate Dean, Faculty and Academic Affairs.

Carmel M Martin, MSc, PhD
Associate Professor of Family Medicine, NOSM, Canada;
Dept Public Health Primary Care,Trinity College Dublin, Ireland.

Stewart Mennin, MS, PhD
Founder, Mennin Consulting & Associates;
Professor Emeritus, Department of Cell Biology and Physiology;
Assistant Dean Emeritus, Educational Development and Research, University of New Mexico School of Medicine.

Beverley Suzanne Ellis, MA, PhD
Principal Lecturer in Health Informatics, School of Health, University of Central Lancashire.

Index

A

Adrenocorticotropin hormone (ACTH), 165
Agent-based counterfactual (ABC) simulations, 41–42
Alzheimer's disease, 22
Anticipatory systems, 73
  failure modes, 74–75
  feed-forward, 72–74
  formal model, 75–77
  modelling relationship, 70
  prototypical modelling relation, 70
  recursion, 71–72
  Rosen definition, 69
Atrial fibrillation (AF), 32

B

Bayes theorem, 61–63
Behavioural health clinician, 235
Braun's classification system, 56–57
Braun's Law, 52

C

Chronic health issues, 36
Clinical governance, 221, 222
Cochrane reviews
  complex interventions
    cognitive behavioural approaches, 188
    computer reminders, 189
    UK health care organisation, 189
  context and transferability, 191–192
  health domain, 188
  and realist reviews (*see* Realist reviews)
  research question, 188
  rigorous research, 188
Complex adaptive systems (CAS), 127–129
  adaptability, 207
  characteristics, 5–6, 243
  co-evolution and adaptation, 220
  complex and chaotic scheduling, 244
  components, 220
  computer modelling and simulation, 215
  definition, 206
  emergence, 207
  emergency department
    diagnostic procedures, 213
    external and internal factors, 213
    human participants roles and actions, 209–210
    information technology, 211
    interactions/scenarios, 212
    interventional procedures and treatment, 213
    Length of Stay (LOS), 214
    time to disposition, 213
    triaging designator, 212
  external constraint, 244
  Gauss and Pareto distributions, 7
  health vortex
    core values and simple rules, 248
    organisational behaviours, 247
    principles, 248
  interdependencies, 207
  non-linearity, 206–207
  non-urgent routine care, 243, 244
  outreach and non-linear modelling, 244
  primary care (*see* Primary care (PC))
  properties of, 9–10

J.P. Sturmberg (ed.), *The Value of Systems and Complexity Sciences for Healthcare*, DOI 10.1007/978-3-319-26221-5

Complex adaptive systems (CAS) (*cont.*)
quality improvement programmes, 221, 222
self-organising dynamics, 8
self-organising networks, 220
technology implementation, 227
Complexity and uncertainty
advanced decision-making tools, 64
Braun's skewed distributions, 52
Braun's classification system, 56–57
Braun's Law, 52
clinical practice
Bayes theorem, 61–63
fractality, 58
linguistic properties, 58–59
Pareto/Zipf distribution, 59
uncertainty = risk, 60–61
distribution, 52–53
family medicine epidemiology, 64
grid, 54–55
improve decision-making skills, 64
protocols, 55–56
skewed Gaussian distribution, 51
Complex systems, 36–37
Complex *vs.* complicated systems, 30
Continuous individualized multi-organ variability analysis (CIMVA™) software, 92
Corticotropin releasing hormone (CRH), 165

D
Depression
co-morbidity, 168–169
depression-inflammation cycle, 170
excessive inflammation, 166–168
homoeostatic hormones, 165–166
neurotransmitter imbalance, 164–165
psycho-oncology, 171
psychosocial environment, 169–170
Directed acyclic graphs (DAGs), 40
Disease and illness, 35–36
disrupted dynamic patterns, 32–35
Dynamic phenomena, 31–32

E
Electronic health records (EHR), 221
Emergency department (ED), 209
diagnostic procedures, 213
external and internal factors, 213
human participants roles and actions, 209–210
information technology, 211
interactions/scenarios, 212
interventional procedures and treatment, 213
Length of Stay (LOS), 214
time to disposition, 213
triaging designator, 212
utilization
billing data, 237
CHFHC patients, 232
double/triple loop learning, 232
EHR, 232
implementation template, 233
medical and psychosocial needs, 235
PAC and UPOC, 237
Patient Advisory Committee (PAC), 232
patient's perception and behaviour, 234
Emergency-ward length of stay (EWLS), 85
Ethical complexities
complex genetic information, 181
DHHS, 178
DHHS Secretary, 183
ethical issues, 181
GH deficiency, 180
health outcomes, 181
Laron Syndrome, 179, 181–182
"normal" human society, 180
P4 medicine, 177–178
SACGHS, 183
Extreme variability
actual distribution, 84
brain-quake, 86–87
conditional waiting time, 86–87
EWLS, 85
expected time, 88
Gauss distributions, 82
grade distribution, 82–83
HRV statistical distributions, 79–80
LFE, 80
median time, 88
normal distribution, 80
Normal statistics, 84
Pareto and IPL distributions, 81
Poisson distribution, 87
return time, 86

F
Family systems theory (FST), 147

G
Growth hormone receptor (GHR), 179
Gulf war illness (GWI), 115–116

H
Health and illness, dynamic patterns, 31–32
Health care system, 3–4
  dynamics of, 14–15
  implications, 17–18
  twenty-first century health system, 15–17
Health system reform
  disease/economy focus, 256
  environmental perturbations, 254
  features, 250
  Framingham data, 250
  gene-disease networks, 256
  healthcare expenditure and health outcomes, 249
  health-focused approach, 252–253
  non-insulin dependent diabetes, 250
  omics networks, 256
  population-based screening, cancer, 250
  psycho-neuroimmunology networks, 256
  quality outcomes framework, 251
Heart rate variability (HRV), 79–80
Heterogeneity mediated system complexity
  bio-heterogeneity
    phenotype and genotype, 109
    somatic cell evolution, 109–110
    stress induced heterogeneity, 110–111
  fuzzy inheritance, 107
  genetic and epigenetic, 111–112
  implication
    adaptive therapy, 114
    Alzheimer's disease, 115
    cellular evolution, 116–117
    GWI, 115–116
    symptoms, 118
  somatic cell evolution, 113–114
  system inheritance, 107
Holism, 8–10
    disease complexity, 23
    ethical complexities, systems medicine, 23
    improving prevention and treatment, 24–25
Human physiological systems, 31
Hypothalamic-pituitary-adrenal (HPA), 165

I
Illness and disease, disrupted dynamic patterns, 32–35
Interactive verbal response (IVR), 148
Intimate partner violence (IPV)
  complex adaptive system, 154–157
  dynamics and predictions
    abusive behaviours, 150
    alcohol attractors, 151–154
    causality, 150–151
    non-linear LZ complexity, 150
    predictable and unpredictable components, 148
    theories of, 148–149
  FST, 147
  intervention, 158–159
  IVR questions, 148
  non-linear dynamics, 157–158
Inverse power-law (IPL) distribution, 81

L
Laron Syndrome, 179, 181–182
Law of frequency of errors (LFE), 81
Living systems, 6

M
Magnetic resonance imaging (MRI), 31
Mental health
  anxiety and depressive symptoms, 140–141
  diagnostic differences, 141
  DSM classification, 142
  dynamics and mental illness, 135–137
  dynamics assessment, 134
  emotional state, 140
  linear and non-linear components, 140
  linear to non-linear dynamics, 134–135
  mood dynamics
    dynamic co-variability, 139–140
    dynamic patterns, 137–138
  non-linear dynamics, 142
  non-linearity correlate, 141
  non-linear systems, 134
Mental models
  definition, 4
  Newtonian model, 5
  reality, 4
  reductionist, 5

Monitoring variability and complexity
altered variability, 99–100
complexity of variability, 101–102
degree of variability, 99–100
extubation, 99
multi-organ variability
CIMVA™ software, 93
harvest set-up and process, 93
HRV and RRV analyses, 93–95
organ failure, 96–98
sepsis, 95–96
uncertainty, 91–92
variability analysis, 92
Multimorbidity
CAS, 127–129
definition, 121
patterns of, 122
systems medicine
biomarkers literature, 126–127
clinical classification, 124
psycho-neuro-immunology and allostasis, 124

N
National Health Service (NHS)
clinical governance, 218
financial balance, 218
holistic approach, 217
organisational maturity model, 218
Non-clonal chromosome aberrations (NCCAs), 108

O
Obesity, 44–46
Organizational performance
agent's knowledge, 199
CAS, 197
complexity science, impact of, 203
core values and purpose, 200
cultural map, 200
culture and time, 202
epigenetic landscape, 202
Intellectual Capital, 197
nearest-neighbour network, triading, 201
NetLogoT model, 197
non-linear improvement, 197
organizational culture, 197
professional experience, 203
Osteopathic medicine synergy, 36–37

P
P4 medicine, 177–178
Primary care (PC)
comprehensive primary (health) care, 240
e-health and service models, 244
interdependent PC dimensions, 240
patient access, 241
scheduling studies
appointment systems types, 242
emergency medical treatment, 242
Internet and mobile technologies, 242
Primary Care Organisations (PCOs)
clinical governance policies, 226
education
characteristics and responses, 224, 225
patient-public-professional partnerships, 223
health professionals, 219
informatics complements, 227
research strategy, 219–220
Probability density function (PDF), 85

Q
Quality and Outcomes Framework (QOF), 226

R
Realist reviews
complementarity of, 193
complex intervention, 190–191
context-mechanism-outcome, 194
RCT, 192
Re-framing health
dynamic entity, 10–11
experiential states, 11–12
somato-psycho-socio-semiotic model, 13–14
Re-hospitalization, 235–236
hospital discharge data, 237
medication reconciliation, 235
qualitative data analysis, 236
risk factor, 237
team-based approach, 235
Restore health, 36
Robert Rosen's anticipatory systems. *See* Anticipatory systems

S
Secretary's Advisory Committee for Genetics, Health and Society (SACGHS), 183
Sepsis, 95–96
Somato-psycho-socio-semiotic model, 13–14

Spontaneous breathing trials (SBTs), 99
Statistical Process Control (SPC) charts, 237
Sympathetic nervous system (SNS), 165
Systems and epidemiology
ABC simulations, 41–42
baseline model, 42–43
computerized simulation approaches, 41
directed acyclic graphs, 40
epistemological approach, 40–41
implications, 47–48
interactions, 39
obesity prevalence, 44–47
simulations, 43–44
Systems biology
complexity science, 22
disease complexity, 23
ethical complexities, systems medicine, 23
experimental design, 25–26
holism, 22
improving prevention and treatment, 24–25

U
Uncertainty, 91–92
Urgent Plan of Care (UPOC), 233
U.S. Department of Health and Human Services (DHHS), 178

V
Variability analysis, 92

The manufacturer's authorised representative in the EU is Springer Nature Customer Service Centre GmbH, Europaplatz 3, 69115 Heidelberg, Germany. If you have any concerns regarding our products, please contact ProductSafety@springernature.com

Printed and bound by CPI Group (UK) Ltd, Croydon, CR0 4YY
01/10/2026
02225951-0014